Justice Is Dead

Jozef Demcak

authorHOUSE®

AuthorHouse™
1663 Liberty Drive
Bloomington, IN 47403
www.authorhouse.com
Phone: 1-800-839-8640

First published by AuthorHouse 6/3/2011

ISBN: 978-1-4520-5026-3 (sc)
ISBN: 978-1-4520-5027-0 (dj)
ISBN: 978-1-4520-5028-7 (e)

Library of Congress Control Number: 2011902651

Printed in the United States of America

All images and characters are supplied by the author and are real people. Copies of faked
records and forgeries on them are from real documents.

This book is printed on acid-free paper.

Canadian Foreign Affairs are a disgrace to humanity *(Author's opinion)*

The way they treat me and other Canadians is a complete tragedy. The findings of my research hit me like a horror movie.

"I don't want to be Canadian anymore," Sampson stated publicly after the failure of Canadian Foreign Affairs to assist him properly when he was tortured in Saudi Arabia. *(Canadian Media)*

"Canadian politicians are the scum of lowest possible nature," Sampson's father, after dealing with Canadian Foreign Affairs. *(Global TV – 16:9)*

"It is like I am talking to the air. I feel my words are not being heard by the Canadian government," Stephan Hachemi said, after dealing with Canadian Foreign Affairs concerning torture and murder of his mother in Iran. *(Canadian Media)*

"Hiseler is worst human being I have ever met in my life," Michael Kapoustin said, after dealing with Canadian Foreign Affairs in connection to his abuse in a Bulgarian jail. *(Personal contact with Michael)*

"It is like listening to a Slovak abuser and talking to the brick wall," I, Jozef Demcak, said, after dealing with Mr. Hiseler in connection to torture I endured in a Slovak jail.

There are others who claim, like I do, that Canada is failing Canadians while supporting interests of foreign torturers, killers, and rapists.

I guarantee that everything in this book is true and nothing but true.

My apology for realistic description of real, true, disturbing scenes, translation of oficial documents and coarse language some people used. Because this is a true story I was unable to avoid them.

Parental guidance please for young book lovers.

ATTENTION!

Prime Minister of Canada.
Prime Minister of Slovakia.
Also European Union, United Nations, Amnesty International,
Human Rights Activists:

"ABUSE and **TORTURE** is **WELL** and **ALIVE**. It will not **STOP**
if you keep looking other way."

Please look at more than two thousand pages - above.
These documents are proofs of:
*Abuse of innocent men, women, and children, *Illegal arrests,
*Illegal imprisonments, *Torture chambers, *Physical torture, *Mental torture,
*False charges, *Forged statements, *Forged signatures, *Destroyed lives
of those who refused to falsely testify, *Suicides, *Murders, *Non existing
and false witnesses, *Corrupted Judges, Prosecutors, Policemen and Lawyers.

Somebody, please look in those documents and do something because -

TORTURE MUST STOP.

Gulag of Slovakia

Located on the main highway to Roznava in the second largest city of Kosice in Slovakia. Thousands of citizens who drive by it do not even realise that they are not witnessing just another office bulding but fearfull Gulag.
Even less can anybody imagine torture chambers, horors and suffering that is hidden behind these walls.

Only if you go in the back of the building, the long, grey, high walls create that creeping feeling of Nazi times.

THEY WILL ARREST YOU.

Illegality of your arrest will be confirmed on official documents. Space, which states conduct or reason for your arrest will be never filled, *(circled)* because arrest was illegal and there was never any legitimate reason for it.

You are innocent, you are jailed, you are abused and nobody will do anything about it. Canadian Government will even defend abusers' cruel, illegal actions.
This is what happened to Jozef Demcak - Canadian citizen when he was abused in Slovak Jail.

★ ★ ★ ★

ČVS:OUV-600/10-1998

ZÁPISNICA O VÝSLUCHU OBVINENÉHO

MENTAL TORTURE

my real signature:

klient   C 95

My FORGED SIGNATURE: C 91

They write some outrageous, idiotic nonsense and forge your signature under it. On that base, they claim that you are stupid, crazy, hazardous criminal, so they are requesting that you be locked up in Mental Institution because you are dangerous to the public.

This type of Mental TORTURE causes huge emotional suffering and can really drive you crazy.

Investigator Demjan was applying this cruel practice on me.

viii

More than 10 years of **Jozef's** struggle to **STOP the TORTURE**: More than thousand documents, proofs, evidence, pleads, complaints, requests, and offers.

Bibiana was fighting for Jozef's life when he was jailed in Slovakia. Now, using her pen, she is **struggling for her safety and freedom**, because Slovaks want her in gulag for telling the truth.

Reaction form Slovak Government: Blind eyes, deaf ears, denials, lies, intimidation death treats.

Reaction from Canadian Government: Blind eyes, deaf ears, denials, lies, degradation, humiliation, even defending corrupted Slovaks.

More than 10 years of desperate hope for justice.

Bibiana miraculously survided fall on eleven Swedish bayonets. *(Photo above)*

Now, for more than ten years, she has been struggling for her safety, because Slovaks want her in jail for speaking the truth.

Jozef, Bibiana and rat Houdini on the stage. If only their fight for justice could go as smooth as their Magical presentation.

Bibiana and Jozef in better times. Just before their
lives were torn to pieces by corrupted Slovak (in)justice
system.

Dedication

I dedicate this book to most important women in my life:

Bibiana, my wife, who risked her own safety and life to fight for my freedom. She was also there for me during my recovery from damages that the abuse in Slovakia caused to my health. Then for five years, she put up with my moods, which were the results of me reliving those horrors again while writing this story.

My mom, Maria, who took care of me as a baby and put me through school. She was in her eighties when she fought for my freedom. Repeatedly, she lost everything, and she has never given up on rebuilding her life. "Never to give up" when fighting for your rights - I inherited from her.

My dad Michal who worked all his life to support us - his family. He is the best human being I have ever met.

I also dedicate this book to an honest policeman who committed suicide after he warned me about danger from other policemen;

Edward Broderick, who became my adopted grandfather and helped me when I was down and lonely, without relatives in that faraway country, Canada; and all people like Good Samaritan Paul Koonar and those I mention in chapter thirty-nine as well as all those citizens who were or are fighting for justice.

Author Description Jozef Demcak B. A.

Graduated at University of Czechoslovakia with Academic Title Mgr.- Magister.

Witnessed first hand suffering of innocent citizens Communist system brought to Czechoslovakia, when his mom and dad were robbed of their small bakery.

It wasn't hard to recognize cruelty of communist system, when it was OK to rob by Government Officials and visiting the church could be used against you.

In 1968, when Soviets invaded his homeland, Jozef escaped to Canada and became High school teacher. After more than 20 years it looked that it was safe to visit mom and dad.

It was too late for Jozef to find out that Slovaks are building democracy by old corrupted communist creeps.

Jozef was kidnapped by police car, kept for ransom in government jail, was tortured.

Contents

PROLOGUE

Miracle in Magic Show

"Human stupidity has no limit." (Jan Verich)

Jasper is a beautiful town located on the east side of the Rocky Mountains in Alberta, Canada. It is the beginning of November in 1999, and skiing season has not begun yet; therefore, downtown stores are not as busy as during the summer or winter seasons.

The Royal Canadian Legion Hall is packed with children and parents. Onstage, Rat Houdini appears in a fire, and then walks on a cane and disappears in a cloud of smoke. He is a rat, all right, but he does not think so. He is trying to achieve all the greatest escapes that Harry Houdini (the world's most famous magician) accomplished long ago. No surprise that the audience is mesmerized.

Jozef the magician is next. Eleven Swedish bayonets are already arranged on the special platform, pointing menacingly to the ceiling. The points are as sharp as the sharpest needle can be. Some members of the audience are invited to check that they are real and sharp. They jump with pain just from touching them gently.

Jozef throws off his black cape and walks over them, stepping between the points. Then he does a handstand over them, rests his forehead on the first one, and concentrates for few seconds; he is ready. He steps up and slowly rests his upper back on the points. One leg goes up and then the other. The impossible is possible. His whole body is resting on eleven points that are sharper than needles.

This is not a magic trick. It is an achievement that is recognized and recorded in Guinness World Records in the bed of nails section. The average bed of nails has six hundred nails. Indian fakirs rested on them many years back. But nobody ever took chances on just eleven and lived to tell about it. With fewer points, more pressure is on each one of them. By all physical rules, the bayonets must penetrate Jozef's body, and he must die. But this is a mind-over-the-body situation. He gets up, turns around, and shows his back to the shocked spectators. His skin is intact. Only after they realised what really happened do they roar in applause.

Three swords about five feet tall are placed above the bayonets. Bibiana, Jozef's assistant is hypnotized for just a few seconds, and then she climbs up and lies on the three swords, high above the bayonets. The audience is already impressed and applauds. But the routine is not over as yet. Jozef reaches and removes the sword that supports Bibiana's legs. Then he removes the one from under her back. Now she is floating just on the point of one sword under her neck. The spectators go wild. The whole platform is sitting at the edge of the stage, and the audience had been invited right to it, to confirm that no strings or any other tricks are used. This is floating without any tricks.

Now, for the grand finale. Jozef reaches to remove the last sword. Just as he is about to touch it, the unexpected happens, and the show that was designed for smiles turns to horror. Bibiana turns a little and falls sideways—straight down onto the bayonets underneath her. Nobody could survive this kind of fall onto eleven Swedish bayonets.

Jozef pulls her straight up and sets her beside the platform. The audience realizes that this is not a part of the presentation, and everybody is in terrible shock, but Jozef is in the greatest shock. They have performed this routine thousands of times, and nothing like this ever happened. He hesitates for a few seconds, not knowing what to do. He looks at the bayonets, which have just taken Bibiana's life. There is nothing for him to live for. He gets really terrified and mad.

"You took her life; now you can take mine as well," went through his mind; he was ready to throw his body over the bayonets.

"Call 911," Bibiana whispers to him. Those are the nicest words he has ever heard in his life. If she talks, that means she is alive.

"Somebody call 911," Jozef yells to the audience. Then he closes the curtain.

"Please refund everybody's admission," he instructs the ticket seller. "God, please help."

Bibiana was treated on-site by Jozef and some spectators. An Associated

Ambulance arrives shortly and takes Bibiana to Seton General Hospital. A trauma specialist also arrives from the hospital to help parents and children to deal with what they have just witnessed.

Some media outlets named the story the "Bloody Magic Show."

CHAPTER ONE

A World Where Justice Has Died and Love Is Jailed

Politicians mix dirt and have others walk in it.

The Vancouver Association for Survivors of Torture (VAST) office was located on the last block of East Hastings Street in the city of Vancouver in British Columbia, Canada.

Vancouver has won international competition as the best city on earth many times. Not anymore. Junkies and prostitutes, with the support of impious city mayors and wicked councillors, were spoiling the reputation the city once enjoyed.

VAST was on the second floor of the old building. The stairs were narrow and dark. There were only two doors upstairs on the right side, if you don't count the fire escape door, which was straight ahead. The first door led into the office of Amnesty International, and right next to it was VAST's office.

They were expecting me, because I had made an appointment by telephone. A lady was already waiting for me. She would be my therapist. Every week, I would meet her in the same little office.

As part of my therapy, we talked a lot. So I knew quite a bit about her. She knew much more about me, because she asked me more questions and she took a lot of notes. She told me that she escaped the brutal system of Iran; she had obtained a university degree in psychiatry, and this fact alone was a crime in Iran if the person who got the degree was a woman.

I never thought I would need that kind of help. After eight semesters

1

of psychology at university, I should be the one to offer help to others; I should not be receiving that help.

It took that terrible accident in Jasper, Alberta, Canada, before I realized that I must seek the help of a specialist if I wanted to be myself again.

You escape a brutal situation, and you are ruined physically and mentally. Torture inflicts big scars on a person, especially if it is also mental torture. Physical torture heals faster than emotional torture, but if you combine both, you get damage four times more serious. You cannot sleep. You cannot eat, but situation is eating you from the inside. You are very, very angry. You feel desperate. You have no energy. Nightmares come every night. You dream that you are back in a hole and that all the horrors continue.

I was fading away. I knew that something must be done or I would be gone forever.

I did not want to fade out. I had some good reasons to stick around.

******

I was not the only person who was grossly abused in prison in that foreign country. There were many other prisoners—some innocent, some not, but many living through hell on earth. They were degraded, desperate, abused.

I promised those unfortunate people that, if I ever get out of there, I would tell the world about what went on in there. They told me I was their only hope, because I was Canadian. If any of them tried to tell the truth, they would be sent back to prison, never to see the outside again. Prison officials would deny the atrocities they were committing. They would punish the whistleblower even more.

It would be nice to see the government of that country step in and punish those who abused me and keep abusing others. Maybe there would be less torture and mistreatment in the world.

There are many people who have suffered gravely, like my family, Bibiana and her family, Jana Visokaiova and her mom and dad, and also others who refused to testify falsely.

Bibiana, my wife, was too young for what she lived through. But she stood by me and fought for me when I was imprisoned, risking her own freedom and her own life. She had to escape her own country, leaving her family and friends behind. Like me, she may never be able to go

2

back to place where she was born. She has done nothing wrong. She only told the truth in a country where telling the truth is greatly punishable sometimes.

Jana Visokaiova was just a little girl who didn't even understand why police tried to force her to talk about something that never happened. She and her family paid dearly for refusing to cooperate with corrupted police.

******

One Sunday morning in 2002, I remembered a little old church on a little street close to where I live, and I decided to visit it again. I used to go there from time to time before I was imprisoned.

I believe in God, but I'm not a fanatic. Whenever I feel like being closer to God, I go to God's house. I pray, but most of the time, I go through my thoughts, listening very little to what the priest has to say. It isn't for lack of respect for the priest or for what he is preaching. Catholic masses repeat the same stories according to the season, and when the priest starts talking about a story that I remember from masses in previous years, my mind wonders away, but I stay with God.

That Sunday morning was different. I could not believe my ears. I always like it when the preacher transfers Bible stories to present life. I learn a lot from this. And that is exactly what was going on. It was like Father Allan was talking directly to me, to my situation.

At first, the priest was reading from the Bible about the suffering of Jesus Christ and other holy people, and then he brought it to the present.

"If somebody inflicts grave damage on you, if somebody hurts you badly, if somebody tortures you, grossly mistreats you, abuses you—do not let it eat you on the inside," he said. "Try to forget, and try to forgive. Mainly, do not think about it all the time. They damaged you before, and now you are damaging your own self. We should fight evil, but we don't have to. One thing is for sure, if you destroy yourself, you will not be able to do anything about it. Look for help if you need it. Help is there somewhere; you just have to look for it and ask for it. Knock, and the door will be opened for you. There will be somebody who will understand."

I'm sure he did not know what I was going through, but it sure felt like he was talking directly to me. I felt like asking him "How did you know about me? I've heard the saying, "Knock, and the door will be opened," so I decided to knock.

All my life, I had depended on myself. But this time, I was down too low. After that accident in Jasper, I thought my life was over. I almost killed the girl I love.

If there was no God or at least no guardian angel present, there was no way in the world that she could have survived that fall onto those bayonets. That means I would not have been around either. I could never have lived with feeling that I had killed the girl who had stuck with me when I was all the way down.

If there ever was a miracle, it was that. Blades of bayonets are about eight inches long. They are made out of hardest steel available. Bibiana fell straight down flat on eleven of them from about five feet higher. Even Dr. Stevens, who treated her in the hospital, was puzzled as to how she survived. Looking at X-ray film, he was just turning his head as he explained it to us:

"I have never heard of anything like this," he said. "This bayonet ended in her neck, missing the main artery by less than a millimetre. If it had cut this one, she could have died from loss of blood in less than a minute. Another went in the direction of her reproductive organs, about six inches inside her ovaries. It looks like it marked some main arteries, but fortunately did not cut any of them. It is a mystery why there wasn't any considerable internal bleeding. A nasty one passed through her left breast, stopping about a millimetre from her lung. It would have been a very grave situation if it had cut her lungs. But the most dangerous one went into her body from behind, next to the spinal cord between her ribs, and stopped few millimetres from her heart. It looks like it even touched the first membrane of the heart. Had it cut her spinal cord, she would have been paralysed and in a wheelchair." Then he turned to Bibiana and finished his story, looking her directly in the eyes, "but had it gone little bit farther, it would have ended up in the heart. You would have been dead right there on the stage. You must be the luckiest girl on this earth. I don't understand it."

I did. "Both of God's hands were there to stop Bibiana's body just before so many life-sustaining organs would have been pricked by those menacing bayonets. You can think anything you want, but only God could have saved her in this situation."

Bibiana was taken by ambulance after that nasty accident. I stayed on the stage to take care of the animals. As soon as I put them away, I rushed to the hospital. The trauma specialist was already waiting for me.

"She is alive," she said, comforting me.

"Can I see her?"

"She is in a coma. X-rays were taken. All we can do is wait. The doctor will let us know if there is any change."

It was a long wait, but the trauma specialist stayed with me all the time, and she kept comforting me:

"The longer we wait, the better for her. It means that she is not getting worse, not losing much blood internally."

It was already morning outside when the doctor came in.

"It looks like she was the luckiest lady on earth. If there is no complication, she should be all right."

Later in the day, I could finally see Bibiana. Needles with little hoses were attached to her; she had an oxygen mask on her face. She was heavily sedated, but she opened her eyes and gave me a little smile.

"Just sleep, baby. You will be all right."

I sat on the chair beside her. I had not slept a minute since the accident. I placed my head on the side of the bed and took a little nap. It was comforting that she was next to me and that she was alive.

Dr. Stevens moved Bibiana to a private room. It seemed like it was a room for a celebrity. It even had a private shower in the corner.

Phones began ringing at admission desk. People wanted to know how Bibiana was. Two days after the accident, the doctor allowed in all the strangers who were demanding to visit. More than a hundred people showed up. Mostly children with parents. They all brought well-wishing cards and flowers. They were cards that those children had made by hand at school or at home and were most appreciated. It was an incredible feeling.

A star almost two feet across was brought in by little children. A photo of all little kiddies was attached to it. It read, "Bibiana, we are glad, you are feeling better. We like you. From the children and teachers of Jasper Nursery School, Nov. 99."

Another message read, "Dear Bibiana, I was at your show when it happened. I was really worried about you. One of my friends started to cry for you. When my sister and I got home, we were crying for you too. Then mom phoned us and said that you would be all right. I was happy and still a little sad. Get well soon. Your friend, Glynnis"

Visitors, flowers, and cards were piling up. It would take another book to write them all. Everyone was wishing her a quick recovery and to come again. We could not believe what a nice community Jasper was. The most moving were well-wishing cards from preschool and elementary school children. They were handmade cards full of drawings and full of love. Those children really mean what they say or write. Everyone was wishing her a quick recovery.

No wonder Bibiana was recovering just like magic. Two days after the accident, she was sitting on her hospital bed, surrounded by flowers and children, chatting and smiling.

It was great for children to see her all right and happy, because no doubt, what some of them witnessed on that stage was very hard for them.

Outside the hospital window, we could see elks walking around as reminders that life keeps going and that we must also try to do our best to go on, even when it feels like it is too hard.

After the accident, I felt like I could not do my show anymore; I was totally lost, but I was glad that Bibiana was alive.

I realized that the horrors I lived through in the Slovak prison had suddenly overtaken my mind as we were performing our wireless levitation. Bibiana is in a very high hypnotic state when floating in the air. She depends on my mind control and support, which require my total concentration, the concentration ability that I lost when abused in the Slovak prison. Loss of concentration was the main cause for that accident.

******

I called Amnesty International. They told me about VAST.

"They help people like you," the man on the phone told me, "people who were grossly harmed, tortured, and who survived."

I was sitting in a room that was a part of VAST. My therapist was sitting beside me in an old chesterfield.

I was amazed how much she knew about what goes on in totalitarian prisons and about what people feel when they get into a terrible situation like I was in. I felt more comfortable when I realized that she knew what she was talking about.

"Did you feel that you were going to die there?" she asked.

"Yes, I have even written my will."

"Was that the hardest part of the whole suffering?"

"Absolutely. At first, you are afraid to fall asleep, because you are scared they are going to kill you while you are sleeping. Later, they make you suffer so much that you wish you were dead. Death is always around you. It is always on your mind—one way or the other. That is what makes your mind suffer most. They know exactly what they are doing. They torture you through your mind and also through physical pain."

******

I needed to get some answers.

How did I, an innocent, law-abiding Canadian citizen end up in a foreign prison, endure torture, suffer disgrace, lose dignity, lose the ability to carry on, and almost lose my life?

Why did Canadian Muslims—suspected terrorists in very similar situations—receive full attention, including investigations and public inquiries, and yet we are still waiting?

How are foreign officials who are corrupted to the core getting away with their criminal activities?

Why does the Canadian government do so little when dealing with those corrupted foreign countries where Canadian citizens are abused?

You will be astonished, like I was. You will discover that some countries that you consider to be safe to travel to are just the opposite. You can be arrested there and tortured, and very little will be done to save you.

You will discover that all politicians do is mix dirt and expect you to walk in it.

This is not a fiction. It is reality.

CHAPTER TWO

The Country Where It's Okay to Offend God, But Not a Policeman

"If you don't steal, you are stealing from your family." (Slovak proverb)

Imagine a country where it is okay to offend God, but if you tell the truth about policemen, they will throw you in jail for a long time. Would you think of a country that is a member of European Union? A country that signed the Council of Europe's Convention for the Protection of Human Rights and Fundamental Freedoms? Hardly. The country I'm talking about neglects basic human rights, jails innocent people, grossly abuses prisoners, and successfully covers up these activities.

Many people already think that all politicians are corrupted. I hope they will respect my opinion. I believe that there is an honest politician somewhere, but I personally have not met one yet.

Those who think that *politics* is really a dirty word are right. You do not realize how dirty of a word it is until you have to deal with it.

The country is the Slovak Republic. That is where our troubles began.

It is what we call "my old country," the country where I was born. It was Czechoslovakia when I was growing up there. From the surface, it would seem that everything was all right. But corruption is deep and nicely covered up.

After the Second World War, the Soviet regime forced the communist system on Czechoslovakia and other countries. The Soviets claimed that they had freed us from Hitler, but in reality, they had also freed us from freedom. The Soviet army has stayed all these years, occupying our land, making sure that, if we want a little bit more freedom, they can suppress it right on the spot without having to come from the Soviet Union.

In the sixties, a man appeared in Czechoslovakia. He was like a prophet from the Bible. His name was Mr. Dubcek. He became the prime minister of Czechoslovakia, and he was from Slovak part of that little country. He got the idea that communists could have a human side. That was too much to hope for. So Soviets arrange a full-scale invasion on the poor, little country. The hope for freedom was ground under Soviet tanks again.

I decided that that was it. I had had enough of that communist crap. The only way to get out of the situation was to escape. So I borrowed $200 and escaped to Austria. Then I came to Canada. I'm still grateful that Canada let me settle here and let me call it my new home. I'm also grateful that Austria opened the door for me on my way to freedom

I will never forget the first time I saw a Coca-Cola sign after I crossed the border to Austria. It was a sign of freedom for many who lost their countries in the hope of finding one with a little more freedom. The craving for freedom was very strong in communist countries.

You can only understand what freedom is if you lose it. People who are born in a free country will never really feel what freedom is unless they lose it and find it again.

It was a great feeling to see the communist system falling down in the late eighties. Finally, I was allowed to visit my family. Leaving the country like I had in 1968 was a crime as far as communists were concern. So for almost twenty years, I could not visit my old country. If I did, I would end up in a communist gulag.

When the communist era was crumbling, I was finally able to visit my old country. It was nice to see my family, friends, and classmates. My dear dad, my caring mom, my brother, and my two sisters—they were all happy to be able to see me again. We had a lot of catching up to do. I bought summer house there, which became my retreat.

It looked like a democracy in Czechoslovakia might be built faster than everybody was expecting.

Then … disaster. Suddenly, from somewhere, a man appeared. He unravelled corruption beyond the human imagination. His name was

Meciar. Before he had been a member of the communist party and of the STB—the feared communist government secret police, which could be compared to the Soviet KGB.

He formed a political party. Almost all communists joined Meciar's movement. It was another time of darkness and major disaster for the country. There were rumours about election fraud that helped him to his prime minister's seat. Mr. Dubcek, Meciar's opponent, died under suspicious circumstances. Meciar became the prime minister of Slovakia.

Imagine communists building a democracy. Everything went the good old communist way and much worse.

Corruption bloomed during Meciar's time. Extortion was a way of life. Entrepreneurs or store owners were subject to extortion. Crooks would blackmail them, hand in hand with the police. Trade workers were hit by high taxes and subject to all kind of permits and conditions.

I was helping the Regional Cultural Community Association to organize the first beauty contest ever after the fall of the Iron Curtain. Beauty contests were not allowed during the communist era. That made me an entrepreneur, as far as they were concerned. I got a taste of what the regular person had to go through just to make a living.

I paid my taxes one day. You pay it at the post office in cash. There was only one window that was accepting money, so the line was very long. It was a hot, summer day; no air conditioning was at the post office. They decided to make it as 'pleasant' as possible for those who were giving them money. So, at the same window, at the same time, in the same line were also gypsies, who were collecting assistance. That way, we were firsthand witnesses of where our money went. Money that we made through hard work went straight on the spot to gypsies, who had never worked an hour in their lives.

On the back of my deposit slip was a warning in a meaning: "If I make a mistake, I will be fined half a million korun." Korun was Slovak money. Five hundred thousand korun was the price of the average house in Slovakia at the time. Imagine losing your house just for making a mistake on your deposit slip.

Meciar divided Czechoslovakia in two. He knew it would be much easier to steal through his movement members without Czechs yelling at them all the time that what they were doing was illegal. Everybody who kissed Meciar's ass became rich.

When Meciar's democratically oriented movement's members stole, they were not fooling around. What are a few million here and few there? It was peanuts. What about stealing millions and also whole factories, together with a few hundred workers? To steal them legally was no problem in the Slovak Republic during the "Meciarismus." All you needed was to be a member of Meciar's democratic movement.

They even created new meaning for building tunnels. In Slovakia, building tunnels had a different meaning. And the tunnels they were building were big. Thousands of jobs disappeared in those tunnels. This is how it works. First, you've got to be a member of Meciar's movement, of course. Then, you pick up a factory to buy. It does not matter how much it cost, because you don't have any money anyway. A few hundred thousand? A million? A billion? No problem. You have not a penny in your pocket? No problem. You can borrow the money from the bank. Your loan is approved in advance, because the bank is government controlled and you are Meciar's boy. That makes you the government's boy. Now, you are the new owner of the factory. There are a few hundred workers on your payroll. What now? You have no idea how to run it. Until now you were just a bum and a stupid one yelling "Viva Meciar." But "Slovaks will not get lost" is what Meciar's most famous statement was, as far as I can remember. The new owner of the business didn't want the factory anyway. He grabbed it, because he just followed the old Slovak proverb "If you don't steal, you are stealing from your family."

The new owner found a way out of his troubles. First, he fired all the management; soon after that, he fired all the workers—every single one of them. Then, all the machinery and all the equipment was sold. Preferably to a foreign buyer. After that, the windows and doors, including the frames—everything is sold. When everything has gone, the job has been finished.

Where once there was a factory, now only empty walls stand; the factory became a tunnel. That is why they called it building tunnels. It was no problem that a few hundred people lost their jobs. Some lost everything, because they were unable to pay their bills. Some committed suicide or died, broken by early death.

Needles to say, that individual who destroyed the factory did not pay his debt to the bank. The bank was welcome to repossess the factory or whatever was left of it—the tunnel. This kind of business was going on under the Movement for a Democratic Slovakia.

"I did not hurt you," Meciar said to the Slovak people on national television when he lost the election and was finally forced to leave the prime minister's seat of Slovakia. What an irony.

Rather, than watch what was happening to my old country, I returned home to Canada. I could not see it anymore.

CHAPTER THREE

Poor man is a Hero; Honest one is Dead

Where do they interrogate dead witnesses? In Slovakia.

My dad died when he was ninety-three. I felt bad, because I could not be by his side during his last days when he was sick. I missed even his funeral, because I was far away in Canada. But when my mom got sick, I decided not to make the same mistake.

I arrived in Slovakia to be by my mother's side when she was sick. She was in her eighties.

I knew there was bad situation in Slovakia, but I had no idea what a big mistake I was making by going there. It was like falling into the middle of a wasp's nest.

The worst people in town had become members of Meciar's government.

They had their hands in appointing all influential positions in towns and cities, all the way from judges, prosecutors, investigators, police and doctors in hospitals to teachers. That created the base for perfect corruption.

They graduated from fraud, extortion, and stealing the whole factories to kidnappings and murders.

Meciar had no problem at all when he had placed in the presidential seat the man who suited him best. Most members of parliament were those who were applauding and yelling "Viva Meciar" whenever he whistled.

Meciar had chosen for president a gentleman from a small town that was almost at the Ukrainian border. His name was Mr. Kovac. Meciar figured out that if he gave the job of president to a man from an unimportant little town, the man would give him no trouble.

Mr. Kovac got sick to his stomach when he realized that, for being appointed as president, he was required to kiss Meciar's ass; meaning he had to jump when Meciar whistled. He decided not to do it.

Meciar was furious when he discovered that this unimportant man from a little town at the end of nowhere is able to think for himself. There were plenty of stupid, dull people in his movement who could have had that puppet job of president of the Slovak Republic, and he had picked up the one who could think. What a drag. He blamed himself for it.

Meciar had to deal with it. Dealing with it was what he was doing, all right. First, he cut down the presidential budget to next to nothing. The president was trying to run the office, but he had no money to do it decently. The presidential residence was located in a castle, but there was not even a stove in the presidential kitchen.

Poor President Kovac learned firsthand what happens when you refuse to kiss Meciar's ass. Meciar's hoppers were smearing the president's name all over. It felt like his name was splattered with human waste on every wall. They were asking for his resignation at every chance they had. Even a ghastly spirit like Lexa was calling for Kovac's resignation.

Meciar had so many puppets around him who danced whenever he pulled the strings. Now he could even pull the navy's rope, and the president would not move. The hardest part of all was that President Kovac was a good dancer before he became president. He knew fast dances like czardas, kozacka, even jumping polka, and now he refused to dance even the slow Argentine tango.

Meciar visited his best puppet at the time, Lexa, and the plan was in place. Soon the president's son, Michal Kovac Jr was knocked out and taken unconscious to Austria. There were rumours that Kovac Jr was involved in some kind of fraud in some European country. So Lexa and his Slovak Informacna Sluzba (SIS) or Slovak spy agents knocked him unconscious and kidnapped him. Meciar was hoping that officials from another country who wanted Jr for fraud would just go to Austria, take him, and punish him. If the president's son was convicted of fraud in foreign country, that should be enough of fiasco and a reason to ask for the president's resignation.

But it wasn't in the stars. Foreign officials did not dance for the

Movement for a Democratic Slovakia. They let Kovac Jr go. He returned back to Slovakia.

Complications developed when all leads of the kidnapping pointed to the SIS, which was controlled by Meciar and run by Lexa, who was not a very good dancer, though he really tried. Lexa danced himself through kidnapping, murder, and forgery, escaping from the Slovak justice system into Africa and staying there on an invalid (forged) passport. He still dances around the corrupted Slovak justice system today.

The real setback happened when a witness to the kidnapping appeared and was even willing to testify. There were other witnesses, but they were quiet because they wanted to live. Testifying against a communist during communism was suicide. It could get you in prison or into a mental institution for life. Testifying against Meciar during Meciarismus was even worse. It could get you six feet under.

It takes an unthinkable amount of bravery to decide to testify against this kind of corrupted manure. He knew the risk he was taking.

So one morning, a car was blown up, and the person in it was burned. It was Mr. Remias. Explosives had been set inside the car's rear axle. Robert had known that, he was on Meciar's death list, so he had kept checking his car, before driving it. There was no way; he could have seen the bomb installed in the axle.

It was a cover-up, not an investigation, that followed after it. The investigator easily discovered, that agents of SIS were surveying and following Remias prior to and also at on the day of his murder. They were following Robert, just like they used to, during communist days. It was done so sloppily, that a number of citizens noticed it, including Remias. They saw cars parked down the street and then following Remias. The licence plate numbers pointed clearly to SIS. When all leads pointed to SIS, the investigator was promptly fired by Meciar. His notes were confiscated, and a new investigator was assigned. The new investigator was also fired by Meciar, and his notes were confiscated, just like the notes of the first investigator. After those firings, even Meciar's strong supporters noticed where the wind was blowing from.

One fired investigator said, "It was one of the easiest investigations. All the evidence was virtually falling into my lap," he said. "It was done by SIS. All of it—the kidnapping and the murder. They fired me when I refused to lie about it. I could lie about Kovac; he was just kidnapped. But poor Remias? I could not lie about the murder of that poor guy. I knew it would cost me my job, but I could not do it."

Meciar promptly pardoned Lexa, and the investigation was scrapped.

After four years of darkness, people had enough of Meciar's crap. There was new government voted in, under Mr. Dzurinda. They cancelled the pardon Meciar had awarded to Lexa. The former head of SIS, Ivan Lexa, was finally arrested. By coincidence, he was in jail at same time as I was.

Lexa was in a Slovak jail when summer break came for justice officials. Prime Minister Dzurinda, the general prosecutor, and other top officials were out of the country. When they returned from their summer holidays, Lexa was nowhere to be found. His cell was empty. While they had been collecting suntans, the old machinery had been working on full speed. Not only had they gotten him out of prison, but he had ended up all the way in Africa, equipped with a bright, new, forged passport. It just so happened that one judge took a break from his holiday to let Lexa out. Nobody knows how much was in the suitcase the Judge received for this service.

Over and over, the circus of Ivan Lexa was unveiled in the Slovak court of justice. Mrs. Remias, Robert's mom, got just one chance to show the way she felt. Meciar was hoping to be the President. His HZDS campaigning entourage visited town after town, trying to get people to vote for him.

The hall was packed. National media was present. Meciar's gorillas and ass-lickers surrounded him.

A little lady with a sour smile and a bouquet of flowers approached the stage. Local people were astonished and frozen. They knew who she was. She calmly approached the presidential hopeful. People were surprised that Meciar's gorillas did not get in her way. Nobody from Meciar's entourage recognized her, so the gorillas did not interfere. Slowly, she stretched her hand as if to pass the bouquet to the presidential hopeful. Meciar stretched out his hand as if to receive the bouquet of flowers from the lady with the sour smile. Suddenly, her smile disappeared, and the expression changed. It became a face that read very clearly, like the pages of an open book: "You murderer." Her hand suddenly changed its motion. Just as Meciar was about to grab the bouquet, the lady's hand moved away quickly. Instead of handing him the bouquet, she slapped his face on each side with the flowers. Nobody expected that to happen.

Then, Meciar's goons attacked quickly. They grabbed the pure, little lady from all sides. They were not sure what to do. They could only think ... they only knew for sure that they had failed to protect their jewel—Meciar. They looked at Meciar desperately, as if they were asking, "Give us a sign as to what we should do. Should we knock her out?" Meciar was all red in his face. It took only a few seconds, but to the gorillas it felt like infinity. Finally, he nodded his head. The gorillas understood; they were to throw the lady out of the hall.

Meciar was shocked. Nobody had ever dared to insult him like that, especially not in front of national media. There were plenty of people who would have liked to see him hang, but they would not dare tell him to his face, especially not with his gorillas present.

It took an unthinkable amount of courage and love for her son to do what Mrs. Remias did.

I admire her and wish her well. I will do my best to try to shake her hand when it is safe to visit that country. I admire her, because nobody had the courage to do what she did. I think that she should be nominated for the Nobel Prize for courage. I also think that there should be statute of her son on the street where he lost his life for justice in Slovakia.

That little lady did something that nobody else would dare do. She stood up with dignity. Believe me; what Mrs. Remias did is really something.

Ten years went by, and Mrs. Remias was still waiting for justice to punish those who murdered her son with the flames of his blown up car. In the year 2006, she still maintained publicly that Lexa, who was the head of SIS, arranged the murder of her son on orders from Meciar, who was the prime minister of Slovakia at the time of the murder. The investigation is still dragging on.

The prosecutor is requesting to interrogate dead witnesses. Prosecutor Iveta Kopcova was looking after this case and put stop to investigation. She was close to Meciar at the time, or she was what I call his puppet.

Later Iveta Kopcova made her most famous decision. She wanted to interrogate witnesses again. Why was that her most famous decision? Because the witnesses were all dead. They were interrogating those witnesses, when she was responsible for it, while they were still alive. For years, they dragged the case on. Iveta Kopcova put the file on a shelf, and the killers put away the witnesses of the Remias murder—not on shelves, like the investigative documents, but under the ground. Now that they were all dead, the case could continue, and dead witnesses could testify again. Not one of them had died of natural causes. That very rarely happens to some witnesses in Slovakia.

Roman Deak had been sitting in his car not far from where Remias' car had been blown up, and Remias had burned in flames. Deak called the police and reported the murder. He himself was murdered in 1999.

Myroslav Sykora was local crook. According to investigative documents, Ivan Lexa, chief of SIS, had ordered him to murder Remias. Sykora is also dead. The reason? Murder.

Peter Krizanovic had information about the whole case and attempted to sell it. He was murdered shortly after Sykora was.

Metti Bubernik. Apparently Vladimir Meciar had hired him to falsely testify on his behalf. Bubernik was killed by a bomb.

Karol Szatmary was a protected witness to the murder and was missing for years. It is believed that a dead body that was discovered underwater was his. Cause of death? Murder.

Jozef Rohac was also charged with the murder of Remias. He is missing without a trace.

Oskar Fegyveres—surprise, he is still alive. He was a friend of Remias, and he also testified as a witness. There was a plan to murder him, but he escaped from Slovakia. After years, he returned to Slovakia. He does not remember anything at all. He does not remember, even, that he had a friend who was blown up in his car. For his self-imposed amnesia and for forgetting it all, he got a job in the Slovak police force. Nobody should blame him for choosing life.

(Information from Slovak magazine *Plus 7 Dni*)

In 2006, Meciar claimed that he had studied investigative documents and discovered that the murder of Robert Remias had never happened. *(From Slovak Media)*

In 2010, Meciar is still MP. He keeps only one institution under his control; that is justice in Slovakia. That way he is sure that, as long he controls the justice system, multiple murders in connection with the assassination of Remias, which Meciar allegedly ordered and Ivan Lexa allegedly executed will never be brought to justice.

When Mr. Mitro became the new chief of SIS, he disclosed secret files to the Slovak parliament. In those files is documented fact that SIS was following Remias all the way up until the time he died. Even after that disclosure, Lexa is still free man, and Meciar still sits in the MP chair instead of in jail.

I would like to nominate Mrs. Remias for the Nobel Prize for having the courage to fight for justice. Because I have no right to request her nomination, I'm asking anybody who has mandate to nominate for Nobel Prize to please do it on my behalf. The case of Remias must be remembered the same as the case of any hero who lost his life for liberty. To point at Meciar and Lexa as murderers took a lot of courage.

Meciar created anarchy beyond imagination. My problem was that I was in the middle of it.

CHAPTER FOUR

The Honest Are Lying, and the Smart Are Stupid

"Do not let anybody shit on your head; open your mouth."
(Slovak proverb)

My therapist at VAST had two chairs for me. One in which I was the way I was in my real life, and a second chair where my real feelings came out of me. The trick worked miracles. When I could not get words out of me, all she had to do to sit me in that "bad" chair. It was almost like there was a split personality in me.

I could not believe the words I was using when my therapist played the tape to me:

"Sometime they kick around our money to impress the world; the other time, they spit shit to impress us. That kind of bullcrap strategy worked well for Meciar in Slovak Republic a few years back. Some Slovaks loved when his mouth was full of shit, and he spitted it straight on Czechs. Canadian Paul Martin was doing the same on Americans, and some Canadians thought it was great.

"Meciar had it easier in Slovakia. It looks, like Slovaks were in better physical shape, and their agility was also superior to that of Canadians. Some Slovaks were catching bullshit Meciar was throwing at them much better than Canadians. Whenever, he was trying to crap on Slovak heads, they managed to avoid it. Skilfully, they opened their mouths and caught it. That is why Meciar won election. There were also rumours that Meciar was much better thrower than Martin, which is the mystery because Slovaks don't play baseball.

"Nobody managed to find out how it is possible that Slovakia, with no baseball experience at all, developed better throwers and catchers than the country with long baseball tradition like Canada. Some experts claim, that it was accidental and only one time occurrence. The others were swearing that Slovaks would be better off, if they learned baseball game, instead of playing with the crap. Slovaks were defending themselves, claiming that Canadians were in advantage, because Slovaks were using only mouth to catch all that crap and Canadians were using baseball gloves. Slovaks claimed they could catch way more crap if they were using gloves like Canadians. Everybody involved had their own excuses. Canadians claimed that Slovaks are better catchers, because they had many years of advantage. Old proverb 'Do not let anybody shit on your head; open your mouth,' was of European origin, so it was in their benefit.

"Fact that Meciar became prime minister of Slovakia … it is bona fide proof that 'shit works if you know how to work with it.' And Meciar is expert in this.

"On the end, both men lost election, which is a proof that there is a limit for how long you can shit on public."

I could not understand it when my therapist played me the tape of my statements. And the language I was using? I was disgusted with myself.

When I was a young boy, I turned to my mom, who had a lot of answers for many problems I faced when I was a child. This time, after the election, we were having supper together at her house. I remember my conversation with her.

"What is wrong with this people? How can they vote for Meciar?" I asked.

"*Butatout*," she said. "That is the answer."

"What do you mean?" I knew that *butatout* meant "stupid Slovak"; it was a word Hungarians used to use. But I did not get her exact point.

"The Hungarians didn't call Slovaks *butatout* for nothing, and Czechs didn't say *blbej* Slovak for nothing." *Blbej* means "stupid" in the Czech language. "They knew what they were saying." Then she continued, "Only *butatouts* voted for Meciar."

I could not agree more. I returned back home to Canada.

My sincere apology to most Slovaks who are smart, honest people and did not vote for Meciar.

******

My dad died when I was in Canada. I was very sad that I was not with him during his last days. When my mom got sick, I decided to spend some time with her. Slovakia was torn apart by the corruption of Meciar's government officials. It was a known fact that there was widespread corruption. I had no idea to what extend it had grown, and I had no idea that I would soon find out the hard way.

I kept a low profile. I was not interested in politics at all. You get what you vote for. That was the way I felt.

My first interaction with Slovak police. One sunny afternoon, I had just placed some groceries in the trunk of my car after shopping in local market.

Two young policemen arrested me and brought me to the police station. The police station had been built during the communist era. We went up a few outdoor stairs, and we were in a small lobby where there was a little window through which they dealt with people

The police accompanied me upstairs to the second floor after they got instructions from the man behind the small window. As I passed doors in a dark corridor, I heard a child crying behind one of the doors.

What was going on in this country? The question crossed my mind. A child cries at the police station? You feel uneasy when you don't know what is going on. You don't want to think that they abuse the children. Later, I found out that that was exactly what they were doing.

The policemen escorted me into an office. Nobody was in it. There were about three office desks, joined together, and some cabinets. Some papers were on the desks. I sat on a chair that was by the door. I waited about an hour.

Not knowing Slovak law, I had no idea that all actions by the police, concerning the child and myself, were illegal.

The police clearly advanced against the Slovak law. Much later, I found out, that they should have sent me notice to appear, and only if I did not show up after the notice could I be escorted to the police station. They also broke paragraph 5, section 3 of the Council of Europe's Convention for the Protection of Human Rights and Fundamental Freedoms, which clearly states that I should have been immediately taken to the judge. Instead, I was held in the town office at the police station.

In time, Policeman Kovac appeared with some papers in his hand. He handed me some papers to read. It looked like a record of interrogation. The heading read "District Police of Trebisov." The document was dated the first of October in 1998 at 1:15. Then there was the name of the child: Jana Visokaiova. I recognized it right away; her parents were friends of mine.

From the document, it was obvious that the policemen had gone to school the day before and interrogated the child Jana. She had described our relationship just like it was.

I read the document and confirmed it: "Yes, it is true."

Then the policeman pulled out another document dated the second of October in 1998. That was that day's date.

I was completely shocked. My stomach was turning inside out. People who do things like that should not be allowed to live; that was my reaction at the time.

The poor little girl, not knowingly, had made a big mistake at her school the day before by telling the truth. She had not said what police wanted to hear, and that is a crime in Trebisov, even now. From the document I was reading, it is obvious that the policemen had returned to the school, taken little Jana to the police station and committed an act that cannot possibly be accepted in a civilised society. Only barbarians could possibly do something like that.

It was a known fact that communists committed horrible acts on their own people, but the communist times were over. The problem was that communists were still alive. As long as they had some power, they were going to use it.

I was only a kid, but I remember it like today. It was after the Second World War. My dad called me to his radio and said, "Listen to this."

My dad listened to the radio every day. His head was almost inside his radio sometimes. It was when he tuned it to Voice of Free Czechoslovakia, Radio Station Free Europe. This radio station was located in Austria, and it was the only one that was broadcasting the truth to the Czechoslovak people. Every other station in Czechoslovakia was government controlled, and people heard only communist propaganda.

It was illegal to tune to Voice of Free Czechoslovakia at the time; that is why my dad had to place his head almost inside the radio, because he had to play it very quietly, so nobody from outside could hear what he was listening to. Later, the Soviets built a strong disturbing station that upset the same frequency and that was the end of hearing the truth for Czechoslovaks.

I learned about communist justice in a very early stage of my life. It was a regular, government-controlled Czechoslovak radio station that my dad had called me to listen to.

"Yes, I'm guilty. Yes, I did it. Yes, I betrayed my country. I deceived my president. I'm a traitor. Yes, I should be punished."

It felt so unreal, so sad, that somebody would be saying something like that about himself.

I turned to my dad. I did not say a word, but there were questions in my eyes, as if I was asking, "What is going on?"

"That is Slansky. He is saying what they want him to say," my dad explained. "Communists know how to make people do what they want them to do. First, they torture him for weeks, disgrace him. And that is why he says what they want him to say. After, they will hang him anyway. That is the communist way. The worst thing about it is that those used to be his friends and colleges who ordered the abuse." Then he gave me the most important advice of my life: "Never mix yourself in politics. Politics is the dirtiest job"

"Yes, I betrayed my country.... I should be punished." It was the voice of Mr. Slansky. I've never forgotten those words. They always come to my mind when somebody says that communists were not so bad. People suspected; people knew; but for years, nobody would dare to even talk about it. Only when communist rule began to crumble and people were able to read what others were whispering. I have read it myself in historic magazines.

Mr. Slansky was the friend and the right-hand man to the president of Czechoslovakia, Mr. Gottwald. He was the head of the campaign when Gottwald ran for the president. Slansky helped him into the presidency. Later, Slansky became popular among the people. President Gottwald did not like that. He felt that Slansky might be getting in his way, so he decided to get him out of the way. Gottwald took no chances. He also cleaned up others who could get in his way. He took after the example of Jozef Stalin, a ruthless dictator of the Soviet Union. Forty million people were murdered under Lenin's dogma, which Stalin continued after Lenin died of syphilis.

******

Back in Slovakia in the town of Trebisov, the policemen were getting furious that this unimportant, eleven-year-old girl Jana Visokaiova wasn't saying what she was suppose to. Some placed the blame on the lack of experience of policeman. Gazdura, He was the young man who had interrogated the child for the first time at her school. Older policemen claimed that, had it been them at the school, they would showed the little snot how to behave. They would have had no problem making a little nerd say what she was supposed to say. She would not just be saying it; she would be screaming it, like in the good, old days.

Policemen did not expect that a little girl, whom they considered stupid, was not stupid and would keep on saying the truth, which would be in the way of them framing me.

Here is a translation of the statement the child Jana said to policemen when they interrogated her at her school on the first of October in 1998 at 13:15.

District Police of Trebisov

Report of interrogation, person younger than 15 years old.

In Trebisov this day (1.10.1998 at 13:15) was interrogated Jana Visokaiova, born 18.8.1987. Student 4a division, Elementary School Komensky's Trebisov. Follow names of her parents, home teacher, mgr. Koscikova Marta.

Witness testifies: For the record, I want to say that I go to fourth grade of Elementary School Komenskeho, Trebisov, and I live at home with my father and mother. One evening, Uncle Demcak said that I could come to visit some time. I'm not sure when exactly it was when I was visiting for the first time. He showed me his house. Then we went to the restaurant for something to eat in his nice blue car. Then he took me home. After when I went there, usually on Friday, Uncle came to get me in his car, and I spent the night. Then Saturday, he took me home. When I'm in Uncle's, I watch television. Uncle shows me albums with pictures from Canada or photos from Miss Slovakia.. I also play in his gym.

Sometimes I play outside with the ball. Also, I skate on roller skates that my father bought for me. As I already revealed, sometimes I sleep there on the ground floor. When I sleep there, I lock my room from inside, because there is crack under the door, and cold air gets in through it. Uncle never yells at me, and he never bites me. He bought me a pink teddy. I go home on Saturday morning or afternoon. Uncle gives me a ride in his blue car.

When I'm leaving, I say "See you." I do not kiss him, and he does not kiss me. Also, he never touches me and never comes to me when I sleep there. My mom and dad know that I go to Uncle's, because he comes to visit us at our residence.

Uncle took three big photos and three small pictures of me. In the pictures, I'm with Bibiana G., and I'm wearing a black–and–yellow dress. That dress is like a bathing suit, because my hands and legs are bare. I made some poses by myself. I rested my arms against the wall. The shot was from behind. Also I was sitting on the bed with my legs crossed, head braced with my hand, and shoes. The third shot was with a bicycle, and I was also dressed. Uncle gave me the things I had on me for the photos. I got dressed alone. Also, I undressed alone in the room where I sleep.

Sometimes we go to eat out of Trebisov after 19:30.

That is all I would like to say. It is based on truth, and after reading it, and without any force, I sign with my signature.

Interrogated: pprap. Gazdura *(pprap. – low ranking policeman or military member)*

Present at signing and reading: Mgr. Marta Koscikova *(Mgr. – Magister title for University graduates in Pedagogy)*
Testify: Jana Visokaiova

From this record, it was obvious that a very low-ranking policeman interrogated the eleven-year-old child at school without the permission or knowledge of her parents. The home teacher was present only at reading and signing. No doubt, the policeman was leading her, by asking questions, and then he wrote down variations of what she said. I'm sure he left out the point that, the first time that Jana visited me, she was with her mom and dad. After she had fallen asleep, her parents had decided not to wake her up and to let her sleep there.

Slovak law says that the parents and/or psychologist or educator must be present for the interrogation of a minor. The policeman was interrogating her alone. The teacher was present only at the end. Also, Slovak law section 158 paragraph 3 orders that this kind of interrogation must be done by an investigator and not by a plain policeman.

From the content of Jana's answers, the whole matter should have ended right there and then. There was nothing wrong. But that is not what the police wanted.

Next is the translation of what somebody made up while the policemen were abusing the child Jana at the police station. Nobody has read it to her. They just gave it to her to sign.

> Addition to the report of interrogation, person younger than 15 years of age. Visokaiova, Jana, born 18.8.1987. 9847 in Trebisov address, 4th grade pupil of Elementary School Komenskeho in Trebisov.
>
> Named was informed, same as at first interrogation on 1.10.1998. She is adding following:
>
> I would like to say that yesterday at school I didn't tell the truth, and when I told my mom at home that the police were after me, my mom told me to tell everything if Uncle Demcak was doing something bad.
>
> Now I want to tell the truth that every Friday when I go to Uncle, at first, I watched television and I played. Uncle always buys me some sweets, and in the evening, he always takes my hand, and I have to go with him to the room where he sleeps. Always,

he takes all my clothes off, places me on the bed, kisses me all over my whole body, touches me all over my whole body—on my hands, on my legs, and between my legs. After, Uncle always lays down on me, kissing me on my mouth, and when he is on me, he pushes something between my legs. When he pushes between my legs his piss piece (penis), what he has between his legs, I am sore, but not much, only a little. I never have blood between my legs after Uncle gets off me. Uncle does it with me all the time, since I have been going to him for about a year. Last time he did it was last Friday. Today, I was to go to him, and he would do the same with me. I don't want him to do this with me, and I tell him that he has his big friend Bibiana for this. But Uncle said that it is better with me than with Bibiana, and he told me, that I must not to tell anyone, because he won't love me anymore and won't buy me anything. Uncle bought me two T-shirts—one yellow that I'm wearing now, and the other is at home. And at home, I have blue jeans that Uncle bought. If I want Uncle to buy me something, I have to go to him, and he also told me that, if I don't come to him, he will come to me. And Uncle promised me that, when he returns for good from Canada, he will marry me. More I would like to say that Uncle never let me out of the house, not even onto the roof to suntan, I had to always be in the house, and I had to always sit in the back of the car so I would not be seen. Uncle would always, when we were going to sleep, take his clothes off. When naked, he shows me his piss piece. He calls it a baton, and always, he shows off what a big baton he has. Uncle does those things many times during the night, and always, when he does those things, his piss piece leaks white, and he sprays it on my stomach and on the carpet. Uncle told me that from that—what is leaking from his baton—the babies are born. I go to Uncle, because he has everything at home—gun and ammunition.

I would like to say that Uncle, when he is going to push his piss piece between my legs, he always pulls on his piss piece primeros or condom, and he has a whole box of them by the bed. I have always told him, right from the beginning, that he should not do that with me, because I was only ten and he does it with Bibiana, but he always tells me that it is better with me.

I have nothing more to add, and what I said is based on the truth. After reading, I agree with this report and approve it with my signature this day 2.10.1998 at 10:45.

Interrogated: Police organ – npor. Sereg Vl. *(npor. Police or military rank)* Testified: Jana Visikaiova

This is the record that Policeman Kovac handed me to read at the police station.

Once I glanced at the date of the other record of interrogation, I was shocked. It came to me that the child's cry I had heard when I had entered the police station must have been that of Jana. I loved that child as my own daughter, and many times, she called me Dad by mistake. And then, I was trying to read. I was having hard time, because my stomach was turning inside out. I've been around for a long time, but I've never seen such a vulgar paper.

The reality is very clear. Yesterday, the child did not say what the police wanted her to say. She only told the truth. The fact is that, the next day, the police decided they were going to show the child they considered to be a little nerd what the Trebisov police were all about. They went to the school, took the eleven-year-old child to the police station, and have done something that no child should live through.

The police needed something incriminating against me, so they figured the little girl would be the perfect subject. To make her say what they wanted? No problem. At least that is what they thought. There were many others, and even the most stubborn ones ended up saying what they were supposed to. They were quite wrong.

Jana was still saying the truth. She was asking for her mom and dad. They said "later," if she told them the truth. Policemen were going in and out of the office. She began to cry, asking for her parents. Her parents had no idea where their daughter was. She had been taken from school to the police station, without their knowledge or approval.

Policemen were in form; there were no witnesses, only the poor child and them.

"You little swindle, why don't you tell the truth?" the older policeman began.

"We know everything. If you want to go home, you'd better tell us everything. Tell us what he was doing to you. He already told us. You'd better also tell us the truth. Tell us what he was doing to you when he took you to his bed," the other policeman joined in.

"Yes. Tell us how he took your clothes off. Tell us where he touched you. Show us where he touched you."   "No. I told you yesterday. He never took me to his bed," Jana tried to explain. "He never touched me."

"You are lying. We already know what he was doing to you. We know where he touched you—all over your whole body, right?"   "No, that is not the truth," the child protested. "Uncle is nice. He never ..." "Don't lie," the first man began to raise his voice.

"He kissed you all over your body. We know it. We know. He told us how he laid on you," said the next one.

"Tell us what he was pushing between your little legs. Was it his dick's head, his piss piece? Did it hurt you? Did you scream?" asked the other.

"Or you liked it." the first man interrupted. "You liked it. That's why you don't want to tell us. What about blood? Were you bleeding?"

Jana was confused. She did not understand what was going on. She cried quietly, turning her head from side to side and whispering repeatedly, "No, no. That's not the truth." "He was buying you sweets, right? Candies, chocolates—you like those. That is why you don't want to tell us, right?"

"No, I don't like sweets."

The word spread throughout the police station. Everybody wanted to see what was going on in that room. Probably almost everyone in the building dropped in to have a little fun or just to see what was going on. The old-timers were having fun. They were used to abuse from communist times. During Meciar's rule, times were even better. Corruption in the government went all the way from the top, right to the bottom. The young policemen did not like what was going on with the child. Some even felt repulsion, but they would not dare show how they felt to the old bastards. They just nodded to each other. So far, it was not going well. By then, she should have broken down and told them what they wanted to hear. They decided to try to create some jealousy, hoping that those tactics would turn things around. "What about his big friend, Bibiana. Did you think he was doing this only with you? He pushes his piss piece in and out of her pussy all day long. You are not the only one, you know. Are you going tell us now?"

"I know Biba. We went to the circus together. And also Uncle Jozef's mom came to the circus with us. After the circus, we went to Hasan Restaurant to get some ice cream."

Getting nowhere, policemen were getting more and more abusive:

"What about his piss piece, his dick's head? Did you like his piece, when he took all his clothes off and walked in front of you all naked? Did you like it? Was it big like this baton?" The policeman took his baton and placed it between his legs.

"Tell us. Tell us the truth," the policeman continued.

He seemed like that he was in charge, because he was trying the hardest, and he was also getting the most frustrated and abusive. He moved the baton up and down. The youngest policemen left the room in disgust. The child was crying. The man was blowing cigarette smoke straight into her face. The smoke was building up in that room. Jana was getting dizzy. She cried louder and louder. The man was getting madder and madder. He was yelling right in her face, cigarette smoke coming out of his mouth as he yelled.

"How many times during the night did he stick his piece into you? We know he used a condom. Did you see white junk leaking out of his baton?" He grabbed his baton again, like before, and pointed to the end of it. "We know he sprayed it on your stomach, right? And also on the carpet, right? Did he tell you that the babies come from this junk? Did he? We know he pulled primeros on his baton. The condom. I know he did." He was pretending as he was pulling a condom onto his baton. "Are you going to tell me or not?" He began hitting his baton on the table next to where Jana was sitting. He was yelling; he was out of his mind.

The child was crying and screaming, her head going from side to side as she said, "No, no, no. It is not the truth. I need to go to the washroom."

"First, you tell us how he screwed you, and then you go to the washroom."

It had been almost five hours, and the child had had no food and no drink. She was not allowed to use the washroom. She could not take it anymore. She urinated in her pants, sitting on the chair right in the office.

"I will show you. I will teach you."

The policeman grabbed her hand and pulled her out of the room. He

31

pulled her out to his police car and drove away. The child was crying all
the way. She had no idea where he was taking her. He pulled into a parking
lot, grabbed Jana's hand, and pulled her into the building. She had no idea
what was going on. He took her into a room where a lady told her to take
her clothes off. She shoved her onto a platform that had strange arms on
the end of it. Jana was to place her legs on the arms, but she was too small
to reach, so the lady just asked her to spread her legs as far apart as possible
while laying on the platform. With some instruments, the lady opened
the child's vagina and looked inside it very closely. Jana had no idea why
or what was going on. She just kept crying quietly and screaming when it
hurt. Then, the lady turned her over and did the same to her rectum.

It was a private clinic for women. It was concluded that what Jana had
been saying for the past two days was clearly the truth. Here is an exact
translation of the doctor's report after the examination.

Doctor's Report - Finding

Name: Jana Visokaiova

Gynaecological Examination Executed This Day,
2.10.98.

Examined on request of criminal police number ORP-
439-15/KP 98 in the matter of abuse of a female child. The
general growth of the child is normal. Secondary sexual
objects are beginning to develop. The menarch/menstrual
cycle has not begun yet.

Gynaecological Finding: Outside parental organs normal.
No pubic hair yet. She is still a virgin. Rectum finding is
proportionate to her age.

Conclusion: Proportionate findings to her age. Virginity
not damaged.

Signed: MUDr. Viera Cserhalmiova, doctor woman
specialist. Private Ambulance Trebisov. *(MUDr. – Title
for doctors)*

The examination proved what Jana had been claiming all along.

There are questions to be answered. Is it acceptable in civilised society to take a child away from school without the knowledge of her parents? Is it human to abuse her at the police station first and then take her for a gynaecological examination without the knowledge of her parents? Why did Dr. Cserhalmiova not get suspicious when just a plain policeman brought the child to her clinic? Didn't she know that a court order would be appropriate if the child's parents were not present or aware of it?

Why did Slovak government officials not step in when they discovered that gross abuse of children was going on in the town of Trebisov? Why did government officials not investigate to make sure that this kind of abuse would not happen to other children? Why did honest people do dishonest activities in Trebisov? Or why did smart people do stupid things? There must be a reason. I could not get it. But I would like to understand.

Or who was behind it? Doctor Cserhalmiova was not an old communist creep. She was not stupid either. She must have been suspicious. Why did she do it? Who was behind it? This is the question somebody must answer, sooner or later.

Jana was taken back to the police station. She had already been in police hands for a few hours. They placed a paper in front of her."Sign here if you want to go home." a man ordered.

She was hungry, thirsty. The room seemed to be turning around. She was dizzy from the smoke that was in the room. Her pants were wet. She had not been able to hold her urine, when the police had been abusing her before.

She signed the paper that they placed in front of her. She had no idea what was on it.

It was clear from two interrogations and a medical examination that there was no single reason to suspect any wrong-doing of anybody. The police wrote just the opposite and gave it to Jana to sign.

It was not easy to read that crap, and it was even harder to translate it into English. Please remember that every single word in this book is completely true, and I have everything fully documented.

It was crap on top of crap on that paper. Later in the case, old gypsy prostitutes were interrogated. Their statements were far less vulgar than that of an eleven-year-old child, who was still a virgin. The man who did this was a pure pervert, an idiot who should be locked up in jail or in a mental institution, but he was still out, creating more crap against me.

Later, when I managed to get a copy of the record and take a better look at it, I discovered a number of broken Slovak laws. Just like the first interrogation, this one was also signed by just a plain policeman. Slovak law section 158 paragraph 3 T.P. was broken. It states that an interrogation of this type must be done by an investigator and not just by a plain policeman. Section 102 paragraphs 1 and 2 T.P. were also broken. They state that an educator or parent be present at the interrogation of a minor. The interrogation should not be repeated.

Section 259a paragraphs 1 and 2 a T.Z. forbids cruel, brutal action by police. All those laws were broken.

I have no doubt that Jana was verbally, psychologically, and physically abused, which is against section 242 paragraph 1 T.Z. Jana was escorted to the police station. According to section 98 T.P., she should have been invited, not picked up at school. That is Slovak law. But the police wanted her to be there alone so they could have free hands to abuse her in order to make her say what they wanted her to say. It was intentional law braking.

Most of all, by law (section 90 paragraph 3 T.P.), the police had no right to deal with Jana at all. According to that law, an underage person can be invited or escorted only by officials from court (a prosecutor) or an organization that cares for underage person. It was an illegal, arrogant act by Trebisov's police.

So many laws were broken. I probably missed some, because I only studied Slovak law for a while when incarcerated in Slovak prison. I concluded that the law is there, acceptable even by my standards. Only if there was somebody to follow it.

Somebody corrupt to the core who believed that he walked above the law must have written that terrible page that was supposed to be the interrogation of Jana. That somebody must also have been very stupid.

Why stupid? How would anybody manage to put a condom on his penis and then spray sperm on somebody's stomach and on the carpet? You've read it in the record of the interrogation of Jana just a little while ago. You would also agree that only a stupid pervert would abuse a child and write the record about it.

I studied at the University P. J. Safarika in Presov, Czechoslovakia, and also at McMaster University in Hamilton, Ontario, Canada. At both universities, I graduated with academic titles. One of the subjects that I studied for four years—that adds up to eight semesters—was psychology of children and psychology in general, so I know a pervert when I come across one. It is a known fact that some perverts abuse victims and take photographs or video recordings of the victims while or after abusing them. That gives them more pleasure when they watch their victims in recordings. That much we know. We also know that they try to hide incriminating evidence. But for a pervert to make a written record of how he abused a child and make it part of the official court documents? That is something new, even for me. He must be ultra stupid.

If, I was writing a fiction, I could not invent anything like this. But remember, this is a true story, which I have fully documented.

But there was something strange, I noticed, in that record of the interrogation of Jana. I have very good memory but also an unusual one. When I have a written page in front of me, I record it like a picture in my subconscious mind. Then later, sometimes when I'm falling asleep, it comes to me in sections. Someone told me that it is kind of photographic memory. All I know is that, when I was falling to sleep one night, it came to me. It was written on the page of interrogation. Jana was saying "Uncle buys me some sweets." At first, it seems an unimportant sentence, especially when the page was full of made-up crap anyway. I knew for sure that Jana does not like sweets. I had the best chocolates from Canada, because my mom liked them. But Jana did not touch them. She was more interested in smoked fish (*udenac*) or fried potatoes with ketchup. So why would somebody write something like that?

Then when I was falling asleep, it came to me. Who buys sweets for children? A pedophile does. Somebody wanted to make me look like a pedophile, and that somebody must have studied psychology. The interrogation record was signed "npor. Sereg Vl." What was the chance that Mr. Sereg, as a plain policeman, had studied psychology? Very slim. That led me to the conclusion that Sereg only signed the paper, but somebody else wrote it. That somebody either studied psychology or was a pedophile himself … or both.

My conclusion was that there was a pervert on the loose in Trebisov who abused children, and he was also stupid. But he was also above the law. He must have been a policeman or an official in the small town who had the police under his thumb. So far, I had noticed that, besides the police, he had used a private doctor, who had examined Jana without a court order. That bastard also had some knowledge of psychology, or he was a pedophile himself.

I don't know who he was. But I want to find out.

****

In a meantime, the police made the deal with local crook who was nicknamed Belavi. He was a local gypsy, small-time crook, and pimp. He was willing to testify anything in the world, as long there was something in it for him. Pimp Belavi was willing to persuade all his gypsy prostitutes to say anything the police needed.

All he had managed so far was to line up a few gypsies that he had procured for prostitution. They were going to the Czech Republic, close to the German border, where German Johns were looking for quick and cheap company. German marks (German currency at the time) were valuable in exchange for Slovak koruna. German Johns knew the advantage of crossing the border to the Czech Republic. It would cost them fifty or more marks for a piece of "love" in their homeland and just ten marks for the same piece, if not a better one.

Gypsy prostitutes did not bring just German money in their purses. They also brought some gifts, which they hid between their legs.

Dr. Bobik was one of the first to discover it. It was when he diagnosed sexually transmitted diseases, including syphilis. It reached almost epidemic proportion in a small town of eastern Slovakia—Trebisov. *(Dr. – Doctor)*

Dr. Bobik was a recognized doctor, a specialist in skin and sexually transmitted diseases. He used to be my neighbour, when I still had my summer house next to his. He was a very nice neighbour. One afternoon, he visited my place to see how it was going with installation of gas pipes in my basement for my new water heater. The installer was our mutual friend. We got to talking about who had the best job.

"You have it made," said the doctor to me. "All these nice ladies around you at those beauty contests you produce."

"Your job is not bad," I address to the plumber. "Your hands get dirty now and then, but look how busy you are and at the big money you are making."

Then we both turned to the doctor and said with a lot of jealousy, "But pussy, looking at pussies … that's the job."

The two of us agreed, with loud laughter, that looking at pussy is the best job on earth. Dr. Bobik just smiled.

The gypsy pimp figured out that I was the best object for what was his hope for a big score. He had gotten tired of small-time crimes, which got him in and out of jail anyway. I owned a nice summer house there.

He also dreamed that I had a pile of money hidden under my pillow. The money he hoped would be his one day. He was known around Trebisov only as Belavi (which means blue in English).

He had a plan, which he hoped could make his financial situation much more favourable. At first, he had his girls call me and offer me a good time. When I wasn't interested, the girls threatened me that, if I do not go with them, they would spread lies around town, claiming that I had gone. They figured that if I wanted to avoid embarrassment, then maybe I would go with them or at least give them some money. The more I kept refusing, the more aggressive they got.

When they spoke only to my answering machine, the gypsies got more and more vulgar, even threatening me.

One day, I met a policeman who had always been friendly whenever we'd met. I told him that the gypsies keep calling me, threatening me, and telling me that, if I didn't go with them, the police would get me. He said he would ask around and let me know.

I phoned him one day to ask him about it. He hung up the telephone as soon as he heard my voice. I got the message.

"Never call me again. Your phone is bugged," He told me. "It could be the end of me, if they find out that I told you about it."

"Don't worry. I did not call from my home. I know that the police listen to my calls."

He was a little relieved but still very concerned.

"The police want you," he told me. "I think you will do best if you return to Canada."

I was getting ready to go to Canada anyway. I usually spent a few summer months in Slovakia and went back to Canada. But I liked to do it on my terms, not because somebody was hunting me.

"Don't be naive; gypsies and policemen are one band. They all want your money—Belavi, his whores, and the police. You see what is going on since Meciar. Just pack your bags and go. We cannot talk anymore. They are watching you."

I was getting ready to go to Canada anyway, so when my reservations came up, I left Slovakia, for my country, Canada.

Before I left, I decided to keep the recordings of the gipsies, who had called and left messages on my phone machine. I also left the machine on, even after my departure.

Much later, I discovered that he was right. He committed suicide. My only conclusion is that, somehow, the police must have found out about his advice to me and made his life unbearable to the point that he could not take it anymore.

The lives of other innocent people were destroyed in just this one case. I'm so sad and upset, because I don't even know his name. All I know is that he was an honest policeman who warned me, and it could cost him his life. Trebisov is a small enough town, and I'm sure many people remember the policeman who took his own life about same time my life was in danger in a Slovak jail.

I will try to place flowers on his grave, once it will be safe to travel to that country.

CHAPTER FIVE

You Want to Be a Judge in Slovakia? You Must Be Idiot First to Qualify

If your car is hit from behind, whose fault is it? Yours! (Slovak judge's decision)

March 2, 1998, was the same as every day. Mrs. Helena Visokaiova walked to school to pick up her daughter Jana. It was only two blocks from their home to school. Their two-bedroom apartment was on the third floor of a big apartment building. Her husband Jan and their older daughter Alena also shared the place. Little Jana was their youngest. Even though the school was close by and Trebisov was not a big town, Helena waited for Jana outside her school every day and walked her home. She loved her youngest girl very much.

"You are my sunshine," I heard her say to Jana on many occasions.

"Jana was arrested," some children leaving the school Jana was attending yelled at her. She frantically rushed to the school to find out what had happened to her daughter.

All they told her was that Jana had been taken to the police station. Not driving a car, she rushed about two kilometres on foot to the police station. She was worried sick. What was going on?   Mrs. Visokaiova yelled at the policemen, wanting to know why they had taken her daughter from school to the police station. They told her that I was abusing Jana and that Jana was denying it. Mrs. Visokaiova replied that she did not believe it. They made a record of Jana's mom's statement. I managed to obtain only the second page of the two-page record. Here is a complete translation:

> Second page of the record of information from Helena V. from Trebisov, this day 2.10.1998.
>
> I agreed with that and also Jana. She wanted to go to Mr. Demcak's place. About the fact that Mr. Demcak photographed my daughter, if that is the truth, I know that he did. I agreed with it, and I'm presenting two photographs, which Mr. Demcak produced.
>
> If I'm to say if my daughter complained some time about Mr. Demcak or if she did not want to go there, I do not have any knowledge about it. I know that she gladly went to Mr. Demcak—that is, she personally wanted to go there.
>
> My daughter never complained that Mr. Demcak would bother her in any way. That is nothing like that Janka ever told me, and I myself do not believe that Mr. Demcak would bother her in any way.
>
> I'm adding that besides the presented photos, Mr. Demcak did not take any other photos. Further, I'm informing you that Mr. Demcak is very kind to my daughter, and I know that he bought some gifts—bicycle, clothes, and some small things. Also, if I'm in a financial difficulty, he helps me without a word; with the sum I ask—it goes about 200, 300, up to 800 korun—and I do not have to pay it back.
>
> We are very good as a family with Mr. Demcak. I agree that, if my daughter agrees, she can still visit.
>
> I have nothing to add, and what I said is based on the truth, and after reading it, I'm affirming with my signature without a request of any changes or additions to this record.
>
> Finished this day 2.10.1998 at 14:54.

Report written by: Present: Testify:

kpt. Stefanak por. Kovac Helena V.

(All small, short words, for example kpt., por., npor. stand for different ranks of policemen and military men.)

The police did not show her the record that the police had made up about Jana and me. The police did not tell her about taking Jana to a private clinic. They did not want her to see police illegal activities. She was shocked when she finally got to see her daughter. Jana's T-shirt was wet from tears, and her pants were wet from urine. Jana cried all the way home and kept on crying after arriving home.

******

Finally, another policeman came into the room where I was sitting while all those horrible actions were taking place. I did not know his name at the time. Later, I found out that it was kpt. Stefanak, the same policeman who had taken part in abusing Jana and interrogating her mother Helena.

"Sorry, to keep you here," he apologized, "It looks like my colleagues are having fun, just making you sit here like this." He put the blame on other policemen. "It looks like all this was just one big mistake. You can go now, and I apologize for all this."

I was very tired, when I got home. My mind was on that poor girl. How much had she suffered? How hard had it been for her? What all had the police put her through? I was thinking of going to visit, but then I thought they must also be tired, so I lay down on my couch.

Soon, there was a ringing at my door. Jana and her parents were at the door. Jana was still crying.

"Sorry to disturb you," the mother said. "We don't know what to do. Jana keeps on crying. She keeps on asking if it means that she cannot come to visit you anymore."

"Of course. Yes, she can come, if she likes. Nothing has changed," I replied.

Jana was a little relieved. She lay down on the soft, foamy blanket by the fireplace. Soon she stopped crying and fell asleep.

We sat at my long dining table—Jana's father Jan, her mother Helena, and me. They were both distressed. Helena was telling me horrors, what the police had done to her daughter. I already knew. I had read the record of interrogation, so I had a pretty good idea. Helena did not know about the record.

Then they asked me if I could write a complaint on their behalf. I agreed. After all, I was the one with an education, and I had the old typewriter. I was also upset by the whole situation.

We decided that in the morning, after she rested, we would talk to Jana again, write it down, and add it to our complaint. The idea came up that the best way to do it was to record what she said. That way we would not forget anything.

It was very late. Jana was sleeping by the fireplace. Her parents did not want to wake her up when they were ready to go home. We let her sleep. I went to sleep in my bed upstairs.

I was the first one to wake up in the morning. There was an old cassette recorder somewhere in my house. I found it and prepared it on the desk in my office. There was a knock on my office door. It was Jana. I turned the cassette recorder on so she would not know that she was being recorded. I figured it would be better if she did not know. She would be more relaxed and tell me the way it had really happened.

In recorded conversation, Jana described the same thing as she had described to her mom. It was quite clear what the police had done during the last two days. When I told her what the police wrote—that I had touch her all over her whole body—her reaction was, "Ouch, they [the police] are so retarded."

On my questioning why she thought the record the police wrote and what she signed was so different from what really happened, she said, "My head was spinning as if I was on a carnival ride. Nobody read me anything. I have no idea what was on the paper I signed."

Another point is very sad. Jana did not mention the gynaecological examination the police forced her to go through. She did not tell me about it. Nor did she tell her mom or anybody else. It had to be very embarrassing for a little girl to talk about it. I did not ask her about it, because at the time, I had no idea that it had happened. Even if I had known, I do not think I would have asked. I can imagine what trauma and embarrassment it would have been to her.

But according to the documents I have, it is clear. The child Jana was put through everything as you've read it. I'm sure I stated that this story is all truth.

I was so shocked again at the conduct of the police when I sat down and wrote the complaint, like I promised Jana's parents when they had asked me to do so.

In the complaint dated October 5, 1998, I described what had happened to Jana and me, how Trebisov's police had illegally escorted us to the police station, and how they had abused Jana. And how my basic human rights were denied.

The police chief of the district of Trebisov simply refused to accept the complaint. He told me that he did not investigate his policemen. I told him that I would file a complaint at a higher institution.

Jana's mother also tried to complain. Her attempts were also refused. She went to the school to inform the principal that Jana was unable to go to school as a result of inhuman conduct by the police. Jana was not eating; she was unable to sleep; and she was afraid of policemen. Her mother was desperate. Terrible things had happened to her daughter, and nobody cared.

I was also shocked that the chief of police did not care that the policemen he was in charge of were abusing the basic human rights of people, including children. Instead, he advised his men to do something, because I was going to file a complaint. And they sure did something. They were not about to let it happen. For more than forty years during the communist era, nobody complained about the police and got away with it. It did not matter what they did. They had the licence to do anything they chose.

That same day—October 5, 1998—right after I attempted to file the complaint, instead

of investigating illegal steps taken by the police, "somebody" arranged a blockade against me at all border crossings as well as at the international airports. The blockade was illegal without the court order.

The trap was set up, and the police were waiting with an ambush.

My fiancée Bibiana got an invitation from the Canadian consulate for an interview regarding an extension of her working visa. I was, of course, to give her a ride to the consulate. The police knew about it because they had had my phone bugged, and they listened to the conversation about our plans for a day trip to Austria. By listening to my conversation, the police had also found out that I was serious about filing my complaint, because I was getting information about it on the phone. I was saying to some people that I would stop in Kosice to fill my complaint on the way back from Vienna.

Somebody in Trebisov managed to arrange blockade against my

43

freedom without a judge, without a prosecutor, without an investigator, without an indictment, even without any record of it. It looks like somebody just picked up the phone, called the federal border police, and took all my basic rights away. It could be the same pervert who abused Jana. It is clear, that this corrupted individual could reach further than the local officials.

On October 11, 1998, my fiancée and I decided to take a ride to Canadian consulate in Vienna, Austria. Bibiana's appointment was for October 12th in a morning hours. Our plan was, to spend the night in a motel in Austria and visit the consulate in the morning. It was 9:30 PM, when we arrived at the border crossing in the small town of Rusovce near the Slovak capital of Bratislava.

The border policeman informed us that we could not continue to Austria, because his computer indicated that there was a blockade on us. He was confused. He said that it was not usual, because it only showed that order to blockade came from the town of Trebisov; it showed no reason, nor who ordered it.

He called the Trebisov police and wanted to know what was going on and what they should do. He was told to keep us at the border.

The border crossing in Rusovce was not equipped to hold people. It didn't have a holding cell. Normally, in that situation, the border guards would have called the Bratislava police, who had a facility to hold people. But somebody from Trebisov had insisted on keeping us at the border until they could arrive from Trebisov to pick us up. They also insisted on the border police not calling the police from Bratislava.

I had no idea then, but it is very clear now. If the Bratislava police had arrived, they would have discovered the illegality of what was happening, and maybe they would not have gone along with the conspiracy of the police from eastern Slovakia. Most likely, the guards of the small border crossing were not familiar with Slovak law; therefore, they went along with the whole thing.

They locked us in the police locker room. Besides metal lockers and two chairs, there was nothing else in the room. We waiting long hours for the police from Trebisov to arrive.

According to Slovak law section 231 T.Z., the restriction of personal freedom can be punished by a sentence of up to ten years. Police were ignoring laws and nobody was concerned about being punished.

Around 7:00 AM—that is more than eight hours after our arrest—two policemen from Trebisov arrived. One of them was the same one who had already talked to me on October 2nd at the police station in Trebisov. It was the same day that Jana was abused. His name was kpt. Jozef Stefanak. The other policeman was mjr. Mgr. Jan Dziak.

They had not one document. There was nothing to suggest that what they were doing was legal. It was kidnapping by the police, using an official police car.

Only a few months later, after I complained that the whole action was illegal, without any legal documents, they wrote one. They called it "The Official Record." Actually, it confirmed that what they had done was illegal.

The record states that on October 5, 1998, somebody asked the federal police in Bratislava for a blockade on my person. It does not state who filed the request or who approved it. It shows that somebody in Trebisov could bypass judges, prosecutors, even investigators and have anybody he wants arrested. Farther down, the record states that somebody had observed that I wanted to leave the country to avoid a criminal investigation. Again, there was no sign of who made the observation or who made the suggestion. There was no trace of any evidence, for this suggestion was never presented. Drastic steps were arranged, based just as they stated on the observation of an unknown person, without any record, name, or proof. Furthermore, the makeshift document says that we were taken from the border to Trebisov by forcible criminal policemen Dziak and Stefanak and that investigator mjr. Jan Demjan took over the matter on October 12, 1998 at 1:15 PM.

Only Stefanak, Dziak, and Demjan signed the document. It is proof that there was nothing legal that would excuse our arrests.

I have an official document dated October 11, 1998, at 9:30 PM. It was from the border police of Bratislava/Rusovce, where we were apprehended. It states clearly that we were apprehended by an order for injunction. No injunction was ever made. It could not be. According to Slovak law section 69 paragraph 1 T.P., an order of injunction is issued by a judge on the request of a prosecutor if it is impossible to serve a notice to appear to the charged person. On October 11, when this document was written, I had not been charged, and no order of injunction had been served to me either. If there was an order of injunction, according to section 69 paragraph 4, I would be escorted to the judge who issued the order, not to the investigator.

All these laws were broken. They arrested us first, and then, they made up excuses. At the time of our arrest, no judge, no prosecutor, not even an investigator was dealing with us, and I have clear proof of all this.

Broken laws piled up one on top of another.

Investigator Demjan was an example of an old, communist policeman who was corrupt beyond imagination. He only knew how to frame people. I have proof that he was unable even to write in the Slovak language. When I complained about something that he had done that was against the law or that something was missing from his investigative file, he simply sat down, wrote it down, and added it to the file. The file was filled with documents named "Official Record," which he made up and signed after I complained that they were missing. But he made very big mistakes on his way to frame me. Because of my continued complaining, Demjan kept on fixing his mistakes, making up stories, forging official court documents, and forging signatures on a decree, probably not ever known in criminal investigation, anywhere in the world. He was making big mistakes. He mixed up dates, names and situations.; therefore, his illegal activities are very easy to see and easy to prove.

It was as if he was doing the same thing he did during communism. He was used to it. He did not feel anything when he framed somebody. We were not the only ones. There were many others. When he changed somebody's life or destroyed it, like he was destroying mine, it was just another usual day. He was a real devil walking on this earth. That was Jan Demjan.

In Rusovce, Stefanak and Dziak forced me, against my objections, to leave my car in an open, unguarded parking lot. We were forced into the backseat of an unmarked police car. By our North American standards, it was little, tiny automobile made by the French carmaker Renault.

It was a rainy morning and still dark outside. Stefanak was driving. He was driving like a typical Slovak. The little Renault was considered a fast car by Slovak standards at the time. He was driving that little toy as fast as it could go. Passing on a wet road when oncoming traffic was approaching was a rule for him. It was just a matter of time until he would end up in an accident. I did not care much about me, but I was very concerned about Bibiana's life. She was too young to die in the hands of this idiotic maniac, who thought he owned the road because he was a policeman from Trebisov.

Then the inevitable happened. He came way too fast to the left of a curve and lost control. Only the guardrail saved our lives. Had it not been there, we would have ended up far down the cliff, and you would never read these lines. It happened just as we were approaching a mountain called Soroska. I knew the mountain very well from my time as a bicycle racer. It was feared mountain among bike racers, and during a race from Kosice to Roznava to Kosice, we had to climb it from both sides in the same race.

The road police from Roznava were called to investigate the accident. Nobody paid attention to us anymore. The driver of truck Avia offered us a ride home. He was going all the way to Trebisov. I told Bibiana to go. After all, they wanted mainly me. Not knowing Slovak law, I decided to stay. These were crooked cops. They could paint it as escaping custody, use it against me, or even shoot me the next time they saw me.

Roznava cops took the car and the two policemen back to Roznava to investigate the accident. We were first-hand witnesses of what had happened, but nobody ever asked me or Bibiana what happened in an accident where we almost lost our lives. Over and over again, I discovered that, when police investigated other policemen, he only covered up the best he could to make it look legal. You cannot even hope for justice in this country, not even in the smallest possible way.

Imagine this, and this is a 100 percent true example. A lady stops at a red light. She is hit from behind by a bus. The impact of the bus makes her paralysed. She is in a wheelchair for the rest of her life. Cops investigate the accident and conclude it was her fault. Because of this decision, she is denied any compensation.

Why such a crazy conclusion about the accident? The bus was registered to the Ministry of the Interior. That means a cop was driving it. And it happened during the communist era, just before communism collapsed; it was normal then. But the communist system fell down, and a so-called democracy was built by the same communists. The lady filed her case again in court. There were new laws, new democratic agreements with the European Union. The only problem was that there were still the same old judges and the same old policemen. The lady was still found guilty of causing the accident and denied any compensation.

All she had done was stop at the red light and get hit from behind. She was still convicted of causing the accident in the Slovak justice system. The incident was published in a Slovak national, government-owned daily newspaper, *Pravda*. The author asked, "Is there anything that can be done when the judge's wrong decision is as clear as a slap on the face?

The answer is no! They call it independent justice.

But what about Canada?

I'm not thinking about judges letting dangerous criminals out, criminals with mile-long records, criminals who would attack innocent people the day they are released. Imagine this example. And it is a true story, like everything in this book.

A recidivist crook who was repeatedly let out of jail decided to break into a school. It was in the middle of the night, so he could not make it through the doors, because they were locked. He decided to try to get in through the roof. He stepped on the thin sunroof glass, which break. The thief falls down into the classroom. He ignores the books, because he got injured.

He decided to sue the school for injuries he received while attempting to rob the school, and he won compensation. The main argument, as far as I remember it, was that there was no warning sign on the roof of the school that the glass was not strong enough for thieves to step on.

This story was in Canadian media. We could not find one single reason, not even an excuse, for this kind of ruling. Next time you need money, all you have to do is climb on any building and jump in or jump off. If there is no warning sign that, if you jump, you may get hurt, you've got it made. Soon, you will be rich.

To put it in plain words, the judge punished the school, and rewarded the crook.

Like I said, we are lucky that it seldom happens in Canada.

I would like to live in times when the safety of citizens will be more important to judges than the rights of the crooks are.

CHAPTER SIX

Mockery of Justice

Why is the child crying? Because she wants to be abused more.
(Slovak police)

After the car accident that was caused by Policeman Stefanak, I was taken to the Trebisov district police station. Again, I waited in an office for more than an hour. It was October 12, 1998, in the late afternoon. No water, no food was offered to me. It had been fourteen hours since my arrest and more than thirty hours without sleep.

Finally, a man appeared with a policeman. He was introduced to me as Investigator Jan Demjan. He was in his fifties. When I looked at him, my first impression was that he might be a decent person. Investigator Demjan didn't look anything like the crook that he was. He was a smaller man—about my size—and he looked like a decent man, but the impression did not last very long. Only until he passed piece of paper in front of me.

It was the accusation. The whole thing was completely fabricated just like the one they had made up about the child Jana. It was so clear to me that they had arrested me to prevent me from filing the complaint, and now, they were making up crap to get me in jail.

Here is what he wrote while I was waiting in the office.

District Office of Investigation of Trebisov

Date: 12.10.1998

Decision:

According to section 160 paragraph 1 T.P., I'm accusing Mr. Jozef Demcak born ... address ... unemployed, of the criminal offence of sexual abuse according to section 242 paragraph 1 T.Z., because there were observations that a criminal offence took place, and there is evidence that at an unknown day, time, and month around the beginning of year 1995, and in spite of the fact that, at the time, underage Anna Demeterova—born ... 1980, address ... Trebisov, Gorkeho ... whom he met at the end of 1994—told him that she was younger than 15, he invited her to his house..., where he offered her alcohol, and gave her a bathing suit so he could take some photos. After the photos, he sent her to the pool that he has in the back of his house, with the intention that she bathe herself. After, he carried her naked to his bedroom. Then he began to kiss and touch her all over her body, and then he had sexual intercourse, for which he paid her 5.000 korun, so she would not tell anybody, but she told her sister, Alena Demeterova—born ... 1981, [same address as her sister]— and when he met both sisters at an unknown time and day sometime in the winter of 1995 at SNP in Trebisov. So he took them both in his motor vehicle and took them to his home. He offered them coffee and alcohol and told them to undress themselves and go to bathe themselves in his pool, and then he took them to his bedroom in his residence, where he massaged them with white cream, and both underage girls were touched on different parts of their bodies, and with the underage Alena D., he had intercourse, for which he paid her 300 korun, which both sisters divided. Before the intercourse, the underage had Alena told him that she was not 15 yet.

At an unknown time, probably in 1995, Mr. Jozef Demcak got to know the Visokaiova family, which included a daughter, Jana—born ... who is a fourth grade student in elementary school. Many times, he gave her rides in his car, buying her sweets, and in 1997 and 1998, he began to take her home for weekends. He undressed her until she was naked, kissed her all over her body, touched her all over her body with his hands, and pushed his sexual organ between her legs. He also gave her a dress in which he photographed her.

Reason: [the whole story was rewritten again]

Instruction: It is possible to file a complaint against the decision at investigator PZ within three days of being informed. The complaint has no postponing effect.

Signed: Investigator mjr. Jan Demjan

Stamp of the District Office of Investigation of Trebisov

This whole accusation was proven completely, absolutely false in an official process. Alena and Jana dropped from the proceedings, denying that they had ever said anything what was written in the accusation. Anna also denied it all. All three stated officially that nobody had ever interpreted for them what was written in the accusation.

I complained repeatedly about this false accusation, but nobody ever investigated such a serious criminal act, which placed me in jail for nine months.

The similarity between this refuse and the crap written when Jana was abused is incredible. Somebody let his fantasy stroll again. The whole contents of the document, and every single accusation in the document were proven totally false.

I sat there, and I could not believe it was real. I hoped it was a nightmare, and I hoped to wake up soon. There was a man sitting in front of me, and I knew that he knew that he had just made up complete crap against me, and he himself was looking at me. At first, I did not realize how serious this crap was, because I knew it was just garbage. Not a single sentence was true. Everything was fabricated from scratch.

Then slowly, I realized where I was. It was the same building where countless innocent people had been convicted during communist times. It was the same country that hung innocent people during the Gottwald era. And this was the son of those creeps who tortured Mr. Slansky and other unfortunate people, convicting and murdering them, even though some used to be their friends.

And this is how they did it.

They make up the sting, and you can read it in their eyes, that they are going to get you." All that was missing in my case was torture. I should never have thought about it. It could be in my cards yet. Not much had changed there. Maybe he was just a stupid scapegoat who had just signed his name under the garbage that somebody else had written down for him.

It took me a very short time to realize the similarity, between, this refuse, and the crap that was written, as a record when Jana was abused at the police station. I have a very good memory. Similarities between those two accusations were uncanny. Both were fiction. Both mentioned sweets, and both were the fantasies of a grossly perverted man. It looked like both papers were written by same person, but they were signed by two different people. Jana's case had been signed by pprap. Gazdura, and this one had been signed by the creep who was sitting in front of me, mjr. Jan Demjan (real name). Two similar pieces of fiction were signed by two different names. Some perverted creep was in fact getting off by writing his own fantasy and using other people to take the blame by having them sign their names to the crap he created. It would be nice to discover who he was.

I realized that they were not about to stop this rubbish soon. I realized that I might need a lawyer. Nobody told me that I had the right to one.

Bibiana walked in to see what was going on.

"Go to the House of Culture," I told Bibiana, "and get me a lawyer, any lawyer."

Lawyer Stefan Hajdu (real name) appeared in the room where I was sitting. The investigator and the lawyer greeted each other as if they were best friends. I suspected that wasn't a good sign. Soon, I discovered that the police, investigators, lawyers, prosecutors, and judges were the best organized criminal organisation in Slovakia.

In reality, I had already been charged, even before I had been questioned. How could that be?

Slovak law section 33 paragraph 1 T.P. says that the accused person has the right to express his views and opinions on all matters and evidence that are against him.

The problem was that there was none. Not one single piece of evidence or proof existed at the time, when, according to Slovak law, I had the right to express my defence against evidence.

The only piece of paper was the one that Demjan had made up and signed—what was to be the charge—but there was not a single piece of evidence to corroborate it. I could not possibly defend myself against something that did not exist.

He wrote the charge, and after that, they looked for those they had named as witnesses.

Demjan began questioning me and filling up an official document.

REPORT OF INTERROGATION OF DEFENDANT

In Trebisov, this day 12.10.1998 at 14:00.

The official form has two choices listed where it should be indicated how the defendant got to the police station:

1. Came on notice to appear day......... time........

2. Arraignment by § …………..Date………..time………

None of those most important spaces were ever filled, because I had been arrested and escorted to the police station illegally.

"2. Arraignment by §" was never filled, even after my repeated requests and complaints in writing. It could not be filled, because there was no paragraph in Slovak law for which I could have been arrested and brought in the way I had been.

According to section 90 paragraph 1 T.P., I should have been served a notice of appearance first. If I did not appear, only then could I have been apprehended, which, by Slovak law, is possible only on the prosecutor's request and after a court order. Then I should have been escorted to the judge who had issued the order. None of this was done.

They were covering one broken law by another, and broken laws kept on piling up.

We already have illegal arrest, illegal accusation, and illegal report of interrogation of defendant, and it was only the beginning.

There were just two names of two sisters in the accusation. No note of their statements existed. They had written the indictments, hoping they would find the sisters and persuade them what to say to fit the indictment.

While I was sitting with the investigator, going through this humiliating process, policemen Dziak and Stefanak were driving around town, looking for the Demeterova sisters. They were going to lecture them on what to say and bring them to the police station.

A complication appeared when they found out that Anna, one of the sisters, was pregnant at the time and was laying sick in a hospital. She didn't want to give any statements. Her sister Alena was also pregnant. She didn't feel like learning what to say or going to the police station, but Stefanak persuaded her and brought her in. A fat gypsy was brought into the office. It was to be what they called a confrontation between the accused person and the witness. In reality, it was a test to see if the liar was also able to lie to your own eyes. They use that statement later in court, and it looks better, because lies were said when looking into the accused's eyes. This woman was unable or was uninterested in saying anything at all.

Investigator Demjan was sitting and typing himself. There wasn't a typist, as was prescribed by regulation. If a typist was there, she would have been a witness to the circus that was about to take place. He decided to type himself in order to be able to type whatever suite him.

Demjan was leading Alena like the dog leads the blind man. They called him an investigator, but in fact, he was a crook. She was saying yes to everything he suggested. It was a complete disaster to watch the creep Demjan at work. "Do you know this man?" he asked.

"Ye." She nodded, speaking in that typical eastern Slovak dialect, coloured by a heavy gypsy accent.

"Did you meet him in Trebisov?"

"Ye."

"Did he take you to his house?""Ye."

The master of interrogation was typing, while speaking it out loud:Here I'm claiming to your eyes that I know you from Trebisov. You were honking at me, and you took me in your car to your house.

The questions continued.

"Did he take you to his bedroom?"

"Ye."

"Did he touch you?"

"Ye."

"Did he touch you there?" He pointed below her stomach.

"On my cunt?" She got confused.

Demjan looked at the lawyer. It sounded too vulgar. The lawyer just opened his arms, as if to say, "She said it. What can you do?" Demjan continued with his expert interrogation. "Did he have sexual intercourse with you?"

"What is that?" It was too high language for her to understand. She knew only vulgar dialect and could not understand what he was asking.

"You know. Did he … " He stood up, walked closer to her to obstruct my view, closed his left hand into a fist to form a hole, and slapped it with his right hand. I could see in her face that the woman was trying, but she still did not get the message. She looked up with questions in her eyes.

Finally, she said, "Ye," but it sounded more like a question than an answer. It was obvious that she was saying yes to something that she wasn't sure what it was. It did not matter to Demjan. He was completely relieved, and he turned around and rushed to his typewriter to put his findings on paper. Then suddenly, an unexpected complication.

Soon after she said "Ye," she looked at us—the lawyer and me— and then she opens her arms and asked "What?"

Demjan was visibly disappointed and even a little mad. It did not matter to him that she did not mean to spoil what was, as far as he was concerned, a smooth interrogation. She only asked because she did not get what a slap on the fist was. It was not her fault that nobody had told her that screwing was also called sexual intercourse.

Demjan was an expert and little setback did not throw him off his stride. He knew exactly what to do. He tried again. This time he did not just slap the hole he made with his left fist, he stuck his index finger right into it. While he was asking, "Did he do this?" he moved his finger in and out three or four times.

"Oh. Fuck." She finally got the message.

The bastard was visually relieved. He rushed to his typewriter and then realized that the chapter was not quite finished. She had only admitted that she had gotten the message of what a finger in a hole meant. He returned to her, nodding his head up and down, and asked, "Did he do it?"

"What?" She looked up again, totally confused, as if she did not know what was going on.

Demjan was already losing his nerves. He was getting red in the face.   "Did he fuck you?" He stood in front of her, his head going up and down like a horse's head when it walks through an Alberta prairie.

"Ye." She finally said what was expected of her.

"And did you tell him before intercourse that you were fourteen?" He kept nodding his head, letting her know what to say.

"Ye," she finally responded.

And creep went back to his typewriter and wrote:

The witness is claiming to the defendant's eyes that he took her to his bedroom, placed her on his bed, and touched her all over her body, including her sexual organs. After, he had complete sexual intercourse with her. She had informed him before intercourse that she was only fourteen years of age.

I was so tired already. I had had no food or drink for many hours, and this was worse than a nightmare. He was sewing the trap right in front of my eyes, and he was not trying to cover it up. We both know what he was doing, and there was nothing I could do about it. My lawyer was not protesting that crap.

I turned to the lawyer.

"What is this?" I asked. "Kocurkovo?" (Kocurkovo was known in a Slovak proverb as a town with no civilisation and no laws at all—complete anarchy.) "Can't you do something about it?"

"This is how they do things here," he answered. "All we can do is write a complaint after."

I will never know if Demjan studied the law at all. What he was doing was terrible and against the law, even in Slovakia. Section 101 paragraph 8 prohibits formulating questions in a way that they contain the answers, which should be revealed only by the witness. It's not that he was just leading Alena; he was making up all the answers for her, and afterward, he was still fixing it up while typing. This was a total mockery of justice.

Then it was my turn to ask questions.   "Did you or your sister attend the gypsy beauty contest in Vagonar?"

"No."

"Are you sure? What about your sister?"

"No."

She wasn't telling the truth, but at same time, she was not lying either. Later, I found out that she was not in beauty contest herself, but her sister Anna was. Anna was the other woman listed in the charge. Alena could not remember that her sister was in the beauty contest. She was later diagnosed by a court specialist with mentally retardation, and she could not remember much of the past at all.

Then the lawyer asked her questions.   "Do you know since when you've known this gentleman?"

"No, I don't know.

"Do you know how old you are now?"

"No."

It was pretty clear: They had picked up a retarded gypsy woman and used her as a puppet against me. Later in court, she really pleasantly surprised me.

Demjan asked me if I had something more to say."I have a good memory, and this is just total nonsense," was all I said about this circus.

The lawyer informed me that by all Slovak laws, they had twenty-four hours from the time I was apprehended to bring me to court in front of a judge.

The policemen decided to bring Jana to the police station The poor girl began to cry hysterically as soon as she heard that the police were knocking on their apartment door. The child's cry was heard all the way downstairs from the third floor, where she lived. The neighbours of the apartment building opened their doors. Some even walked out to see what was going on. They had heard what had happened with the child at the police station just a few days before, so they came to see what the police would do with the child that time.

The policemen, Stefanak and Dziak, obviously decided that it might be better if they backed off. It would not be a good idea to drag a crying child to the police station while all those people were watching.

Later, as I was gathering evidence of all this terrible, corrupt, criminal crap, I came across this horrendous thing they called the official report. Here is the translation in short:

District Directorate of the Police Force

Department of the Criminal Police of Trebisov

In Trebisov, this day 12.10.1998

The Official Report:

October 12, 1998, we were sent by Investigator J. Demjan to secure the underage Jana Visokaiova for interrogation. Her mother Helena Visokaiova told us that she would not leave her daughter alone for interrogation. She was told that an interrogation would be done (of course) with the presence of a psychology specialist, and of course, she can come with her underage daughter. For that daughter, Jana said that she would not go in for the interrogation, and her mother right away reacted that, if daughter was not going—respectively did not want to go—then she would not force her to go.

It seemed like the daughter would go alone, but when her mother said that she would not let her go alone, then the child refused to go (The child obviously did not want to talk in front of her mother). The conversation with the mother took place at the front door of their apartment, and Mrs. Visokaiova told us that she would not let the daughter go to the interrogation alone, so the girl yelled that she was not going, from where we heard the cry of the underaged.

Notes of: mjr. Dziak and kpt. Stefanak

This is an example of how repulsive and arrogant some people can be. They were just one millimetre short of claiming that child was crying because she wanted to go to the police station to testify alone but that her mother would not let her.

Jana had been at the police station. She had been abused to the point that it was the worst day of her life, and it caused a lot of damage to her mental health. Then the same policemen were trying to claim that she would like to go alone and be treated to some more cruelty but that her mother would not let her. I don't think that there is a limit to human arrogance.

Soon, the whole family of Mr. and Mrs. Visokaiova, including their daughter Jana, paid dearly for not playing by corrupt police rules.

***

The investigator had already written a request for my custody. Every request or decision written by whoever was the same. Everybody was simply rewriting what had been made up from A to Z by the crooked investigator Demjan.

Demjan needed to get to my house to look it over. If he knew, what my house looks like on the inside, he would be able to make up the stories, for what would be presented as a record of interrogation of the Demeterova sisters.

He made up the story. They bypassed the prosecutor, and Judge JUDr. Jan Milko issued the search warrant. As the reason, Demjan had stated that there was a suspicion that there might be some photos and video recordings that might be important for a criminal investigation. It did not matter to Judge Milko that there was not a single piece of evidence to corroborate that kind of suspicion. There was never even a statement of where the idea had come from.

The search of my house began on the same day, which was October 12, 1998, at 9:45 PM. According to Slovak law and also the European Convention for the Protection of Human Rights and Fundamental Freedoms, I should have been free already for more than two hours.

All Slovak laws, whether concerning injunction, apprehension, or any other restriction of freedom, are the same on one point. The person whose freedom is restricted must be in front of a judge within twenty-four hours or be let go free. I was not. The Slovak laws, Slovak constitution, the charter of rights, and European agreements were broken.The police were going through all of my personal belongings. They brought a big black video camcorder and recorded the whole interior of my house. They also had a regular camera, and they were taking photos as well. All of this was in order to show the gypsies so they could describe the interior of my house.

Sometimes, there were some funny situations, but they were not funny for me at the time. The policeman who was carrying the big video camcorder placed it down on a table to rest his arms. Another young one walked in and thought it was my camera.

"They put the camera on a tripod, you know, when they take a porno" he said to his older colleagues to impress them with his great observation.

"It is not his camera," the older one corrected him. "It is ours. We brought it here."

The *nuno* ("stupid" in Slovak slang) had been fooled by Demjan. He had actually believed him that I might be producing some videos. The fact was that, to that date, I had never even owned any video cameras. But the *nuno* did not give up.

There were a few VHS tapes on my dresser next to my VHS player. Of course, the policemen were collecting them all. Then *nuno's* big time to impress his superiors came again. He spotted one empty box, from which the cassette was missing. He grabbed it, lifted it high over his head, and yelled so everybody could hear him.

"One of the tapes is hidden somewhere. Here is the empty box."

"Big discovery," I said.

Then I pushed the button on the VHS player, and missing tape came out. All my tapes were about Canada or were some recordings from Miss East Slovakia Beauty Contests, which I was coproducing with the local cultural society. There would be no sign of porn in my place at all. Demjan had made it all up so he could enter my house and look it over.

Than came the big time for Demjan. In my office, there was an old antique gun, which my uncle Juraj Demcak had brought from Argentina as a gift for my dad, his brother. Demjan took the photos of where the gun was located. It was clear that the gun was sitting beside the closet about two feet away. But in his report, he wrote that the gun was behind the closet to give the impression that I had hidden it there. He was so skilled in changing little words, but the difference in meaning was very big.

When the policemen entered my rec room, they lost their speech. I had built it out of rocks. It was the combination of a cave and a glass house. There was a fireplace made out of rocks in the shape of a monster. The fire was burning in his mouth. A hot tub was also set in rocks. In the corner was a blue bathtub, and across from it was the shower in a natural cave setup. Next to the blue bathtub was a pond with a miniature castle high above it on the rocks. Water flowed down the rocks all the way to the pond. It was great to rest there after a whirlpool, listening to the sound of the water fall. I had spent countless hours building the room, picking out the rocks piece by piece, welding the frames for glass, and designing it all. It was to be my summer retreat for my retirement.

All the policemen were shocked when they walked in. By then, some of them suspected that they were being used by Demjan. They had already searched most of the house and found no sign of anything that they were supposed to be looking for. You could hear a fly; that's how quiet it was down there in my "cave." All the policemen just stood there, looking. Some felt envy; some felt respect for the man who had built it. It seemed like they were not sure if they were allowed to speak in a place like that.

Then one of them whispered very quietly, "Can you believe it? A place like this in Trebisov?"

After that, I could sense the feeling that there was no point to continue the search. One by one, the policemen began getting ready to go. Nobody believed that the man who had built that room had the interest or time to do something illegal. They didn't even bother to search my basement, my indoor garage, or my wine cellar. There was also big double garage outside, which nobody bothered to look in. There was a different feeling in the air that was coming from the men. They had attended to the search as their duty to Demjan's request. It was like there were saying, "We've had enough of this. Let's go home." No doubt, those who could think realized right away that they were being used by Demjan for his dirty job. Slower thinkers realized it later, especially when they found out who was behind it all.

What about the judge, Jan Milko? Was he proud of himself that he had issued a search warrant in spite of the fact that there was not a single piece of evidence to support what Demjan was claiming in his request?

CHAPTER SEVEN

The Judges Are Corrupt, the Prosecutors Are Stupid

Where do they fabricate the charge first and then fabricate evidence to fit the charge? In Slovakia.

We were alone in the office after the search of my house, when Policeman Demjan said, "I need your keys."

"I don't have them. I left them at home."

He got really upset. He had plans for my keys, and I had left them at home.

"Why did you leave the keys at home?" He yelled. "I didn't tell you to leave those keys at home."

"I already know you; I know that you are crook," I yelled back at him. "You need my keys so that you can bring your gypsy friends to look over my house, right? I knew it; that is why I left them at home. Your gypsies are liars, just like you. You and the gypsies—you are all the same, one gang, you shitface." I was tired and pissed off, and I did not care anymore, so I let him have it.

"I will take them [the gypsies] there [to my house] anyway," he fired off. "You are not as smart as you think. You will pay for this. You are not coming out if you don't pay. I will destroy you."

I thought, *He has forgotten that times are changing, slowly but surely. Framing the innocent is like eating daily bread for him and for bastards like him.* This was an example of a pure, corrupt communist pig. I will never forget the look on his face and the words:

"You are not coming out if you don't pay. I will destroy you." I would like to know how many people he had already destroyed and how many he would still destroy in the time to come. He enjoyed the power that enabled him to destroy people's lives. An evil devil walking this earth—that was who Demjan was. I guarantee it.

Two policemen took me to a holding cell. There was only a hard bench and no blanket. It was almost the morning of the next day. I guess I clanked out.

The young policeman walked in. He stayed behind the bars, which divided the cell across.

"The budget is thirty korun [about $1] for your meal," he said. "Would you like salami or ham on your sandwich?"

"Salami and milk." I had not eaten for a long time, but I still did not feel like eating. Too much aggravation, too much hassle, too many people that I didn't want to see.

I knew I had to eat to survive.

That same day (October 13, 1998), two young policemen walked to the cell and opened the barred door. I recognized them from walking streets of Trebisov. They were not at all like the communist old-timers. They were nice and polite and well groomed; their uniforms fit them properly.

"We are going to escort you to court, sir," said one. "We have to use these. Sorry, it is regulation." He was showing me the handcuffs. I placed my hands in front of him.

"It won't be necessary," said the other policeman, then he turned to me and asked me,

"Sir Demcak, you will not try to run, right?"

"No, of course not."

"Handcuffs are not needed," he instructed his colleague, who hung his handcuffs back on his belt.

We walked through the underground parking.

"Is somebody picking up your keys?" One of them asked me.

"I left them at home."

"But I saw them at the front desk. The lady asked me if I should take them to court."

"Could you please get them for me? I don't know how they got there. I left them at home."

One policeman went to get my keys.

"Demjan said he will still need them," the policeman told me when he returned.

"He is going to take those gypsies to my place," I said, "to look it over, so they know how to testify."

The policemen did not say yes openly; they just nodded their heads as if to say "We know." These were young policemen who knew what was going on. They did not like what was going on, but there was not much they could do about it. The most they could do was show some compassion or respect, like not placing handcuffs on my hands. I remember that gesture, because the feeling from most of them, especially the older policemen, was much different. It was a feeling like "Finally, you are here, now you are going to pay."

If Demjan had ordered my keys in the morning, he knew I was not going home, even before I faced a judge. Everything was set up against me. Somebody had arranged it nicely in advance.

This was already after the search of my house. The only reason for getting my keys would have to have been to bring the gypsies to my house to look it over. Demjan had it all planned out in advance.

******

It was 1:00 PM. I was escorted in front of a judge. The judge's name was JUDr. Jan Milko—the same judge who, late night yesterday, had ordered the search of my house without any legal documents from the prosecutor. Did he know about section 75 T.P., section 76 paragraphs 1 and 4 T. P., section 69 paragraph 1 T.P., and other laws concerning human rights and freedom? Did he read those laws and not understand them? Or he did understand the meanings of those Slovak laws and choose to ignore them, like the old communists were doing? Or did somebody—the pervert who had abused the child Jana—ask him to go against the law?

The fact is that, according to all those Slovak laws, I should have been a free man for more than fourteen hours. There is no exception to that. And I was not asking if he had ever heard about the European Council Convention for the Protection of Human Rights and Fundamental Freedoms or the Slovak constitution, because maybe he had not bothered to study them. He had broken all those laws without any problem. He had proceeded as if the law did not exist, and that kind of judge was going to serve justice on my head. The future looked black for me.

In the court was Judge Milko, a typist with a typewriter, my lawyer, the prosecutor, and the two policemen who had brought me in. In a Slovak court, the typist does not type what is said. She always waits until judge dictates what should be written down.

Even the prosecutor was bogus. mgr. Maros Sabo was sitting in prosecutor's chair. He was very young. "mgr." is the title of an educator, which I have as well. That means that Sabo should be teaching children at school not prosecuting me. How he had gotten that chair beats me.

Judge Milko had a pile of documents in front of him; it looked like four hundred pages or more. Where had they come from? And what was written on that pile of documents? I was very surprised.

Investigator Demjan was trying very hard, but he had had only one afternoon and one night to gather whatever he could against me. With his typing using just his two index fingers, I estimated he could put together as many as twenty but no more than thirty pages. So where did those four hundred pages come from?

I look closely at the documents, and sure enough, the documents were already joined together and sealed. Normally, the documents of an investigative file are joined after the investigation is completed. No doubt, the judge had the investigative file from some other case and those few pages that Demjan provided were stash inside that file.

All they wanted was to lock me up, and then the investigator would have enough time to fill up whatever was missing. Good trick, Judge Milko. I bet nobody before me caught on to you and that kind of trick of yours.

Maybe I would not have noticed that dirty trick right away if it weren't for Marx and Lenin. I had used the same trick while studying at university. The subject of Marx-Leninism was absolutely compulsory in each semester, and nobody could get around it. All of my essays about Marx-Leninism were only one page long. It was very boring for me to study, and write about something that I believed was total nonsense. I did not want my professor, Sudruh Molcan (sudruh was used by communists instead of Mr. or Sir), to notice right away that all my dissertations were one page only. Most students had forty to fifty pages; some even had two hundred pages or more. Instead of reading the whole book and making a study of it, I borrowed the dissertation from Jan Gajtko, my roommate in the university dormitory, and I made my essay out of his essay. Since I usually worked on it just the night before the deadline, I ended up with only one page for each dissertation. Just like Judge Milko, I stashed that page in some old pile of papers to make it look as if I had a few pages of work done. The trick worked only while the papers were sitting on my desk, while I was glancing at them, while we were discussing the subject, or when professor was just walking by. I was going to write some more pages later, but I never got around to doing it. In the end, I ended up with ten essays on just ten pages. On the final evaluation of my work, professor Molcan wrote beside other things, "All Demcak's essays were only one page long."

There were only few people in court, but Judge Milko did not want anybody to notice that he had virtually nothing to send me to jail for.

There I was, standing in front of the judge. I feel like spitting in his face. What could this man think, when he was using such a primitive trick? Did he think that I would not see what he was trying to do? I felt like telling him how I felt, but I thought I'd better not. He was the one who was going to make the decision about my fate. He was openly corrupt. Who knew what he might do.

> I wonder how many times he had used that kind and similar tricks before and after me. That wasn't the only trick Judge Milko used in my case. In court, he dictated to his typist, skilfully joining one sentence with another in order to change the meaning of the sentence, to make his illegal steps look legal. He dictated to typist what was supposed to be what I said in court:I was apprehended by police on 11.10.1998 at 21:30 at Bratislava/Rusovce. The Decision of Charge was given to me, so I understand the charges against me.

From this, it is understood that the Decision of Charge had been given to me at my apprehension, as was required by law. It never happened that way. The fact is that it was given to me hours later, after I was brought back to Trebisov and after Demjan fabricated it.

Judge Milko was using same trick Demjan was using. Skilfully joining sentences to get a different meaning—the one he wanted.

Judge Milko not only stashed documents from my case into another file to make it look big, the documents he stashed and used against me were illegal to use in court according to Slovak law. He should have read section 158 paragraph 3 T.P. and had somebody explain the meaning of this law to him, if he had had difficulty to understand it. This paragraph of Slovak law orders that the information that was taken from the child Jana should have been taken by an investigator, not by the plain policeman, pprap. Gazdura, on October 1, 1998.

The same applied to the interrogation that had taken place the next day, when the child Jana had been taken from school to the police station where she had been grossly abused. Again, only a plain policeman, npor. Sereg Vl, had signed the document. According to Slovak law, none of them was competent to interrogate the child. But that is not all. Section 158 paragraph 5 T.P. forbids using these documents in court completely, because the information had been gotten before the investigation by an investigator had officially begun.

So Judge Milko was using against me documents that were obtained illegally by incompetent policemen, and those documents were also illegal for use in court according to valid Slovak law. That is still not all.

What about the fact that not even one single document that was presented to the

judge by Demjan had been registered. None were numbered, stamped, or marked, which is proof that none of those documents had been registered at the Office of Registry. That fact made all the documents that were used against me in court invalid and the whole proceedings illegal.

I believe strongly that the Judge did know all that, but he knowingly went against the law for a reason that he should explain.

What about the prosecutors? Did none of them notice that the whole case was just a scam? Basically, they could not.

I have an official document that states that prosecutor JUDr. Maria Pacutova, *(JUDr. – title for graduates in law)* on October 12, 1998, refused my complaint against the investigator's charge. I had my suspicions, and I was right. I closely examined the document and found out that she had not seen it at all. Somebody had fabricated the document in her name and signed it "instead of her." Most likely, she was surprised that her name appeared there at all. The big question is: "Who fraudulently used the prosecutor's name against me?" It was one of first forgeries, and many more followed.

I offered to present telephone recordings as proof that the Demeterova sisters and their pimp did blackmail me, and now they are listed as witnesses against me.

I also offered the invitation from the Canadian consulate as proof that I was going to Austria for only one day; therefore, the suggestion that I was escaping was absurd. No chance was given to me to present my proof, but the fact that proof was not there was later used against me.

Did Judge Milko understand Slovak law section 89 paragraph 2 T.P., which clearly names sound recordings as admissible proof in court? Legal evidence and proof were not considered, but the illegal proof was used. That was the judgment of Judge Milko.

Section 92 paragraph 2 T.T. says that to the person who is accused must be given the chance to speak about the charge in small details, mainly concerning the charge, to describe situations that diminish the charge or contradict it, and to present proof.

Here, I was offering proof, and here was the law that had clearly been broken.

The prosecutor and judge were responsible that everything goes according to the law. The judge was corrupt, and the prosecutor was phony. His name was Maros Sabo. During the whole procedure, he did not say a word. He only said yes when the judge asked him questions. He said less than the retarded gypsy Alena Demeterova had said at the confrontation. The judge asked him, if he wanted to detain me according to section 67a. He said yes. 67b? Yes. 67c? Yes.

That was it. The whole prosecution. No reasons, no evidence, no proof—and he never spoke again in the court that afternoon.

At the time, I wondered why my lawyer, JUDr. Hajdu, did not protest clearly that the whole proceeding was illegal.

Investigator Demjan, and Judge Milko were covering the child molestation case, which had happened at the police station, and the lawyer Hajdu was not objecting.

And what about the complainer? Did anybody ask how this case began in the first place? Nobody had filed any complaints against me. Nobody had claimed any damages, so why was I there? Did anybody in that court understand any law at all? Had anybody read the chapter "Basics of Criminal Responsibility" in the Slovak law book *Criminal Law*? In that book section 3 paragraph 2 T. Z. reads: "A criminal offence in which the level of danger for the public is small is not a criminal offence, in spite of the fact that it shows signs of criminal offence."

If the judge was influenced by somebody to make that wrong decision, than that somebody should have read section 169a paragraph 2 T.Z., which warns that if you wrongly influence a judge in his responsibilities, the minimum conviction in the case like that would be three years, and it could be as high as ten years.

And in his decision, the judge wrote that both Demeterova sisters were accusing me, in spite of the fact that Anna had not even been interviewed at the time at all, and not one single document was in his hands about her at all.

Can anybody comprehend that?

I objected, Your honour, with my passport, I can prove that I was in Canada at the time when, according to the charge, I'm accused of committing the crime in Slovakia."

Judge Milko had no problem with that either. He simply himself changed the dates to fit times when I was in Slovakia. Now different dates are in the charge and on the court documents. Is that the problem in Slovakia? No!

And how do you explain this sentence from his decision?

> The acts that we suspect that he committed allegedly happened in 1995 and 1996, then he went abroad, and then from July 1998 when he returned. There is suspicion that he was committing those acts without any break. That is why we fear that he may continue in them even now.

I would be ashamed to write something like that. From 1996 to 1998, two years passed, but according to the judge's understanding, two years was no break at all.

To make it complete, Judge Milko shocked me one more time. When I objected against the conduct of the police who abused the child Jana Visokaiova at the police station, he called me to his bench, pulled out the bottom part of the document, which was supposed to be the interrogation of Jana Visokaiova at the police station, and showed me the signature of the school principal ("RNDr. Marcela Ferkova, Principal, Elementary School Komenskeho). They wrote that she had been there during the interrogation, the reading, and the signing. That would make her an accomplice to the abuse of a child she was responsible for.

I was totally shocked. That document had been shown to me at the police station before. I had read it, and I was most disgusted that nobody was present, only the police—no parent, no educator, no psychologist. I'm a qualified educator, and I knew for sure that somebody should have been there, even by Slovak standards, and was not. That was why I had written a complaint against it. And here, he was showing me that the principal had signed it as if she had been there.

I knew it was a lie, like all of the procedures, and I knew I was helpless to do anything about it. There was no way that the lady principal could have been there when the brutal abuse of the child was going on. Somebody had forged her signature.

Judge Milko knew exactly what he was doing. He made sure that, even though there were only a few people in the court, they would not realize what he was doing. That was why he did not read any documents in court. How could he have read that gross record, which was de facto proof that the child Jana Visokaiova had been abused at the police station? How could he have read that completely senseless record that the investigator had written during the confrontation with the retarded gypsy Alena Demeterova? Or how could he have let me play the recording that would prove that the gypsies whose names were in the charge against me were also the ones who were involved in blackmailing me with their pimp? And the police were their accomplices then. He kept it all skilfully under the cover, but two policemen who were in the court noticed it anyway. I knew I was in trouble.

Judge Milko ordered that my detention be enforced in the prison in Kosice.

On the way to a holding cell, one of the young policemen said to the other, "I did not think he would be imprisoned. There was nothing against him. Everybody in Trebisov knows that gypsies were blackmailing him."

CHAPTER EIGHT

Welcome to My Nightmare

Is it one hundred jokes by George Burns? No. It is one hundred broken laws by Jan Demjan.

Soon, I was sitting in the backseat of an unmarked police car. I knew the road very well. As a bicycle racer, I had passed that hilly road countless times. The biggest hill is called the Dargov.

On the top, there was a big statue called the Statue of Soviet Heroes. A big Soviet soldier stood in the middle, and two small people were on each side. The little people represented Slovaks. German soldiers had a strong hold on these heavily forested hills when the Soviets were chasing them back home in the Second World War. Thousands lost their lives there. Gratitude should be given only to those soldiers who placed their lives on the line., not to those who occupied Slovakia and other countries for more than forty years.

As I passed the sculpture, I remember my two uncles who also lost their lives in the same war, fighting for freedom. They were Frantisek and Stefan Milovcik from the town called Secovce. Both were young, and they voluntarily joined the army. One of them lost his life right in Dargov's hills while defusing mines. A mine went off right in his face. The other uncle was shot by a German soldier two days after the war was over. The German soldier was hiding in the bushes and had not gotten the message that Germany had surrendered, and the war was over. He surprised a group of young Slovak soldiers who were celebrating the end of the war by a campfire. The German sprayed them all with machine gun bullets. My uncle was one of them. No statue was erected for those two young men or for many other Slovaks who lost their lives, fighting for freedom. The communists forgot about them.

I was not paying attention to what I was doing, when I realized that I had taken my handcuffs off. I'd done it many times before when I had demonstrated escape techniques as part of my magic show. I was going to hand them to my escorting policemen, but I decided that I'd better not. Who knew what their reactions would be. They could even punish me for the little joke. I put the handcuffs back on my hands.

At the gulag in Kosice, a guard took me downstairs to a storage room. The guard took all my clothes. He placed the prison wardrobe—a pair of socks, green boxer shorts, a blue shirt, a black hat, a blue sweat suit, and brown sandals—on a platform, along with a pillow, a blanket, bedsheets, orange pyjamas, a spoon, toothpaste, and a toothbrush.

He let me keep my book. I had taken it when they were searching my house. It was the first book that I had gotten my hands on. It happened to be the last book by George Burns, *100 Jokes*. Believe me, the whole situation was not a joke at all. If I called the situation *100 Tortures*, *100 Criminal Acts*, or *100 Broken Laws* by Jan Demjan it would have been a much more realistic title.

It would be much better for me, if I were writing fiction and not a true story. Believe me; it is not easy for me to write about the horrors that went on behind those walls. It is all coming back to me, like the worst nightmare, even now. But I have no choice but to write. I was not the only one who was abused in that gulag. There were many more. The worst part is that the abuse is continuing today. By writing about it, I'm hoping to help other prisoners who are also being abused. And other children who are being abused, other witnesses who are being locked up just to shut them up—like I was. I'm hoping that, by bringing this into public knowledge, help will get to those unfortunate people. Guilty or innocent, the civilised world must not let abuse like this go on.

Please keep in mind that this is a true story. Not only is it true, but for every allegation in this book, I have evidence to prove it.

I was escorted to a cell. There were four bunk beds in the far corners, two below, and two above them. The space between them was about three to four feet wide. A little window just about two feet by two feet was in the far wall. The glass was painted a light yellow, so not much light was getting in. The bars on it were about an inch in diameter. You could not walk to the window, because other wall-to-wall bars were about four feet from the wall where the window was located. That divider was called a gater—that means a complete bar wall from the cement floor to the ceiling. In the right corner, right behind the door, was the toilet. It was all open. Only a little board about two feet wide divided it from the rest of the cell. On the other side of the board was a sink. Next to it was a small metal closet that was attached to the wall. There were four small sections in it—one for each prisoner—of about one foot by one foot by one foot.

Next to the closet was a small, metal desk and four metal stools. There were two openings in the heavy, metal door. One was a plain, peephole. The other was a feeding opening, just big enough for the average plate or small pot to fit through. Both openings were controlled only from the outside.

The prison had been built by the communist government. It was located in the middle of the city. Kosice was the second largest city in Slovakia after the capital, Bratislava. The city of Bratislava was on the west side of the country, and Kosice was on the east side.

The front end of the prison was located on a very busy street, which was the main drag between Kosice and Roznava. From the street, you could not see that it was a prison at all. It looked like any other business. A small sign read "Provincial Court, Kosice." Thousands of motorists who drove by it every day had no idea that they were passing the gulag of the new times.

The building was U-shaped, with the sides facing very small roads with hardly any traffic on them at all. The back part of the complex was just a brick wall about three stories high. Old faded signs read "No parking!" That high wall was the only clear indication that it might have a jail behind it.

They took prints of all my fingers and thumbs. Soon after that, they took my photo—a front view and both sides. After that, I was escorted to a dark room, where benches were along both walls. I was ordered to take all my clothes off. The feeling was terrible, because I had no idea where I was going or what was going on. All kinds of things were going through my mind. *What are they going to do? Where are they taking me? Are there torture chambers behind the door? Why am I here alone? Why do they want me to take all my clothes off?*

The door opened, and behind it was a large, brightly illuminated room. There were people dressed in white. There were some ladies and also men. I was relieved. It was the medical examination. Then I realized that I was walking into a room of strangers, including women, completely naked. I was a private person, not used to promenading naked in front of people.

As far as nudist beaches are concerned, I've visited one only once. It was the famous Wreck Beach in Vancouver, British Columbia, Canada. I lived not too far from it and heard that a few thousand people went there every summer. I decided to check it out. There were two reasons why I never went back. The first was that the sun was shining from the wrong side. I like it when sun is shining from the ocean. Secondly, I was not impressed with some weirdos who were walking around, staring at my "apparatus," as if they had never seen one before.

Imagine this. You are on a beach where everybody is naked. But some weirdo still hides in the bushes, and when some girl walks by alone, he jumps out, flashing his "equipment." Can you believe this? I decided that kind of environment was not for me.

Back in the gulag, the nurse marked down information about me and took my blood pressure. I had other things on my mind, so I did not notice if she also checked my "machinery."

Four new prisoners were also brought in for examination. All four of them were gypsies. Two of them were well built and were not paying any attention to their "tackle technology," which was hanging below their stomachs, swinging from side to side in pendulum motion as they walked into the room. It was obvious that these two had been there, done that.

The other two gypsies were just the total opposite. They were very young and shy. Using both hands, they were desperately trying to hide their "gear instruments." They almost managed to do it; only now and then did a little smoked "European wiener," or "pigeon-size egg" protrude from behind their palms. Most likely, it was their first beauty contest.

I would think that jail medical staff in Kosice could allow for prisoners to use at least towels for this kind of procedure, so that human dignity would be respected. Also sitting on chairs on which other naked prisoners had been sitting before me is not what I consider hygienic. You could not expect any consideration during communist times, because jails had been run by tyrants. But a more civilised society should not allow that kind of abuse. I felt completely degraded at the time. Promenading naked in a brightly lit room with ladies, men, and gypsies present was shameful time for me. Little did I know that it was only the beginning.

I was asked to cough while doctor was closely watched my "natural paraphernalia." I remembered this examination from years back when I had been admitted to the Czechoslovak army. So I knew it was part of the standard examination and not just a trick of the examiner's to validate my "tools."

When a man coughs, his "tackle gear" jumps up. That is not why the examiner asks him to cough. While examiner is on his knees, he is observing if the "slag hammer" of the prisoner actually jumps. If the "hammer" does not jump as required by regulation, it means that the proper connection had been lost and that a "tune-up" is required. The worst scenario of this malfunction could be that "penetration" would not be possible.

In reality, the examiner watches both sides of the lower stomach, and coughing helps him to diagnose if the patient has a hernia.

After that, the examiner stuck a needle in a blood vessel in my left arm. All my life, I have been afraid of needles. It is to the point that I let the dentist drill my teeth without anaesthetics.

This time, the examiner gave me no choice. I closed my eyes and hoped it would be over soon. But the needle was in for what seemed to me like an eternity. My hands and feet became cold. It felt like millions of ants had gotten into my brain. He was just draining the blood out of me until I lost consciousness. He drained almost all of my blood.

I imagine that they carried me out naked, because I was in a waiting room when I woke up. A guard was slapping my face.

"Time to go," he said.

I was dizzy, but I managed to pull my sweatpants on and stick my feet into my sandals. Hobbling, I followed the guard to a lift. Inside the elevator, there was already another guard, who was escorting a gypsy prisoner. I was lost consciousness again. As I came to, the gypsy prisoner was lifting me up.

"Sir, sir, wake up," he was yelling into my face. Then the guard slapped my face.

"That is how you do it," he said to the gipsy. "This will wake him up faster." He was going to slap me from the other side, but the gypsy blocked his hand with his elbow.

"Do not do it. The man is sick," he yelled into his face.

The guard reached for his baton.

"You f-----g "more" [a nickname for gypsy], I will show you who is … " He was going to give it to him, but the guard who was escorting me stepped in.

"Cool it," he said. "He is a foreigner." He pointed at me. The aggressor just looked at me with disgust. He hung his baton back on his belt. The gypsy helped me pull my sandals back on, and I hobbled to the cell.

It was the first time but not the last time that a gypsy showed compassion for a human being, the human side of a person, the side that many guards and other officials in justice and politics lost or never had. This young boy was a little taller than me, but he chose to risk his safety for me, for somebody he had never met before. He had stood against evil, while two biffed-up guards with the biggest batons hanging at their sides were present. Who knows how it would have ended up if I had been another Slovak or another gypsy. And who knows what happened to him after that, when I as a foreigner was not present.

In that state of my situation, I did not even thank him, which really bothered me a lot. I thought, *I will thank him when I see him again.* I had no idea that I would almost never be able to do so. The whole system was run in a way that you very seldom see any other prisoners. That gave guards free hands to abuse, without any witnesses or without giving prisoners the chance to complain to each other. But by accident, I got my chance to thank him. It was much later, in the elevator again, when I was on my way to another medical examination. I was already in the elevator when the guard brought him. He recognized me right away.

"I helped you when—"

"No talking," his guard yelled at him.

"Yes, I remember. Thank you," I said.

"Didn't you hear me? No talking." This time, the guard yelled at me.

That gypsy is on my list as one of the people I would like to see again so I can really show my gratitude or just see how he is doing. In a desperate situation, a little gesture means a lot, because you feel the difference much more. On the one side, a gypsy is a crook. Most likely he was a small-timer, like most gypsies are. But he had a human side to him, and it came out. On the other side, there were two guards. Both guards had only crap inside of them. I still don't understand where that kind of person came from. How could they watch me when I was falling down in pain, and neither of them moved a finger?

I could hardly wait to fall on the bed after they drained blood from me. Somebody was banging loudly on the steel door. Then he opened the feeding hole and yelled through it.

"No lying on the bed."

I did not know the rules of the house yet. One of them was no resting on the bed during the day. I had no energy to get up. There was very little blood left in my system and no food or liquids to replenish it. So I rolled off the bed, fell on the cement floor, and passed out.

When I woke up, another gypsy was over me trying to get me to drink some water. I was already on the bed. I guess he had lifted me off the floor and placed me on the bed while I was "sleeping." He also tried to feed me. Supper was in a camp-style aluminum pot. It must have been delivered while I was still in a dream world. It was noodles with poppy seeds. It was actually my favourite meal. It could have been a little bit sweeter, but otherwise, it was okay.

"You must eat," he said, "or you will not survive here."

"Who are you? Where am I?"

"I'm a prisoner, just like you. We are both in jail. Why are you here?" he asked.

"They brought me here, I guess."

"I mean, what you have done?" he asked again.

"Gypsies were blackmailing me, so they sent me here."

"Oh, I understand." He got the message right away. "You must be rich."

"The police and everybody are against me. They think I have a lot of money because I'm Canadian, but they are wrong," I explained.

As soon as I told him that I was Canadian, his attitude changed. He took me by my sleeve to the corner opposite from the toilet and began talking very quietly. He pointed to the ceiling and placed his fingers over his lips, as if to say to talk very quietly. I got the message. The bug must have been there.

"If you have a lot of money," he said, "you are not getting out as long as they think that you have money or anything at all. That is the law here," he was whispering in my ear.

"But I haven't done anything," I objected.

"They don't care if you are guilty; they only want your money." He had just proved what Investigator Demjan had told me just the day before yesterday."

"You will pay for it dearly," he'd said. "You are not coming out unless you pay. I will destroy you." I remembered it very clearly.

"Why are you here?" I asked him, for a change of topic. "Two murders," he answered. "I'm Fero Holub."

He passed me his hand. His name did not tell me much, mainly because I had been in Canada when his case was famous in the Slovak media. He told me the story about how his brother had been killed by some crooks, about how they had tried to kill him as well, and about how he defended himself. In the process, he killed two of his attackers. It sounded like a bedtime story or self-defence to me.

"It was self-defence all right," he agreed when I told him my opinion, "but my family still owns the house, which is why I'm still here. The police already have all my money, and now they want the house of my parents. But they are not getting this one."

"What do you mean, they want your house? How can they take your house?" I wanted to know.

"Are you stupid?" he asked. "Where are you living? On the moon? You don't know what is going on in here. Everybody knows it. They keep you here in an investigating prison until you sell everything you have and give them all the money. Then they convict you anyway and send you to normal prison. Normal prison is heaven compared with this one. Here is hell on earth. You will see. Especially if you have money, a

house, or anything."

He filled me in on the situation very well. In time, I found out, from different people and my concrete situations, that he was right.

The prison had two parts. One was called the investigative prison. In that section were the prisoners who were awaiting their trials. These were people who had not been convicted of any crimes yet. That meant, according to Slovak law and all international agreements, they were still presumed innocent. But it was a place and time when corrupt justice officials would drain money from the prisoners. Once the prisoners and their families were completely broke, there was no longer a reason to keep them there. They would be convicted, whether they had committed any crimes or not. Then they were sent to the section of the jail for convicted prisoners. When they came out, they and their families were completely broke—financially, spiritually, and mentally. The system worked perfectly. Most officials were involved, and they were much better organized than any criminal organisation, including the real Italian mafia.

"If Canada will fight for you, you have a chance to get out of here. Broke, but alive. Promise that, if you get out, you will let the world know what is going on in here."

"Of course, I will," I promised.

Then he told me horror stories that I thought, at first, were the imagination of a gypsy who had been in a jail for a long time and needed some attention. *Sure, it could happen in communist times, but now?* I thought. The more he told me, I realized that he would have to be really good fiction writer with an imagination like that. Realizing that he was not Stephen King, I began to believe his horror stories of what was happening in that prison. Later, I discovered from other prisoners and my own experience that all those unbelievable fairy tales of abuse were reality not the fiction of somebody's imagination. They were sad but real.

He also gave me very valuable advice:

"Never complain about anything," he said, "and never ask for anything. If you complain here about something, they will make it worse. If you ask for something, you will get just the opposite."

Then he reached deep inside his underwear and pulled out a little, folded paper. He unfolded it and pulled apart a postal stamp, envelope, and paper.

"Here. Write home, and ask them to send you envelopes, writing papers, and many stamps. Stamps are a high commodity here. And be careful what you write; they read all mail. Do not seal your envelopes. They will seal it for you after they read what you write. And don't forget to let everybody know what is going on in here when you get out."

"I will, and thanks for the advice and the stamp. When I see you again, I will return your stamp to you."

"You will not see me here anymore."

"Why not?"

"They have a system here that you do not see the same person twice," he assured me. I could not see how that could be—to be in the same prison and never to see somebody again. Soon I found out that they know how, and they do it just as well.

Surprise, surprise; later, I was reading a Slovak national magazine who Fero H. really was. Allegedly, Fero and his brother were running an organized crime ring under the beautiful High Tatra Mountains. They lived in a town called Spisske Podhradie. Allegedly, there was a war with another organized crime group, in which Fero's brother was killed. Fero apparently revenged his brother, by killing two of the enemies. What exactly happened, nobody knows for sure.

Before I went to sleep, I sat at the table and wrote:

Dear Bibiana! Tuesday, 13 October 1998

As you see, one phone call, and it was enough for me to be here. Talk to the lawyer, and ask what you can write and what you cannot. He will advise you, because they check all the mail. Make a drawing for Milan so he knows where the car is so he can bring it home.

I miss you very much. I hope I will last few days here. The last days were full of stresses and disappointments. You can write to me here.

Turn off the phone's answering machine, and you can answer the telephone, because now you are the landlady of the house, just like you wanted to be but without the landlord.

So far that is all.

Love, dodo.

P.S. Please water the flowers. The upstairs ones only to the bottom plates, and the rest just normal.

Please mail me from my bag: 3 skin creams, razor blades, shaving cream, shampoo, toothpaste, soap, writing paper, envelopes, stamps, ½ kilo of sugar. The parcel must not be heavier than 5 kilos. Also vitamin C, plastic cap, tea, cookies, magazines, elastic bands for magic, a brown bottle with liquid, and cotton balls. You must write my date of birth under my name on the address. Thanks.

That was my first letter to my love, Bibiana.

I was very tired, but my sleep was very light. Every once a while, there was a loud sound on the door. It sounded like somebody had unlodged and then re-lodged the lock on the door. It seemed like it always happened when I was about to fall asleep. Not one good sleep did I have during my stay in that prison.

CHAPTER NINE

Neo Gulag

Torture? No. Gross abuse. No. Just no comfort. (Canadian politics)

The guard unlocked the heavy, steel door, and I was in a room that was to be my home for who knew how long. It was exactly the same room, like I had had for the past two days, except that two prisoners were in it. One was a gypsy. His name was Jan. In a friendlier form, you could call him Janco, which was pronounced Jancho. He was a dark-skinned gypsy. The other prisoner was a little younger. His name was Miro. He had black hair and a full beard. Only after the velvet revolution and the official (not real) fall of the communist system, would they allow longer hair or beards in a prison. More than 80 percent of the inmates in a Slovak prison were gypsies. That was why all the prisoners I had met so far, except Miro, were gypsies.

Janco was very polite. "My name is Jan Gore. I'm from Kosice, and I'm here for robbery," he introduced himself in the usual, customary way in prison.

In case you are imprisoned in Slovakia, it would be good for you to know that there are many customs. It is considered polite behaviour if you remember to say your full name, where you are from, and what brought you in. Do not lie about your crime, no matter how gross it is, because when Judge mailes some court documents to you, everybody is very eager to read them. It is one of very few ways to get excited and entertained. These are only the first rules in there, so do not think that you are all ready to go in. There are many more policies to make you a good prisoner. I will fill you in as they appear.

The second guy was Miro, a small-timer from Michalovce. And he was in for breaking and entering and forgery.

Another rule is seniority. Whoever has been in the longest got to choose his bed. Usually, the bottom bed was preferred by guys with more seniority. That was where Jancho was, of course. He had been in that cell, without a conviction, for almost three years, not counting the years he had spent in prisons for previous convictions. He was what was called a recidivist.

But he packed his bed and moved it to the top one. Not knowing at the time that the bottom bed is for privileged people and that I should be honoured. I told him that it was not necessary, but he insisted, and made up my bed for me where his was before. I think that he recognised that I was little different than prisoners he was accustomed to.

Jancho was as polite and considerate as a gipsy could be. In his manners, he beat many guards and also some white people. When he found out that smoking bothered me, he did not take it lightly. Each time he wanted to light up a cigarette, he climbed up onto the top bed and blew smoke straight toward the window. Even though, the bars of the gater were about one metre from the window, most of the smoke went out, and it did not affect me as much. By climbing up onto the top bed, he was actually risking punishment, because we were not allowed to touch our beds during the daytime.

The only setback was that he rolled his own cigarettes out of a tobacco called Taras Bulba, which was the cheapest tobacco you could buy. It also stank. If you combine terrible tobacco and whatever paper, including toilet paper or newspaper, that he could roll it in, the result was that it stank like cholera. Later, when I found out that there was a little window downstairs where, once a week, you could buy some groceries and cigarettes, I offered to buy him normal smokes so I would not have to smell that terrible stink of the Taras Bulba tobacco. Jancho was so grateful that he would not have to smoke that stink anymore that he offered to do all the chores I was required to do in the cell for me.

The wake-up call was at 5:30 AM. We had until 6:00 to make up our beds, wash ourselves, and dress. At 6:00, the warden of our section made his daily visit. By the sounds at neighbouring doors, my cellmates knew exactly when he was going to enter. All three of us lined up behind the door and across from the toilet. With the loud noise of the locks and latches, the big, steel door opened and a big, at least six-foot, man walked in.

Other guard always stayed outside the door for safety. In case of any problems in the cell, he could run and call for help. Like all guards, he wore the Slovak army uniform. Nobody knew his name. There were no name tags or numbers on any of the guards. That way, a prisoner was unable to report the name of a guard who abused him. Inmates called the warden only by his nickname, Mojo. While most guards had smaller batons, he had the largest; it was L shaped. In his hands, he had a book, in which he was writing. "Anybody for shopping? Mail? Keep your cell clean." That was all.

I learn a lot that day.

I could buy some groceries once a week for whatever money I had on my prison account. Bibiana had to send me finances for me to be able to buy some groceries.

Every second week, there was worship downstairs in a makeshift chapel. I could sign up, and if I was picked up by the warden, I would be escorted there. Space was limited.

I could write home but not seal the envelope. They want to know what I was writing. If I received mail, they opened it for me to be "helpful." Regulation said that they should only look inside to see if there was some object in the envelope. But they did a much better job, so they read and/ or copied the letters. Once a month, I could receive a parcel, but it could be no heavier than five kilos.

Once a month, I could have visitors, but no more than five people, and visits were subject to police approval.

No typewriters, no musical instruments, no hobbies, no telephones, and no currency were allowed at all. The only luxury was a submersible electric heater to boil water for tea or coffee, but there was only one per cell. Electricity came on at suppertime for a limited time only.

Every day, except during statuary holidays, we had the right to go out for a walk, which could be up to an hour long. Twice a week was a shower, which was compulsory. Once a week, we could exchange our shirt, socks, underwear, and pyjamas. From wake-up time until 5:00 PM, you were not allowed to lie down or sit on the bed. No climbing on the gater or looking out the window. No talking through the wall to somebody in a neighbouring cell. No talking to anybody, anywhere, except your cellmate. No taking anything at all when leaving the cell. No radios, no alcohol, no drugs, no medicine, no money, no sprays, no vitamins, no, no, no … no end to nos. The only contact with the outside world was through mail, but only if they sent it for you.

It was a horrible realization—the power people can have over others. And what if that power ended up in the wrong hands? That's how Lenin, Stalin, Hitler, and others were made.

Suddenly, you were cut from your life. Nothing existed any more. You were no longer who you used to be. Your work stopped. Your family, your friends, your love, your pets—everything was out of reach. You got up in the morning, and there was nothing for you to do. It was an empty feeling. Everybody who was in the room had the same empty feeling getting out of them. You were not used it. Your brain was deteriorating, because its use was limited. The worst part about the whole thing was when you knew that you had done nothing wrong at all.

******

Heavy locks moved with a loud noise, and the big, steel door opened.

"Demcak. Visitor," a guard yelled.

He took me downstairs down a long corridor. Doors were on both sides of it, and behind them, office-style rooms were located. The guard showed me to one. An office desk was in front of a large window. The glass of the window was milky, but shadows of standard-size bars were visible behind it. A few chairs were also along both sides of the room. A little metal cabinet was on the left side. I had no idea what was in the cabinet, because the door was shut. My lawyer JUDr. Hajdu was in there, sitting behind the desk. He got up. We shook hands. "How are you," he asked first.

"Surviving, so far. What is going on?"

"The first thing we should do is apply for bail."

"I don't want any bail. I haven't done anything. Shouldn't they have something against me before I need bail?" I was still naive, not realizing where I was. It was the system of old communists, and they needed nothing to be able to hold me. "Did you see that gypsy Alena and how the investigator was leading her? They can't take that seriously. And that judge—how could he write that I was committing a crime without a break when, in the same sentence, he wrote that I was out of the country for two years? Is he stupid or what? And what about the crime? Can you complain or do something about it?"

"Yes, I will," he said. "And the search of your house? Their jaws clamped shut. Empty on that as well. I still think that we should file for bail."

"I want to see something against me before I pay bail. There cannot be anything, because, I have done nothing at all. And those gypsies—they were blackmailing me, and I have proof. I have proof from my telephone recordings, and the judge did not pay any attention to it. Can you please give one message to Bibiana?"

"Sure, I will."

I hesitated a little, because I did not trust him, mainly because he was such a chum with the investigator. But then, I decided to take my chance. "Please tell Bibiana that the tape with the gypsies' voices is in the bathroom behind the sink."

I was going to tell him that some money was also there, but I decided I'd better not. It was a logical conclusion that, when she looked for the tape, she would find the money as well.

When I remodelled the bathroom, I made a little hiding place behind the sink. It was fireproof and not visible at all. That was where I hid my valuables. The best bet for me was to wait until Bibiana had the tape and money, and then I would give her further instructions.

I realized that I made a mistake when I refused to apply for bail right away. I didn't know that all officials could be corrupt. Who would believe it? Would anybody believe it even now, if I didn't have proof for everything I'm writing? I thought, *The first honest person who gets the investigative documents in his hands will send me home.* How could I know that there was nobody honest in Trebisov's justice system? During his second visit, it was clear to me that JUDr. Hajdu would not move a finger against his friends in his town. Trebisov was a small enough town where everybody knew everybody. When I was arrested, people talked a lot about it. No doubt, many knew who was behind all of this. I decided to look into the possibility of JUDr. Fercakova. At least she was from Kosice and not from Trebisov. She was the one Fero Holub recommended to me when he was my roommate for a few hours during my first day in prison.

I should have listened to Fero Holub, when he advised me not to complain about anything. As soon as the warden Mojo find out that I was allergic to cigarette smoke, we received a new roommate. The new cellmate smoked virtually nonstop. Even in the middle of the night, he would light up. That was very harmful for me, because of my allergy. My nose bled every time he lit a cigarette.

The new roommate was also a "corridor boy." A corridor boy was a prisoner who was also a caretaker of the prison corridors. He washed long hallways, cleaned the warden's office, disinfected the shower, and did other chores. Three times a day, he pushed a cart with food and passed it through the little windows on the cell doors to prisoners while a guard accompanied him. Suspicions among the prisoners were that many corridor boys were also informers. I contacted JUDr. Fercakova by mail. She sent me a form, and on October 21, 1998, I signed the agreement and gave her the power to represent me.

******

Soon, I began to realize what was going on in that investigative prison. Now that the system had changed and some people owned some land, properties, and even some money, neocommunist, corrupt officials were taking whatever was possible from them.

In investigative prisons, they used abuse to make prisoners more willing to pay. Psychologists and other scientists took part in inventing and improving the torture.

It was created in the old communist system to punish political prisoners. Stealing was not a big crime then, because almost everybody was doing it. But if you said something against communists or the system, you were in big trouble. If you managed to get out, you would never try to speak up again. Millions were never seen again in the Soviet Union.

Even politicians in democratic countries avoided the subject of torture. It happened to me when I returned to Canada and realized how arrogant the Canadian liberal government was. An official from the Department of Foreign Affairs was trying to persuade me that what I had been put through in the Slovak jail maybe wasn't torture but only gross abuse. When I was willing to settle for gross abuse, he continued to water it down, suggesting that maybe it was only mistreatment. Later, it was just not comfortable in that jail. This after my health and my life were ruined in there. I was getting sick to my stomach just listening to him. That was how our politicians, who lived off our tax money, treated us. Try to tell this kind of person with a closed mind about mental torture. They will secretly think that you are mentally retarded, because they are unable to understand it.

There was a faint hope for me to survive. The Meciar's HZDS or Movement for a Democratic Slovakia lost the election. The government of Mikulas Dzurinda won. Dzurinda was not one of the corrupted excommunists. Hopefully, he would deal with it. Bibiana would send me all the fighting tools. I had my pen, paper, and stamps, and I was not about to sit and rot in that hole.

We were full—up to capacity—in the cell. That meant we were four of us, and everybody had a story to tell. Everybody had been abused in one way or another. In every case, justice officials broke laws. They acted like the law did not exist at all.

Hi Bibiana, 15.10.1998

I hope you have all the keys. When I was leaving, the investigator had the key to the house. It was a big mistake that you gave them keys. You must not believe anybody. He brings dark ones [gipsies] there to look over my house, so they remember it. You do not have to talk to anybody. Simply refuse it. Don't forget that things are being invented against me. It isn't truth, of course. I hope you understand it.[…]

Say hi to my mom. Explain to her, mainly, that it is not the truth and that, if there is any fairness, it will be proven. I'm not convicted. I'm in investigating prison, and somebody is trying to drown me.

Watch everything, and be very careful.

It was not pleasant to see when you were talking to people who are trying to drown me, and then you gave those keys to them. If they made copies, they will come into the house whenever they choose. All locks to which they had keys should be changed. Keep the door to the basement locked, and leave the key in the lock. It will be needed to put together a larger amount of money, in case bail is needed. Tell Milan to stop building and start saving, because it goes for his brother. The bail will be returned after court. Most likely, all kinds of thoughts and doubts are going through your mind. If you believe it, then you don't have to come, and you should not come to see me. You know best, because you are always with me. I know the truth the best, but I'm quiet for now, because I don't believe anybody.

It will be hard period for you, but a far cry from as hard as for me.

Do not write anything about the case. It does not interest me, and they could use it against me. I have nothing to hide. I've done nothing, and I'm here.

Thank you for now.

Love, dodo.

P.S. Is the car at home yet? Send 1000 korun by money order to my address.

I was very desperate. There I was on one side, and the corrupt Investigator Demjan was on the other. Bibiana was in the middle. Only I knew what a creep he was. Only I knew that everything against me had been fabricated by him. She had no means of knowing. She had to decide who to believe. Him or me. And I expected 100 percent trust. It was stupid of me to write that sentence, and I still regret it: "If you believe it [what Demjan was saying], then you don't have to come, and you should not come to see me." That is what I wrote.

I had to be very hurt to write something like that. I should have at least given her time until things were clear or at least explained, The way she handled the whole situation was amazing, and I will never forget it.

The regulations of the prison stated that, once a day, except on statuary holidays, we could go for a walk outside. I thought we would go out to the yard and walk around with the other prisoners like I had seen on television. I was wrong. If it was that way, the prisoners could talk to each other, and stories about abuse would spread. The less people knew about it, the easier it was to suppress, and/or have everyone distrust somebody who would like to talk about it. The communists thought about everything when they built that gulag. Abuse in prison during communism was widely known, but proving it was impossible. Those prisoners who knew first-hand about the abuse could only whisper about it. The others heard about it later, most of the time, after they had been convicted and moved to other wings or to a completely different prison. They were so glad to be out of the gulag of horrors that they would not dare to talk about it. They were so afraid of being brought back that they were glad just to be able to be quiet about it.

After they are out of prison, everybody knew, one complaint and you were back. And the reason? Because you complained. That was exactly why I was in then. I'm not the only one who is innocent in that gulag. You can bet your life on it.

And the whole gulag had been built precisely for that purpose: to be able to cover it all up.

Gypsy Janco, Miro, and I from cell 218 went for a walk.

The sun hurt my eyes. Instead of a yard, there was a line of twelve steel doors. The doors were very similar to those of the cell doors. They had peepholes and also little openings, like the feeding holes. The cell feeding openings also had other purposes than passing in food. They were also used to put handcuffs on some prisoner's hands, if they were considered to be dangerous to the guards. They stuck their hands out through the opening, and the guard placed cuffs on them.

Outside, we were in fact just in another cell. The only difference was that this one had no ceiling, no windows, and no furniture. The walls were about four metres high. On the top, was what looked like chicken wire, so it reminded me more of a chicken coop. "Chicken coop" was what I called it from then on. So in reality, you were going from one cell to another. You were still isolated from everybody, just like in a cell. Conversation with other prisoners was impossible. The feeling that you were always secluded added tension to an already stressful life.

There were two high watchtowers. The guards could see into every chicken coop. Talking to neighbours over the wall or to prisoners through the windows of the building was strictly prohibited. A five-story building was on two sides of the yard in the shape of an L. Two other sides were protected by the brick wall that was about three stories high. Escape was virtually impossible.

"Mr. Magister, come with me." (*Magister - Mgr. is an academic title for graduates in pedagogy from the University of Czechoslovakia. It is on the level of a master's degree in Western English-speaking countries.*) The guard was an older, typical communist creep. He took me to two big, plastic barrels of garbage. They were both about three-quarters full.

"Take this one, and empty it into that one," he ordered me.

The logical conclusion was that it could not be done. Unless you were a magician. I remembered that, besides being an educator, I was also a part-time magician. But I was not about to do a performance for that creep. I just picked up the barrel and push the bottom of it into the other to press down the garbage as much as I could. Then I dumped as much rubbish as I could into it. Some of it fell on the ground.

"Oh, you dropped some. Too bad. Now you have to pick it up." He said it with a slice of happiness in his voice.

Not knowing the rules and laws, I was just about to pick up the refuse with my bare hands when something told me, *Hold it, this is not the communist system anymore.* I got up and looked at him. His face was happy. It was apparent that he was enjoying his power over a helpless man. His happy face turned to a stern one when he noticed that I was going to say something. The old military rule was that you fulfil an order first, and then you can ask a question. This rule was transferred to prison by retired or discharged soldiers who took jobs as prison guards. It had been a long time since I had been in the service, so I decided to ask first.

"Does Chief Warden know about this?"

"About what?" His face turned red.

"That you make prisoners pick up filthy waste with their bare hands?"

I could see that he was boiling on the inside. He turned around, opened a little door in a little container, pulled out a shovel and a broom.

"You can use this, if you want."

I cleaned the garbage. He took me back to chicken coop. I understood his gesture, which signalled, "Just wait. I'm going to get you, when the time comes." He sure did his best to do it.

Abuse had been normal during good old communist times. Now it had to be covered up. It would have been a totally different situation, if I had question the garbage situation when the prison had been run by fully communist rules. I don't want to think about what he would have done to me then.

Dear Bibka, 21.10.1998

I have come to senses a little. I was so destroyed from the beginning by that injustice that I was afraid of losing my health. I'm beginning to believe that I may survive, but I need

God's help, so please pray. We are four in a cell, just like in a school dormitory. We have enough time here, and also we have food. We play cards, and I also exercise. It helps me with the stress. The worst part is that I miss you.

I hope that you are taking it in a sporting way, as always, and that you will not give up on me.

I'm sure that the lawyer told you about my situation.

Write me what the situation with my keys was. How did they get to this man? Do not write his name; just call him "man." I want to know if he returned to my home again, and how exactly he got those keys, and how he returned them, and if he came to the house alone.

By alarm system in the house it could be established what happened. If he did not return keys, then ask for them. Nobody has the right to have my keys or to go into the house. Don't let anybody in. Do not talk to anybody, and don't believe it if somebody tells you that he wants to help me or you.

If some gypsy asks for money, do not talk to him, but remember him, and write to me about it. Do not call the police for now. I hope nothing like this will happen. But be sure not to walk alone, especially not after dark.

The lawyer told you where the money is. Hide it well or give it to Milan. He will pay the bail. If it is not enough, then Lubo from Hriadky may lend some. In the same place, you will find the cassette. Make some copies with Rado, and hide some in a safe place. If you have any problems with the alarm system, Mr. Benetin will help you. His number is somewhere on the desk. Believe that it will be over soon.

You will get a permit for a visit that means that 5 people may come. I think that only you and Milan should come. My mom should not come. It will be too hard for her and also for me.

I know that you are taking care of her. I hope you will stand up against it all.

Love, dodo.

It was so hard for me even to think that my mom might come to prison to see me. She suffered so much in the hands of the communists for more than forty years. She always faced them with dignity. And by then, she was in her eighties, and to go through this? I thought it would be too hard for her. That was why I asked Bibiana not to call my mom. Later, I discovered that my mom was much stronger than I thought. She stood for justice then, like she had all her life.

CHAPTER TEN

Investigator Demjan Is a Liar,
a Cheat, and a Crook

When is a child happy? When she is abused. (Slovak teacher)

A skinny, tall prisoner advised me that I could borrow the book *Rights and Punishments*.

"You can borrow it from the corridor warden," he said.

So I did that the next morning. The problem was that there was a time limit on it, because there was only one copy for the whole wing. Right away, I wrote to Bibiana to send me one, and she did. The book had only 160 pages, but it was very informative. It listed all basic paragraphs of criminal law and criminal order.

I began to study Slovak law, and that was when I was completely stunned by what I discovered. Every single step that the police, prosecutors, and judge had taken until then had been illegal. The law in Slovakia was acceptable, if anyone went by it.

I wrote numerous letters.On October 20, 1998, I wrote a letter to Judge Milko of Trebisov. I reminded him that he had sent me there illegally. I named some laws that he had broken, and I also named the paragraph by which he could let me out of there, this time legally.

On October 30, 1998, Judge Milko sent me a note that he had remitted my request to a district prosecutor. The judge proceeded in the opposite way. Section 72 paragraph 2 T.P. orders that the prosecutor passes requests to the judge, not the reverse way.

The office of the district prosecutor responded

on November 4, 1998, by dismissing the request, because of a fourteen-day minimum limit between requests. That was total nonsense, not to mention that it was also illegal. Just like in the previous circumstance, somebody, not the prosecutor, had written the decision. Three weeks before somebody had used prosecutor JUDr. Pacutova Maria's name and signed instead of her. In the same manner was used mgr. Maros Sabo's name. Both signatures were not readable; therefore, it was a logical conclusion that Policeman Demjan was doing all of those forgeries, because he was handling the investigative file. One thing was certain: the prosecutors did not write them.

I was lucky I had my darling Bibiana fighting for me outside. I had discovered her talent, and she had become a full-scale assistant in my magic show. We presented magic performances in virtually every city and in the bigger towns of the Slovak Republic. Then we travelled in Canada for two years, presenting our magic show.

In the world of magic, the magician and his assistant were very closely connected. We communicated without words, using the subconscious mind or invisible signals. In dangerous routines, like floating, we protected each other. On the stage, we were both connected as if we were one person. Logically, we became very close.

Our ability to communicate through the subconscious mind became very handy and useful in our fight against the corrupt officials of eastern Slovakia. I was in jail, and she was my extended reach outside. I wrote many letters to her while in jail. It amounted to more letters than the total I had written during my whole life. In fact, I did not have to write any letters at all. Most of the time, she picked up my messages and ideas as I was thinking them.

As an example, during the night once, I thought, *she is going to need a fax machine to fax complaints and requests.* So in the morning, I wrote to her to buy herself a fax machine. Just as I was passing the letter to the warden to be mailed, the warden handed me one from her.

"Last night, I got the idea that I would need a fax machine, so today, I bought one," she wrote.

She picked the idea up at the same time as I was thinking about it. That went on during my whole stay in the gulag.

It also worked the other way. I remember the time when I was thinking that I might need another lawyer. Then overnight, I decided that, the next day, I would get one. That was the night when Bibiana wrote to me:My darling,

You have to change your lawyer very fast. Maybe right now. I just came from him, and I will give you just one advice: change fast. Think twice!!! One sentence made me sure about it. I quote: 'We can prove it.' Then he corrected himself,

"I mean, they can. I have no interest in proving it.' That was quote of the lawyer JUDr. Hajdu.

JUDr. Fercakova, my new lawyer, came to visit. I estimated that she was about my age. I explained the whole situation to her from the beginning.

She just turned her head and said,

"What a mafia in that Trebisov."

It looked, that she may be looking after my rights much better, than JUDr. Hajdu.

On October 30, 1998, I wrote to Investigator Demjan, requesting that he finish the investigation and arrange another interrogation of myself. I offered again my evidence. I named the laws by which he was required to investigate, like section 164 paragraphs 2, 3, and 4 T.P.—which required him to investigate as quickly as possible, gather evidence against and also for the defendant, and obey the law—and

section 2 paragraphs 4 and 5—which required him to respect the human rights guaranteed by Slovak constitution.

I also listed laws that he was breaking.

I let him know, that I was aware of the fact that his friends, the policemen, were looking for more gypsies and persuading them to falsely testify against me, which was illegal, and according to section 158 paragraphs 1 and 2c T.P., he was obligated to investigate his partners, because their activities were punishable by at least three years and up to ten years.

I also requested that he serve copies of the request to the judge, the prosecutor, and the person who was helping to create false testimony against me.

My last request was to verify, if there were still reasons for my imprisonment, according to law, section– 72 paragraph 1.

I wasn't expecting much from my letter, because I knew what a corrupt creep he was. I only wanted to remind him that what he and Policemen Stefanak were doing was illegal. I was hoping that it might slow them down a little when they realized that there was a law against it and that I knew about it.

******

Demjan did not waste much time fulfilling his first promise to me when he said that he would take those gypsies to my place anyway. Bibiana went to visit her mom for a weekend. The police were watching her movements. They gather gypsies and brought them to my house. It was never clear if Investigator Demjan was there in person, or if he just sent policeman Stefanak and his partner to do that illegal job. The policemen were surprised when the alarm began to sound. They had no information that I had an alarm, which was connected to a police station but to a different branch. Within minutes, a police patrol car was at my house. When they discovered their friend policemen there, they took no action, leaving the policemen and gypsies there.

The gypsies and policemen looked over my whole house. In his false accusation, Demjan had written that I had carried the gypsies to my bedroom, which was upstairs. That part of the house, the gypsies had no clue about. That was why it was necessary to bring them to my house and show them what the upstairs looked like. Policeman Stefanak also needed to look my house over, because he was the head coach of the gypsies, whose memories were less than that of a chicken. Before every question period or court appearance, Stefanak collected his gypsies in his police car and drove them wherever needed. He repeated to them what they were to say, over and over and over again. The poor gypsies tried to say it right, but they were unable to, because of their short memories.

After they left my house, they locked the door, but the alarm stayed on, because you needed to know a secret combination to reset it.

When Bibiana returned home, the alarm was still beeping. She called the number that was attached to it. It was police who were looking after it. They informed her, that yes, the alarm had signalled, and a patrol car had been sent to my house. The police had looked over the house from the outside, seen nothing wrong, and left.

Later, I filed a complaint, stating that the police had broken our written agreement; so they denied that the alarm had sounded at all. In a case like that, they were to report it immediately to my parents' house, where my also brother lived. They did not do it, because my parents' house was just two blocks away, and somebody from my family could have been there in one or two minutes. They would have discovered the gypsies and their colleagues, the policemen, in it. They did not make sense at all and would lie straight to your face.

I received "The Record of Interrogation of a Person Younger Than Fifteen Years of Age."

From that it was clear that Investigator Demjan went to school to interrogate the child Jana Visokaiova again, in spite of the fact that the law (section 102 paragraphs 1 and 2) recommended to proceed with the interrogation of minors very gently and in a manner that the questioning wouldn't be repeated again. The child had been interrogated twice already: once at her school and once at the police station, where she had been abused to the point that she had urinated in her pants. The school was where all the dirty work was taking place. Demjan should have done this questioning before he wrote the charge against me. Now his intention was to get the child to say at least something to fit the charge.

He exposed the child to two and a half hours of grilling.

The child was crying as soon she was informed that the police were at the school again. For two and a half hours, over and over, Demjan asked the same questions: "Did he do something with you?"; "Did he do anything to you?"; "Did he kiss and feel your body?"; "Did he do something with you at night?"; "Did he photograph you naked?"; Can you swear that he did nothing to you when you were going to sleep?"; "Did you sleep naked?"; "Did he sleep naked?"; etc.

Two and a half hours of tricky questions that were not suitable for an eleven-year-old child. Does it sound like a sex lecture? You bet. She denied all the crap the police had written in their report while abusing her at the police station just a few days before.

Demjan confused the child about the date she was taken to the police station. Imagine this kind of trick: Demjan took the calendar and showed the child the square that read October 9, 1998, and suggested that the previous interrogation at the school had taken place then. There was no way the child could possibly have known the date, especially when just pointed at in the calendar. All squares are the same in a calendar. The child agreed. But Demjan had picked the wrong date purposely to confuse her. He asked some more questions, and then, he said, "Oh, I chose the wrong date. It was not this square but this one." The child agreed again. All the squares were the same anyway. It did not matter to her anyway. But it was very important to confuse her like that. In confusion, she could not possibly have realized that he was pointing to the date (October 2, 1998) as the day she was taken to the police station and abused. So Demjan had written another lie, as if the child had been talking: "…what I was saying happened on October 9, 1998, happened on October 2, 1998 after the interrogation at school."

Are you confused about those dates reader? Imagine how confused the eleven-year-old was.

The confusion worked; the child did not realize that October 2, 1998 was in fact the day she was taken out of school to the police station.

Bravo, Demjan. You managed to confuse an eleven-year-old child. But if anybody asked, how would he explain the record I have, the record that shows that the police also took her to a gynaecological examination, which was dated October 2, 1998? Was that examination also done at the school? Was it legal to interrogate the child three times without the knowledge of her parents?

Demjan wanted to know the sleeping arrangements when she slept over.

"I was sleeping on the right side, as you walk in the room," she said, "and Uncle was sleeping on the left side."

Imagine what he wrote: "On this bed, we were sleeping together. The way I was sleeping was on the right side of the bed as you get into the room, and Uncle Demcak was on the left side, where he had the counter."

The sneaky word that he stuck in was "together." The bastard knew very well that, between the bed on the right side of the room, where child was sleeping, and the left bed, where I was sleeping, were two additional beds. He knew it very well, because he had personally looked over my bedroom during the search of my house, taking videos and photos of it. And he went ahead and made it look as if we had slept on the same bed. How could the child notice that kind of trick? Bravo number two.

The child testified that I had done nothing wrong at all. Period. But Demjan turned around and claimed to Judge Milko that, if I was let out on bail, I might influence the child as a witness. Since she claimed in my favour, I could only have influenced her to testify against me. And Judge Milko approved this total nonsense.

In her testimony, the child called me "dad." It only underlined my claim on my first day in court when I said that "We developed a child/father relationship, which never changed." Later, that was emphasized by Jana's parents and the court psychologist.

You can always find something good in every bad, if you look for it. I was looking, and I found it. At least he did not stick the baton between his legs, like his colleague had at the police station. He was a liar, and a crook, but he was an investigator. How many innocent people had he framed like this? Who could believe that I was the only one?

Demjan didn't think that he had done enough damage to the child as yet. After the interrogation of Jana, he took to questioning her classmates; all were ten and eleven years of age. He interrogated Anna Lukacova, Lucia Barancikova, and Marek Mazurkovic—all from the same school and the same neighbourhood as Jana. He kept asking the children if they had heard that Mr. Demcak had undressed and touched Jana, and he asked other suggestive questions that were not suitable for children.

These were children, damn it! Could the bastard get any lower? Can anybody imagine what it did to the child, when those children at school and in the neighbourhood began talking about and teasing her? Could the creep imagine how she felt? The child Jana Visokaiova was destroyed emotionally and socially and was unable to sleep or to attend school. Policeman Jan Demjan destroyed her life, because he wanted to destroy mine.

Her home teacher, mgr. Marta Koscikova, stated officially, "Jana is not a problematic child, and her mother is well concerned about her, accompanying her daughter to school and waiting for her after school." That was until policemen Demjan, Stefanak, and others stepped into their lives and destroyed everything that the Visokaiova family had.

Did Demjan understand section 101 paragraph 8 T.P. when he asked children if they had heard that Mr. Demcak was undressing and touching their friend Jana? "You must not give the witness questions, in which are mentioned circumstances that should only be obtained from the witness' statement." He was asking and giving the answers, which was even against Slovak law.

What about Trebisov's educators, who signed as having been present while this child abuse was in progress?

RNDr. Marcela Ferkova, the school principal, was not at the police station when the child was abused. But it is written in a document dated October 22, 1998, that she was there. This document was a plain forgery and was listed as an addition to Jana's previous statement. That day, Demjan was asking eleven-year-old pupil, Anna Lukacova, if she had heard that I had undressed and touched Jana's body. If principal Ferkova was there and also at the police station when Jana was abused and thought it was appropriate and legal, then she should quit her job as a school principal and seek a psychiatric examination as soon as possible. In that written statement that she allegedly signed, she should have asked Jana why she was changing her story. Didn't she notice that the child Jana was telling exactly the same story at her first and third interrogations? The one that was different was the grossly vulgar one, the one that was proof that the child Jana was abused by the police.

What about mgr. Anna Pekarcikova, a teacher at the same school, who signed as the present pedagogue, when Demjan asked Lucie Barancikova and Marek Mazurkovic those obscene questions? Isn't the presence of pedagogue at the questioning of children required exactly in order to stop corrupt officials like Demjan from inflicting damage on the children?

I have message for mgr. Marta Koscikova, who was Jana's home teacher. First, I want to thank her for telling the truth when she was questioned by Demjan on October 22, 1998. You said that "Jana is not a problematic child, and her mother is well concerned about her, accompanying her daughter to school and waiting for her after school."

I don't understand your other statement, when you said that "From the time the underage [Jana] was interrogated by the policemen about Mr. Demcak, she always smiles, and is in a good mood." My goodness, what kind of crap is that? It is like saying that Jana could hardly wait until she would be taken again to the police station and to a gynaecological examination a few more times. That way your statement would fit better into the incongruous Demjan-style monuments.

I saw with my own eyes that happy mood, because I was still out of jail then. It was hours of crying, inability to sleep, or going to school. Did you forget when Jana's mom came to school and informed you and your principal that Jana could not attend school, because she was not well as a result of what the police had done to her?

She did not show that kind of happiness when Dr. Stancak came to examine her, as he stated in his report that the "child was crying as soon as she was informed, that another grilling was coming up." She thought he was a policeman. That was why she was desperate. I really want to know why you wrote such a lie. Would you be happy if what happened to poor Jana on October 2, 1998, at the police station happened to you or your child? She was abused at the police station after she was taken from your classroom, and nobody—not you or the principal—stopped the police. Would you be smiling if the police took you, when you were a child, against your will to a clinic where a doctor would spread your rectum and vagina, looking inside them close up with a flashlight? You wrote that, after all this abuse, during which she urinated in her pants, Jana was happy and smiling. Covering up for the police will not prevent them from doing that to other children; they could be yours. All I wanted you and your principal to do was disclose who asked or who forced you to say such lies. If you did not write that, and your signatures were forged, you are obligated to say so. I spent nine months in jail trying to stop the abuse. Jana's life and the lives of her parents were destroyed. Don't you believe that they deserve to know the truth?

So far, so many people had told lies and broken laws, and I was trying to find out why. I had a hunch that somebody had had to force these people to have that kind of polluted behaviour.

What happened to Jana, her parents, me, Bibiana, and our families was a crime against humanity, and I shall not rest until it stops.

CHAPTER ELEVEN

Horrible Damage from Mental Torture

Where do Slovak police look for evidence? In children's asses.
Blast. Kuka is a virgin.

On October 26, 1998, I received my first visitor since I had been incarcerated. The little stalls were in line, all enclosed with unbreakable glass all the way to the ceiling. There were about fifteen of them. On one side sat the prisoners, one by one. On the other sides were five chairs, because up to five people were allowed to visit. In the middle of the glass was a circle of tiny holes about three millimetres in diameter, through which you tried to talk to your loved ones. You had to talk very loudly to be able hear each other. That made it certain that "bugs" would record the conversations clearly. Those communists had thought of everything. Only a one-hour visit once a month was permitted, and only if the investigator agreed.

My brother Milan and Bibiana were sitting behind the glass wall. I was very sad to see Bibka again. We had spent a lot of time together before that. I do not think there was ever any time longer than an hour when we would be without each other while touring Canada with our magic show. The same was true when we were touring Czechoslovakia while producing stage presentations.

My main plan was to let her know what to do with the audio recording my telephone answering machine had made of the gypsies, while they were blackmailing me. I did not want to write it, because the guards were reading every word of my mail. They could inform corrupt officials in Trebisov, and they could confiscate the tape. It was very important evidence, and I did not want to lose it.

Bibiana placed her ear against the glass around the tiny holes, and I whispered through the little openings.

"Did you find everything in the washroom?"

"Yes, I did."

"Make a few copies. Five or more. Give one each to different people you trust for safe keeping. Do it today. Then, make a detailed record of it in writing. Everything you hear. For example, if you hear laughter, write it down. Give a few copies to my new lawyer. She should bring me some also. I'm going to fight it from here."

"And I'm going to fight from here," she assured me. I believed her, but I had no idea what a great fighter she was or how long it would take.

An hour went very fast, and they were gone. I was again alone behind the thick walls of the gulag. As soon as I was escorted back to my cell, I sat down and wrote to Bibiana.

Hi Bibka, 26.10.1998.

You just left, and I'm writing [...]

A lot of warnings were in that letter. I began to worry about her safety. I realized it more and more. They were trying to destroy me to get money from me and to keep me quiet. What were they going to do with her if they realized that she was helping me? The last thing I wanted was for her to get hurt or even worse by trying to help me.

In the meantime, well-working machinery began functioning in order to destroy an innocent person. Unfortunately, that person was me. The system was a combination of emotional and physical abuse.

Communist justice officials knew that it worked like the best Swiss watch.

For example, abuse by mail? Is it possible? It is very effective, and it works way better than anybody could imagine. Unless you live through it.

In February of 2006, Mr. Bhupinder Singh Kang committed suicide after receiving a series of letters. The mail was not from some criminals who were blackmailing him or who threatened his family. Neither had it happened in some third-world country or Russia or Chechnya. It was Canada where it occurred. To be more precise, it was Vancouver, British Columbia, and the senders were WorkSafeBC. Mr. Kang was injured in a traffic accident eight years before, and he was depressed and despondent from dealing with government officials. Through some kind of lack of common sense, they were sending him different letters from different officials, requesting different assessments, including a psychological assessment. They drove him to desperation. His anxiety reached the state that he urinated in his pants on the way to the interview. That reminds me of the child Jana when she was abused at the police station. She also urinated because of the abuse. Surveillance was also in place, to see if Kang was cheating or if he was able to work.

These government administrators did not try to destroy Mr. Kang, and he was not locked up in a prison, but I have not the smallest doubt that, unintentionally, they caused his death. It was a clear illustration of mental abuse. Was it manslaughter or negligence, causing death? In my opinion? Yes. Was anybody punished for it? I doubt it. This—and there were many other cases—only points to the fact of how detrimental mental torture can be. Mr. Kang could have been cured and worked again, if he had received the proper assistance. Instead, he had received the kind of treatment from Canadian officials that made his condition even worse through psychological abuse, driving him to suicide. In other words, WorkSafeBC officials abused Mr. Kang to death. That is why it is crucially important that government employees be familiar with the power of the pieces of paper they write on. It can become a deadly weapon.

Try to understand how damaging mental abuse can be if inflicted by people who focus on it and are trained to do it. That kind of abuse, combined with physical torture, was systematically used on me and other prisoners in that Slovak prison. I have no doubt that it is exploited against other prisoners today. That is why I'm writing this story.

Imagine a gulag where guards intentionally abuse prisoners, and they know what they are doing. They know their business, because they have been practicing mental torture for many generations. In Russia, it was studied and practised for more than ninety years. After the Second World War, people from Eastern European countries traveled to the Soviet Union to learn first-hand how to do it. And first-hand, I learned how effective it is, when they put me through it.

Prisoners who lived through physical torture recovered much faster and to a higher level, after they were released from prison. On the other side, prisoners exposed to mental abuse had a much longer span of recovery. Most did not heal at all and died broken men.

The damage of mental torture affects the body from the inside out. That means that damage to the body is visible last. Healing takes place in the reverse order, which means that the visible marks of harm disappear first, but on the inside, the healing of wounds take a very long time, if it ever happens. Ten years afterward, I'm still negatively affected.

In prisons in all ex-Soviet countries, as well as all ex-Soviet satellite countries, mental torture is still active in the present. It is going on simultaneously with other types of abuse. Together, they are much more efficient, and inflict much greater destruction to the human body and mind.

******

At home, Bibiana made a few copies of the recording that was left on my telephone answering machine by gypsies who were blackmailing me before. She distributed the tapes to a few safe places. The contents of the recording was so gross that Bibiana was not able to make a written copy of it. She asked her brother Rado to do it for her. Many vulgarities were used in eastern Slovak slang and gypsy jargon. They were so horrible that I myself had a hard time translating them into the English language.

The most difficult task for me in writing this book was that of describing the cruel abuse that was going on. To describe the cruelty or translate some coarse language and keep a level of respect for my readers was virtually impossible. I apologise for the vulgar language that follows. Please remember that this is a fully documented, true story.

Here are the highlights of the translation of the recording.

At the beginning, there were a few calls of a so-called invitational nature, like the next one.

Prostitute 1 (Eva): "Jozef, don't be mad, but I must report you, and do you know why? Because when I want to meet you, you don't want to meet me."

Since I did not agree, their pimp tried to be more persuasive.

> Pimp: "Hey, listen here. If by any chance you don't do what they [his prostitutes] say, then you know you will end up dreadful. Comprehend me? Understand me?"

> Because these tactics did not work, they started to be even more abusive.

> Prostitute 2 (Anna, nicknamed Kuka): "Hey one, one,

one. Hey, can you hear me? You maggot. You homo. You debility."

With time, the coarse language also mounted, and it became full-scale extortion.

Pimp: "You fury, you stupid pig, you fascist, you mantinel, donkey, donkey, ass, stupid gypsy. Stick your cock in your mother, you fruit one."

Prostitute 2 (Anna): "There he is, there he is. Tell him fury."

Pimp: "Demcak, I will report that you are smuggling women to Canada, and here you bother women, and you photograph them naked. I will talk to you once alone. I swear to God, I have the evidence. I will report, report, report you, I swear to God. I will report you for all those women. And those photos go to the West. You go to the mother's cunt. You will get rich on the account of gypsy women for one hundred korun. So, boy, this is all over. Be quiet, be quiet, be quiet [he was talking to his friends, who were making noise in the background]. They have pimps already. Listen here, listen here, they have pimps already. Boy, you are finished.

"Either I destroy your car or you pay as much as it should be. Is that clear, or should I stick my cock in your mother? Boy, I will give it to you. We know everything. The girls are able to report you, normal to cops. They will claim that's them, and they have those photographs. Eva has those photos, you know what photos. As she is alone in the house, you know those photos, you know about this, boy. It is not blackmail, it is just using, boy.

"You will crack [pay]. Hey, you placed the snake on Kuka, you homos, you are not fucking? Or yes, or smoking girls ... [more vulgarities follow] ... you think I'm joking. You will go in cunt for this. You will pay, and you will crack."

The same pimp another time: "Hi, Joe. Listen here. I'm

calling you as a good friend. Joe, I have one good message. You have here one big problem. So I hope you don't want to go to jail. This is not blackmail, but it is a smaller service that I want from you. I will call on you. I think. I think we will come to an agreement; we are sensible people, because I'm not whore, and I hope that you are not whore, and we will nicely come to an agreement. I will call you tomorrow at the same time. Hi."

Prostitute 1 (Eva): "How are you? Good, I know. Yesterday … I know very well that you have heard that I called you yesterday. I will call you every day until you answer. If you do not answer, I will go to your place, and you will see. I will go, I will go to your place. Me and Kuka, we will smash your balls and your whole home, I'm telling you nicely, if you will not come, or if you won't be at home, if you won't talk to me and apologise and so on, I will call cops, and they already have my photo."

[More vulgarities]

Pros. 1 (Eva): "I will place my pussy on your mouth, also Kuka with her naked ass, she will sit on your head. She will sit with her pussy on your bald head."

Pros. 2 (Kuka): "You homo, fuckin' cock, I will report you now, you will see. That is what you do with us. You never want to meet us. Today we are going to destroy your house. If you are at home, I will kick down your door. I will steal your snake. I will go to the cops with the snake. You don't believe me; you will see. I'm telling you nicely, you head; you will see, I will tell everybody that you wanted to lick us. You don't believe me; you will see. You homo one, fuckin' cock. Who are you making cocks of? Of me? I'm farting and fucking. Father is coming. I will put Father on the phone. You frog, your head is like a rabbit. Your hair stands, like that on my pussy. You homo one, you don't fuck, you … So you don't want to fuck. Dzigi, migi, figi. Natasha returned from the Czech Republic. She was fucking very fine. When you meet her, you will place your tongue under her. I will always call you until you answer, and I want to talk to you, because the message … I don't know if it is the truth, and now Eva is going to talk."

Prostitute 1 (Eva): "You frog, you donut, you cock, you, frog. I was not fucking in the Czech Republic. Joj, how great I was fucking, normal, and everything [goes]) on your mouth."

Another time:

Prostitute 2 (Kuka): "Again, you are not at home. I'm going to destroy your house. You don't believe me; you will see. And if you are at home, I will yell that you '*nastrunil*' me [vulgarism in gypsy slang that means something like tuning]. I will tell cops that you *nastrunil* me up. I cannot talk, because my boyfriend is coming. So hi, you fucking cock."

From those messages, it was more than clear that I was refusing to meet them or to talk to them. It was also very obvious that they were threatening me and trying to extort money from me. When it was apparent that I would not cave to their demands, the gypsies kind of eased off, and the calls were fewer in number. None of them was underage; therefore the idea of using that line had never crossed the gypsies' minds. That is, until the police bugged in. It was the police who brought up the idea to use the gypsies and use the underage scam.

The police were listening when the gypsies left those "friendly" messages on my telephone answering machine. In a normal situation, they should have arrested the gypsies for extortion, the threats, blackmail, and whatever else, but they did not. Instead, the police used the gypsies as their new partners.

The police had a much better tools than the gypsies had. They had police cars, guns, jails, and cooperative prosecutors and judges—even the lawyers and jail guards.

The police were also watching my movements. They were hoping for big money.

In their first attempt, the gypsy Kuka was to be their first tool. She was still in elementary school. Kuka was little with short hair—not a very attractive gypsy—but she was somehow dressing sexily for her age, especially, when strolling around town after dark. I don't think she was a bad girl at the time at all. She only gave the impression that she was, because she was a gypsy and because she was friendly with older gypsies with bad reputations and also because of the way she was dressed.

In fact, I had met her once at that time. I had stopped my Pontiac at a tobacco stand by the train station to buy some newspapers and magazines. I bought the papers through a little window, without going inside. It was only about five steps from the place where I had parked my car; therefore, I thought there was no need to lock the car. I had even left the engine running. When I returned, there were two young gypsies sitting on the backseat of my car. I had never talked to them before. Only much later did I identify that it was Kuka and Andrea. While in my car, they were begging me to give them at least a short, little ride. My Pontiac was a very unusual car in those days in that town, so it was not unusual for some people to ask me for a ride. Those who know how persuasive gypsies can be will agree that, to get them out of my car, I had no choice but to fulfil their dream. I took them for a ride the distance of one whole block. It was from the train station approximately three hundred metres to the next crossing, where Mr. Hasan had his ice cream stand on the left. I dropped them off at that crossing. The girls were very happy and left my car joyfully.

Kuka became the tool the police were looking for. Somehow the police heard that she and Andrea had taken a ride in my car. It is obvious that the girls told some friends. It is possible that the police spotted it because they were watching me. All I know is that, soon after, the police paid her a visit at school. At the time, they left Andrea out, for some reason, but they tried to recruit her later. Kuka was the perfect subject, because she was almost fifteen years of age but not quite yet. Fifteen was the age when you were considered an adult in Slovakia. You got a citizen ID, and of course, it was the age of consent.

The police visited Kuka at the school she was going to. As you can see, schools are the favourite places for police to exploit children. The parents are not there, and principals or teachers do not dare to prevent police from doing their filthy work there.

The police did not expect that even Kuka could fool them, even without the intention of doing so.

When the police arrived at the school that morning, the lady principal welcomed them as usual.

"Kuka slept with Demcak. We are here to investigate," the older policeman informed the head of the school.

Kuka was escorted to the office, and the principal left to let the cops do their duty in private. The police did not beat around the bushes at all.

"You slept with Demcak," one of them told her straightforwardly, as soon as the principal had left.

"No. No, I did not."

Slap! A huge hand ended up on her cheek. Kuaka's head turned to the side, driven by the power of the policeman's hand. Green snot shot across her face, all the way to her ear. She began to cry out loud with a typical gypsy sound. With her head down and crying, she was saying, "I did not. I didn't sleep …"

Slap. A hand hit her on the other side.

"You slept with him."

It was the snotty side of Kuka's face that the policeman had hit, but the slapper had not seen it, because Kuka's head had been turned down and to the side. He looked at his snotty hand with disgust and wiped it on the principal's desk from the bottom and finished wiping it on his pants.

"I did, I did," she said, crying, to avoid more slaps.

"Take her," the slapper ordered his partner, who was until then just watching with repulsion. He was the younger policemen, and he was not exactly amused by the persuading tactics of his older partner.

The story became a big joke among the policemen, mainly because of the big, green snot the policeman's slap had produced: "How is your hand today?"; "Did you disinfect it properly this morning?"; "Is your hand still green?"; "If you not lazy, your garden is green."; "Sorry, I decline to shake your hand today. Next time you go questioning, don't forget to wear your gloves." Those were the lines of conversation at the police station, mainly by older policemen. The younger ones and those with character felt rather sorry for the poor little girl.

My friend the policemen told me about it when he was advising me to go back to Canada, because the police were sawing a doghouse for me. Trebisov was a small town, where almost everybody knew everybody, so the snot story came out and was the talk around town for a while after. Later, it was also recorded in court documents, which I have a copy of. I also asked Kuka about it when I had the chance to question her officially, when she was used against me by the police. It was part of my plan and my determination to prove police brutality. I knew they would deny everything, unless I had proof. Even if the evidence was right in front of them, they would lie to your face and deny it without any hesitation.

The younger policeman took the crying Kuka by the hand and led her out of the principal's office. When passing through the teachers' lunch room, the teachers from the whole school were already gathered there to hear the news of the year.

"She slept with Demcak," the older policeman proudly informed the congregation. "We are taking her to the doctor." The teachers could hardly wait until school was over so they could trumpet the news around town. And news like that went around Trebisov better than by the best communication system in the world. Kuka had not reached the doctor yet, when the buzz was around the town that Demcak had slept with Kuka. A lady teacher from the school Kuka was attending was also the wife of a very good friend of mine, Minko. They were also my neighbours.

"You are in big trouble," she told me. "You slept with Kuka."

"Who is Kuka? I don't know any Kuka."

"Don't lie. She just admitted to the police at my school that you slept with her."

That was around 4:00 in the afternoon. Kuka was just waiting for the doctor to look between her legs for evidence.

On the way from the school, the police had to pass Kuka's home. She was crying and wanted them to stop at her house. Her mother was outside on the sidewalk. Kuka began to cry on full blast when noticed her mom. They stopped the car on the side of the street next to her.

"She slept with Demcak. We are taking her to a doctor," The older policeman informed her mother.

"You pig; didn't you have somebody else to sleep with other than Demcak?" The mother let her have it right away.

"I did not sleep with him. I did not sleep—" She cried even more, astonished that even her mother didn't believe her.

"Don't you lie, you whore, and I'm going with you."

Poor Kuka was taken crying to the hospital. By then, the dust, snot, and tears had made the mess of her face. It was very sad to look at. The hospital was usually packed with people. Everybody was looking at the crying girl, wanting to know what was going on.

"Demcak slept with her," the older policeman arrogantly passed information on to some.

And then, the blast. The doctor looked between Kuka's legs, and then turned her around and examined her rectum. Just to be sure, he examined the vagina one more time a little more closely than the first time. The doctor nodded his head from side to side and then turned around.

"She did not sleep with Demcak or anybody," the doctor informed Kuka's mother.

"But the policemen told me that she slept with Demcak," The mother protested as if she could not believe it.

"I told you," Kuka cried.

"She is still a virgin. Nobody slept with her."

The report of the examination reads:

The result of the examination is negative. The vagina has not been touched; she is still a virgin. The rectum is normal, average size for her age and dimensions. To date, nobody has had intercourse with the girl yet.

Everybody was shocked.

The mother let the policemen have it. Every swear word that there was in the gypsy and Slovak dictionaries was tossed in the direction of the policemen as she passed them, holding Kuka by the hand. Even some Hungarian profanities were not spared. When she was done, she took her daughter home.

There are a few ironies in the destiny of life.

1. Knowing the nature of gypsies, I don't think that her mom ever apologized to Kuka for betraying her by believing the policemen and not her.

2. Nobody will ever comprehend how it happened. The gypsy girl who walked around town late at night with older friends, wearing skimpy outfits, and was still a virgin—impossible to believe. At most, she was almost fifteen. The average age of sexual activity for most gypsies could be estimated around twelve or thirteen, if not earlier.

3. Kuka will never know what a shock she gave the policemen by still being a virgin. She had fooled everybody. Nobody was more surprised and disappointed than the policemen. They had not counted on the possibility that Kuka might not have been touched yet. All their plans with me had to be postponed,adjusted and taken back to the drawing table again.

4. Kuka will never know that she actually saved me. I'm still trying to comprehend how close I was to being drowned by the police right then. The police were sure everything was in place. The rest would just be child's play. It would not matter who had had sex with her, as long as somebody had. It would have been framed on me, and not even holy water could have

cleaned me up. Her virginity saved me. If Kuka had not been a virgin and if she had still been a few days underage, it would be a straightforward business for the police. The perfect frame. Now they had to regroup and come up with a different strategy.

As an educator myself, I must ask how much damage the police caused to that young girl by abusing her at school and dragging her to a gynaecological examination at a time when she was young and still a virgin. I'm not asking if the police caused damage to her or not. I'm asking how much they caused, and I'm doing so intentionally, because, as an educator qualified in two countries and in two languages, I guarantee that damage was done.

After the encounter with the police, she never returned to school again. So I must ask how much that abuse by the police had to do with the fact that she became a prostitute. All I know is that the damage was done, and somebody should be punished, because cruelty must stop.

The police will never stop, unless the government acts.

That was not the only time when the policemen in Trebisov had searched children's vaginas and rectums for evidence. In both cases, it had been done without any reasons or legal basis. In both cases, it was done without a court order and only on requests made by primitive policemen in the town of Trebisov, Slovak Republic. In the case of Jana Visokaiova, it was done even without the knowledge of her parents. Kuka's mother was lied to by the police.

Those policemen involved in looking in children's asses for evidence were not any better than what you usually discover in anybody's ass.

So I sent another request to the Slovak government this way. Since one hundred polite complaints did not work, this time, I will try it in language they may understand:

"Slovak government, please do something to stop the abuse of children by police in your country. I will not rest until you stop perverted policemen from looking into children's vaginas and rectums for evidence, without a court warrant or the knowledge of the children's parents, and until you punish those who have already done it."

CHAPTER TWELVE

The Judge and the Investigator
Are Bloody Brothers

Who are the three stooges of Slovakia? The three judges.

Soon after the underage Kuka was abused by police, I returned to Canada to fulfil business engagements. It was two years before I returned back to my old country. My father had died, and my mom was sick.

The police were determined to continue their unfinished business,

"We know well everything you have done" was probably the most used phrase by the communist police. In a society run by tyrants, it was very scary when an official tells you that. Right away, you think about what you may have done and who knew about it. Even, if you didn't recollect right away what you had done in the past, you were afraid to ask. So you would do what policemen were asking you to do. If there was somebody who was sure that you had done nothing wrong at all and resisted, there was a back-up line: "We know your opinions, and we know how you think." After that line, you were right up against the wall. Communist prisons were full of people who had been told what they were thinking. They called them political prisoners. Try to understand how communists could know how somebody thought. In communist days, you were required to prove that you were innocent. How could you prove that you were not thinking what they claimed that you were? It was a helpless situation.

In jail, the machinery to destroy me had already begun. At first, it was to be through my mind. Officially, that is called mental abuse. All my requests or complaints were turned down promptly. Responds were all very similar in almost all points. Every one described alleged crimes as if I had already committed them. In all correspondence, the senders repeated them twice for greater effect. I knew I had not done the crimes, but it hit me quite hard. Each time I received that kind of mail, my blood pressure shot up. The same effect it had on all prisoners when they received similar notes.

Every letter listed the reasons for my imprisonment, even if they were absurd or illegal. At first, I wondered if those judges could read at all. Then I thought that, if they could read, then they did not understand the meanings of sentences, not to mention the law. Afterward, I realized that they were totally corrupt.

It was very stressful to see so clearly that what they were delivering to me was stinky bullcrap written on white paper. None of the documents were signed by the judge. The documents were signed by the person who had written it, and I could never read the signature.

I received similar crap, dated October 21, 1998. I realized that I was in bigger trouble than I had thought. This was not from a district judge from Trebisov, but from a provincial judge from Kosice, and if that judge went hand in hand with corrupt officials from Trebisov, looking for the justice would be very hard. That could signal that whoever was behind it all might have influence on judges even at the provincial level. I sure would like to know who that person is.

Crap after crap I was receiving from different judges, prosecutors, investigators,

and Demjan. New names were added to my list of corrupt judges.

From the district of Trebisov, it was JUDr. Jan Milko; from the provincial court, it was JUDr. Jan Liska and JUDr. Ondrej Brdarsky; and so on. A new name and a new question: how many people could that pervert influence?

Each time I received those absurd decisions from different people, it was like a cannon blast to my head. Even now, it is very difficult to look at these papers. And the question always comes to my mind: "Where does this kind of people come from? What or who makes them so hopelessly corrupt?

It was totally shocking. I had three judges involved already, and nobody cared that not a single paper had been registered. That meant that I was kept in jail just like that with nothing legal or valid. That was a real reason to worry. They could do anything they wanted. All they needed was to think of it. By their decisions, you would think that they were not judges but the three stooges.

It was hard, but I was still surviving. Then came full-scale mental torture by Policeman Demjan.

Once or twice a week, I received a new accusation from him. He accused me of almost every crime that exists in the criminal book. Not once did he mention where the ideas came from, and no evidence was ever presented.

Policeman Demjan accused me of drug trafficking, and requested a special police team from Bratislava to search my car. Nothing was discovered. Before, when they searched my house, not even an aspirin was in my home.

He had already accused me of producing porn when he had requested a warrant to search my house. He did not provide any indication of where he got the idea. By law, those requests had to go through the prosecutor and be approved by a judge. There was no such a request, no judge's order in the investigative file at all.

The request to search my car was signed by Investigator Anton Viscur from the district investigative office in Trebisov. How he got involved in this and where he came from was not known to me. It could be that his signature was also forged, like many others. Demjan and Policeman Stefanak travelled all the way to Rusovce, where my car was, to search it.

A number of specialists of the district criminal police of Bratislava were involved in searching my car, including two dogs specially trained to search for drugs: por. Mesaros Robert, mjr. Gigle, mjr. Kapicak, strzm. Marczy, pprap. Garay and his dog Syrt, kpt. Kubinec and his dog. Pprap. Horvatova was also there. Demjan requested and received cooperation from all those policemen based on absolutely nothing. How could that be?

The result of the search was the same as that of my house. They found nothing.

Demjan sure wasted many people's time. All that time, he knew that he was making everything up. The police in Bratislava should ask for judicial orders when dealing with somebody, especially somebody from Trebisov. This was the second time in my case when policemen from Bratislava were doing dirty work for corrupt policemen from Trebisov. The logical conclusion is that they were not even aware of it, but they failed to ask for the papers that are required for such a procedure. The first time was when we were apprehended without a warrant, and then my car was searched without one as well. It was a horrible feeling when I realized that they might have planted something in my car.

All this had a devastating result on my health. They kept accusing me first. When I was cleared from the allegation, they did not let me know. It just built in my mind. The stress was very hard on my blood pressure. And because of the cigarette smoking of my cellmate, to which I was allergic, my nose bled every day. The food in that jail was terrible, so my body was unable to replenish the blood I was losing. My health was leaving me.

Investigator Demjan and Judge Milko were like blood brothers. I should call them bloodthirsty brothers. Any crap Demjan made up was approved by Milko. Some accusations Demjan bypassed the judge for.

By fabricating false charges, Demjan was committing a very serious crime. According to section 174 paragraph 2 T.Z. and section 158 paragraph 2c T.Z., the minimum punishment is three years in jail, and it could be as many as ten years. No wonder Demjan was doing everything he could to shut me up, because I was the one who was bringing his illegal activities up. Judge Milko also proceeded as though there was no law at all. Most likely, Demjan was his friend, and he did not want him to be punished. If this was a fiction, I would call them blood brothers. Some other writers would call them bloody brothers. If this wasn't a true story, I would call them all of the above. Because this is a true story, I cannot call them any of this, because it is against the law in Europe. Free speech in Europe has restrictions and penalties. You are not allowed to express your opinion if it offends an official. Not even if what you are saying is true.

The two interrogations of the child Jana were proof that I had done nothing wrong. Under normal circumstances, Demjan should have asked the judge to release me. Instead, he changed and turned around Jana's answers and used them against me. Judge Milko approved Demjan's requests immediately. He didn't even wait until the statements were verified. Judge Milko punished me by already ordering more restrictions on me in jail on November 11, 1998. Only on December 2, 1998, on my request, did they talk to Jana's family.

Demjan lied to Jana's mom's face and used tricks on her. The judge's decision had already been decided almost three weeks before. It appeared that, when Demjan whistled, Judge Milko jumped. It did not matter how absurd Demjan's requests were.

Demjan and the judge claimed that I would influence Jana, so they broadened my restrictions in prison. By doing so, they made it impossible for me to apply for bail.

Judge Milko formulated that Jana, "besides other things, said that Demcak allegedly told her mother that, if the police came to school, she should not talk to them and that she should not attend the questioning at all." An important point, in this case, was what "other things" meant— those things that the judge chose not to name. It was a disaster of justice.

Prisoners cry and are driven to misery when that kind of unfairness is continually placed upon them.

I was devastated myself when I received these fabricated decisions. They were sent to me in many different forms. Each of them described all fabricated accusations twice. That system was elaborate mental abuse. I knew that, by the judge's request, I was going to be moved to a different cell with more restrictions and that all my mail would go through Demjan's filthy hands. On the top of that, the possibility of bail was also out because of this arrangement. I was punished more, because the child Jana Visokaiova and her family testified that I was innocent. My innocence was used against me. That was the justice in Trebisov.

Policeman Demjan kept accusing me of other new crimes.

When my new lawyer and I filed a complaint against Demjan's illegal actions, a prison guard went through my documents and confiscated those from Demjan. But they had been recorded in other files, and I managed to get them; therefore, I can prove all the mental torture anyway.

I discovered a special guard going through my papers.

"Isn't it against prison regulations to read my investigative documents?" I asked him.

"I'm not reading; I'm just glancing," he said with irritation in his voice. It was already known to all the guards that I had studied the law and regulations and that I even understood their meaning. It was getting to them that I dared to want them to go by the law and regulations. The regulation states that guards are not to read the private or official correspondence of prisoners, but they can glance into envelopes to see if there were some restricted items. That gave them the excuse to keep glancing and reading whatever they chose.

I filed a written complaint with the chief warden. I stated that I was abused and some documents had been taken and were missing from my bag. He came and told me, "You cannot prove it."

I realized that it was the truth, what the prisoners had been telling me all along. "He [the chief warden] is only making sure that, whatever crimes are committed by the guards, the prisoners cannot prove. A few prisoners warned me about it. Warden should have made sure that the laws were being obeyed. Instead, he was only making sure that any wrongdoing could not be proven. And he was quite open about it.

That was another shock when I realized that even the prison officials were going hand in hand with corrupt officials on the outside, exactly the same way as during communist rule. I could see more and more problems coming my way. I had to ask myself if the hands of the pervert who had abused the child Jana were reaching all the way into the prison.

All this lawbreaking and the more and more accusations against me had a terrible effect on my mental and physical well-being. Whatever I did, the dread was always on my mind. I was tired, but thoughts were in the way of my sleep. I was forever afraid of what else they were going to make up against me.

And there it was. The next correspondence from Demjan almost knocked me out.

I received a letter from Demjan dated November 4, 1998, in which he requested a psychiatric examination by two specialists, MUDr. Stefan Safku and MUDr. Maria Kilianova. They were both doctors or psychiatrists from Kosice, the same city where I was incarcerated.

It would not have been so bad if my memory wasn't so good. I remembered the times when mental institutions were full of normal people in all the communist countries. Some had been driven to desperation, by confiscation of their possessions, and sent far from their homes.

If communists wanted somebody out of their way, there were only three possibilities for the poor victim: jail, a mental institution, or death. In jail, there was still hope for some of them to get out. In a mental institution—no way. You were there for life. Completely normal people died, forgotten, in many of those dreadful establishments. Most of them were housed in old castles or large residences of rich, upper-class citizens. The owners had been chased away, and their estates and their assets had been confiscated. The buildings had been abandoned and run down by the weather. When the communists came to power after the Second World War, there were too many people they needed to get of their way. The big buildings were just what they needed, especially because most of them had high brick fences around them.

The communists confiscated whatever they wanted from people. All businesses—big or small. Farms of all sizes. Domestic and farm animals—horses, cows, calves, you name it. Farming equipment and machinery were all being confiscated and taken away, as well as the farmers' fields.

I was a very young boy when all this was going on, and I will never forget it.

The most ruthless of all was the case of the old lady who lived across the street from where I used to live. She was hanging onto her cow, when the communists dragged it away to the Unify Farmers Yard called the JRD. Her husband had died just a while before, and she had no family left. Her cow was her whole life and her only company. She had taken the best possible care of her cow, feeding and watering it, and allowing it to accompany her on the way to the pasture in the summer. In return, every morning and evening, she received fresh milk for homemade, white coffee. There was always some milk left to make fresh butter and for the neighbour's cat, which jumped the fence every day for his bowl of fresh milk. I used to go there to buy fresh milk for our family. In a special milk container called a *kanticka*, I brought home one or two litres of fresh milk. She never forgot to pour half a litre of fresh, warm milk into a metal cup called a *harcicok* for me to drink. It was a free bonus for walking to her place in the early morning and evening. She bought herself fresh bread at a private bakery called At Svatosha's. The same as at most farmer's places in those days, her cow was also sighted in the back section of her house. The barn adjoined the house. Cows were very big assets for everybody in those days.

She cried and hung onto her cow for as long as she could. Then she fell to the dust, her hand reaching after her cow, which was dragged away, not to be seen again. I was there, as I was every morning, to get milk for our family. I helped her to her feet and brought her to her empty house. She was crying so hard, she was losing her breath. Tears were in my eyes then, and they are even now, when I'm recollecting this true story, which left the scars in my conscience throughout my life.

The old lady did not stop crying. Soon she was gone. A policeman, who was imported from a small village, moved into her house.

"The communists got rid of her because they needed the house for STB member," my father told me when I asked him what had happened to the old lady. "She is probably up in Garani or some other mental institution." Garani was a mental institution just a few kilometres from Trebisov. It was up on a hill in an old castle. Very few people have seen what went on up there behind those thick walls of the building. All we knew for sure was that people who were sent there did not come back. Institutions like that were scattered throughout Czechoslovakia.

After what happened to the old lady, please do not try to tell me that there are good communists.

"Be quiet, or you'll end up in Garani," my father used to warn me whenever I swore at communists.

There were many others whose lives were destroyed around the country, just like that of the old lady. The grandfather of my classmate Mr. Lopatnik, who lived "Na Zahumni" in Trebisov, also disappeared. People whispered that the communists took him *na cechi*, meaning to the Czech Republic to a Labour Camp. Nobody knew for sure. He had refused to sign that he would voluntarily become a member of the Unify Farmers Organisation and give them everything that he owned.

There were some who resisted as long as they could, like Mr. Mancos' family or Mr. Bumbera's family, and many others. These were the people who worked every day until midnight and rose at 4:00 in the morning to work on their farms. They worked like that for many generations. Then the communist bums showed up and wanted them to sign everything over to them.

Slovak communists found a way to deal with those who refused to sign away their soul.. Here comes a new idea and a new word in the Slovak vocabulary: *kontingent*, or quota. That meant you could keep your cows, pigs, chickens, and whatever you had, but the milk, eggs, meat, and whatever you produced would go for the *kontingent,* meaning you gave it freely to a communist-owned businesses, which would sell it. Not a penny went to farmers for their produce.

Nothing was taken into consideration. Not the fact that, in different seasons, animals produce different amounts. The communists came, counted how many cows, chickens, or whatever a farmer had and stated how much milk, eggs, or other produce the farmer had to bring for the *kontingent.* There were huge fines, if somebody's cow did not produce the amount of milk the communists prescribed. Absurd? You can bet your life on it. The whole system was designed to make sure that die-hard farmers could not meet their quotas and could then be fined. Once they could not pay their fines, their assets were confiscated with that excuse. People cried and fainted when the communists came to repossess their belongings. In the end, not a single farmer survived. Many died shortly afterward from sorrow and grief. In some cases, including the case of my dad, the subconscious mind saved them. Many of them, like my dad, did not remember the day when the communists came and took everything they owned from them.

"I was lucky that they did not take my business away from me," My dad usually replied. It was irony, but we did not remind him that the place where he was an employee was not his anymore. Remember that this is a true story.

Another heartwrenching situation was that of Mr. Rusnak. His son used to be my classmate at elementary school.

When it became obvious that the Unify Farmers Organisation would flop, the communists gave back small parcels of land to people to grow some vegetables and some fruit to avoid starvation.

Mr. Rusnak had his parcel just on the other side of a small stream called the Trnavka. Most people in Trebisov called it the Kanalish. The parcel that the communists let him use was just bare land when he took it over. For years and years, he planted a large number of fruit trees. Every tree was like a child to him. He named every one of them and talked to them as if to his best friends. After years of work, his parcel became one of the best orchards in the area. The trees were the biggest and nicest in the whole province. In the meantime, Mr. Rusnak grew older himself, the same as his grove.

Then it caught the eye of some communists. The idea lit up. "The communist party of Trebisov is returning the land of your orchard to the Government of Czechoslovakia," the official note read. Mr. Rusnak was astonished. His family had to explain to him over and over what that meant. After the war, the communists pronounced that all land belonged to the state. Not even a square meter was owned by anybody. That way, they could do anything they chose with the people and with their lands as well.

It was the second shock to Mr. Rusnak in his life. First, they had taken it all from him after the war, and then, they took his beloved orchard. He would have been dead right then and there, but his subconscious mind saved him, as it had saved Mr. Mancos and my dad.

It works the same way as when somebody loses a limb. When the pain is unbearable and could kill him, the person loses consciousness. That way, the person survives.

Mr. Rusnak's mind would not let him realize that he was no longer the owner of his orchard.

Nobody expected that the communists were not finished with him yet. The worst was still to come.

The trees were cut, and cottages grew in Mr. Rusnak's orchard. High-ranking communists from Trebisov divided his orchard into parcels that fit exactly for them. Communists destroyed about half of the fruit trees in a process. It was no longer the nicest orchard in the province. The main reason they had chosen Mr. Rusnak's orchard was because they had liked his trees. Then they went ahead and destroyed them. It was highly cruel and selfish conduct by communists from Trebisov.

Mr. Rusnak was getting old very quickly when he watched helplessly as they destroyed his beloved orchard. He was watching, and he could not understand why they were cutting his trees.

"Why are you cutting this Hrusku tree? It was a good tree," he said to a man who was cutting Rusnak's beloved pear tree down with an axe.

"You can f--- it now," the man answered.

Mr. Rusnak's health grew weaker and weaker. But whenever he felt better, he took about a two-kilometre walk to what he still considered his orchard. He still attended to some of his trees that needed care. He still remembered his trees' names. Most of the communists had no idea how to care for trees anyway. He never harvested any of the fruit, except if he picked one or two that he munched on.

He was sitting in the shadow of an apple tree when a communist member noticed him.

"Hey, Rusnak, what are you doing here?"

"I'm taking care of my orchard," the old man answered.

"It is not yours anymore. Go home, Rusnak."

"But it is mine. I planted all these trees, you know."

"Just go home, Rusnak. They are no longer yours."

A meeting was called of the communist party of Trebisov. The urgent agenda was

Rusnak's orchard.

"Something must be done. Rusnak has the nerve to think that the orchard is still his," the man reported his findings to the communist party council of the City of Trebisov. The rest was simple:

"Who is for it? Raise your hand. Who is against? Nobody. Everybody is for it. Thank you. It is a bylaw now."

The very next morning, a note was delivered to Mr. Rusnak's family. They were responsible for making it clear to Rusnak that his orchard was no longer his. They were to look after him and make sure that he no longer walked there and attended to trees. The penalty was listed in case the order was not obeyed.

It was a terrible, cruel decision of the communist party; in order to punish a poor old man, they robbed him of his property for the third time. It fulfilled its purpose. Mr. Rusnak died a broken man shortly thereafter.

You would think that tragedy was finished. Not so if communists were concerned. After the velvet revolution, the communist system fell down in Czechoslovakia. No so quickly in Trebisov. A new law was introduced at the beginning of 1990s. They called it restitution. According to that law, all lands confiscated by the communist era were to be returned to their original owners if they applied for them. If the owners were not alive any more, there lands were to be returned to their families. That was the law. Not so fast in Trebisov.

The claim for the orchard, on behalf of Mr. Rusnak's family, was filed by his daughter-in-law. By Czechoslovakian law, all buildings on that type of garden were to be portable, with no regular foundations, only suitable to store gardening equipment. Guess how many communists in Mr. Rusnak's orchard complied with the law? A law that they had legislated themselves? You are right—none. They defied their own laws. They built full-scale cottages on permanent foundations. And they were not about to obey the laws that the new or even the communist government had legislated.

There she was, Rusnak's daughter-in-law on one side, with a bunch of communists on the other. She was applying for the land that her family had been robbed of twice. The law was clearly on her side. It stated that the lands were to be returned to their original owners. On the other side were the communists, who did not want to give up what they called their gardens with all their cottages on them. You are right—she had no chance.

The first democratic government was only appointed for two years. Then Meciar and his movement came to power. The old communists were back in government chairs. Full-scale anarchy followed. The Rusnak application was dragged through courts and turned down in the end by an old communist judge. He defied the law, just as he had done during his whole career in his communist judicial chair.

The main argument from the communists' side was that the cottages were stable on permanent foundations. The fact that they had been built so illegally was acknowledged but not taken into consideration.

The most shocking and truly ironic examples came when I attended some meetings of the City of Trebisov council, concerning an application to return one of my family members' property. In fact, the city council was voting whether to return the property or not.

"You are voting whether the town is going to obey a federal law or not. Nobody has the right to vote on something that is the law already. The law is the law," I tried to explain to the council. Nobody seemed to understand.

My present problem was that I was being held in prison by people who did not just understand what the law was but abused it when it suited them.

CHAPTER THIRTEEN

They Will Drive You Crazy and Then a Shrink Will Send You to a Mental Institution

Mental torture is more effective and causes graver damage than physical abuse.

It was an enormous shock to my mind when I received a decision dated November 2, 1998, and another one dated November 4, 1998, by which I was informed that I would undertake psychiatric examinations by two psychiatrists of their choice. I knew that it was the corrupt policeman Demjan who requested it. The first note was the request for it that was sent to the court, and the second one was the request for examination sent to the psychiatrists themselves. Both were written by the person, who had no clue about Slovak law. They sent the notices separately to have a double impact on my brain. It was sophisticated mental abuse.

The whole of both requests was written in a way as if I had already been convicted of everything. Section 2 paragraphs 1 and 2 T.P. exactly prohibit that kind of procedure. Those paragraphs are listed in Slovak law under "Basics Rules of Criminal Process." One would hope that at least basic law would be known to these bums. Just in that decision, section 2 T.P. was broken nine times.

Just glancing at those papers, I got the bad feeling that they were attempting to put me in a mental institution. Knowing about all those innocent people who ended up in those castles that everybody called "Crazy Houses" created fear in my consciousness.

When I read the questions that the psychiatrists were being requested to answer, I was sure that was it. They are going to try to lock me in a mental institution and throw the key in manure. The following were the accusations against me, which also appeared as questions that the psychiatrists were to answer:

1. Does the charged mgr. Jozef Demcak suffer any mental illness? While committing the acts did he suffer some mental disorder?
2. Could the charged mgr. Demcak, while committing his acts, recognize the danger of his action for society and control his actions?
3. Is the charged mgr. Demcak able to comprehend the sense of criminal acts? Could he, at the time of committing the acts, understand the sense of a criminal investigation?
4. Does the charged mgr. Demcak suffer some sexual disorder?
5. Is the presence of mgr. Demcak in society, in light of his activities, not dangerous for society, was it necessary to order safeguard treatment and in what form?
6. Outline all other circumstances that will accrue during the creation of this expert evaluation that would be important for a criminal investigation

Knowing everything the communists had committed against innocent people, it was like lightning to my head. My blood pressure shot up. Profuse bleeding from my nose followed. I had heard that they were doing this to people. Then they were doing it to me, and I saw how it was done and how it felt. Believe me, the feeling was pure horror. I felt how the victims felt. It was much worse than I could have imagined it.

All they needed was one corrupt psychiatrist, and I was gone. Question five asked if my presence in society, in light of my activities was not dangerous for society, if it was necessary to order safeguard treatment, and in what form? If the answer was yes, I was going to an institution and might never be seen again. Countless normal people had been thrown in those institutions and had become mentally ill in those crazy castles. Electric shocks, wrong medications—terrible things I heard about those places.

These psychiatrists, court specialists that corrupt officials would choose and pay for their services—they were going to decide my future. What were the chances that they would be honest in my case? How could I possibly know?

After the first shock, I studied the decision again and again. It became more and more clear to me that it was most likely that somebody really was behind it all. Somebody who had no idea about the law but who knew more about psychiatry. Demjan could be just a scapegoat, doing his primitive twisting and forging, but he would know at least to write "allegedly did so and so ..." Whoever wrote that decision did not. I would have expected Demjan to know next to nothing about psychiatry, but the writer of the decision against me knew quite a bit. It was already formulated in such a way that it would inflict a big injury on my consciousness. It was put together the same way as the second interrogation of the child Jana. It was brutal and cruel against me. No doubt Demjan was a big part of the scam. He was signing all the documents, leading witnesses, and twisting their statements, but somebody more powerful with a knowledge of psychology must have been behind it all. How else would the decision get around the prosecutor or judge? The investigator had to deliver his decisions to the prosecutor, who had to check them over, correct them if necessary, and then place them in front of the judge. The judge then had to decide. That was Slovak law. All there was a suggestion dated November 2, 1998, and signed by Demjan, and a decision dated November 4 and also signed by Demjan. No prosecutor or judge.

There was a glimpse of hope for me. When I studied the decision, I noticed the birth dates of two psychiatrists who had been assigned to examine me. MUDr. Stefan Safku had been born in 1941. MUDr. Maria Kilainova had also been born in 1941. I had been born in 1941. My conclusion was as follows: We were a generation that remembered when democracy had been drowned by communists. We had studied all the communist theories, because we had had to, but we had taken it with reserve. Our parents, uncles, and other older family members, who had been robbed by communists, kept telling us that Marx/Lenin teachings were bullshit. We had seen the atrocities the communists brought on innocent people. Our generation was not stupid. I was counting on the hope that the psychiatrists who were going to examine me were smart enough to know that it was only a matter of time until the last bunch of corrupt communist officials would lose their powers, and the truth would win. I imagined that, like me, most of my generation could hardly wait until the communist bastards would have no more power to destroy people's lives. If the psychiatrists who had been assigned to examine me had been ten to fifteen years younger, my prognosis would have been much worse. At least, I was hoping, that doctors will write the truth about me.

Later, I noticed that even my new lawyer, JUDr. Fercakova, had been born in 1941. What a coincidence. Four of us had been born in the same year. That meant that we had been attending different universities in Kosice at the same time. It was also possible that we had attended the same university dances and other celebrations. University dances happened weekly, with live music led by Mr. Sabados with Mr. Caba on the drums. It wouldn't be very probable that we had even danced together, but who knew. I had attended almost all of the university dances during my five years there, and I had danced with countless girls.

All these hopes were diminished very quickly. Soon, I discovered that Demjan also had a backup plan. Six days after the first order to have me examined by two psychiatrists, I received another order. This time, I was to be examined by a court expert in psychology as well. The order had been written by the same person who had written the first one. All of the sentences had been formulated as if I had already been convicted. It had been written in defiance of Slovak law. Again, it hadn't gone through a prosecutor or a judge. No such evidence was enclosed in the investigative file. Somebody had again bypassed the law.

Here are the things that the court expert psychologist was requested to do:

1. To execute a psychological examination of the intellect and personality of Mgr. Jozef Demcak.
2. To execute a psychological examination, with a focus on a probable sexual disorder of the charged mgr. Jozef Demcak.
3. To outline all circumstances that would emerge during an examination that might be important for a criminal investigation.

My biggest concern was the person who was going to examine me: Doc.PhDr. Andrej Stancak Csc., born September 20, 1924. He was a court expert with three academicals titles, and he was also a professor at the university, specialising in clinical child and adult psychology and the psychology of sexuality. His high qualifications were not my concern. It was his age that prompted my concern. He was seventeen years older than me. That would make him a young adult when the Slovak communists had committed the most horrible atrocities against our people. He could have been a part of it. No doubt, he was a member of the communist party. As such, he would have been required to produce false assessments that would have been used as reasons to place innocent people in jails or mental institutions. If he had been doing it for all those years, he would have done it so many times that he would be completely use to it. From a psychological point of view, people who do something wrong for a very long time persuade themselves that it is the right thing to do wrong. The result is that they end up believing that what they are doing is correct. In some cases, they could even pass a lie detector (polygraph) test.

My greatest concern was the possibility that the pervert from Trebisov who was after me might know Dr. Stancak and try to influence his findings. I believed that he had already influenced a number of people. So why not Dr. Stancak?

The more accusations I received, more I was worried about the whole system. One of them was an order for the psychological evaluation of the child Jana Visokaiova. It was dated November 17, 1998. The poor little girl had been interrogated three times already. Now she would get another interrogation. My conclusion was that Demjan, in his two-and-a-half-hour interrogation of the child, had not managed to get her to say something against me, so he had hired a specialist to do it for him. I felt really sorry for the child, and I was afraid that the psychologist might find a way to fabricate something that could be used against me. My fear increased when I found out that that examination would be done by Dr. Stancak only. On the same date—November 17—Demjan wrote another two requests to the psychologist Dr. Stancak to have him evaluate the gypsies Alena and Anna Demeterova, the two sisters who were being used against me. From the questions that the psychologist was requested to get answers to, I concluded it to be just a tool to frame me and make it look, if not legal, then at least official.

Here are some examples of the directions or questions:

> 3. To establish to what extent Alena Demeterova is able to reproduce truthfully incidents that she lived through and whether her statement in front of the investigator can be considered truthful.

Here was an attempt to have the psychologist approve the record of interrogation, which he wasn't even present for. Section 107 paragraph 1 T.P. states that he, as an expert in psychology, should not evaluate evidence. And that was exactly what Demjan was asking him to do, even though the warning that he should not do it was written on the next page of the same request.

The most cynical was the formulation of the next item the psychologist was to address:

4. In case Alena Demeterova's answers are truthful, find out what kind of effects on her mental development those actions that she lived through may have resulted in.

A similar order was requested for her sister, Anna Demeterova. To put it in plain language, here were two adult prostitute gypsies, who were blackmailing me with their pimp, and the officials were trying to fabricate the possibility that I could harm them in an emotional way. Here I was jailed, and one of the reasons that was being fabricated was that I caused damaged to prostitutes by refusing to go with them. I refused to believe it was happening to me. At the time, I was totally devastated. Could it get any worse? You bet.

My new lawyer, JUDr. Viera Fercakova, came to visit. She was born same year as I was. That made her fifty-seven at the time. She was slightly on the heavier side, but with her impressive boobs, it did not show as a setback. Her blond hair could have used styling more often, but when it was done and when she was dressed up, some gentlemen could still turn around to take a second look.

I described my whole situation, from the time I was illegally arrested until my present situation in the prison.

"What a mafia it is in that Trebisov. You are lucky they did not throw rape at you." That was her first reaction. She was so right about that. Later, I realized that they tried even the rape.

The next day, she filed two requests. One went to the district prosecutor's office in Trebisov; she was requesting my release from prison. The second went to the Office of the Supervision Ministry of the Interior. In that one, she requested an investigation of the illegal conduct of members of the criminal police in Trebisov.

Following is an exact translation of the request to the Ministry of the Interior that she filed on my behalf.

> Office of the Supervision Ministry of the Interior, the Slovak Republic
>
> Request for criminal investigation of the criminal police of Trebisov
>
> 11.10.1998, I was imprisoned by the district court of Trebisov according to section 242 paragraph 1 T.Z. Investigated by district investigative office of Trebisov # OUV 600/10-1998.

The criminal police were involved in this case at first. They arranged a restriction against me travelling abroad without reason. They acted illegally in the case of Jana V. who was interrogated many times and was forced to testify against me. Her parents asked me to write a complaint, which I was unable to file because I was imprisoned. I was imprisoned in order to make me unable to file my complaint, so I'm sending it through my lawyer.

The names of the policemen involved are not known to me, but there will be no problem identifying them through the investigator involved in this case.

I assume the criminal police broke the law. The criminal police knew that I was traveling abroad on invitation from the Canadian Consulate to arrange a work permit for my fiancée. I have proof of this. They also knew that I was blackmailed by the so-called damaged in the case that it is directed against me.

I also assume that the 24-hour limit for my apprehension was broken by 14 hours.

I assume that it is a case of violation of the duties of a public servant, so I'm requesting an investigation into this case.

In Kosice, 16.11.1998 mgr. Jozef Demcak

The other request was to district prosecutor's office.

District Prosecutor, Trebisov.

Suggestion for release from prison.

On 11.10.1998, I was imprisoned by section 67 paragraph 1a T.P. I believe that it is necessary to verify my present situation, because, in my opinion, have not committed any illegal act.

Enclosed is a written documentation of telephone recordings, in which I was blackmailed by the Demeterova sisters, who were trying to extort financial resources and who can be clearly identified from these recordings. I'm pointing to my answers at my interrogation that I know them, and from the recording, it is clear that they were extorting money. This cassette, which I offered already at questioning, was not accepted by the investigator, in spite of the fact that it is proof that the whole case against me was clearly fabricated by the Demeterovas and members of the criminal police of Trebisov. I filed a complaint with the Ministry of the Interior against the actions of criminal police who are investigating in this case.

It has already been proven, from the questioning of Jana Visokaiova, that I have not committed any unlawful act.

Even before any charge, I was restricted from travelling abroad. I'm enclosing a document, proving that, in October 1998, I was to travel with my fiancée Bibiana G. to the Canadian consulate in Vienna, where I had been invited. I'm enclosing the document in the English and Slovak languages. I was to return immediately back to Trebisov.

Because of that, the reason for imprisonment by section 67c cannot be applied. In 1968, I went abroad. After 1989, I was returning home, because I was working abroad, but I have a sick mother in Trebisov, so I was regularly returning home. The whole charge is nonsense, in my opinion, so I do not attempt to hide from it. I want members of the criminal police to be punished for their actions against me. The parents of allegedly the damaged Jana V. requested that I write complaint against the criminal police, a copy of which I'm also enclosing.

Nonexistence of a reason for imprisonment, according to section 67c T.P., I mentioned above. Not to mention that incidents in the charge cannot be the truth, because from August 18, 1996, until July 18, 1998, I was not in Slovakia at all. I have never been punished, and I'm engaged and have a normal life, so I do not see any reason why my statements cannot be considered as a basis for this case, when the rest of the statements are untruthful and total nonsense.

On the basis of those reasons, I'm requesting to be released from prison.

In Kosice, 16.11.1998

I was pleased that at least my lawyer was doing something. I was not sitting around with my hands resting. At the same time, I was writing complaints on my own. Typewriters were not allowed in that prison, so I had to write everything by hand. Every letter took a long time, because I was writing in print, and that is time-consuming. I was also describing everything in detail, so my letters were two pages long on letter-size (A4) paper.

A few letters I wrote on November 16, 1998 included one to Mr. Schuster, the mayor of the city of Kosice; one to Mr. Dzurinda, who had just won the election and become the prime minister of Slovakia; one to Mr. Pitner, who had just became the minister of the interior; and one to Mr. Carnogursky, the minister of justice. All of them were newly appointed officials. My hope was that, once they settled in, they would start cleaning up the corruption of Meciar's government, which had been left blooming like flowers on a cherry tree in springtime.

In small elements, I illustrated the frame fabricated by Demjan, the abuse of the children by the police, the blackmailed against me by the gypsies and the police. Most of all, I begged them to help, because my health was getting very weak and because I was afraid of losing my life in that prison.

I was not aware that my fiancée Bibka was also sitting at home, typing requests for my release from prison. I'm still moved when I read some of her letters, like the one dated November 17, 1998, sent to Judge Jan Milko, under the title "Request to Immediately Speed Up of the Case of Jozef Demcak." She described the whole situation in the best way possible under the circumstances and with the information that was available to her. All of the important points were in that letter, from the false charges by the investigator to the blackmailing by the gypsies to the stalling of the case. What pissed me off was the fact that she had to be so polite. Of course she had no knowledge what a dishonest, corrupt man this judge was. She was asking for my release from prison from the man who had intentionally and illegally placed me there. There was the young innocent girl, dealing with an older, corrupt communist judge, asking him to help. It was the irony of life. After such a long time, I'm still very moved by it, and I will never forget it..

Investigator Demjan was busy as usual. He received a complaint from my new lawyer, stating that his charge was absurd because I had been in Canada when I was supposed to have committed the crime in Slovakia. His partner in the scam against me, Policeman Stefanak, got very busy as well. He was strolling the town, looking for anybody who would be willing to testify against me. He managed to persuade other gypsies from the same group that had been blackmailing me before.

On November 18, 1998, Demjan signed another accusation against me, using three different gypsy prostitutes.

As I was reading the new accusation, I noticed that whoever was writing all these decisions had to be a corrupt, stupid idiot. Not only was he writing like I had already been convicted but he was leaving clear evidence that he had no idea about Slovak law and that he could not even remember what was going on before. It was a total macabre of laws and regulations from Investigator Demjan and whoever was helping him frame me.

Three new names were added to the new charge against me. All of them were gypsy prostitutes from the same blackmailing group. Demjan and Stefanak had concluded that more was better. But it resulted that more people meant more lies, more broken laws, and more contradicting statements. Two new sisters were added, Natasa and Eva Pukiova, as well as Andrea Karickova. While the sisters Natasa and Eva were in a herd of prostitutes, who were blackmailing me and had the same pimp, Andrea had some honesty in her conscience and was not a prostitute. She refused to be part of the scam and refused to participate. To avoid harassment by the police, she moved to a small village and did not want to have anything to do with the whole thing.

The new charge was a much larger fantasy than the first one. Somebody was getting off on writing lies about me. It was not at all a case for justice, just a case to put as much dirt as possible on me.

It was possibly the cruellest application of mental torture.

The crimes were fabricated first, and then the police tried to make the gypsies claim them. It was to happen long before then, when they were underage. It did not matter that I was in Canada at the time.

Intercourse was virtually out. It was no longer effective. The licking of whole bodies, including sex organs, was in. Whoever was writing those lies decided that blow jobs from the gypsy prostitutes would be more degrading to me than just simple, plain sex.

Receiving these accusations one by one, with grosser and grosser descriptions had a horrendous effect on my mental state.

Investigator Demjan was so great with educating the gypsies that all teachers should be ashamed of themselves. He turned the women, who could not remember how old they were at the present time, into women who could remember how old they had been a few years ago. Under Demjan and Stefanak's supervision, they became geniuses with perfect memories. Every one of them was fourteen years of age on the days they met me. It was true, of course, only on the paper Demjan created.

The story that he fabricated went like this. Every one of them told me as soon as it was possible that they were fourteen years of age. Fifteen is legal age for someone to consent to sex in Slovakia. That was why everyone was fourteen at our first meetings. By Slovak law, you must know that the girl you have sex with is underage in order for it to be considered unlawful. So according to Demjan's creation, all meetings went something like this:

"Hi, I'm fourteen years old."

And my response was "Hi, take your clothes off."

In another situation, after I was informed that the girl was fourteen, my reaction was "It's okay; I want to try you out."

Demjan created a total monster out of me.

In all Demjan wrote twenty-five times that the girls had told me that they were only fourteen, and I still did not get the message that it was unlawful. I became a complete idiot in his statements, and the girls became geniuses.

Like anybody who fabricates something big, these coaches also made some big mistakes. They funnelled the most important number into the gypsies' heads very intensively. If they were able to remember at least one number, the situation would be safe. The magical number fourteen was the number to be remembered. Some had difficulty remembering it anyway.

No problem; Demjan knew what to do.

"Did you tell him, that you were fourteen before you entered his house?" That kind of question usually did trick. All she had to do was say yes. It did not matter to him that that kind of leading question was against Slovak law.

Demjan said: "Natasa Pukiova. Explain if you told Mr. Demcak how old you were and if he asked you in the same room as you were telling Andrea Karickova that you were fourteen."

But he created a problem that made the gypsies look even more stupid than they really were. Demjan and his assistant coach must have had big problems with basic mathematics.

It was clearly established and confirmed by me and the gypsies that I met all of them on the same day, at the same time, in the same place. It was when they came to my door to rent some costumes for their contest. By Demjan's creation, they all told me that they were fourteen. Not just once—it appeared twenty-five times, just in Demjan's paperwork. The problem was that there were four years of difference between their ages. Basic mathematics tell me that they could not all have been fourteen when they met me. But Demjan made it possible. Even Natasa Pukiova, who was eighteen at the time, was suddenly four years younger. He made a real miracle, that Demjan.

"How could they all be fourteen if there are four years of difference between their ages?" The gypsy who was in the cell with me asked. He was reading the investigative document, and he noticed these obvious discrepancies. This was a gypsy who had been in and out of jail all of his life, and he had noticed it, but Demjan hadn't. If you do not believe me, here is his real name: Jan Gore from Kosice. On the other end are Demjan and Stefanak from the police department of Trebisov who bluntly wrote it down and presented it to prosecutors and judges, and everything was fine. Nobody noticed the impossibility of the statements. There was no end to the stupidity. The problem was that that was the kind of person who was keeping me, and a number of others, in prison.

To prove his everybody-was-fourteen theory, Demjan invited into his investigation the opinion of a person whose judgment could not be challenged by anybody. Demjan made him a court authority, a criminal expert, a specialist in estimating age. He had obtained his "court authority" qualification by being a criminal himself and through his repeated presence in courts, where he was convicted for various crimes. Demjan used that man's capacity in age estimation.

He was to be Demjan's star witness. The importance of his expert opinion was undisputed, because of Demjan's traveling all the way to his residence. His home at the time was UZVJS Presov—

to be more precise, the Slovak prison for convicted criminals in Presov.

His name was Gejza Tancos. He was another gypsy and was a friend of Eva Pukiova. At the time that she visited my house with her friends, she had told me that her friend was in jail and that she would like to mail him a photograph of herself. She was sixteen at the time. I was sure, because I requested to see her citizen's ID because her intention was to rent some clothes. I took one picture of her with an old Polaroid camera and gave it to her. Soon, she mailed it to her friend Gejza.

Demjan was desperate to obtain at least a single photo, because he had stated a number of times in his false charge that I had taken photos of the girls before intercourse. He had nothing to corroborate his accusation. He travelled all the way to the city of Presov to get it. It was beside the point that it was completely legal to take that photo. She was already of age, and she was also dressed. The women were denying that I had ever taken any photos of them. They were also denying having sexual intercourse. The charge was proven complete false, and there was a ten-year punishment for making a false charge.

Luck was out even on that. Gejza had mailed it to Eva's brother, Radoslav Puky, who was a resident of Kralova, Banska Bystrica, which was, of course, another jail in another town of Slovakia.

Demjan used the gypsy convict Gejza's knowledge and expert opinion and had him estimate what Eva's age was a few years before. Can anybody guess the answer Demjan wrote down?

You are right. Of course fourteen. What else?

But if he was able to count at all, he would get exact numbers, and the estimation of the expert Gejza would not have been necessary. As Gejza stated to Demjan, he had been imprisoned in 1995. That was when I met Eva and took that one photo of her. Eva had been born in 1979. By simple mathematics, she had to be sixteen in 1995. Her friend Anna was a year younger, so she was fifteen. Both girls were of age by Slovak law at the time I met them. Her sister Natasa was two years older; therefore, she must have been eighteen at the time. So where was the crime? Even if I had done those degrading lickings and not passed out, the crime would have been impossible, because they were all of age at the time. All that and many other pieces of evidence of my innocence were not acknowledged by the officials involved. All was focused on convicting and embarrassing me.

Could that be happening to me? It was. And various accusations were presented to me at least twice a week. Every one was like a cannon blast to my head.

The following are facts that were fabricated and used against me as mental torture:

1. I was apprehended trying to escape to Canada. Accused at least ten times.

2. I was mentally ill. Accused two to three times.
3. I have been mentally ill before. Accused two to three times .
4. I was unable to recognize that my actions were a danger to society. Accused two to three times.
5. I was unable to recognize what criminal activity was. Accused two to three times.
6. I was unable to understand what a criminal investigation was. Accused at least three times.
7. I could be a sex maniac. Accused at least three times.
8. I would be a danger to the public if I were on the outside. Accused at least four times.
9. I needed preventive treatment. Accused at least three times.
10. I raped children. Accused at least four times.
11. I took pornographic photos of children. Accused at least three times.
12. I produced videos of child pornography. Accused at least three times.
13. I was a drug trafficker. Accused at least three times.
14. I murdered somebody. Accused at least twice.
15. I should have been locked up in mental institution. Accused at least four times.
16. I had sexual intercourse with two gypsies simultaneously. Accused at least six times.
17. I licked the whole bodies and sex organs of many gypsies. Accused at least ten times.
18. I was told that the gypsies were fourteen and had kinky sex with them anyway. Accused at least twenty-five times.

Never was there any indication where any of the ideas came from. There is no need to say that there was never any evidence or any corroboration of any of this ever presented. There was absolutely none.

Policeman Demjan simply made up the accusation and sent it to prison, and the guards handed them to me, peppering me with words like: "You pervert, you are never going out, … you are going to shrink house " and so on.

Demjan was pretending that he was investigating allegations that he had fabricated, and in many cases, he employed a number of specialists who had no idea that they had been duped and used by him.

Imagine what something like this does to a person in a strange country. Even local prisoners were losing their minds, driven to total desperation and horrible acts of self-mutilation, like cutting themselves with razor blades, burning themselves with boiling water, or breaking their bones.

I regret with all my heart that the Slovak government and the Canadian Foreign Affairs office turned deaf ears and blind eyes when I demanded that something must be done to stop it.

CHAPTER FOURTEEN

They Could Only Understand Farting

They named broken laws and, right afterward, claimed that they couldn't see them. (Slovak justice representatives)

I was very upset when I received the order to be examined by two psychiatrists and a psychologist. The request had been formulated in a way that, if you read it, the meaning you got was as follows: "Here is a convict who has done these criminal activities with children, and you are to decide if he is normal, if he was normal when he committed those horrendous crimes, and if it is safe to have such a criminal walking our streets.

I sat there in my cell, shaking with nervousness, and my life was disappearing into the hands of people I had never met before. The worst part was the waiting and waiting while I received accusation after accusation.

I wanted to get it over with, so I wrote letters to those who were going to decide if I was normal or if I was a monster as described in the documents signed by Policeman Demjan. I requested that they come as soon as possible, because I was losing my health. I could not take that mental torture any more.

Finally, I was escorted downstairs to the office. A lady and a gentleman were sitting behind the office desk. They both stood when we shook hands.

"Jozef Demcak," I introduced myself.

"I'm Dr. Safko, and this is Dr. Kilianova," the man said, pointing to his partner.

"We received your letters, so we came as soon as we could," Dr. Safko informed me.

They were exactly my age and looked like it. They were dressed up well. I felt like a homeless man in my prison garb.

Dr. Safko was the head physician in a psychiatric hospital in Kosice. Dr. Kilianova was a children's specialist in the same hospital. They did not strike me as monsters who would destroy people's lives. Dr. Safko did the most questioning. In front of him, he had a copy of the order for my examination, which had been signed by Demjan. He shook his head from side to side when it came to how the questions and the whole thing were formulated. It was all as if I had already been convicted.

We recalled our times as university students. That was a the first time, since my arrest, that somebody had treated me with human dignity and respect.

Dr. Safku apologized when it came to asking me sensitive personal questions.

"Sorry," he said, "but I must ask you about your sexual habits."

"No problem. I understand." I had nothing to hide, and it was obvious from the requests by the framer had to be Investigator Demjan, who had stated in his request that he was suspicious that I had a sexual disorder. It was inevitable that sex must come up in the conversation. I told them exactly how it was.

It came to light that Demjan had given them only parts of his investigative file to study. He had given them only those pages that he considered most damaging for me. The whole record of my statement, which had been made at the court, had not been showed to them. That was the part when I offered evidence that the gypsies were blackmailing me. They were not about to be fooled by that primitive man. The next day, they requested the missing pages, which were given to them. They also made a record of Demjan's illegal action in their assessment; therefore, I have proof of this and others of Demjan's machinations. He had also fooled the psychologist, Stancak, and the judges.

We said good-bye after it was all over. They did not say anything about how I had done. I had normal feelings, slightly on the positive side, but I was also worried, mainly because Demjan and whoever was helping him had picked up those psychiatrists. All I could do was wait and see.

******

My heart bounced when my name was yelled after the heavy door opened.

"Demcak. Psychological examination."

Finally, I was going to meet the feared examiner with three academic titles.

Doc. PhDr. Andrej Stancak, Csc, had been born in a small town that would be hard to find on the Slovak map; it was Pecovska Nova Ves.

As a champion bike racer, I had crisscrossed Slovakia many times on my bike, but I had never heard about town by that name.

The guard showed me the same office where I had been examined by the two psychiatrists just a couple of days before. I had not the smallest doubt that the room was bugged.

Nobody was in the office. I sat at the office desk. Soon, the examiner walked in. I got up.

"Good day, sir Docent, my name is Jozef Demcak." I left my magister title out.

He offered me his hand. "Docent Stancak. Sit down, please."

The man was an old gentleman. He did not look his age, and he was very well dressed in a dark blue, three-piece suit with a very light blue shirt and a tie matching the colour of his suit. Either he had come from court, or he had dressed up to show superiority or just respect. It was also possible that he was just a well-dressed man. One thing was for sure—I felt like a rug man, wearing that worn-out prison costume.

"I have done hundreds, if not thousands, of examinations like this, so if you try to lie or try to fool me, it is not going to work." That was his opening intro.

"Sir Docent, I have nothing to hide and no reason to lie. Everything was fabricated against me. I have done nothing wrong," I told him; it was in my opening statement.

"Sure you have not. You undressed that girl and slept with her in one bed."

"It is a lie," I got up and yelled at him. "I was under the impression that you came to examine me and not to tell me those bloody lies that Demjan is writing and sending me every day. If you already have a diagnosis of my mental health then we have nothing to talk about." I got up and was ready to leave.

"Sit down, please. Sorry."

It could have been his trick or something he had believed from the false charges or the testimony of a child whom Demjan had tricked, twisting her sentences to make it look like we had slept on the same bed.

In every single letter Demjan sent to me in prison were descriptions in details of what horrible things I had done to those poor girls.

All I knew was that I was ready to go back to my cell; I didn't realize, at the time, how dangerous that move could have been for me. He could have written that I was some kind of psychopath whom it was not possible to examine; therefore, I was dangerous for society. Had it happened during the communist system, I would have stood no chance. I could see Demjan writing the suggestion to place me in a mental institution with pleasure and Judge Milko approving it with a grin on his face, trying to look serious. My life's destiny would be stamped. It was horrendous how much power over other people such corrupt people had.

After I sat down, he changed his attitude and proceeded with the examination. I felt exactly like I was taking a university exam again. The last exam I had taken like that was about thirty years before. After I told him what had really happened—how and why they were making things up about me—he gave me an assortment of psychological tests, as well as tests of personal intellectual level, functions of memory, structure of personality, and psychopathological changes. There were visual puzzles of different shapes, different ornaments, structures, and large numbers of questions.

Approximately two or three times, I hesitated with answers in the part with different ornaments. He did help me with little hints. That was the part where I got a little sweat on my forehead. I tried to explain that I was under a lot of stress in jail, so it was harder for me to concentrate. He did not buy my explanation and reacted like an uncompromising professor.

"You either know it, or you don't," he told me.

I guess he had not spent any time in jail yet. Obviously, he thought about it later, because in his written evaluation, he did recognize my point. He wrote that some functions were lower at the present time as compared with the intellect, as a result of the different personal situation. If he had not recognized my point, my evaluation of him would have been much lower than it was in reality.

In my opinion, every expert who examines prisoners is not expert at all, unless he spends at least three months in prison as a simple plain prisoner. It should be a mandatory part of the education of those who want to be court experts.

Then, they could understand what is going on in the minds of prisoners.

When it was all over and we stood up to say good-bye, I told him that it was very hard for me in prison and asked if he could give me a little sign as to how I had done on the examination.

"There is nothing wrong with you," he said. "There is something wrong with some other people. I also saw those gypsies." He shook his head from side to side and smiled. "It is a laugh. I'm not sure why you are here," he said. Then he waved his briefcase with papers in it and said, as he left, "This may help to get you out of here. I hope soon."

I had a satisfying feeling after that experience. The man was intelligent, and he knew his business. At seventy-four, he should have been retired by then. But the money he made by doing those assessments must have been handy. It was also satisfying that three more people would know what was happening to me in that prison. No doubt, they would tell their spouses, friends, or neighbours that I was being held for ransom as an innocent man. They would be whispering about it, but sometimes a whisper could go a long way.

My new lawyer filed two complaints—one to the Control Organ Ministry of the Interior in the capital city of Bratislava and one to the district prosecutor in Trebisov.

Both requested investigations into the illegal activities of the police and into my unlawful imprisonment.

I wrote to the corrupt Investigator Demjan and the stained Judge Milko in Trebisov, as well as to Mr. Pitner of the Ministry of the Interior, Mr. Carnogursky of the Ministry of Justice, Mr. Dzurinda who was the prime minister of Slovakia, Mr. Schuster, who was then the mayor of the city of Kosice, where I was imprisoned and who I named the future president of Slovakia, before he became one. To all of them, I described in detail the illegal activities of the officials in eastern Slovakia and my poor health as a result of prison treatment. And I begged them to help. Besides Demjan and Milko, they were all the highest, newly appointed officials of Slovakia. I wrote to all of them, hoping there would be at least one of them who was honest about his promise to fight the corruption unveiled in Meciar's government. So I waited for replies from them and for the results of the evaluations by the three court experts who had examined me recently.

While waiting for the results and replies, I had a little time to get to know my roommates a little better. One was the gypsy Jan Gore (his real name); I call him Janco. He had lived in an apartment with his girlfriend in the gypsy part of Kosice before he had taken up residence in the gulag many years before. He had been in and out of the gulag ever since. That time, it was running on almost three years for him.

Once, when we were talking on the subject of teeth, he said,

"When you are released, I hope you will leave your toothpaste for me. It smells great." Janco had begun the conversation.

"Sure, I will. But you don't need it, because you don't have any teeth left."

"Oh yes, I still have four left," he said proudly, pointing to the back of his mouth. "One on each side up and down makes it four. Right?"

"Yes, if you are sure that they are still there," I agreed.

"Oh yes, they are there—a little wobbly, but still there." He reached inside his mouth to check and to prove the point. "It looks like I have only three left." He showed me one tooth, holding it with his right thumb and finger. He had just taken it out.

"Why did you do that?"

"I didn't mean to. It was just hanging there. I pulled all of them just like this."

There was not any blood at all. I found out that, as a result of stress, those prisoners who relied just on a prisoner's food had the same problems. Their teeth got wobbly and fell out, just like rotten pears.

"They [the prison officials] refused to fix my teeth for me. They wanted eight hundred korun," Janco said sadly.

I decided to cheer him up a little.

"You don't need teeth. At least when you lick a pussy, you will not bite it." It worked; we had good laugh.

That reminded me of the great dentist, Biluscak. Not only was he a great dentist who never used X-rays, but he also had two beautiful daughters, Eva and Milada, who used to be friends of mine.

Janco Gore spoke in a special language, which was a mix of eastern Slovak slang, gypsy slang, and even some regular Slovak words. He told me his sad life story.

"You know, I never ever done anything wrong, and I'm here." He began with his first visit to the gulag. "No, it is no justice. Sure, we robbed the prick, but I didn't do it. I only kept the knife to his stomach, but I didn't stick it in, did I? I didn't do it. Me not trumpet, I no cock. My friend did it. He took his briefcase, not me. I was here, and he was out, the prick head. We divided the money later. What could I do, if he took his briefcase? We split it fifty fifty. Thirty thousand each, and I got three years for it. You see, I'm innocent. I told them I no trumpet, I no cock. You think, me fucking cock, but me no trumpet. I never done nothing wrong, and I'm here."

He thought for a while, as though he was trying to think whether there was anything at all that he ever done to be there in the gulag. Then he continued,

"No. For sure, not one bad thing ever I done wrong. I'm completely innocent. Of course, I fucked her, the whore. Who wouldn't? She was only fourteen, but how could I know how old she was? You don't ask for ID before you screw somebody. Do you? Even if I did, I wouldn't have been able to see it. It was dark outside.

"I fucked her like this."

He brought his hands up to his waist and showed that he held her butts with both hands, moving them back and forth. "I held her ass right here. She liked it, the whore, but her fucker did not like it. She lived with him, and he ratted on me to the cops. The police said, 'you fucked a fourteen-year-old, you go to jail.' I sat for a year for that, but as I told you, I done nothing wrong at all. I no cock, me no trumpet. And now, look, almost three years, and me no break the law at all."

Then he thought for a while to figure out how it was possible that he had been clean for almost three years. Then it came to him slowly.

"Of course, I was here for all this time. But why am I here? For nothing. The guy—my friend robbed him, not me. They call him the damaged or the defendant. He didn't show up for court four times, and they kept me here. He no care we took his money, that is why he no show for court. Maybe my friend persuaded him not to show. And she told me, I could get eight years for it. The whore."

"Who told you you could get eight years?" I inquired.

"The judge. I changed whole senate. It is unlawful for the judge to threaten me like that. I told them they were prejudiced against me, and I canceled the whole court senate and asked for a new one. They said they would consider it and sent me right back here. Eight years, and for what? For nothing. I didun do nothing at all. Sure, the damaged told them that I held a knife to his belly. But he also told police that he didun see what it was. I no cock. It could have been my finger I pushed to his stomach. How could he know? It was dark there. I didun grab his bag. He did it, the friend of mine. The cock. What could I do? He took his bag and run.

And I'm here, and he is there—outside. You see? I told you, I done nothing wrong. I'm not a fuckin' cock. I'm no trumpet. All he had in his bag was three thousand. That came to only fifteen hundred each. You see, I done nothing wrong, and I'm here like a fuckin' cock. I told the lady judge."

Janco dropped to his knees hard on the cement floor. I thought he had broken his knees or the cement cracked. But he had felt nothing, and the cement floor was not damaged.

Then he continued,

"I was on my knees like this, telling her that I was innocent, and she was telling my wife that I could get eight years, and for what? I told her, I did nothing. And my wife? She disappointed me like this: she lives with somebody now. I was stealing for fourteen years for her, and now she fucks him. We have an eight-year-old daughter, the whore. She fucked me around, and now she fucks with him. But I will show them, when I get out. I will come right back here." Janco punched the floor with his fist..

"Right here. But I will show them. She lives with him now, the whore. She is fucking him on the bed I bought for her with money from my first robbery. I've stolen for her for fourteen years, and that's the thanks I got from her, fucking whore. I bought furniture for her from my second robbery, so she could be comfortable, and you see ... fucking whore. But I will show her. I will pull a scam on her that she will remember for the rest of her life. I will write to welfare that she is not giving any money from the family allowance to our daughter. I will show her. And him, her fucker, I will crack his head like this." Janco hit the cement floor with his fists together, forming a ball. "I know I will be right back here, but I no care. I will show them."

The story went on for much longer, but it was all very similar. It showed the life of a recidivist, who was spending his life inside. Like most prisoners, he spent years in the investigative prison, where his mind went away from doing absolutely nothing. You wake up and sit on a stool for eleven hours. Your mind and body are sitting, day after day, year after year. You cannot be normal.

After doing it all of his life, he really believed that he was doing nothing wrong. Exactly the same thing was happening to the Slovak officials in the justice system. They believed that it was normal to place the innocent in jail and destroy him. They didn't feel sorry for their victims at all. The difference was that people like Janco were paying the price for their wrongs, and the officials were getting paid for theirs. So who is worse?

Janco told me a few times how he had replaced the whole court senate, because the lady judge

broke the law. Then he yelled the same story from the cell to his prison friends, who were walking outside in the chicken coops. He also yelled the same from the chicken coop to those who were peeping from cell windows.

I didn't pay much attention to it, thinking that he was just making up the story to feel important in front of his friends. I did not think he was familiar with any laws at all. But I was wrong.

I was studying Slovak law extensively at the time. With shock after shock, I was discovering that absolutely nobody in the justice system even knew that the law was the law and that it should be followed.

Then I came across the paragraph that states that no judge, nor any member of senate, is allowed to discuss the awaiting punishment or any other details from the court proceeding at all until after the person is convicted.

I realized that that was the law Janco was yapping around all that time, claiming that the judge had broken it. It got my attention a little.

Then he received a decision from the Supreme Court of Slovakia. From that, it was clear that Janco had in fact requested orally a cancellation of the senate, because the judge had broken the law and because they were prejudiced against him.

The judge of the Supreme Court of Bratislava listed, in the first part of the decision, the laws and paragraphs that forbade judges and members of the senate from disclosing any possible punishments that he is considering until the time of sentencing. Those were exactly the paragraphs that the judge had broken.

Then the judge concluded, "Not seeing that the law was broken, I'm returning the case back to the same judge and senate."

Janco's destiny was set in stone. He was going back to the judge he had complained about. She would deal with him very "friendly and rightly." The most disturbing fact was how the controlling organ or higher court dealt with complaints. First, they named the laws that had been broken by officials, and right after that, they stated that they had not seen them or that they did not see that the law had been broken. That was one of the most used phrases as an answer to many of my complaints. If somebody had a chance for justice in Slovakia, it is only an exception. That is my conclusion.

I was going to try to smuggle that written decision out to show what they called justice in Slovakia, but I was out of luck. I asked Janco for the document. He was very upset because of what he had done with it, and he even blamed me for not asking for it earlier.

Most documents were done the old fashioned way—that is, by inserting a bunch of papers with carbon papers between them into the typewriter. For that purpose, they had papers that were so thin that you could almost see through them. That's just perfect for some other purposes. And that was exactly what Janco had done. He had run out of cigarette papers and had been rolling his tobacco, the Taras Bulba, in toilet paper. When we ran short on toilet paper, he used newspaper. That was when the documents arrived. After reading them, he cut them nicely into a little bit larger size than the original cigarette papers, and one by one, he blew what would have been evidence out through the window.

In his heart-opening speech, you probably noticed that, besides swearing, Janco repeated many times that he was not a trumpet. I did guess why it was, but I decided to verify it.

"You always say that you are not a trumpet. Why?"

He thought for a while, and then, with a little shyness in his voice, he said,

"It is because of my fart. That is why the convicts gave me that nickname, but I'm not … "

When Janco farted, it was the sound of very high tune. In fact, it almost sounded like a trumpet.

"You think that you have to do it so laud? We are here, but we are not convicted yet, so we are still innocent people. You also told me that you are innocent. We should act like innocent people, and innocent people fart, of course, but they do it quietly, because it is private. Think about it." I think he did think about it, because I did not hear the trumpet any more. Later, when we received another roommate, I heard Janco telling him, that we were not convicts yet. And there was no loud farting in our cell anymore.

Janco thought some more and decided to explain why his manners had gotten so low.

"Look, I'm not a trumpet, I only cap-ca-rap. *(Stealing)* I'm not like those murderers. I would cut their cocks off while they're alive or hang him alive or drown him alive in hot asphalt. Or the one who fucked his own daughter. And they throw a net over you, and then you are here. They throw the net on me, and I'm here, and the one who was raping them is outside. If I had a speech where the government is, I would tell them that they are, without proof, locking people up. They "shup" in prison, fuck in jail, isn't it broken law? Where are we? Now they fucked me, they made a cock out of me; they fuck with me in jail; they make pure debility out of me. I am becoming a total cock in this gulag. And squats and push-ups, so what are you doing? So I'm pissing." He poured his heart right out. And the whole message was that they imprisoned innocent people and destroyed their lives.

I don't know what happened to this man, to me. I had thought that Janco had some manners, like not farting like a trumpet. Some years ago, not far from here, while in a university dormitory, it was a different story.

In the 1960s, about five kilometres from my involuntary residence was the school dormitory of a university called the Pedagogicky Institute. It was a wing of the Faculty of Pedagogy, P. J. Safarika in Presov. For five years, it was my residence while I studied to become a school teacher of natural science and psychical education. We had four beds in the room, too. The difference from the gulag arrangements was that the beds were in the four corners, instead of bunk beds, like we had in jail. We also had normal windows with no bars on them.

As students of psychical education, our minds were competitively oriented. We had all kinds of competitions. Beside the boring ones prescribed by school programs, we also had more popular ones to fill the darkness of long evenings in the cold winters. Every Thursday evening, it was a competition much favoured. The contest of (excuse me) farting, the most popular once it took off. It started in our room (#215) and later widened to much larger interest. Since it had begun in our room, I considered myself one of the founding or pioneering members.

The competition had two parts: loudness and length. In short, we named it a contest of "L. L." Somehow, the contest leaked out of our room, and soon it became the official competition of the whole hallway. There were about fifteen rooms on the second floor, and many rooms sent their champions to the finals. There were even spectators coming in from other floors.

There was, of course, strenuous preparation by the athletes. It consisted of eating the ends of black bread and raw onions to enhance their abilities to reach to the highest of achievements.

As in all top sporting events, this one did not proceed without scandals. Those who were the most serious contestants even brought small electric hotplates to their rooms and cooked big white beans to improve their capabilities. For a long time, they kept it secret so as not to help the competition. White beens increased competitor's chances of winning the much prized trophy. When it was finally disclosed, it was pronounced that it was using achievement enhancement substances; in simple language, it was doping. The senate, consisting of three judges, came up with a different conclusion. After deliberating for more than three hours, they concluded in a written statement that "The defendants did not fulfil all signs of criminal behaviour; therefore, no further fart investigation was necessary." As for the reason for their conclusion, they stated, "On the basis of evidence available to us at the deliberation, the panel of three judges concluded that white beans are not listed as forbidden achievement improvement substances in sports; therefore the defendants were cleared from any illegal actions.

It was never proven whether the Slovak justice system acquired this phraseology from our competition or whether it happened the other way around. One thing is sure—both of them are worth a fart.

At first, the contests were held in our room. Later, as the popularity increased and the room was too small to accommodate all who were interested, we moved the event to the janitorial storage room, which was much larger. Besides few brooms, some mops, and some buckets, the room was virtually empty. There was a small participation fee, and an entrance admission fee of five korun (about 15¢), but we still maintained the venture as a nonprofit organisation. All proceeds went to buy more precise equipment for the contest, as well as trophies for winners. To keep in line with the communist ideology, no cash was ever awarded as a price for the winners. If cash had ever been awarded, we could have been arrested for promoting a professional sport, and that was illegal during communist rule.

After studying Marx-Lenin philosophy, we discovered that it was not as complete an ideology as was claimed by its followers. We were unable to find out, if it was legal to fart under the picture of the first secretary of the Soviet Union, Leonid Breznev, which was hung in most government offices. We did not attempt to ask our professor of Marx-Lenin ideology, Docent Molcak, this question, because we hoped to graduate from the university, and a question like that could jeopardise the attempt.

The number one hit was called the blast. It was simple and easy to measure and was foolproof as far as the results were concerned. We placed a very sensitive noise measuring machine right beside the competitor's blast hole. The decibel machine delivered undeniable results. The highest number on the dial established the winner.

The number two hit was called the straddle. It was much more complicated. The equipment and procedures required for fair competition was as follows:

For the actual contest, the competitor could compose a position of his choice, but access to the hole was mandatory. He had to pull his pants and freshly laundered underwear down off his balloons. Only butt cheeks were allowed to be exposed. Revealing the barrel or fireballs was strictly prohibited in order to maintain the seriousness of the competition, as well as to not distract or influence the honoured judges.

A clear plastic ruler was placed in line of the outlet as close as possible. An arsonist placed a lit match—made in the United States of America—right in the obvious line of the exploding gasses. The judges watched closely to see what number on the ruler the blue flame reached during the explosion. Logically, the highest number on the ruler won.

In case of a discrepancy, the senate, which consisted of three judges, retired to a private chamber, where they voted by secret deliberation. All decisions were reached without unnecessary delay, most of the time right on the spot without cheating, lying, forging, or breaking any laws or rules. No innocent person was ever punished. It was a big contrast to the judicial officials in Trebisov, where my case was dealt with. The Trebisov officials could learn how to bring about justice from our event in the university janitor room. Needless to say that I have a much higher respect for the officials who overlooked justice during our farting game than for those in Trebisov and all others who were involved in my case.

Had the prosecutors and judges taken part in our contest, they would learned how to understand the law and how to write sentences, because those in my case were unable to do so. They disgraced the whole justice system in Slovakia.

Even though we respected all the rules of the communist ideology of Marx, Lenin, and a picture of Breznev was hanging on the wall, our contest did not have a happy ending after all. When university officials discovered our contest, they did not recognize the learning factor the event could be for appointed judges in Slovak courts.

Our school officials could not even understand the meaning of mitigating circumstances.

The only word they were able to understand was *fart.*

CHAPTER FIFTEEN

The Agenda of the Highest Representatives at the University: Farting

What can you do when somebody is pissing on your head?
Duck.

When word leaked out about our special event one Thursday in 1964, there was a secret meeting in the principal's office. Present were the Principal, the vice principal, the vice principal of discipline, the chief of the dormitory, the professors, and a few most trusted members of staff. The agenda was the fart. The professor of the Slovak language, Mr. Koloda, was sent out as a secret agent to investigate it. Our counterintelligence service informed us that a spy, a specialist in farting, was coming. We made the appropriate arrangements. Our competition that Thursday was promptly cancelled. All promotional materials, as well as the pictures of Breznew and Gottwald in the janitor room, were removed from the walls, and the chairs were scattered in rooms across the second floor and downstairs in the boiler room. All evidence was removed. The door of the innocent-looking janitor room was left unlocked so the fart detective could easily discover that nothing illegal was going on in there. All of us had innocent faces already rehearsed and ready. Our hope was that the fart investigator Professor Koloda would discover the not guilty room and report the findings to his superiors.

But after his futile discovery of the empty room, Mr. Koloda decided to investigate even the farter on his own initiative. He decided to sniff out what was going on in the headquarters of the farting event, which was our room.

This important secret action reminds me of a similar one in Trebisov. I have official documentation that points to the fact that the police in Trebisov also had a secret meeting. They were discussing a secret order to search my house, hoping to find some naked asses or even some pussy. Demjan called it pornography. The result of that search? Not even a fart. Investigator Demjan was discovering fart after fart in his expert attempts to frame me. More often, he did not even discover the fart.

After cancelling the event, we were relaxing on our beds, having serious conversations as usual. Dezko, from the village under High Tatra, was sleeping on the bed by the door, and Jano, from Secovce (no relation to the gypsy Janco who was in my cell), had his bed by the window. On their side, behind the wall was the washroom for the students of the whole second floor. My bed was located on the other side of the room by the window, and Suller was sleeping on that same side by the door.

Since the contest had been cancelled, we were talking about topics as far as possible from farting. We were an intellectual bunch, all hoping to be professors one day, and there were a lot of more intelligent topics to talk about.

To underline our intelligence, farting was not even permitted in our room. That was not easy on Suller that evening, because he was all prepared for that night's contest, which had been cancelled for unprecedented reasons. But rules were rules, and when pressure built in his stomach from the heavy black bread and the raw onions, enhanced by big white beans, Suller had to run to the door and let it out—in the hallway.

As I mentioned, our room was located right next to the washroom. The washroom was very large. On the left side were showers with unlimited hot water. In the middle was a long sink for washing and shaving. On the right side near the window were five toilets, and near the door were urinals. There were about six of them, because they served almost one hundred boys, so they were quite busy. It just so happened that all six of them were attached alongside Dezko's bed—of course on the other side of our wall. Those who knew buildings made out of panels during communist times will know that the walls were thin, and sound insulation was next to none. We could hear every time somebody relieved himself on the other side. Fortunately, there wasn't any stink coming into our room.

We got used to the noises coming from the other side when somebody was moistening the pot or filling up the toilet. For months, we did not pay any attention to it. That is until that fated evening, when Jano suddenly yelled, "Desko duck!" It was a warning scream as if the wall were coming down. Suller and I sat up on our beds to see what was going on.

"Somebody is pissing on your head," he said. And sure enough, we all heard a spraying noise coming from the other side. We had a great laugh. I have no idea why or how Jano discovered that new "intelligent topic." I said that farting was not the only thing we knew to talk about. It went on for a while, and each time somebody opened the "hose" on the other side, Jano found a new innovative way to warn Desko. He yelled warnings like "bend," "drop," or whatever to warn the poor guy.

The future looked dark for poor Desko, and it seemed that there was no way out of this new *slamastika*. It was customary in our room to defend yourself, if a joke was on you, by returning it back to the joker, but of course, with a much bigger impact, if possible. It seemed hard to top that one. But Desko did not give up easily.

Suddenly, he yelled, "Jano, run!" He yelled, with even greater inspiration than Jano had, because Jano's warnings had begun to sound worn out. Anyway, Suller and I reluctantly sat up anyway, just to be polite.

"Somebody is shitting on your head," Desko continued.

At first we did not get it, but once we understood it, there was a good point in Desko's idea and legitimate reason for a good laugh. It had taken Desko a while and a pile of Jano's insults shot at him, but he had figured out the point of his defence.

On the other side of the wall where Jano's bed was were all the toilets that served the whole second floor. We could hear them flushing, and we could hear all those natural noises that come with that anatomical and physiological feat. Now the laughs were on Jano, and it was Desko's turn to warn him when somebody was engaged in business on the other side of the wall. And he had enough words stashed in his head to warn Jano.

Poor Jano had to gather all of his farmer's brains for his defence, or he would go to sleep that night with his black hair painted a little brown. It would be a disgrace for him, as a farmer's son from Secovce, that some skinny, blond boy from town that nobody had heard of might taint his shiny black hair. He was not the kind of boy who would give up easily without a fight.

When Desko informed him again, "Jano, dash. Somebody is shitting on your head again."

Jano already had his answer ready: "Shitting, shitting, but rinsing with clean water. But you ... they even masturbate on your head."

That was undeniable proof that we had much more dignified topics to talk about than farting. We were a funny bunch. Our jokes usually went until very late every night. Those were probably the funniest times of my life. Jay Leno from TV's *The Tonight Show* could learn a lot from us. The saddest part of it all was that it was to be over soon. The old proverb says that "nothing lasts forever." So true.

The important thing for Jano was that he could go to sleep peacefully and, especially, with clean hair. Maybe with clean hair. But peacefully? Not so fast.

Destiny is not predictable.

Between those laughs produced by Jano and Desko were many other jokes. On the top of it all, Suller was running, opening the door, sticking his balloons out in the hallway, and letting it all go out with a thundering echo in the hallway. There was no farting allowed in our room, remember? That action just added the pepper to our laughs. Suller had signed up for the competition, so he had been all charged up. All that preparation, all that strategy was wasted. He had been hoping to win that priceless trophy in the competition that had been cancelled on short notice.

And then disaster. With the already rehearsed routine of a professional, Suller opened the door again, stuck just his butt out the door, and let out a fart as loudly as he could manage under the circumstances. He slammed the door behind him, but the door opened immediately.

At the same time, Desko yelled at Suller, "Hey, that is no fair. You are shitting outside, but the stink follows in right behind you."

We thought that the door had opened from the impact of Suller slamming it. But it was not so. It was much worse. In fact, it was Professor Koloda who had opened it. He was the one who, as a secret agent, was sent to check on our contest. Because, he had not discovered it, he had decided to come and check on the organizers' quarters. Talk about bad timing. Needless to say that the professor's nose was right at the door when Suller let his blast out. As if that was not bad enough, Desko added to it by saying, "the stink follows in right behind you."

The professors were real authorities in those days. They were also members of the communist party. Showing them honour and distinction was compulsory. This incident signalled that a huge tornado was coming our way. Believe me, nobody was laughing in that room. Laughter was out of our lives for a long time. You just don't fart in the face of your professor, and you don't call him a stink under any circumstances. Accident or not, it made no difference. You just did not do it. Period. Suddenly, our hopes of becoming professors one day disappeared just like a fart. The moral of the story for Suller was the same as the one that is obligatory in the army: "Make sure to check the area before you shoot." As for Desko, it was, "Always check who is opening the door, before you yell an obscenity." Neither of them had lived up to these lifesaving rules.

As if this was not bad enough, more disasters were coming our way. Sometimes, when something starts to go wrong, everything seems to collapse. Our problem was that our high intellect was notable in almost everything that we did.

For about five months, we had not swept our floor; instead, we had covered it up. The janitors only took care of the hallways and washrooms. The students were responsible for keeping their own rooms clean. All papers went nicely down: newspapers, magazines, scrap essays, wrapping paper, and pieces of cardboard from parcels we received from home. All just on innocent stuff. In a few months, the floor was covered nicely with about two to three feet of a nice, soft coat.

As Mr. Koloda opened the door, with Suller's and Desko's welcomes, he only stepped on the clean floor in front of the door. The clean space was there because the door opened inside, and with the motion, the door always pushed papers to the side. The professor stood there for few seconds, as if he had lost his breath. I guess he was trying to pretend like that he had never seen anything like that before. Then he turned around and closed the door behind him with a very gentle movement.

That would have been the right time for a good, real laugh, but none came out at all. We knew the storm was coming down, and there was not much we could do. It was getting late, but there was a hope that, if we could have the room spick and span by the time Professor Koloda spread the story and the chief of the dormitory arrived in the morning, we stood a chance of getting some mitigating circumstances.

But how did you get rid of about a truckload of paper overnight? The strategy was set up very quickly. There was no time to waste. We would take bed sheets, pack as much paper in them as possible, and run to the boiler room, where we would burn it all. It was three stories down to the basement. There were four of us. About fifteen to twenty trips each and we could do it. We were in good shape; it should have been no problem. When the chief arrived, all he would discover would be our innocent faces, looking at him from under white bedsheets.

It was a good plan, but it was not to be. Just as we finished our lightning planning, it was over just as fast as the plan was endorsed. Not even fifteen minutes had passed since Mr. Koloda had left when somebody knocked on our door. We all froze. Other students did not knock gently like that, if at all.

When the door opened, it was much worse than any of us could have imagined. In the doorway stood the school principal, two vice principals, the chief of the dormitory, Professor Koloda, the security door guard, and some other trusted professors. They all tried to fit on the clean patch of our floor, but it was virtually impossible. Some stayed outside, just stretching their necks to look in over the shoulders of their colleagues. Nobody said one word to us. We were like wet dogs that had been in a hurricane for a week. They were just shaking their heads and whispering to each other. Like Professor Koloda before, they were pretending that they had never seen anything like that before. Then they left without saying good-bye, just like Professor Koloda had before.

The question was how had they all gotten together late at night and so quickly. They had all been in the principal's office, deliberating about our farts, and they had sent Professor Koloda to look into the farting. Instead of farting, they received a mountain of surprise.

We knew we were in big trouble. Taking down the paper overnight would not save us anymore. It could even be used against us, as the boiler room was out-of-bounds to students. All we could do was wait and pray.

At 8:00 AM, all four of us stood on the red carpet in the principal's office. The principal, the vice principal, and the chief of the dormitory were present. The Soviet leader Breznew and the Czechoslovakian president overlooked the whole meeting from the wall.

Our fate was already sealed. They had done it the same way they have been doing it in justice until today—"about us and without us." They were not interested in anything that would make our situation a little bit better. No mitigating circumstances of any kind were considered at all. They could take into consideration that the room was not very big, so it was easy to fill up. Or that under the beds, the paper was thinner than on the floor. Even the fact that we did not dispose of any organic materials that could rot or decay was considered.

The verdict had already been decided.

1. All four of us were expelled from the dormitory. We had to be out by the end of the month.
2. Everyone would be fined 100 korun each (about $3.50), which would pay the janitors to clean our room.

3. Dismissal from the school was pending and was being deliberated.

It was like a nightmare, of which I have a very blurry memory. I remember some words that were mentioned. Words like fire hazard, flees, ticks, rot, mould, and some other pests. None of them were found, of course. They were named only as possible hazards. We took it as a fair punishment as far as being expelled from the dormitory was concerned. But the question about being expelled from the school weighed very heavily on our minds.

That same day, janitors from all five floors came to assess the situation. They looked in our room and also pretended that they had never seen anything like that. After shaking their heads, they left. Shortly, they returned with huge laundry baskets. After deliberation, they left with their baskets empty. Shortly, they returned with large bedsheets. I guess that was also our idea the night before.

But the sheets received the same treatment the baskets had. The bedsheets also left empty-handed. Soon they returned, and all five of them were holding huge brooms and mops. Consequently, the mountain of paper moved slowly, step-by-step, down the long corridor. Like five ladies, the janitors were following it and pushing it in front of them with their brooms and mops, all the way down three floors to the basement and then all the way back to the boiler room, where it was burned. Not a trace was left of it.

That day, there was also a tragedy in the history of Slovak sports. Our new, rising sports discipline was also killed, even before we had a chance to submit it to the Olympic Committee for consideration for it to be added to the list of Summer Olympic games. Neither had we had a chance to submit our results to the *Guinness Book of World Records*.

The chance to invite Slovak judges and prosecutors to the event, so they could learn how to apply justice or how to understand the law in a democracy was also slaughtered. No surprise.

That was not the only time the communist system killed all new and free ideas. They never even got the point that we were only having fun. We were never serious when we were having fun. We were just doing pranks, without hurting anybody or anything. There was no vandalism, no broken laws—not even broken rules. Nobody informed us of the rules about what was required to keep the room clean. "No papers on the floor" was added to the rules only after our case. We were tired of all the boring, black-and-white life that the communist system had forced on us. Our case was talked about at all the universities in Kosice. But the laughter stopped when inspections of rooms at all dormitories were ordered because of our case.

Only after I escaped to Canada did I find out that pranks by university students were common practise there. I also discovered that our pranks were next to nothing to compared with those pulled by Canadian students. We did not hang a Volkswagen car on the highest bridge like students in Vancouver did. What is a little paper in the room to compare with a prank like that? Just a simple fart.

I had a more serious problem looming over my head. How was I going to tell my mom what I had done? It was all taken care of.

Our parents had already invited. My mom attended from my family. She even cried in the principal's office. Maybe it helped, but I'm not sure. Maybe it was the combination of her crying and the fact that I was a champion bike racer, who was representing the country at some international races at the time. The fact was that all four of us received permission to finish the school semester. Everybody said that we were lucky, because we had not been completely expelled.

But there was no compromise on the dormitory. The verdict was uncompromising: we had to be out by the end of the month. All four of us scattered wherever we could. Jano went to his brother's bachelor apartment; Suller and Desko found a room at one of Suller's cousins' place; and I moved to a room rented by a friend of mine, Imro Imrich. He was also my teammate from Lokomotiva, the cycling club in Kosice.

Jano and I were model students until the end of the year. It was the main condition of being allowed to continue to study the next year. Maybe that was the reason we were even allowed back into the dormitory the next September. For some reason, we were not placed in a regular student room. I suspect it was as punishment for our behaviour during the last school year. They gave us the janitor room. The irony was that it was the same room where we had had our contests. The janitor room was much larger than a regular student room. It had three windows instead of one. It also had a cement floor. Later, we were told that no other students wished to reside with us and that was the reason why we were there. We did not mind at all. At least we had a much larger room and a lot of privacy. But it was not a smooth ride for us after all.

There were some tall, partly broken dressers in our room. We were told that we could take them down to the basement if we didn't want them. Instead of taking them down, we brought some more up from the basement. Having a nice, large room with three windows, we decided to improve our living quarters. We lined up the dressers, so that we created a hallway in our room. The doors of the dressers faced hallway, and the backs faced into our room. To cover up the ugly backs of the cabinets, I covered them with large pieces of paper and painted beautiful pictures on them. I loved to paint, so it was real art. To get into our room, you had to open one of the tall dresser's door and walk through it. You had to know which door to use; otherwise, you had to check every door to find out which one it was.

We had inspectors checking on us often, as our reputation had been tainted because of the activities from the year before. The inspectors were the principal, the chief of the dormitory, or teachers on duty. Everything was fine. Some even praised our creative talents. Our room was clean and cozy. Until the storm hit again.

One evening, Mr. Somer decided to pay us a friendly visit. We would have given him a friendly welcome, but his size got in the way. Mr. Somer was the vice principal of our school. That was not a problem. The problem was that he would tip the scales at far more than three hundred pounds, if he ever attempted it. At 158 centimetres tall, most of those three hundred pounds had grown around him, like a Firestone tire.

Not that he did not try. He really did—sideways, forward, crossways. Those were hopeless attempts. He could not make it through our dresser door. Again, it was our fault. It made no difference that we jumped up and moved one dresser to the side to let him in. The fact that, in the process of moving the closet, we had to tear up half of my artwork was not good enough. The embarrassment of Mr. Somer was against our account.

After the whole process of meetings on red carpets, we still ended up well off. The only punishment we received for Mr. Somer's size was that we had to immediately return all the dressers back to the basement storage room. We were allowed to keep one, the same as all other students.

We felt lucky after all. It was very close to the end of our way to academic titles. The same day, we carried all the closets downstairs to the storage room. Our room became a total disaster, because it looked big, bare, plain, and normal. The only thing left of that was a good laugh whenever we remembered how Mr. Somer had tried to get into our room. But we didn't dare talk out loud about the situation until after we had graduated.   I think what saved us was that Mr. Somer was visiting us alone. If some other representatives had been present, the embarrassment would have been too much to let us go without much graver punishment.

CHAPTER SIXTEEN

Can You Pee on the Ceiling? Try It.

Janco is murdering himself.

Janco Gore was a dark-skinned gypsy man who had spent most of his life in prison. He was a very young boy when he got into jail for the first time. That was still during communist rule. His opinion was that it was very bad when the communists had controlled prisons but that now it was even worse.

He remembered when there were still tinted glasses outside the windows to block the prisoner's view of the outside world.

"You could not see anything—just milky glass," he said. "Then, as communists were falling, somebody kicked one glass through the bars and broke it to pieces. Then another one in the next cell and the next and the next. In a few minutes, almost all the glass was in pieces. It had all happened to welcome the New Year, and fireworks were going on outside. It was a lot of trouble to replace them, so they installed gaters inside the cells. Then you could see out, but you could not get to the window. All you could see from my cell were the walls that surrounded the prison."

Every Tuesday and Friday, it is shower time. It was quite a different feeling, because I was not used to showering in one large room with a few men around and one or two guards watching through the window. There were a few shower heads installed in the ceiling of the shower hall. A guard in an adjoining room controlled the water temperature and flow. He watched what was going on through the window.

There were three of us from our cell and three gypsies from a neighbouring cell—two young boys and one older guy. The two young ones were washing each other's bodies very enthusiastically. I guess the older guy didn't like the fact that he was left out. I guess he needed some attention. As the two were soaping each other on one side of the room, one of them realized that warmer water was spraying on his back. He turned around suddenly to get more sprinkle on his face and chest. Then he realized that the attention-seeking cellmate was relieving himself right on him, holding his instrument in his right hand. I believe that it was an innocent prison prank, because everybody, including the guard behind the window, was laughing except for the guy who was getting the extra spray.

I was not impressed at all, because his spraying achievement was a far cry from those we had practised in our high school washroom some years back. The goal we were trying to achieve was to hit the ceiling with our natural spray. It wasn't an official competition at all. We were just trying to pee as high as we could. The top achievement, of course, was when you hit the ceiling. Hitting the ceiling could be compared to a home run in baseball. A boy's school washrooms in those days had wall-to-wall areas for relieving inner pressures. Only a few of us were able to do it. There was no way you could hit the ceiling with just the natural pressure from your internal organs. Those who did, in fact, achieve it were able to do so only by using a special technique.

Here are some directions if you wish to try it in a restaurant washroom or in a locker room. If you are right-handed, pull the skin of your instrument over the end of it and squeeze the end of the skin with your left hand. The thumb and index finger are most recommended to do the job with the greatest efficiency. You are trying to achieve the same effect as when you try to spray your vegetables with the hose that has no nozzle.

Fill up the natural bag you just created with urine. The skin will form a pouch that will remind you of a balloon filled with water. For the best result, fill it with as much urine as your bag can hold. Then you are ready for action. With your free, right hand, squeeze the "balloon," while controlling the size of nozzle with your left hand. Set the nozzle to a small dimension, which will produce the best result. If you follow those directions precisely, you will most likely hit the ceiling. The results are certain, but by no means a money-back guarantee.

I had never told this story to my young wife in order to maintain my reputation as a decent man. But when I promised that I would write the truth in this book and nothing but the truth, I meant it. That is why I'm writing exactly the way it was, and I profusely apologise for the contents of some parts that may be offensive to some readers. Therefore, parental guidance and reader's discretion are required.

As I was writing this facts, suddenly, my wife began to yell obscenities at me and even at all men.

"Peeing on the ceiling? That's what you were doing? Aren't you ashamed of yourself? "You are disgusted, all men are disgusted."

I did not notice that she was standing behind me and reading what I was writing. Otherwise, I would have barred her from reading, because her mom wasn't present, and parental guidance is required for young book lovers. Maybe, she was just jealous because there was no chance she could do it herself.

The following advice is for men only: If you ever hear from some woman that she is able to do everything a man can, all you need to say is "Try to pee on the ceiling." Before a challenge like that, though, be sure that you practise first to make sure that you can do it, in case your wife or girlfriend says "Put your urine where your mouth is."

Our high school washroom stank horribly. It was our favourite place to hold men-only meetings. It was the only time and place in school where Janko Scerbik could smoke. Jan was our classmate, and smoking by students was strictly prohibited. It was a favourite subject of some teachers to chase him around. The teachers knew he was blowing smoke, but Jan kept denying it. Professor Kelly was a young teacher who had been trying to catch Jan with the steaming stick in his hand for a long time. It was something like when the cat took pleasure in catching the mice, or the dog enjoyed chasing the cat. Jan escaped being caught for a long time.

Meetings in school washrooms were also banned.

It was in the cold wintertime, when we had a meeting in the washroom on the second floor of the school. Jan was puffing his smoky circles as usual. Suddenly, our watchman ran in and yelled the warning, "Kelly is coming!"

We all jumped on the wall-to-wall urinals, pulled out our nozzles, and innocently pretended that we were relieving our inner pressure.

With movements of skilful expert, Jan Scerbik did what he always did in that kind of situation. He was not about to waste the second half of his cigarette. He pressed the cigarette against the wall to put it out and placed it in his top jacket packet. He was going to jump on the wall-to-wall urinal and pull out his shooter, like everybody else, but it was too late.

Professor Kelly opened the washroom door. Everybody was quietly standing side by side, pretending that only innocent pissing was going on in that room. Unable to jump on the urinal, Jan had chosen the second-best choice. He walked toward the door as if he had already finished his business and was innocently leaving the room. But an obvious obstacle arose.

Feeling all the smoke in the air, Professor Kelly stood in Jan's way and asked the obvious question, "Are you smoking Scerbik?

"No, no, I'm not, honestly."

Professor Kelly noticed a little smoke coming from Scerbik's top jacket pocket. Finally, Kelly thought to himself, *I have caught him right in the action. I wanna see how he gets out of this this time."*

With two fingers in front of Jan's eyes, the professor asked with the voice of a winner, "And what is this?" Then, with the smooth movement of Detective Sherlock Holmes, he turned over his two fingers and reached right for the evidence. In a rush of excitement because he had finally gotten the sinner, Professor Kelly forgot the old proverb:

"Where there is the smoke, there is the fire." He jumped in pain and pulled his fingers out very quickly. Then he shook off the burning cigarette, which had stuck to his fingers. The worst part about this was that we could not laugh right on the spot. Professors had huge authority in those days. It did not matter what happened, you just didn't laugh at a professor in those days. Period. We had to wait until the professor had left the washroom, and then, we could let it all out. It was a good laugh for years to come.

Jan was waiting for a call to the red carpet in the principal's office. But the call was not coming and it never arrived. I guess Professor Kelly decided that the best thing to do was to not report it any further. If he had, the story about how he had discovered the burning inferno would have also come out in the professors' lunch room. His attempt to cover it up wasn't very effective anyway. Soon, the story spread from mouth to ear among the students and then to the ears of Mr. Giba. Mr. Giba was the caretaker, which made him the school authority right under Principal Galaj. He told the story to some people, and soon, the whole school was laughing about the inferno in the pocket.

Jan became a small hero, even though; he did not plan the trap.

In the prison shower, I noticed lines on Janco's chest. The lines were going from his neck to his shoulders and all the way down to his waist. The lines were so even and strait that it looked as if somebody had made them with a ruler. They stood out quite brightly, because they were a lighter colour in comparison with Janco's dark gypsy skin.

"What happened to you," I asked after we returned back to our cell.

"I fell from a pear tree and scratched myself."

I used to love climbing trees as a kid and had also fallen down a few times, so I knew how the scratches looked after a fall. Nothing like those on his chest, that was for sure. I knew that he was lying, but I did not push him about it. It made no difference to me, if he wanted to keep the secret.

Then a new prisoner was placed in our cell. As soon as he entered, he warned Janco, "No more cutting yourself, more." "More" was a nickname for a gypsy. "Or I'm asking to be taken out of here."

That was when I found out where those straight lines on Janco's chest had really come from. The new cellmate told us how Janco had taken a razor blade out of a shaver one afternoon and cut his chest from the top to the bottom.

"There were just two of us—me and Janco. He was sick, but they would not let him lie down. Janco lay down on the bed anyway. He began cutting himself like you cut a pig. I ran to the door and pressed the panic button. It was all red—Janco and the bed. I fell on the toilet and was throwing up right into it. They took their time coming, because we were just two gypsies in the cell, so who cared? I kept getting sick and pushing the button, and he kept cutting his chest. I began kicking the door and screaming as loud as I could that he was killing himself. The prisoners next door reacted and started to yell as well. Soon, the whole wing was screaming.

"Finally, the guards opened the door. You could not see him anymore; he was all covered in blood, including his face. They just wrapped him in the bedsheets and blanket and took him out. I never saw him again. I thought he was dead. Boy, it was long ago, but my stomach still comes up in my throat when I think about it. I woke up in the middle of the night, screaming."

The man was really red in the face and all drenched in sweat as he told us the story.

"Fell out of the tree, right?" That was all I said to him.

Janco was just looking down. He was ashamed of what he had done. I wouldn't have minded knowing why he did such a thing, but I did not ask because I could see that he wasn't up to talking about it at the time.

Now I know why he did it. I know the pain when you are sick and they don't let you lie down. It feels like you just want to die to make the pain to stop.

The new cellmate, whom I do not want to name for his safety, told me a few more stories that sounded like they were from horror movies. It was very hard to believe that it could have been happening right there and in those times. But later, I heard it from other prisoners and felt it on my own skin. That was not the last story of self-mutilation that went on in the prison. Torture of the human mind resulted in body mutilation, which the prisoners inflicted on themselves. At first, I could not understand how it was working, but later, I felt it on my own skin.

The next day, I went with Janco for our hour-long walk in what I called the chicken coop. When we returned, our new cellmate was gone.

"They transferred him away because he knew a lot and was talking too much," Miro told me very quietly, the way he always talked. "They are going to teach him a little lesson."

"The room is bugged. That is how they know. Right?" I wondered.

"You can bet your life on it," he said. "That is why they took him away. They don't want you to know what is going on here. In case, you get out of here and go to Canada. You may talk around there about what kind of place this is."

Around the same time, I had been studying my law book and I had come across section 33 T.P.

I began yelling like I was out of my mind,

"I don't care that room is bugged; at least somebody will hear that I'm innocent. Look at section thirty-three. I have the right to explain all my circumstances, and my statement is the most important. Can't they read? I'm innocent, and nobody listens. Where should I yell it so that somebody can hear me?"

"Yell it up there," Miro pointed to the ceiling, "or to the toilet. It is all the same."

I bent over the toilet and yell into it, "Hey, can you hear me? You have to hear my voice—section thirty-three. This is no democracy if I'm innocent and I'm here. Nobody listens."

"Where should I yell it?" I got up and asked Miro again.

"Be quiet. The room is bugged," Miro warned me.

"I will yell it anytime, anywhere," That time, I turned to the ceiling, and with my hands forming a loudspeaker, I yelled, "Hey, up there. Help. I'm innocent. Section thirty-three. Help. I'm innocent. Help."

Bachar (Bachar – guard in jail slang) opened the feeding door: "What is going on here? Are they biting you?"

"No, I'm just saying that I'm innocent and that somebody must listen. Don't you know paragraph thirty-three?"

"You're crazy. Take it easy." He slammed the door.

I was not so crazy. I was only checking to see if the room was bugged. Now I knew for sure that it was.

A few days later, we were playing cards again. When I needed to get away from studying the law and writing complaints, I joined my roommates for a few games of cards. The cards themselves were the old-fashioned type and must have been there for generations, because they were soft and completely worn out. That was when Janco began to talk about the time he began to butcher himself.

"I was very sick with a very high fever. They escorted me down to the clinic. The doctor gave me some pills, but he refused to prescribe permission for me to lie down. So I had to sit on the stool, but I had no energy. I was falling down. The pills made me even more sick. The next day, I requested to see the doctor, but they refused. They told me that I had been there yesterday and asked if I thought that I would go there every day. I got sicker. My head was like a balloon, and later, the whole body felt like it was going to burst. I could not stand it anymore, so I decided to let the pressure out."

"What happened after?"

"The doctor placed a brown liquid all over me and bandaged me all over. They kept me there for one day and sent me back to my cell. I was alone. He was gone. The doctor did not let me lay down anyway. The only time they let you lay down here is if you are dead. You don't get anywhere here, no matter what you do. Nobody cared that I was cut all over. "

"You made a mistake. You cut yourself in the wrong place—where nobody could see it after you were dressed up. If you had cut yourself where they could see it, like on your face, maybe they would have shown more interest." I only said it as a joke, but I did regret saying it later, because Janco took my advice more seriously than I thought was possible.

Miro was brought back to my cell. He was a small-time crook from Michalovce, which was a little bit larger town about sixty kilometres east of Kosice. He had broken into cottages around a man-made lake called Sirava. More than two years of total inactivity had made him almost a vegetable. For eleven hours of the day, he sat on the stool, almost motionless. The rest of the time, he lay on the bed, looking at the ceiling or into the pillow. He got up promptly to get his food at eating time and then went back to his inactivity. He never went out for a walk in the chicken coop. His back was totally deformed from long hours spent in a sitting position.

The deformation is disease called scoliosis, which means that you cannot straighten your back all the way.

******

I began getting some answers as reactions to my complaints. It was one disappointment after another. I did not expect any good news from Trebisov, because I knew that I was dealing with purely corrupt individuals. But I was hoping for some positive reactions from the top, because I believed that the new government would try to build the democracy. I was also hoping that they would start doing something about the widespread corruption. My hopes were crushed when I received the first answers. Imagine this:

On November 16, 1998, I again wrote a number of complaints to the prime minister of Slovakia, Mr. Dzurinda, as well as Minister of Justice Carnogursky, Minister of the Interior Pitner, and the future president, Mr. Schuster.

Bibiana wrote to Judge Milko and Ministry of the Interior Pitner. The Ministry of the Interior informed her that they were forwarding her request to the Office of the Inspectorate.

JUDr. Fercakova, my lawyer, wrote to the inspectorate of the ministry of the interior and the district prosecutor of Trebisov.

In all of the complaints were descriptions of all the broken laws and the twisting of the facts by Investigator Demjan, who was keeping me in prison under terrible conditions illegally. Many different officials were informed. I was hoping for one ... only one single honest person who would check into what was going on and step on the corruption. There was none.

This is how it went:

The future president, Mr. Schuster, responded in five weeks. I was informed by a letter dated December 28, 1998, that he had requested that Dr. Mazak from the Ministry of Justice investigate my case. The result? None. I have never heard from Mr. Mazak.

In exactly one month (on December 16, 1998), the Office of the Prime Minister of Slovakia informed me that they were requesting that the Ministry of the Interior investigate my case. It was the same office that my lawyer had also sent the complaint to.

My letters to the Ministry of the Interior and the Ministry of Justice were mailed to the Office of the Provincial Prosecutor in Kosice. The provincial prosecutor mailed them to the district prosecutor in Trebisov. In plain language, they requested the same corrupt people who were breaking the laws to investigate themselves.

And look what the so-called prosecutor Maros Sabo did. He apparently dismissed the requests of both ministries for the fourteen-day limit between requests, even though it took almost two months, since the requests made their ways through the different offices and back to Trebisov. In other words, this so-called prosecutor, with no degree in law, dismissed the requests of the highest institutions of the country. Something was telling me that somebody was doing the job for him and just using him like a puppet.

District Judge Milko never responded to Bibiana's letter, which she wrote from her heart. Bibiana had no idea that it was he, Judge Milko, who himself was responsible for all the corrupt actions, because he knew all of it and sent me to prison anyway.

Finally, the Office of the Inspectorate of the Ministry of the Interior in Bratislava sent somebody to investigate. The problem was that they had an office in the city of Kosice, which was only about forty kilometres from Trebisov. So almost all the policemen were friends. Imagine one policeman investigating the other. The even bigger problem was who they sent to investigate. It was pplk. JUDr. Dzurcaninova Alzbeta. Imagine a poor, little lady investigating old, corrupt-to-the-core bastards.

Judge Milko, kpt. Stefanak, mjr. Demjan, mjr. Dziak—they all acted against the law. Then there were the small fish, like prosecutors JUDr. Maria Pacutova and mgr. Sabo, who were just used in my opinion. And on the top, there was that somebody who, I knew, was behind it all—somebody who must have been the big fish.

They all had one big interest: to cover up their illegal actions.

Against them all was one little lady. They knew who to choose.

She came to see me and wrote down most of the broken laws and all involved. Then she, talk to Demjan and Stefanak, who told her another bunch of ridiculous lies. No explanations were given on many important points, for example, on how the blockade on me was arranged without a judge, a charge, or even the name of who had requested it.

The most ridiculous statement was made by Policeman Stefanak, who claimed that the gypsy sisters Alena and Anna Demeterova had answered the questions spontaneously. He forgot to say whether they were singing in harmony or against each other.

The little lady investigator, Dzurcaninova, covered herself. In her decision, she stated that she had studied only "parts of the investigative file." The complete file did not exist at all. So why did she not state these facts in her report? If she had, I would have been released. Who persuaded her to break the law? Who asked her to turn a blind eye to clearly broken laws?

The number of corrupt people now moved even further out from Trebisov. In her decision, dated January 25, 1999, she decided to put away her investigative document, because, as she stated, "the police did not fulfil the subjective or objective deeds of breaking the law ..."

(In Slovakia when officials don't want to make any negative decision against their colleagues, they place the documents on the side and this is it. They call it – "put away.")

That and many similar lines were used by all so-called investigators who were asked to investigate their colleagues and who never found them responsible for their corrupt and illegal activities. Policemen walked above the law, and that was only one of many pieces of evidence. A citizen in Slovakia had no chance for justice at all.

The little lady investigator was sent back again and again to investigate the illegal activities of Investigator Demjan, and she kept putting the decisions away, because she was unable to spot any broken laws.

How could Mrs. Dzurcaninova miss that?

On March 19, 1999, she was questioning Investigator Demjan. The interrogation was written in the file of the Ministry of the Interior's Office of the Inspectorate under the following mark: CTS: UTS-39/05-PO-1999. In it, Demjan claimed that the "claim of Bibiana Gombosova that, after searching the house, he requested by telephone the keys of the house and the car, which were on the same ring, and that she gave them to him is not true."

But look at what the same Demjan claimed when she questioned him again: "After agreement by phone with Bibiana Gombosova, on the day of October 13, 1998, he requested the keys....

On October 16, 1998, he returned the keys to Mr. Demcak's brother, Milan Demcak." Could she miss that kind of lie that Demjan had told her straight to her face and that she had written down by herself? Impossible! Why did she cover up for him? She still concluded that Demjan did not break any laws. Lying to an investigator done by a policeman was against the law. This statement was written on June 4, 1999, and was filed under: CTS:UIS-39/05-PO-1999. They could take that kind of investigator and stuff them. One was a liar, and the other covered up for him—open corruption.

November 18, 1998, was a big day for Investigator Demjan. His colleague kpt. Stefanak was working tirelessly. He persuaded three gypsies to falsely testify.

The first charge against me had proven to be completely false. The Demeterova sisters had been virtually hopeless witnesses, so the police had decided to try another three. Policemen Demjan and Stefanak thought that more was better. But that backfired. As Demjan fabricated their statements, he confused even himself. How do you synchronize the statements of three women whose memories were very limited?

The new accomplices to Investigator Demjan and Policeman Stefanak were Eva Pukiova, Natasa Pukiova, and Andrea K. The Pukiova sisters were full-scale prostitutes with a pimp who had attempted to blackmail me a few years before.

Andrea K. was only their friend. She showed more class than any official I came in contact with. While the judges, prosecutors, and policemen had no problem with lying and cheating, Andrea refused.

Demjan wrote statements for all of them. Here are fully documented answers from Natasa Pukiova and Andrea Karickova. They were explaining how they had together gotten to my place for the first time ever at the same time on same day, after they had met me in town:

Jozef Demcak

Natasa: It was in May
About 9:00 PM

At the employment office

He came in big, white car.

We took a shower after we got out
of bed

I had a skirt and shorts All three of
us were in the bed

He didn't give us any money
Only two of us went there

Andrea: It was in the fall or winter
About 1:00 PM

At the train station (about one Km
apart)

He came in small blue car
We showered before we went to bed

We both had housecoats on
She went into the bed first, and then
I did

He gave us 500 korun each. There
were three of us; Kuka came with
us

Not a single match. Everything was different. Only an idiot would even consider using something like that in a court of law. But Demjan had no problem doing it.

That kind of crap had to be verified and approved by the prosecutor and the judge. Nobody had noticed any discrepancy in those statements at all? Was it possible that people like that were actually sitting in important chairs, with serious faces, pretending that they were serving justice in the name of Slovakia?

Can anybody imagine how I felt when I was getting these kinds of decisions from people like that? Or that I was locked up on the basis of that kind of statement? It was a killer for my mind.

I received a decision, dated December 3, 1998, that stated that only the statements of these women were now the reason I was kept in jail. It was signed by the district prosecutor, mgr. Maros Sabo. On top of that, he wrote that his decision was final and that it would not be possible to file a complaint against that kind of crap.

I wrote to the provincial court in Kosice; I named nineteen pieces of evidence that had been investigated and documented by Investigator Demjan, and all of them were proof that I was innocent. Separately, beside every piece of evidence, I wrote nineteen times "INNOCENT" in big letters. I thought that even the stupid or partly blind would have to get the point. For that, they could not make up any stupid excuse to keep me locked up.

They did not respond at all. That was how arrogant they were. Perfect, complete corruption.

CHAPTER SEVENTEEN

Why Are All Those People Behind Bars?

What intellect is required to become a policeman in Slovakia?
That of a caveman.

The sisters Anna and Alena Demeterova were the first two partners of Investigator Demjan, and Policeman Stefanak on the way to frame me. It was confirmed and became obvious that these two gypsy sisters were kind of senseless and ridiculous witnesses. Whoever was helping the two policemen could not realize that, because his own intellect was not much higher than that of the gypsies, they were relying on. The only thing the policemen could do better than Alena and Anna was write. It was not a big deal to write better than those two sisters, because they could not write at all.

I have here in front of me an official investigative document that was used against me in a court of law in Trebisov, Slovak Republic. It is called "

Record of the Questioning of the Witness Anna Demeterova, dated 12.10.1998." This is the one with 293 mistakes, (give or take a few; more likely add some more) and about ninety fabricated things—smears and lies—on a stretch of two and a half regular pages. It was signed "Investigator Demjan."

The officials of Trebisov were content that he was still suitable for the post of an investigator in the name of the Slovak Republic.

What about the simplest mathematics? Did that man have any knowledge in math?

I have in front of me another record signed by Investigator Demjan. In this document, three women apparently claim that, when they visited me together on one day, in the same place, at the same time, they were all fourteen years of age. The problem was that according to their birth dates, which were written on the same document, there are three years of difference between their ages. Anybody who can do plain mathematics can tell that that is not possible. Demjan simply wrote that kind of ridicules nonsense, signed it, and passed it on to the prosecutor, and the prosecutor passed it on to the judge, who used it against me. Nobody saw any problem with this.

Why would they keep a man like that in the function of investigator? Could it be that it was because he was willing to fabricate anything against anybody and lie to everybody's faces? That is the only conclusion I can come up with.

My apologies to all the policemen in Slovakia, including those in Trebisov, who are normal, regular people, doing their jobs honestly.

What about the prosecutor—or should I call him teacher?—Maros Sabo. These documents had to go through his hands to make it all the way to Judge Milko. Every normal teacher would return this kind of creation back to Demjan to rewrite it as homework.

What about Judge Milko? Was he content that he had ordered me to jail on the request of a man whose writing and mathematics were almost the equivalent of a caveman's?

Most people would think that this is not possible. That maybe, I'm producing jokes. But I'm not a joker at all, and this is not a comedy. This is a tragedy that is documented word for word. It is the tragedy of one man, fighting for his life against men like these.

Can you imagine how I felt when I received these kinds of documents, on the basis of which I was kept in jail? It was a killer. If they could do that, they could do anything at all.

They were like patients in a mental institution, locked behind bars. Looking out at visitors, one would ask another, "Why are all those people locked behind bars?"

Didn't these people realize what it meant to lock somebody behind bars, knowing that he was innocent?

Demjan should have been behind bars for all of the illegal activities he committed and to keep him from hurting other innocent people.

Demjan requested an examination of me, the child Jana, the Demeterova sisters, and others, but he was the one who needed an examination more than anyone else.

I'm not an expert, like Docent Stancak, but I have had eight semesters in psychology at a Czechoslovak university and about same at a Canadian university. I feel that I would qualify to make an unofficial assessment. After studying about a hundred pages of work made and signed by Demjan, all well as his conduct while dealing with me, my mother, and others he came into contact with while I was incarcerated, I came to the following assessment:

Name: mjr. Jan Demjan

Born: 25.2.1950 in Tokajik, Slovakia.

By the post that he holds as an investigator of the police in Trebisov, Slovakia, one would believe that he had finished high school, but it is questionable whether he graduated. If he did, it is a great mystery how he passed spelling and writing in the Slovak language.

After school, he most likely worked somewhere in the fields around his place of birth.

In the past, communists searched small towns for creeps who would be willing to come to bigger towns to persecute innocent people, because the locals were ashamed to do so. It must have been an ideal opportunity for Demjan to get away from working on a farm and to get into the city.

That could have been the turning point in Demjan's life, when he joined police force. He moved from stocking manure to stocking papers—the worthless illegal papers that he calls investigating reports, decisions, charges, interrogating records, and so on. Most of them were fabricated stories that were used to place innocent victims in jail.

For years, he has been, and still is, jailing innocent people.

He is not choosy in his methods.

Since his knowledge and intelligence is very limited, he is unable to gather enough legal material for convictions; therefore, he uses every illegal scheme to convict everybody, including completely innocent people. Lying is his way of investigating. He lies everywhere that it suits him. Lying straight to your face is no problem for him at all. Even when he knows that the person he is lying to is aware of it, he can still look him in the eyes and lie some more.

He does not understand the meaning of the sentences in law books at all; therefore, he keeps breaking the law with almost every step he takes in his investigations. The lies and broken laws are straightforward and easy recognizable, even by primitive individuals.

The forgeries of signatures that he illegally produces are so bad that they are recognizable even by the naked eye.

He influences witnesses during questioning; he twists their answers right on the spot as he types. Afterward, he unlawfully makes up whole pages to suit his needs. Any witness who is willing to falsely testify is his friend.

No innocent or guilty person ever has a chance for a fair investigation when in his hands; therefore, nobody has a chance for a fair trial.

On the other hand, if a guilty person pays ransom, he has the special preference.

His ability to investigate facts is minimal. On the other hand, he has only to make up and twist the facts to get innocent victims behind bars.

Conclusion

Mjr. Jan Demjan illustrates signs of psychopathic behaviour. This is obvious in cases when he is able to imprison innocent people without any regrets at all. The man is without the conscience of a human being. Chances are that he takes pleasure in destroying people's lives. This makes him feel like a powerful man. It is a substitute for a lack in his physical abilities.

The only feeling that points out that he was of the human race is his fear of the thought of what may happen when some convict he sent to jail on the basis of fabricated evidence will get out of the gulag. The fear that that one will look for him sits in his head and keeps him from having a good night's sleep. This fear was not diagnosed as paranoia or as a sort of unreasonable obsession because it is based on a rational platform. It is a known fact that prisoners who committed the crime usually accept their punishments. But those who are sent to prison innocently and on the basis of false and fabricated evidence usually never forgive or forget. They will remember the man who sent them to prison forever, especially those whose lives were destroyed based on his false evidence.

His personal mental abilities are on the border of a mental primitive with no consciousness at all.

In my expert opinion, he should be committed to an official psychiatric and psychological examination to establish:

1. if Demjan understands what the law is for or what it is all about.
2. if he understands that the forgery of official documents, the fabricating of evidence, the jailing of innocents, and lying in official documents is illegal and punishable in a democratic society.
3. if he realizes the damage he causes to innocent people he sends to jail on the basis of fabricated documents.
4. if his conduct isn't dangerous for society as whole.
5. if protective treatment is required for this dangerous individual.
6. if he should not be locked up in an institution for the same amount of years that innocent people spent in jail on the basis of false evidence fabricated by him.

Signed by mgr. Jozef Demcak, BA *(Bachelor of Arts)*

What are the chances that he will ever officially pay for his illegal activities? Next to none.

What are the chances that some individual will pay him back for destroying his life? Fair.

I received a copy of my psychological examinations. The first examination was completed on November 18, 1998, by Docent Andrej Stancak. I was really worried about him, because of his age and because of his reputation as a destroyer of prisoners. Following are his findings, exactly as he wrote them on his computer. and then translated. Some parts that were repeated, I have left out. The report was on thirteen pages.For the District Office of Investigation, Trebisov.

> On the basis of your decision from 8.11.1998, under sign CVS: 0UV/10 - 1998, chr.
>
> Jozef Demcak— born 20.7.1941 … Trebisov—underwent this psychological examination.
>
> After the actual examination and after studying the investigative documentation, I'm providing the following expertise from the specialty of psychology and human sexuality.
>
> Opening Statement:
>
> In that part, he rewrote the false charge as it had been fabricated by Demjan. Then there were questions that the expert was supposed to give answers to.
>
> In the "Study of the Investigative Document" part, the expert actually rewrites some recorded of statements of the witnesses. In my case, that was what policemen Demjan and Stefanak had put together.
>
> I think that Docent Stancak noticed that something was wrong when gypsies became geniuses overnight. I'm sure that Investigator Demjan and his accomplice rewrote or improved all the statements of the gypsies to fit each other.
>
> I would like to hear what Docent Stancak was thinking when he read the statement with almost three hundred

mistakes on two and a half pages. I would also love to know if he noticed anything wrong with the sentence that Demjan wrote that said, "He applied massage cream and then he licked it off the whole body ..."

One thing is certain: Demjan did not show him the record that was made when the child Jana was abused at the police station. He tried very hard not to show it to anybody. Psychological examination of Jozef Demcak took place in prison in Kosice. He cooperated positively, reacting willingly to requests. In the family anamnesis, he stated that his father died at the age of ninety-two. His mother is still alive; she is eighty-two. His parents were entrepreneurs.

He is the second of four children. There have been no mental illnesses in the family, no illegal circumstances, and no hereditary illnesses that could harm mental ability.

As a child, he overcame only the usual infectious diseases. Until present, he has been practically healthy. He graduated from high school. After high school, he studied at Pedagogical University, specializing in physical education and natural science. After university, he worked as a teacher in Vojcice. In 1965-1966, he attended compulsory military service and functioned as commander of a troop. He was an active bicycle racer, in which sport he became a provincial champion. He was also active in other sports.

Emigration

After the invasion of the Warsaw Pact military, he decided to emigrate. Canada offered him political asylum. For two years, he worked in a factory, producing plastic materials. At the same time, he was studying the English language at night lectures.

By completing lectures on the English language, he was able to start working in his own profession. He worked at the YMCA as a swimming instructor, and in the form of further education, he obtained the qualification of Bachelor of Arts in physical education and natural science.

In 1975, he became a teacher of physical and health education at a high school in Toronto. He also became an entrepreneur. He opened a store, selling sports equipment.

Beside this, he was active in magic. He produced various stage productions, including at schools. From 1979 until 1989, he produced stage productions full-time.

His common-law wife helped him with these productions.

He had lived with his spouse for fifteen years. They had son, who is now twenty-two. Because of different problems, they split by agreement.

Since 1985, he has lived with another woman, also as a common-law relationship. No children have been produced by this association. Both women were white and younger than him, one by five years and the second by seven years.

Return to country

In 1989, he decided to return to his "old" country because of his parents, who were in very advanced age and also because he had considered living in Slovakia when reaching his old age.

He saw an advantage in this, because his pension from Canada would enabled him to live comfortably.

Psychosexual development

From his young adulthood on he has liked women with full bodies—from the age of fifteen. His first sexual contact was at the age of eighteen. He knew many women; among them, there was also a gipsy. He had an intensive sexual life. There was understanding in his first relationship, but he was also unfaithful sometimes. It was similar in his second relationship. After arriving to Slovakia, he had a partner who was twenty-five years of age. They understood each other. Also sexually. He is considering a serious relationship, because they are in intensive correspondence contact.

Circumstances of investigation

Underage Jana Visokaiova. He has known her father from childhood. He was friends with the whole family. Jana visited him with her mother. Sometimes she spent the night, but he was like a father to her.

On her birthday, he took some photos of her. She was dressed in an exercising outfit.

He estimated that she spent the night about nine times, from Friday to Saturday. He gave her a good-night kiss, but he never touched her body. He bought a t-shirt for her, and he brought a sweater and blue jeans for her from Canada. To her parents, he gave about 800 korun for Jana.

Meeting the gypsies.

Toward the end of 1995 and the beginning of 1996, four gypsies visited his house with a request that he help with a beauty contest that was to take place shortly. He let them in and showed them some costumes. He told them that there were rental fees of 100 korun for each costume ... Anna D. was in the house approximately three times. Once, she was with her sister Alena. He offered them Coca-cola. He never offered them alcohol. He never touched them, licked them, or had sex with them. He knew that Anna was at least fifteen, because she had a citizen ID. He had no information about the ages of Alena or Eva.

He knew the age of Jana.

He never gave any money to them, except once when Anna pulled from him 100 korun. He denies giving them 5000 or 300 korun to licking them or for sexual contact.

Activity in Slovakia and Canada

After arriving in Slovakia, he built a house, where he has a hot tub, a shower, an exercise room, four big beds in the bedroom, and a water bed.

In 1992, he was in Canada for six months, in 1994, for about four to five months, and in 1996-1998, for almost two years. He goes to Canada to produce magical productions for certain schools. The productions are financed from the admission, which is about $1,000 to $2,000 Canadian.

He is able to do it because he has a licence and pays taxes.

He has an apartment with a Vietnamese man, where he also stores his props and exhibits of animals of the jungle, which he uses during lectures at schools and also during stage productions.

In three years, he will be at retirement age, and his pension can be sent to him from Canada.

Contradictions in statements

He claims that he didn't give them any money, except when Anna pulled 100 korun from him. Anna D. stated that he gave her 5000 and also 300 korun when she was there with her sister. [It has been proven that Anna D. never said that I gave her the money. It was Investigator Demjan who made that up in the statement he fabricated.]

Most probably, it is the truth, that the girls, who were in puberty without consideration of age, were forcing the visit. Probably for food, the possibility to bathe, the sexual initiation of the host, and most of all, financial interests, of which proof is enclosed from a telephone recording machine.

In general, girls with very low moral cultures and low education begin heterosexual activities that end up in prostitution.

A reaction in an adult man on unripe objects neanidophile is not a variation of a pedophile. In case he has done what they said, he was motivated as a neanidophile, which belongs to the heterosexual formula. [Here I need to say that neanidophile means heterosexual—in other words, normal.) Even though, the expert explained it right on the spot, it was used against me anyway. The fact that I was normal was used against me by the stupid, who did not understand the meaning of it.]

The different situation was with the underage Jana Visokaiova, who hasn't reached puberty. She told her friend about an erotic experience with the defendant, which she did not confirm during her interrogation, nor during the psychological examination. Most probably it was pseudopodia fantastic, or a wish.

The defendant explains his relationship with the underage girl as being a natural father's feelings. Her parents knew about her being at his place and spending the night.

From a psychological point of view, it appears that the motivation of this relationship is based on natural parental feelings that weren't fulfilled in his previous life in his first relationship, from which he has a twenty-two-year-old son with whom he has practically no communication.

Clinical situation

The defendant is properly oriented presently, time-wise, and personally. He is presently experiencing sleeping difficulties (light sleeping). Thinking about the situation, he is afraid of blackmail by the pimps of some girls. There are no signs of mental illness. Additionally, no sexual disorders of any kind were discovered during the psychological examination. He is a heterosexual person with an interest in younger women when they are forming their womanly personalities.

His attitude toward the investigation

He believes that he did not commit any illegal act, he did not do what he is accused of. He regrets being "stupid" when he came into contact with the gypsies for the first time, when they came to get information about beauty contests.

Results of diagnostic tests

The expert used a battery of psychological tests to establish the level of intellect, memory functions, structure of personality, and psychological changes.

Intellect. Intellectual abilities are above average with an IQ of 117. Memory function is lower in comparison with intellect in practical tasks as a result of nervousness caused by his present situation.

His personality is balanced, with phlegmatic temperament. By these signs, it can explain the fact that he is not careful when making interpersonal contacts.

No tendency to lie was discovered. No tendency to describe a situation to his advantage or to describe in line with social expectations.

Affectivity. Some points of affectivity are not differentiated enough in comparison with intellectual level, education, and life experience. His nervousness is higher now, which is a result of realistic distress caused by telephone threats.

In clinical symptoms and by psychological measurements, there were no differences that would show signs of any mental illness.

An unrealistic evaluation of his lifestyle can be explained as difficulty in getting use to his new environment, but he still has generally acceptable cultural expectations.

Conclusion and assessment

The defendant Jozef Demcak is not from a problematic family.

He emigrated to Canada for political reasons.

After returning to Slovakia, he built a house, with a hot tub, a gym, and a water bed.

He lives with his fiancée Bibiana Gombosova."

He denies the act he was accused of and admits only to non-erotica contacts.

His intellectual abilities are above average. His personality is without any changes. His sexual activities, of heterosexual form, are normal for his age. A sexual disorder was not diagnosed. Other personal problems that could cause difficulties with distinguishing right from wrong or with being able to control himself are not diagnosed.

Following are the answers to the questions of the investigator.

1. By psychological examination, it was discovered that the intellectual level of the defendant is on a level above average. The function of his memory is without any problem.
2. By psychological examination, no sexual disorder was diagnosed. He is a heterosexual individual.
3. No other circumstances were discovered during the psychological examination.

Signed: Doc. PhDr. Andrej Stancak Csc. Stamped.

I was glad that he did not drown me and that he wrote it the way he diagnosed it. I do not agree with his assessment of my IQ. He did not give me enough tests to make it accurate. I was also under tremendous stress at the time. The jail wasn't exactly a proper place for an IQ test. The result of the test I took at McMaster University showed an IQ of 159, and I was not trying my best then. Docent Stancak assessed it at 117, which, as he stated is above average, but I think he degraded me there. But it is okay, because it was never important to me. I believe in the saying that my older sister Bozena once told me: "We are the way God created us."

I would like to advise Docent Stancak, not to use high words like "neanidophile" when his assessment is made for primitive people, like Demjan and his associates. They used that word against me, not knowing what it meant. I still like young women, and I'm not ashamed of it at all. That doesn't mean I'm going to break the law because of it.

******

MUDr. Stefan Safko, Csc., and MUDr. Maria Illinova wrote their report together. I was worried about it, because Demjan had chosen them. But I was also hopeful, because they were my age, and our generation was not so stupid or as corrupt as those after us.

It was actually a pleasant surprise. I was right in my hopes. They wrote it the way they had discovered it. It was a very similar result as that from Docent Stancak.

It was eleven pages of psychiatric and sexuality expertise. While Docent Stancak had created his work on a computer, these specialists wrote theirs on a typewriter.

Report begins with "Study of the Investigative Documents" section. In that part of the document, it was confirmed without any doubt that Demjan was illegally manipulating the investigative file the way it suited him and committing forgery.

For number one, he did not show them the statement from the district court, in which I offered the tape as proof that the gypsies were blackmailing me.

For number two, the record of the statement of the child Jana, made at the police station where she was grossly abused by the police, was not showed to the experts at all. Neither was it shown to Docent Stancak. If the psychiatrists had read it, they would have easily concluded what the policemen were doing to the child.

For number three, Demjan showed them his masterpiece with almost three hundred mistakes, which he had dated October 12, 1998. That was the day of my arrest. The same as Docent Stancak, these experts did not realize that Demjan had made it up and backdated it.

For number four, he had forged the statement by Alena Demeterova by changing her answers. When she was asked "Do you know how old you are?" she had answered "Maybe seventeen." Later, Demjan changed "maybe" to "yes." But he did it after the experts had already rewritten that part. So it was absolute proof of Demjan's machinations and his forgeries of official documents. And, the copy I received in jail read "maybe" and not "yes."

Back to the actual examination, which I have translated in detail:

The defendant was escorted for examination by the prison guard. During the examination, the defendant was correctly oriented in all fields of life. On questioning, he answered correctly and to the point. He willingly participated in the examination.

Psychomotor and mimic reactions are slowed down.

The abilities of his brain are above average. Thinking is without pathological changes. His memory is without any defects in remembering, accumulating, and restoring.

There are signs of instability in social adaptation; otherwise, we did not discover any psychopathological signs.

Dependence on alcohol was not discovered. Neither did we notice any hallucinations, errors, or signs of psychosis.

Sexual Examination

According to anamnestic facts, the neurological development of the defendant during his childhood was normal. Sexual activities began around eighteen to nineteen years of age. He lived with his common-law wife for fifteen years. Sexual activities were regular. They had one son.

At the present time and for the last four and a half years, he has lived with his fiancée Bibiana Gombosova. She is younger than he by twenty-five years. They have sexual activities about once a week.

About the accusations, he states that he did not commit any crimes. Mr. Demcak claims that the charge was fabricated, that they want to pay him back what they threatened by phone.

Sexually, he is normally developed. The sexual norms point to normal heterosexual development.

Tables of sexual activities point to normal sexual function.

After sexual examination, we did not discover any sexual disorders. The alleged crime was not motivated by a sexual problem.

Conclusion and Assessment

Through expert examination, we found out that the defendant is not from a problematic family. He finished Pedagogical University and worked as a teacher. In 1968, he emigrated to Canada. He returned in 1990. He is self-employed at the present time.

He lived with a partner in Canada; now he lives with his fiancée Bibiana Gombosova.

He does not smoke; he uses alcoholic drinks only on special occasions. He never uses any drugs. He has never been criminally punished.

As a child, he had only the usual infectious sicknesses but not any serious diseases. He was never treated by psychiatry. His name does not show up in The Records of Psychiatry.

By objective psychiatric diagnosis, we discovered that his mental abilities are above average. In affectivity is some instability. Thinking, responding, and remembering are without any disruptions.

Sexual functions and sexual activities are comparable for his age. No sexual disorder was discovered.

At the end, there were answers to the six questions that had been written as if I had already been convicted. Demjan and whoever was helping him had had satisfaction in writing them in that illegal form. Even these court experts' heads were turned by this detail. But they answered the way the questions were asked:

1. The defendant Jozef Demcak, at the time concerned, did not have any mental disorders, not even a temporary mental illness.
2. He was able to recognize the dangerousness of his actions and was able to control his manners.

3. He is able to understand the logic of unlawful behaviour, and he understands that illegal activity is punishable.
4. We did not diagnose pedophile tendencies or any other sexual disorder or deviation. His behaviour was not motivated by sexual disorder.
5. His freedom, from a psychiatric and sexual point of view, would not be a danger for society. Protective treatment is not required.
6. Use of alcohol and drugs were not discovered.

The assessment was completed after counselling by section 106 T.P. In Kosice, 23.11.1998.

Signed: MUDr. Maria Kilianova MUDr. Stefan Safko, Csc.

Two stamps followed their signatures.

Two different examinations by three specialists agreed that I was a completely normal person, without any problems. The only difference was that my intellect was above average. They agreed that my freedom would not be dangerous for society. It is logical that they concluded that I had not committed any crime.

After this you would think that they would consider letting me out, at least on bail. Not so. Demjan kept these findings out of everybody's sight. His plan was to keep me in indefinitely. He kept it even out of my sight for a long time. That kept my anxiety eating at me for a long time.

CHAPTER EIGHTEEN

Three Devils at One Table.

"Jozef, if you die, they win; you lose." (Janco Gore)

Every step that Investigator Demjan took was more proof that I had never committed any crime. Three court specialists—two psychiatrists and one psychologist—whom he picked up by himself, diagnosed me and confirmed that I was innocent and that my freedom would not be a danger for society.

Demjan kept it all to himself. He even did not show the results to me for a long time. They do anything they choose to people, and nobody is stopping them. It was already nine years after communists had officially fallen. You would expect at least some change.

A new inmate was escorted in my cell. They placed him in my cell to "help" me with my allergy to cigarette smoke. He virtually never stops puffing.

"I'm somebody, Zdeno P."

We shook hands. He was also what they called a corridor boy. Three times a day, he was called out to the hall, and he passed food through the little opening in the heavy cell doors. He also did other janitorial duties on the whole floor, including cleaning the guard's office. Since he never went out for a walk in the chicken coop, it was possible that he was an informant who had been sent to my cell to smoke my guts out and to get something out of me that could be used against me.

His crime was apparently that he was too strict with his teenage daughter, and she had not liked it. She liked to hang around with her friends, and forgot to come home for the night. Sometimes, for a few days. As a father, Zdeno made some strict arrangements. He locked her in her room. With the help of her friends, she found a way out of that situation.

Soon, the father was in jail, and the girl was free to do what she was dreaming of. He was charged with sexually abusing his daughter. He denied it profusely. He had been locked up even before anybody had asked him any questions at all. Exactly the same way, they did it with me. They locked him up first and then began the investigation. Everybody who is locked up is convicted. Nobody I talked to had ever heard that the police had ever made a mistake. They were perfect people. They always made evidence to fit the charge.

Poor Zdeno. He was getting all kinds of statements, and everyone— from the beginning to the end—described twice how he had molested his daughter. Each time he received another paper, he was about to collapse. Tears were in his eyes when he showed me those papers. What crap they made up against him. I felt for him, because I was getting similar letters from Demjan.

When his daughter got tired of running around, she returned home and told her mother that she had made everything up.

In court, Zdeno's wife reported to the lady judge what her daughter had admitted to her. Boy, she got it from the judge,

"Aren't you ashamed of yourself?" the judge asked. "Your husband molested your own daughter, and now you are lying to get him out. If you tell the lie once more, I will have you arrested for contempt of court. It is he who told you to lie for him, isn't it? I will teach him how to influence witnesses."

She already had him convicted, even before the conviction. Even before, she had talked to the girl. Instead of somebody talking to the girl and asking questions to find out the truth, the judge forbade Zdeno's wife even from talking about what had really happened. He had already been locked up for a very long time, and they were not about to admit that it was all by mistake.

He returned from court completely ruined. He was all yellow in the face, crying, his hands shaking. He could not even stand up or sit on the stool. He was crawling on all four and falling down on the cement floor. It was only noon, and there were still five hours before he could rest on the bed.

"Finally, she told the truth," he told me the next day, "And the judge doesn't believe it. I'm going to kill myself."

In a few days, he received a greeting card from the same judge. He was accused of obstructing the investigation and influencing the witnesses. She ordered imprisonment for him according to section 67b, meaning that he would be transferred to a different cell with more restrictions. His mail would be going through the investigator's hands, and he would read every word of it. The investigator would decide who could and who could not visit him, and the guard would be with him in the booth during visiting time.

Soon after we returned from a walk Zdeno was gone. They always transferred somebody out of cell that way so you could not even say good-bye. You came back, and the person was gone. You wondered what happened to him. It was part of the system that added to the stress of the prisoners. Every little detail had been worked out.

I was in bad shape myself. Living under stress had had terrible effects on my health. I was bleeding from the left side of my nose. It was a result of the smoke in a room, high blood pressure from stress, and receiving crap from the investigator and other officials to whom I had written, asking for help. A pain in my back became unbearable. I also felt heat in my brain, and my heart was giving me problems with an irregular beat. My front lower teeth had become loose.

I had been completely healthy just a while before. Now, I was ruined. Even marks on my skin appeared. I could not believe how fast my hair changed colour. I had had some salt around my ears when I was arrested. Now, I had white all over.

I had no idea how fast mental abuse could take over the body. This system designed to ruin human beings worked miracles. I was totally astonished, when I looked in the mirror.

Seeing and hearing other prisoners suffer was like a catalyst to all the awful things that happened to your own body and mind.

The worst news was the prison doctors. You had to be dying before they would prescribe that you could lie down.

We were sitting in the waiting room, waiting to see the doctor. The door was open. The gypsy who was sitting in front of the door was able to see inside. He yelled, "Hey, we have a nudist contest here."

"Shut up. No talking," the guard yelled at him.

Six new prisoners were promenaded into the doctor's office. All of them were gypsies. As usual, there were female nurses, a female and a male doctor, and a female psychiatrist.

A skinny, tall guy, by the nickname Giraffe was also there. He had been in the "hole" for eighteen days by then. *("Hole" – solitary chamber. Some of them designed for abuse and torture)* He had six more days to go. He had received twenty-four days in the hole for passing a cigarette to another prisoner through the window—pretty banal offence for such a strict, inhuman punishment. His eyes were sitting deep and big; black circles were all around them. His health was on the verge of collapsing. The doctors were making sure that he stayed alive; therefore, they checked on him every day.

"Anybody need a thermometer?" A guard asked.

"I do," Giraffe said, with whatever voice he had left. The guard did not hear him. Later, as the guard walked by him, Giraffe touched his arm and asked again. "I need a thermometer."

"You don't get one. I asked you before, and you did not say yes, so you are not getting it."

"I said yes, but you did not hear me."

"You did not."

"I did."

"I said you did not. Are you calling me crazy?"

"He said yes; I heard him." I had no stomach for that crap, so I said it. They picked any stupid thing to abuse prisoners with.

"You keep your mouth shut, or you will end up in the hole with him," the guard yelled at me first, and afterward, he gave Giraffe a thermometer anyway.

"Thanks," Giraffe said.

"Like to take chances?" a prisoner sitting next to me whispered.

I knew I could get into trouble for that. Some guards were gods there. At least that was what they thought. Giraffe was the guy who had given me the advice about the possibility of borrowing the law book during my first walk in the chicken coop, so I owed him one.

Igor Gregor told me Giraffe's story.

"They believe he has a lot of money, and they want it. But they are all wrong. He has not a penny to his name. He was only a 'horse' in a scam."

"What you mean, a horse?" I was not familiar with the prison dialect, so I asked.

"They pulled a scam, a forgery for a hundred fifty million korun

[About $80,000]. Not a big deal. Slovak politicians were doing it every day. The only problem was that only the politicians, like Meciar and his ass-kissers, were allowed to steal. But Giraffe was only a horse. That meant that the crooks only used his name, his identity, for the scam. They gave him a few korun, but he had to escape. He escaped to Romania. They promised him more money later but did not deliver. He ran out of money in Romania and returned. He was all dirty and full of fleas and ticks; he was glad to be in prison.

"Normally, he would have been out in a year or two. His problem began, when he bragged in his cell about all that money he has stashed somewhere. He was just trying to impress other bums. But one of the bums was an informer. The informer reported it to the officials, and now they want all that money for their own pockets. So they are torturing him—in and out of the hole—to break him down. They keep asking him where the money is. He cannot tell them, because he has no money at all. The problem is that they don't believe him. So they will keep him here until he tells them where the money is. Which will be never. If they think you have money; you have no hope of getting out until they get it. The poor guy—he is going to die here.

That was the way it was. The investigative prison was the place where the officials pulled all the money out of the prisoners."

Next day I saw the lady doctor. I began to tell her all the problems I was having: "… red marks on the skin, pain in the back, an abnormal heartbeat … I feel heat in my brain—"

She stopped me right there.

"Do you think that you are here to fix up all your health problems? You are here to be punished, not to get well."

"I came to prison completely healthy."

"Sure, you did," she said to me, and then she turned to the doctor in charge and yelled to him, "He is making things up."

"What is going on?" The doctor came to see what the problem was. He was the same bloodsucker who had almost drained all my blood on the first day that I was in this prison.

"He is saying that his brain is hot."

"No jokes here. Give him cream for his stains and send him home." He was pointing to the red marks on my skin.

The lady doctor brought a pail the size of a four-gallon container, almost full with a dark brown cream. It looked just like the grease I use when servicing the bearings on my car. With a wooden stick, she placed some of the grease on a piece of plastic and handed it to me.

"Use it twice a day." That was all for my first examination.

My story about heat in my brain confused them. It was so unbelievable for them that they concluded that I was making everything up, so they sent me away without checking my other medical problems. I would think that, as doctors, they would know something about the physiology of the brain.

Later, when I told a prison psychiatrist about the heat in my brain, she had different knowledge on the subject.

"It is completely normal to feel heat in your brain under these circumstances," she explained. "

It is because you are fifty-seven, and you have been arrested for the first time and because the situation here is dreadful."

"What about not sleeping at night? Fainting? Falling down?"

"That is also normal. If it did not happen in your situation that would not be normal. It is happening to all those who are innocent in here."

"Are many innocent people here?"

"Oh yes. The place is full of innocent people here. Oh, I did not say that." It was then that she realized that she had told me something that she was not allowed to.

"I did not hear anything." I placed my finger on my mouth. I believe that there was a bug in the room, because I have never seen this psychiatrist again. When I asked to see her again, I was told that she did not work there anymore.

The huge stress and terrible food caused terrible damage to my health. Worst of all was that, from 6:00 AM until 5:00 PM, you are not allowed to rest.

You have to eat very fast, because in two to three minutes or so, they pick up the dishes, and they don't want to wait. If you are not finished by the time they collect the dishes, the next day, you get only half the portion, so you can finish it on time. Being a slow eater, I was in trouble with this system.

When Janco noticed how fast I ate the first time, he pulled out an empty, oval, fish can and told me to empty the food into it. That way, I could take my time, forcing that terrible tasting food into my stomach.

When I lay in bed, I could not stop thinking about all those terrible things they were doing to people, day after day. I was also worried what all might happen to me. One night, as I got up from my bed to go to the toilet, I lost my balance. I hit the bed across from mine, then the desk, and then the chairs, which were on the side where the toilet was. Everybody woke up and noticed that I was going really downhill. Janco helped me back to my bed. I was really worried. The last time I had lost my balance like that was when I was a kid and had gotten off a carnival ride. But even then, it was not as bad as this time. Never had anything like that happened to me before.

I knew how important walking or any other movement was when you were locked in for a whole day. The next day, as usual, I went for a walk in the chicken coop. I could not stop thinking about the situation, I was in. It was as if I was losing consciousness. Everything was blurry, fuzzy.

I noticed Judge Milko. He was sitting in a black robe, but his face was extremely white. It was as if it was glowing, like he was saint or some kind of total, unlimited power. Two devils were next to him. They were on both sides of him, as if they were whispering into his ears. Their red horns were almost touching Milko's face. They were also glowing like a red fire. The one on the left side, I recognized right away. The expression on his face was just like that of a rat. I recognized him immediately. Demjan. It was Investigator Demjan. He was on the left side of Judge Milko, whispering into his ear.

On the right side was a much more devilish-looking evil. You would think that this had to be Lucifer himself. Besides the fact that his horns were much larger than Demjan's, he also had a hoof on one leg instead of a shoe, and he also had a thick tail protruding from under his black jacket. I did not recognize who it was right away.

But as the mist cleared a little bit, I looked into his face, and I was shocked. It was him. I kept asking myself, right from the beginning of the case, "Who is that pervert who makes honest people do dishonest acts? Who is it who makes smart people do stupid things, or law-abiding citizens participate in illegal activities? I kept asking myself that question over and over again. He had never come to my mind, because I had not seen him for years. So I had even asked my subconscious mind to help me find out who it was. I guess my mind was giving me the answer. And there he was. Whispering right into Judge Milko's ear was Jan Danko. If there ever was a devil walking on this earth, it was him: Jan Danko. You can bet your life on it. Wasn't that something? Three devils at one table.

That fat, deformed, dung beetle, whose *trombi* ("mouth" in Slovak) was deformed from licking Meciar's ass. Nobody could call him a human being. It was becoming a little bit clearer, why everybody danced the way he played. Three devils, and every one of them had the same first name, Jan. Three devils with the same first name and a lot of power were making plans for how to destroy me.

All the police force with their guns, all the justice officials with their power, and even the prison officials with batons were on their side. They were destroying people's lives, and the government was doing nothing to stop them. On the other side was me, locked in a cell, sick, and the only weapon I had was a pen and paper. What were my chances? Hardly any.

Dreadfulness, awfulness, and terror overpowered my body as the images of those three devils suddenly appeared in my mind while I stood in the chicken coop. I could not move anymore.

A cool stream of air overcame my body. It felt like I was being dusted with a very fine snow or with tiny crystals of ice.

Suddenly, I saw Janco. Funny. I was looking down at him as if I was standing on the top of a ladder or flying on the hot air balloon. I did not feel cold anymore, and all my problems were gone. I felt relieved and was happy.

Just watching Janco down below felt somehow strange. He was shaking somebody, who was lying on the cement floor. I could not see very well who it was, because Janco was somehow in the way. It looked like he was punishing the man who was lying under him and crying at the same time. I noticed that tears were running down Janco's cheeks as he yelled into the face of the man he was punishing.

"You cannot leave me here alone. Wake up! If you die, I'm going to kill myself. They want you dead. If you die, they win, and you lose! Jozef, Jozef, don't leave me here. You don't want them to win. Remember what you said? You said you are going to get them."

I saw how he was frantically shaking and pressing the chest of the man lying on the cement ground. It was not an expert-like press, the kind that paramedics usually generate, but it was a hysterical movement that made the lifeless body of the man lying on the ground jump up and down. At the same time, Janco was yelling up to where the lookout tower was.

"Help. Jozef is dying. Help."

I glanced at the tower and saw the guard just looking down, like nothing was going on down below. The thought went through my mind "Why is that guard not calling for help if a dying man is lying on the cement ground?" Then I wondered why Janco was calling my name. I looked more closely, and sure enough, the body lying on the ground that Janco was shaking was my body. I looked one more time at the guard on the tower; he was just looking down. It pissed me off. Then I felt Janco screaming into my face.

"Jozef, Jozef, they want you dead. If you die, they win, and you lose."

Funny. I was no longer looking at him from the balloon. Instead, I was looking at him from underneath. I smelled the strong stink of tobacco. It wasn't the smoke, just the stink of a mouth that had destroyed tons of tobacco in its past. I saw Janco, this time clearer than before. His face was all wet with tears, but he had a little relief on his face.

"Oh, I thought you died." He began kissing me. "He is alive," he yelled up to the air.

Then, the obvious came to me. It was me lying down, and it was my spirit that was looking down at my body.

I guess it was a totally hopeless situation—my little spirit inside one sick body against three devils there in Trebisov. Then, as I watched poor Janco acting frantically, not wanting to lose a friend, the spirit decided to come back.

"They want you dead. If you die, they win, and you lose." Knowing myself, that sentence could have had a lot to do with the returning of my spirit back to my body.

Janco helped me up and gave me support on the way to our cell. I was very weak, but I listened to Janco's story. He told me that as I had stood in the middle of the chicken coop, I had turned all yellow. My face and hands had just changed colour. Then, I fell down onto my back, completely stiff. That was when he had begun his "professional" but successful lifesaving procedure.

There were three things that I learned that afternoon. One was that Janco had saved my life, which I was very grateful for. Two was that the guards would let me die, without calling for help. And three—which is very important to me—was that I definitely and finally realized, for sure, that spirits really do exist. There was no way I could see how Janco was shaking my body, if not through the eyes of my spirit. That was for sure. Remember, whether you like it or not, if there are spirits, then there is also a God. Neither have we ever seen. It is possible that what we call the subconscious mind is, in fact, a spirit.

Janco had saved my life. We had been in a cell together for quite a while and had gotten used to each other. He always came for a walk in the chicken coop with me. As I mentioned, Zdeno never went for a walk. That was why I was suspicious that he was informant. Janco got on my nerves sometimes anyway. When we walked around in the chicken coop, he spat right on the walls. It was repulsive. But when I explain to him that gypsies were also people and that they could act like humans, he got the point and stopped spitting completely, just like he had quit trumpeting. He liked how, little by little, I was changing him into a nice person, and he had begun to enjoy it. If some other "pig" was placed in our cell, he was the one who taught him human manners. I've heard him saying, "Just because you are a more [gypsy], it doesn't mean you have to be a pig." He never let me do the so-called *rajony*—that means, whenever it was my turn to wash the cement floor of our cell, he did it for me. I personally would not have minded washing the floor; at least I would have gotten some needed exercise. But I did not want him to be disappointed, seeing how happy he was when he could do something for me.

It was a very short time that we kept company with each other after he saved my life. Soon afterward, Miro, Zdeno, and I were called out and locked into the hair-cutting cell. Miro had already guessed what was going on.

"They are transferring the poor guy," he said. And sure enough, when we returned, there was not a sign left of Janco. He had saved my life and become a nice person, with acceptable manners. Now, most likely, they had placed him in a cell with other gypsies, who were as bad or even worse than Janco was when I met him.

Only twice more have I ever seen that guy. The first time was shortly after he was transferred to another cell. I was walking in the chicken coop.

"Jozef." I recognized his voice right away. I looked up and Janco was hanging on the gater of his new cell, looking down into the chicken coop, where I was walking.

"Janco," I yelled back, once I spotted him hanging up there.

"No talking," a guard yelled at me.

That was the whole conversation we had together. I was quite lucky that the guard on duty was one with some human feelings left in him. Otherwise, I could have been punished much more harshly. All I received was a strict warning, since it was my first big, punishable act. I still spotted how the guards were pulling Janco off the gater. He was hanging on, looking down for as long as he could. Who knows what kind of punishment he received for breaking the rules by looking out and talking.

It was few months later when I saw Janco for the last time. This time, it was in reverse. I was on the gater, and he was walking in the chicken coop.

I was practically a model prisoner, and I never took chances by climbing on the gater and looking down to the chicken coop at other prisoners walking. The punishment you could get for it was not worth it. My roommates took chances quite often.

"Janco Gore," one yelled while looking down. I wanted to see him, but I did not want to take the risk. One of my cellmates volunteered to stand in front of the door to block the peephole, in case the guard looked through it. I looked down, and there he was. He looked completely ruined. His hair was all white. But the most shocking was the huge, open scar on his nose. It was already healed, but the nose was practically open vertically, from about middle of his forehead all the way to the tip of his nose. It was a horrible sight.

Later, I heard that Janco had done it to himself shortly after he was transferred from my cell. He had requested to be put back with us, but they refused. He was very distressed. In desperation, he had taken a razor blade and cut his nose right open. His wound needed to be sewn, but all they did was place some Band-Aids on it to stop the bleeding. It took a long time and a lot of pain to heal. The result was a big, open scar on his face.

I felt terrible about the whole thing. He should have been convicted and sent to a normal prison long before. Instead, they had kept him in that hell for almost four years by then. I even blamed myself for it. Remember what I had told him when he described how he had cut his chest in lines from his neck to his waist? I had told him "You cut yourself in the wrong place where nobody could see it. If you cut yourself where they could see it, like on your face, maybe the prison officials would show more interest." It was only a joke. I hope he did not take it seriously and did not cut his nose because of it.

I agree that he committed a crime when he robbed or stole a few korun from somebody. I agree that he should be punished. But I do not accept, and I protest, the way he was being kept for years in that investigative prison and the way he was abused there. He should have been convicted and sent to a regular prison. After all, he was a gypsy, but most of all, he was a human. He also saved my life.

I really feel sorry for him and would like to know how he ended up. But the system in that prison was designed in a way that it was very hard to find out what was going on in there. Now that I'm out, I'm trying to find out. It is a long journey against evil.

CHAPTER NIGHTEEN

The Most Brutal Bastard Who Ever Walked the Streets of Trebisov

What is the greatest advice? A winner never quits, and a quitter never wins.

I was convinced that there was a real reason why I had been returned to this world. It had been so relaxing when I was floating. Now, I was back in a place that I did not want to be in at all. All my problems and worries were back. And they were much bigger than they had been a while back.

I knew about Investigator Demjan and Judge Milko, who had appeared in my mind as evil, but the third one was a real devil. Jan Danko, in my opinion, was the most primitive bastard who ever walked the streets of Trebisov. Everything fell into place, like when you finish a puzzle.

Ever since my arrest, I had been looking for that pervert with power, the crook who made smart people do stupid things and honest people do dishonest things, somebody who knew something about psychology but was stupid in the law … and there he was.

A bastard beyond imagination. Why had I not thought of him earlier?

During communist times, officials had to look in small villages for those who were willing to spy on people and abuse citizens in larger towns, because the locals refused to do it. The same was the case with Investigator Demjan, who had been imported from a tiny village that nobody has ever heard of to Trebisov by communists to do dirty work.

Not so in the case of Jan Danko. He had been born and raised in Trebisov. That did not slow him down in abusing his own town's citizens. In fact, he had dedicated his life to that cause. He had studied some psychology. He was so stupid that he was pushing himself to join the communist party at the time when the communist system was actually collapsing. His graduation work praised the communist system as a great idea.

After the velvet revolution, when the communist system crumpled in Czechoslovakia, he joined a political organisation called The Public against Violence. This organisation was strongly focused against communists. He, as a communist member, had slithered into that anticommunist organisation like a poisonous snake.

When visiting Trebisov, I had been totally shocked when attending The Public against Violence meetings. This deceptive, selfish, greedy psychopath was sitting as the head of that organisation in the district of Trebisov. The irony of this was that communists like Danko were "building democracy" in many other parts of Slovakia.

Danko turned coat whichever way the wind blew. As long as he could abuse somebody, he was satisfied.

I had joined The Public against Violence to open some people's eyes.

Danko did his job like a true communist would. Once again he had the power to do what he really loved best—abuse citizens in Trebisov. He saved the jobs of all the high-ranking communist officials.

When we voted for something, he distorted our decisions behind our backs. He dictated to the administrator, Petro, just the opposite of what we voted for. He reported whatever suited him to the capital city, which was forgery at the government level.

When I personally discovered what he was doing, the members called an election. One week before the election date, a bunch of new people suddenly joined our movement. Nobody knew where they had come from or why they had joined. I had my suspicions, and I was right. They were all old communists; they all voted for Danko; and, of course, he won again. After the election, we never saw those who had voted for him. When I brought the scam up, other members got very upset. Mr. Filip and his whole group of members from the second-largest town in the district, Secovce, decided to leave the movement if Danko stayed as the head. Danko retreated after all, and Mr. Kacinec became the new head. But Danko, like a good communist, never forgot about this disgrace.

For a time, he kept away from any public functions, but he was working like a bee on a warm, spring day. He wrote articles in the local paper and had somebody sign them for him, because his name had been fused with disgrace. To destroy my reputation was number one on his to do list. Without me, who knew if his black, illegal actions would ever have been discovered?

With the help of local House of Culture and Bibiana, I had created the largest entertainment productions in the history of the town. People had a good time, and most showed respect. National and local magazines, like *Life*, *Plus 7 Days*, and others, described me as David Copperfield of the east. My achievement was also recorded in the Guinness World Records.

This ate Danko up on the inside. Like an arrogant psychopath, he set his plan in motion, which was to destroy my reputation. While national and local media ran admiration stories about me and my productions, Danko spread stories of just the opposite, which were total lies. He "broadcast" them in the local pub.

The first unwelcome story that he made up was that I had stolen money and all my cars and that Interpol was looking for me. It didn't take much in town like Trebisov to turn that little buzz into a full-scale story.

When the Interpol story died, Danko had a new one ready.

"Demcak did not escape the country because of political reasons. He had no political reasons at all. Demcak slept with a gypsy, and he escaped because he did not want to pay alimony for his son."

It took only a day or two for that story to get out of the pub to become the buzz of the town. But later, people began asking questions, like "Where is the son?" or "Who is the gipsy?" Since none materialised, people realized that somebody was letting his big mouth out for a walk.

Danko was doing his dirty work right on the surface then. He could bullshit very fluently. The crap came out of his mouth just as smoothly as the water in the Danube River.

I should know how smooth the water under that bridge is, because I almost lost my life there.

One summer day, I noticed two guys, who jumped off the bridge and survived. I loved heights, and diving was my favourite sport. Seeing those boys survive, I could not resist. Looking down, I had never ever seen such a huge and smooth mass of water as was moving under that bridge of Danube River. Probably for the first time, I was really afraid. But stupidity did not let me back off. I closed my eyes, and let destiny decide if I would live or not. Feet first, I went. It felt like forever to get back to the surface. I was in the last moments of holding my breath when the current finally let me up to the surface. Later, when I read that a well-known singer had lost his life there doing a similar jump, I realized how stupid I had been to do it.

In Bratislava, Meciar had divided Czechoslovakia so that he had free hand to do what he desired. Slovaks had a burden of corruption, anarchy, arrogance, and abuse on their shoulders. When I saw top officials sitting around Meciar on TV, my stomach turned inside out. And when some of them began speaking, it was impossible to survive. The stupidity was boiling over and over. Lie after lie, crap after crap, and I couldn't figure out where they had gone for all that shit. It hit me like a train under the English Channel. It would be suicide to listen to them any longer. That was when I returned home to Canada and stayed away from Slovakia for two years.

Danko was Meciar's dummy on a higher level. Durisin – also native of Trebisov was Danko's own puppet. Danko sent him to Bratislava to serve as a member of parliament. Durisin even agreed to sign his name to some stories that had been fabricated by Danko about me. Danko always hid behind somebody when he made up his stories. He made a total prick out of Durisin. The poor guy Durisin never rehabilitated himself from the time when Danko made him MP, which made him a dickhead for the rest of his life.

Danko became the boss in Trebisov. That gave him the power to do what he loved best—destroy people's lives. He privately reorganised the town. Like in old times, you had to be a communist to be a judge, a prosecutor, an investigator, a school principal, a chief of a hospital, the mayor of the town, and every single post that was under government or town control. He fired everybody who was not with him and replaced them with those who were willing to be his puppets.

He began with those who were sitting at the table when he was pushed out of his chair as the head of The Public against Violence. Mr. Backovski, who was the head of the school district at the time, was fired. Mr. Filip, who was the head of the district of Secovce, was fired. Mr. Biro retired quickly from his job so he could not be fired. Mrs. Rohacova, who was the head of the House of Culture, was fired. She paid because she had been cooperating with me in producing district beauty contests. Mr. Kacinec, who had taken Danko's chair after he was ousted, ended up in jail. And so on.

The only person, Danko could not touch, at least for a time, was me. I did not hold any government-controlled job, so I could not be fired.

"Demcak has AIDS."—suddenly, that was the news in the town of Trebisov. That was his best invention to date. It lasted the longest of all three—stolen money and cars, a son with gypsy, and now AIDS. There was not even one case of the infection in the district at the time, so it stirred quite a bit of anxiety around the area. I noticed; a lady in a local store picked up the bill with the tips of her fingers when I paid. Even my best friend, Vilo, came to my place all worried, asking if it was true.

Others that I had some contact with, even as little as shaking hands, were calling and asking questions. They wanted assurance that they did not have to get examined. Telephones in the local laboratory for infectious diseases began to ring. People were inquiring if it was true about AIDS and what they could do to avoid it. They were informed that it was just more crap. Even the pub-goers, whose thinking usually wasn't on a very high level, figured out what he was doing.

Like a big shot, Danko entered the pub and yelled, "Drinks on me for everybody." I must underline that the pub was not very big—about forty to fifty people at the most. But it was a good base to start a story. The drinker went home and told his wife. She went to work the next day and told everybody she saw. In a town where everybody knew everybody, the news went fast.

Sure, everybody drank what Danko ordered in a pub. But as soon as he leaves:

"What a dickhead," you could hear in the buzz around the pub.

His late sister, Anicka would not speak a word to him at all. She had been my classmate in high school, and she was one of the smartest as well. She was a pharmacist in the town of Michalovce, but when she came to our class reunion, she spent the night in a hotel, because she could not stand his presence.

It took people a while, but they did get it after all anyway. Whatever I had, I had gotten by honest and hard work. But whatever he had, he received by licking Meciar's ass and by destroying other people's lives. That of an arrogant psychopath was the only legacy he was going to leave behind.

Then his dream came true. He had all that money, and most of all, he had me in jail. All of those judges and prosecutors he had appointed would do as they were told. The buzz, around town he made up before was nothing to compare with this. Licking a whore's pussy? That is a story nobody can top. And he had me in jail. How could I deny it? How could I fight it? I had to be done for good.

"A winner never quits, and a quitter never wins," a gentleman who owned the whole circus down in California once wrote on a picture that he gave me as a souvenir. It was just him and his brother—two people struggling to keep the circus going. They could not afford any help, so it was just the two of them to set up the big top and present the whole performance by themselves. I was also struggling alone with my magic show at the time we met. It was long, long ago, and I haven't thought about it for years and years. Funny how thoughts return to your mind when you need them. "A winner never quits, and a quitter never wins." How true. Remember it.

I remembered that when I really needed it most. I'm not sure about a winner, but I'm not a quitter. So I was not going to quit. I told myself that over and over again, when the times and my efforts were totally hopeless.

All the complaints that I had mailed to the highest institutions in Slovakia had ended up in the hands of those who were acting illegally with a request that they investigate themselves.

In my mind, it was approximately like this, "Hey, Janu Demjan, what are you doing there? What, are you stupid? Demcak says you broke the law. I don't see it, but you investigate yourself and punish yourself."

I felt like that was the way they were responding to my complaints.

I kept on complaining, and they kept on breaking the law.

CHAPTER TWENTY

It's Okay. We Just Have a Liar Here. Nothing Special.

Does Investigator Demjan ever tell the truth? Only by mistake.

On November 26, 1998, Investigator Demjan paid a "friendly" visit to my residence in jail. It was to be an interrogation to widen the old accusation, adding not one but three liars. He brought with him his friends, who were gypsies. It was to be a rehearsal for them to see if they were able to lie to my face and consequently do the same in a court of law.

For the gypsies, it was just a good time. They got a ride in an unmarked police car to the big city of Kosice. They got a free lunch in a restaurant at the taxpayer's expense. All they were required to do was tell a few lies.

Lying would not be a problem for them if only they did not have to remember something. Remembering anything at all was the main obstacle for them.

I was taken to the same office downstairs where I had been taken before to meet my lawyer. In the office were the typist, Miss. S. Volochova; my new lawyer, JUDr. Fercakova; and, of course, Demjan. I had already received his decision, dated November 18, 1998, so I was expecting him to bring three new liars with him. He had tried to bring more, but Andrea Karickova had refused to come. But, including Demjan, that still added up to four liars.

Of all the gypsies he had taken as partners, he was the best liar. Added to it his machinations with the child Jana, the gypsies' interrogations, the forging of court documents, and illegal entry, with the gypsies, into my house, it would be hard to beat him as far as a crook was concerned. I was totally disgusted just to see his face.

All my medical and emotional problems just disappeared, and I felt like my energy returned. I was face-to-face with the psychopathic bastard who was using every lie and trick that he knew to frame me and destroy my life. Finally, I would get to tell him what I thought of him.

"Were you going to shoot me? Go ahead. Where is your gun?" I began to yell at him as soon as the guard left the office. I turned toward the door, where everybody's coats were hanging. I grabbed his coat, as if to look for his gun to give it to him.

"Here, I'll give it to you. Go ahead, kill me. If that is all you need."

My lawyer ran to grab me, to calm me down. The coat fell on the floor.

"Take it easy. There is no gun in his coat. He had to deposit it at the entrance office."

She led me to a chair on the left side of the office and sat beside me. The guard, who had been listening behind the door, opened it.

"Is everything all right?"

"Yes, yes," my lawyer assured him.

Demjan stood in the left corner behind the desk, where Miss. Volochova sat behind the typewriter. Her head was all the way down; she never looked up or at me. She felt what Demjan was doing. Only the blind and deaf would not feel it.

Demjan wanted Ms. Volochova to read his accusation.

"No need to read this crap. I have a good memory. I remember every lie in it," I jumped in, before she could even begin reading. Instead, I began dictating to her.

"I'm objecting to the sexual part of accusation, because it is bullshit fabricated by him." I pointed to Demjan. "The old, rusty gun part, I'm not objecting."

"Do you know the witness Natasa Pukiova?" Demjan asked.

"I'm almost sure that she was one of the gypsies who visited my house at the beginning of 1996 under the pretension that there would be a gypsy beauty contest. They looked over my house, because the house had been converted for business to train women for beauty contests and modeling.

"My fiancée Bibiana Gombosova was in charge of the coaching part of the business, while I was responsible for writing scripts and directing stage presentations. We explained our services, introduced our facilities to our possible customers right at the first visit. We both have business licences and permits to run the named business.

"There cannot be any sex accusations whatsoever. The same goes for the second one, Eva Pukiova, and the third one, Andrea Karickova, and all those who are going to be looked for in the future by the same policeman who kicked in these three.

"This policeman is trying to cover up his own criminal activities. In my opinion, the present investigator is familiar with everything. His accomplices, other policemen, were also acting illegally. He is damaging me in order to save those policemen, and he keeps on overstepping laws—I mean, he keeps on breaking laws. I don't know how it is getting through the prosecutor and the judge.

"As far as the old gun goes, I'm telling you that it has been in our family for as long as I can remember. I discovered it again in the attic after my father died. I took it to my home with the intention of finding out if it works. I think that my uncle brought this shotgun, as a gift for my father, from Brazil, where he worked as a young man. I would like to stress that the gun is not mine. It never was mine. My father used to own it. I never used it. I would like to stress very strongly that the gun was not discovered behind the dresser, like he wrote. It was leaning against the wall in front of everybody's eyes. He," I pointed at the investigator, "wrote 'behind the closet' on purpose to cause me more damage, to make it look as if the gun was hidden behind it. That is how crooked he is." I pointed at him again.

"I meant that the gun was behind the closet from where we were standing," the investigator tried to excuse himself with another lie. I could not stand even to be in the same room with him, and him lying again to my face was too much to take.

"You are telling us that you are so stupid that you don't know the difference between behind and beside? I'll show you, so you can learn it."

There was a little metal closet sitting against the wall. I got up and pointed to the right side of it.

"This is beside, and this is behind." I did not mean to, but as I tried to point to behind it, I pulled the closet too hard, and it fell down on the floor with a big noise. My lawyer JUDr. Fercakova ran to me, grabbed my arm, and sat me back in my chair.

"Take it easy. You will get yourself in trouble."

After that, she held my shoulders to keep me down.

"Is everything all right?" The guard opened the door again.

"Yes, yes," my lawyer assured him.

"He is breaking every law possible. He is not an investigator; he is a criminal. Write it down,*"* I addressed the typist.

Demjan dictated to the typist, "The investigator is asking to record that the defendant claims that the investigator is breaking laws against himself, in his opinion."

Even there he was twisting the facts. It was me, not him, who insisted on marking it down, but he made it look like it was he who was asking.

All four of us signed the document at 10:50 AM.

Right after that, they brought in what they called a witness. This was Anna Demeterova. Her name had appeared in the very first, original charge that had been made up even before anybody had talked to her. Then the police had discovered that she was sick in a hospital, so they had to wait until she got well. She was the one who got slapped by the police when she was in elementary school. Remember?

"You slept with Demcak!"

"No I did not." *Slap.*

After that, they looked in her vagina and in her rectum for evidence.

Now, she had long hair and looked much older. After all, she had had two kids since. I had already studied the script of the recording the gypsies had left on my telephone answering machine, so it was not hard to guess who she was.

"You are Kuka, right?" I asked as soon as she sat down.

"Yes."

"What's going on? Why are you here?"

"It is he. He brought me here, and Andrea is out. She does not want to do this anymore." She was talking about one more gypsy the police had tried to bring into the case.

Demjan interfered right away. He wanted to start before she gave away more revelations about his dirt. Later, I found out that all three were to be charged with some small crime, and they had been brought there to lie under the threat that, if they didn't, they would go to jail. Policeman Stefanak and Demjan had prepared them, so they would know what to say.

In the first part, Demjan led her sentence by sentence to say something discriminating against me. It would be waste of time to repeat it all, so I will take only the most important parts. Of course, she said that she had no idea what year it was when we met for the first time, but she knew that she was fourteen.

In the first charge, Demjan had written that I had had intercourse with her. She denied it, but she agreed with Demjan about the blow job. She said that she came to my place alone about twenty times every week. That sounds like she was living with me. Doesn't it? How could that be? I was living with my fiancée Bibiana, at the time. Logic tells me that a week has seven days. She had to have been coming to visit about three times a day.

Then Demjan reminded her that Eva P. was going with her as well. The poor girl had forgotten that the police had changed her partner. Demjan had made her sister, Alena, be her partner in his first accusation, but when Alena changed her mind and refused to go along with the scam, Stefanak had found Eva Pukiova, and Demjan had listed her as the new partner for Anna. On Demjan's suggestion Anna agreed that Eva was with her at my place and that I gave her about 100 korun (about $3), and sometimes 20 or 30 korun to buy some cigarettes.

On questioning by my lawyer as to whether she told her mother or reported it to the police, she answered,

"No, my mother had no idea about it. And nobody else knew, except Eva Pukiova." Anna forgot about her sister, Alena, who was to be in my place with her By Demjan's false claim.

"I never reported it to the police. Even now, I have not reported it to the police, I have no idea why the policeman from the criminal section [Stefanak] came after me when I was pregnant in the hospital, and later, the investigator—this one here who is confronting me—the investigator was there alone."

Demjan reminded her that her sister was also at my place. She agreed to that as well.

I got the message right away. At first, the police had picked up her sister, Alena Demeterova, to be Anna's partner and to collaborate her stories. Then they had replaced Alena with a more willing witness, Eva Pukiova. Alena was dropped from the case on the request of Prosecutor JUDr. Bicko. But after she was dropped, she was still used against me illegally anyway, without being brought back to the case. Because Demjan was manipulating the whole process back and forth, forging investigating documents, he had confused even himself to the point that he had no idea what was going on at all. He had created complete anarchy—made in Trebisov.

Back at the confrontation, the investigator wanted me to react to what Anna Demeterova said.

"Yes, it is true that I know you and you were in my place, but what you are saying is not true."

At 11:45 AM, Demjan ordered a noon break. We could have gone until 12:00—noon—but obviously, Anna needed some more coaching before she could say too many things off the script.

At 12:55 PM, the crap continued.

"I don't want to talk to her anymore. I just want to ask her some questions." I had decided to ask questions that would be on record as proof that Demjan's charge was fabricated on the very first day of my incarceration.

"Your name is Kuka, and your sister looks very different, since I saw her last. Right?"

"Yes, it is me, and it is true that my sister has changed very much."

"Did you go to the beauty contest?"

"Yes, it was in May, when I was fifteen."

"Did your sister know that you attended the contest?"

"Yes, she knew."

I had cleared the only discrepancy in my first statement. If Alena had said that she was familiar with the contest, I would have known who they were. But because she had denied it, there was no way I could know.

Next, I cleared the fact that we had met for the first time at the newspaper stand when they had jumped in my car, not the way Demjan had made it up in his record, where he had stated that it was on Gorkeho Street, which was on the other end of town. My intentions were to have as many absurdities and lies as possible recorded.

"Remember the very first time we met, when I was buying a newspaper, and you and your friend jumped into my car, asking me to give you a ride in my car? At your insistence, I took you both for a ride for about four hundred metres, and then you got out. Is that right?"

"Yes, it is truth."

The fact that her friend stole a bathing suit from me, which Anna had sold back to me for 100 korun was also confirmed and recorded.

"You wanted me to take a photograph of you, but I refused and told you that I would not do it until you showed me your ID. Tell us if I took a photo of you."

"It is true that you did not photograph me, because I did not show you an ID."

Then Demjan jumped in and added, "Because she was not fifteen then."

You could kill a bastard like that; he was using every single chance to twist and add something against me. Right then and there in front of my eyes, he was playing dirty to hurt me. I would have hoped that the lawyer would have stepped in at times like that, but no. That was the way they were framing people, and the lawyer just let them do it.

"Did I have sexual intercourse with you?"

"No, you did not,"

Demjan felt like he was losing the battle, because he had written in the charge that we had had full intercourse. So he stepped in and reminded Anna, "What about licking? He licked you, right?"

She smiled a little, as if she had forgotten what she was supposed to be saying.

"You only licked me."

The investigator felt like it was his turn to score, so he said—notice how suggestive his sentence is—

"Tell him to his face if, when he was licking you at those times like you told us, he knew how old you were. If yes, tell him to his face how you told him."

"He had no idea how old I was."

It was a slap to Demjan's face, because even if I had licked her, which I had not, I would have had to know how old she was to make it illegal. That was the Slovak law.

"Were you present when I had sex with your sister?" I realized that I had worded the question Demjan's way—in other words, the wrong way, because all she had to say was yes, if she decided to lie. I knew for sure that she could not have been there, because I had never had sex with her sister. But Demjan had noticed his chance, and he was not about to miss it.

I noticed that Anna was looking to the corner, where Demjan was standing, with questions in her eyes as if she did not understand. I glanced at him in his corner, and he was jumping, waving both his arms over his head, like a stork waving its wings when trying to take off from wet swamps. His head was nodding up and down, like a horse's head when walking on the trail to the river for a drink. His head was signalling her to say yes, and his were arms signalling for something big.

"Look at the asshole, at what he is doing," I said to my lawyer, pointing at him.

"Excuse me. What are you doing?" she inquired. He clamped down, but the damage was done. Anna got the message.

"Yes."

"Was he trying to fly?" the guard asked me after it was all over, as he escorted me back to my cell.

"What you mean?" I was not sure what he was talking about.

"Demjan was waving, as if he was trying to fly."

"Oh that. He was signalling to his gypsy friend Anna what she should say."

The guard just nodded his head in disgust.

"I can't believe these men in Trebisov," he concluded.

There was no way I could kill the asshole there, but I sure felt like it at the time. I decided just to prove more lies, if I could. First, I had to distract her, to make her forget that she was expected to be lying there. So I asked an unimportant question first.

"Was your sister Alena working as a whore on a corner in the Czech Republic?

"No," she lied. Everybody knew that they both went to the Czech Republic to work the streets. She told a lie, so there was a chance that she would tell the truth to my next question.

"When did Alena tell me how old she was?"

"I don't know."

Demjan had written in the charge that they had both told me together that they were fourteen, just before intercourse. I had cleared another lie.

"Did I ever give you alcohol?

"Yes, it was apricot."

I should have use the word "spirits," or "moonshine" instead of "alcohol," because she confused juice with alcohol. I dropped the subject so as not to upset her. If I did, she might have told more lies, just to spite me. I needed to confirm that they had kept calling me and forcing me to meet them and trying to blackmail me.

"Were you present when you called me on the telephone and were asking for money?"

"Yes, it is true that I called and swore, but I did not ask for money. I was not there when some man called and asked for money. I have no idea how many months back it was when we met you went to Canada." It was good enough for me. I had proof that she was calling me, and also proof that she had no idea when we met.

"Did you ever tell anybody that I had sex with you when you were in the last grade in elementary school?"

"No."

"Were you taken to the hospital from school when you were fourteen?"

"Yes. I was a virgin. The policeman was also after me at that time about this case."

I had enough proof that the whole first charge had been totally fabricated, because she had denied everything that Demjan had written in the charge, point by point. I also had proof that she was approached and forced to testify against me as a child, when she was thirteen or fourteen, at elementary school. It was at the time that the police were trying to frame me for the first time. But that scam had collapsed when Anna was found to be a virgin; therefore, they could not use Anna in the scam against me.

Now, that she was an adult, nothing was in the way of trying to use her again.

They brought Eva P. in next. It was so clear that Demjan had prepared her during the lunch break. He tried very hard to make it fit what Anna had said. It would be stupid and a waste of time to repeat how Demjan led her to say whatever he wanted her to say. Let's just say that I was not surprised when she said such nonsense—that they had both been in my bed, that I was between them, and that I was licking them both all over their bodies. I was not surprised, but I was pissed off. What was I? A body licker? Another interesting statement was that I apparently told her, that I would marry her when she turned fifteen! She also said that I bathed them and gave them pyjamas to wear.

It was my turn again to address that nonsense.

"I have nothing to say about what she said. Only one thing: that it is not truth."

The record reads: "The charged is not talking; he only wants to ask questions."

"What colour were the pyjamas?"

"White with stripes." I concluded that I might have a problem, because Eva could even think on her own. There was not a single set of pyjamas in my whole house, because Bibiana and I never wore any, and Eva had made up even a colour and stripes. It only told me that she knew what pyjamas looked like. Maybe she had some at home.

"Did you want me to take a photo of you?"

"I did not want to." Then I realized that she would lie even about things that did not need to be lied about. The fact was that she had begged me to take a photo so she could mail it to her boyfriend, which she did. He was in jail at the time. She was wearing a full body suit, so what was the lie for? She had come prepared to lie, so she lied even when lying was not required.

"Did I take a photo of you naked?"

"No, I was in a bathing suit with a curtain."

"When did you tell me that you were fourteen?"

"Right at first, when we were going to your place in your car." How could that be? The four of them walked to my place.

"Why did you decide to report me now?"

"I did not report you." I knew she had not reported anything, but I needed it to be recorded. Nobody had ever reported anything, because there was nothing to report. Every word had been fabricated by the police.

"Tell me if the policeman the with beard [Stefanak] came after you and requested that you testify against me?"

"Yes, the policeman was after me." Demjan added to that on her behalf, He said: "And I spoke voluntarily, just like I'm doing now to your face."

"Are you going to stop this?" I asked him in Slovak and added in English, which he could not understand, "You asshole." Whenever I needed to relieve my frustration, I did it in English, so nobody could understand it. I was not generally a swearing man. I admit that I swear only at the special occasion.

"Do something. You see what he is doing," I said to my lawyer. I guess it reminded her that she should do something.

"Do you know when you finished school? In what year and how old you were then?"

"No, I don't know when. But I was fifteen."

In the recording that they left on my telephone answering machine, she was the one who had said "I must report you to the cops, and you know why? Because when I want to meet you, you do not want to meet me." My refusing to meet her must have upset her to the point that she was willing to say anything.

Eva's sister, Natasa P., was next; she was already eighteen when we met. Look at how Demjan outlined the whole answer for her by giving her answers instead of what should have been questions. This is exactly how he said it, and it was recorded in the document.

"Here he is in front of you, face-to-face. He is claiming that it is not true that he was sexually abusing you from 1992 until 1995, when you were underage, or that he was licking you all over your body and on your sexual organs. So you tell him to his face, how it was, where it was, and if he knew that you were not fifteen years of age."

He made up the whole answer for her. From this, it was just confirmed that the idiot had made up the story about licking the whole body. Who else with a normal mind would lick the whole body of a gypsy prostitute?

The worst part was that my lawyer was there—not even a sign of an objection. That was the way they did justice there.

I was already sick and tired of that crap. It was totally below the level of any pig to even react to anything like that. He brought those women from Trebisov just to say yes to his fabricated lies. The

important thing was for me to clear some important facts, which included if I had committed the crime. She confirmed that we met for the first time, outside, when they were leaving the nightclub called Vagonar. Than they went to the dance at Community Hall. They were all at least fifteen at the time, because a citizen's ID was required at both places.

Licking or not licking was not important any more. I asked only one question. I did not think she would lie about it, because she would not have any idea why I was asking.

"I only want to know who met me first. You or Kuka?"

"Kuka knew you first."

That was good enough for me. I had plenty of proof already that Kuka was fifteen when she met me. Plain mathematics proved that Natasa was eighteen at the time. If Demjan had persuaded her that she could have been fourteen, then he had a big problem with counting and the law. Not just that he had persuaded them to falsely testify, he had also made them younger by a few years.

It was my time to say something about what she had said.

"I'm denying everything she said, the whole content. I'm insisting on my statement."

It was a huge punishment to my soul to listen to all those lies and to see Demjan manipulating those women and changing what they said, while dictating what they said to the typist. We were there, and he was doing it in front of our eyes. Imagine what he did when he was alone and nobody was watching.

This was the way it went. Policeman Stefanak looked for and found those women, who were willing to falsely testify against me. They called it seeking out witnesses. I called it searching for liars. Stefanak knew those who were trying to blackmail me with their pimp, the gypsy Milan Tancos (real name). Policeman Stefanak offered them cooperation and gave them the first lecture of what they needed to say. He also assured them that, if they did it, the outstanding charge against them would be dropped. In an unmarked police car, he brought them to Investigator Demjan, who gave them more schooling and rehearsal. They called it questioning. Demjan could write down anything he could think of, because they couldn't read, and they would sign anything at all. I called it a document of bullshit and lies.

Then they brought them in front of me to find out how they would do when lying straight to my face. This process was called a confrontation. In fact, it was the same as a dress rehearsal for lying. After that, they were to repeat those lies at the premiere—they called it a court of justice. The whole process stank and made me sick; it was used all over Slovakia and in many post-communist countries.

He had all those documents on the desk and was looking through all of them. None had numbers on them, so he had difficulty finding any particular ones.

My lawyer JUDr. Fercakova was also studying some documents. The dates on the records of interrogation of the three new assistants to Demjan got her attention.

"You interrogated them on November 18? How come you did not let me know?" She asked Demjan.

"It was too late. I could not get you on the phone."

"That is a lie. I talked to you that same morning, requesting that I be present at the questioning of every witness. It is your duty; it is the law to let me know. No. This I cannot believe. We were talking on the phone that same morning, and you made a secret of it. What did you need to cover up? When are you going to do something according to law?"

She had been taking it easy and letting him get away with many things before, but lying to her own face had somehow gotten to her, and she was really upset, so she was letting him have it.

My energy was drained. I could not see clearly, but I had something in my mind that I needed to clear. It was the record of that horrific interrogation of the child Jana Visokaiova, when she was abused at the police station. It had also been used against me, illegally, as a reason for my incarceration at my first appearance in court. Since then, in studying the law book, I had discovered that it was totally inadmissible in court by law and also that it had been taken by an unqualified policeman instead of an investigator. Since Demjan had been manipulating the investigative records, I wanted to be sure that it would not get lost through Demjan throwing it intentionally into the garbage.

"Can I see a copy of the interrogation of Jana Visokaiova from October 1 and October 2, 1998?" I asked Demjan.

"Which one?"

"The one that was taken by policemen at Jana's school on October 1. And the one that was taken the next day at the police station."

"What do you need them for? They are not legal in this case." My lawyer was trying to explain to me something that I already knew. I had no idea that she did not know that they had used them against me at the first hearing.

"I just want to see them. I have the right to see every document that is used against me. That is the law." I was getting really upset.

"But they are not admissible in the investigative records." She was still persisting, which really pissed me off.

I began screaming.

"I want to see them. The judge was showing them to me in court as evidence and as a reason for jailing me, and I want to see those documents."

"What do I hear?" Now she turned her question to Demjan. "Did you present those documents to the court?"

"The little one [Jana] did not want to talk, so we used them," Demjan tried to explain. He looked like a school kid who had been caught cheating. That really set off my lawyer.

Then she began to scream at him.

"I cannot believe this. I have seen many things, but never anything like this. Did it ever occur to you that this is against the law? Can you do anything according to the law at all? I put up with you placing all these ideas into these women's heads, manipulating documents, but this is going too far. It is all against the law. On top of that, you lie straight to my face." Then she turned to me and suggested, "We are going to apply for another investigator. This man is hopeless … terrible. He cannot do anything right. He is not investigating; he is totally prejudiced against you." She closed her papers.

"I tried to tell you that many times, but you would not believe me. But if we switch investigators, it is going to extend the case for a much longer time, isn't it? And how do we know that the new one will be an honest one?" I had been thinking and had concluded that I would let Demjan finish his dirty work, and then I would complain about it at a higher institution and in court.

"Show me those documents," I requested again. "Where is the investigative file?"

Demjan was standing behind the desk, looking at the pile of papers sprayed all over the top.

"Is this investigative file? This is the investigative file. Look at it," I pointed to it, addressing my lawyer.

"Is this the file you are keeping him here with?" she asked Demjan. None of the pages were numbered; none were registered. He was standing, all red in the face; his arteries were getting really big in his neck.

I was screaming at him,

"No point talking to him. You are a liar and cheat."

"Is everything okay?" the guard opened the door again.

"Yes, we just have a liar here. Nothing special," I explained to him this time.

Demjan was looking and could not find Jana's records. To me, it was clear, like the sky over the Saskatchewan on a sunny day. So far, they had kept it of sight whenever they could, because it was proof of police brutality in the case of that child.

"I'm not surprised he doesn't have it." Then I turned to him and yelled in his direction,

"And don't bring any more gypsies here; you can keep those whores for yourself. They are just like you—liars, all of you."

The time was up, and we had to quit.

"Please make sure to get those records, and bring one copy to me. You will see who you are dealing with when you read them."

"I think I already know," she agreed.

I went back to my cage, my energy completely drained. To be there with that asshole, listening to those lies, was like a nuclear bomb for my soul. Shortly after I returned to my cell, I began sneezing and feeling just like I had before I had gone downstairs. Strange that I did not feel like that when I was facing that creep and those liars. I felt like tearing his head off.

I was sure that Demjan was coaching those women during the lunch break. I noticed that Eva was saying similar lies to what Anna was saying. There was no way she could have just done that without Demjan lecturing her. Ms. Volochova, who had been typing it all, seemed like a decent young lady. Ms. Volochova had witnessed all of the coaching of those women by Demjan. I was sure that she, being a young lady, was sick of what he was doing. I placed her on my list of witnesses. But, of course, Judge and Prosecutor did not present her in court. They knew that she could tell how Demjan was coaching those gipsies. The reason for not presenting Ms.Volochova in court was never disclosed to me, in spite of the fact that, by law, I had the right to call witnesses of my own choice.

There was a small chance that she would tell the truth. But that was a chance I was willing to take.

CHAPTER TWENTY-ONE

"The Child Wishes to Be Raped." (Docent Stancak)

Who tells the truth in Slovakia? Psychopathic liars.
The Destruction of the Visokaiova family.

Soon after I was face-to-face with the four liars—Demjan and the three gypsies, Anna Demeterova, Eva Pukiova, and Natasa Pukiova—I received a copy of the psychological examination of the child Jana Visokaiova.

It hit me hard, because I felt like I was her father. The poor child had already been interrogated at school, abused at the police station, dragged to a gynaecological examination, interrogated again at school, and given a psychological examination. Her reputation had been destroyed by Demjan asking children at her school if they had heard about me touching her. Her feelings had been disturbed by the police who abused her. All the girl had done was tell the truth, and she was paying dearly for it.

The examiner was Docent Stancak, the same man who examined me and all the gypsies who had been brought into my case by the police.

The examination had been performed at her school again and, again, without the knowledge of her parents. School had been used for all the dirty work by the police.

Jana began crying as soon as she was brought to the school library where Docent Stancak was waiting. Once she calmed down, she undertook the intellectual and psychological examination.

Again she confirmed—this time for the third time—that our relationship was entirely father-daughter like.

She stated that we had never slept in the same bed, because she had always slept alone. Demjan had written just the opposite in the charge.

Sometimes, I had given her a good-night kiss on her cheek but never on her lips. She had never kissed me either. I had never felt her body, and she had never slept naked. During three interrogations, she had repeated the same claims. But Docent Stancak, a trained psychologist, was paying attention to what Demjan had stated in the charge, which he had written even before he had talked to Jana. Demjan had also written that some child had allegedly said that Jana had said that I had raped her. I knew Jana well enough to be certain that Jana had no idea what "rape" really meant at her age at all. No doubt Demjan had made it up.

Mr. Stancak concluded that no rape had ever happened but that Jana had said it to the other child because of a so-called "fantasy," which meant that she was claiming something that she wished for. In plain language, in this particular case, the eleven-year-old child was wishing to be raped.

Just when I had thought that there could not be any more outrageous bullshit, they came up with this. Little did I know that it was just the beginning.

I had had respect for Stancak before, because he had written quite a close assessment of me, and then he spoiled it all like this. The child was wishing to be raped. Can you believe that kind of conclusion? He had to be out of his mind to even think about something like that.

I knew that Demjan was manipulating the investigative documents and fabricating statements. Therefore, nobody knows for sure what he showed to Docent Stancak to make him conclude something like that.

All around, Docent Stancak concluded that there was absolutely nothing wrong going on between Jana and me. He also concluded that she and her statements could not be used in a court of law against me. There was nothing wrong with that as far as I was concerned.

I was with Docent Stancak long enough to see that he must have noticed what the police were doing, but he had a reason not to write it down. If he did, he would have in fact accused the police who had hired him. He would have had to accuse his employers of a very serious crime, if he was to write the truth. It would have been his last expert examination. A worse scenario could be that he could have ended up in jail next to me. I was in jail because I had accused the police of doing just this and also because they wanted my money.

By now anybody could guess what Docent Stancak did. He placed the blame on the poor little girl. He concluded that child had told that story because of her fantasy. I believe that Docent Stancak knew that it was not the child's fantasy but the fantasy of the police who were wishing for at least one—at least one single—thing that I had done against the law. But I had not obliged.

The worst fact about this was that Docent Stancak had written that from Demjan's suggestion, which had been made from the alleged sentence of a third person—another ten-year-old child. This so-called fantasy Docent Stancak had not confirmed through his own examination. There she was, Jana Visokaiova, sitting in front of him. He did not examine her to see if she ever said what Demjan had written. He did not even examine if she really had a fantasy of being raped. Instead, he wrote it down, which was something that could destroy the child's life.

Docent Stancak concluded that the fantasy would not have any negative effects on her psychological development. But he also suggested that she should be examined by a child psychologist and a child psychiatrist, because of the signs of the fantasy. I thought that he was doing the examination. Where was the sense to it? I guess it was too long ago when he had attended school, so he forgot that everybody who was normal had some kind of fantasy. Only dead or insane humans had no fantasies. That was what bothered me most. Imagine the child, who had done nothing wrong, and then she was the one to be examined—not those who had abused her, not those who had fabricated all those horrible stories about her. Was that justice in Slovakia?

From my cell, I mailed multiple requests for him to provide an expert analysis of some of the documents. I was going to have him do an analysis of the document from when Jan was abused at the police station. But Docent Stancak never replied.

I asked myself how much damage that wrong statement would cause to the child Jana. Later, I discovered that this suggestion gave corrupt officials another tool and excuse to persecute the child. And a persecution of the child it was.

Oh my God.

Months later, when I was released from prison, I discovered what damage that one seemingly unimportant suggestion from Docent Stancak had caused to the child. That was the suggestion for another examination.

Remember that the family of Jana Visokaiova refused to falsely testify against me. Something like that couldn't be forgiven. The wheels of Trebisov justice were working just based on that.

Visokaiova family, including the child Jana, was evicted from their apartment onto the street. They became the first homeless people in Trebisov's history. Their stepdaughter Alena Gradosova received their apartment. Jana's mother Helena Visokaiova swears even today that the apartment was in her name until eviction.

The father, Jan, the mother, Helena, and Jana—their eleven-year-old daughter—slept in the open basement of the apartment building. No water, no heat, no window. The police were cruising around, looking for the child. The child was hiding and crying; she could not go to school, because she was afraid of the police. The parents were trying to protect their daughter. One morning, the police grabbed Jana on the street and took her to a mental institution for examination just like Docent Stancak had suggested. She was locked up there for three months. From there, she was taken to another institution. That lock up lasted for three years. Her young life was virtually destroyed. Jana left Slovakia for UK. Each time she sees policemen, the abuse she was put through at Trebisov police station goes through her mind again. She suffers till present, hawing nightmares.

Jana's mother, Helena Visokaiova, attempted to commit suicide with a butcher knife. Jana discovered her covered in blood and called ambulance. Her father died an early death, heartbroken.

The Visokaiova family had been a completely normal, average family before the policemen, Demjan and Stefanak and others, stepped into their lives and demanded false accusations. Their normal lives were officially confirmed by the statement of Jana's home teacher, and is recorded in investigating file.

Helena and Jana survived and hope that, one day, the corrupt policemen and officials who destroyed their lives will face justice. That is the same justice that I'm hoping for by writing this story.

Docent Stancak also conducted examinations on the gypsies who were used against me. The two sisters, Alena and Anna Demeterova, as well as Eva Pukiova were examined.

The cases of Alena and Anna Demeterova were very similar. As Docent Stancak stated, "Both sisters are mentally retarded and illiterate, with low and dull mental capabilities. Family members have been convicted for various crimes.

"Both sisters became prostitutes on the level of streetwalkers. They provided their services on the streets of the Czech Republic, mostly for German costumers. They both have two children each, acquired through prostitution.

"Alena is mentally retarded, mainly in the moral field."

What's interesting is the next statement by Docent Stancak.

"Overall brain abilities are at the level of mental dullness. All functions of memory—infusing, holding, and retrieving—are below average. Even under these brain functioning abilities, the witness is able to reproduce events that she has lived through but with various mistakes in details."

The next line is even more interesting.

"The amount of Anna's lies is in comparison with her age population."

I must be stupid, because here I was completely lost, even with my higher-than-average IQ. Could you imagine what policeman Demjan could make out of that? He could conclud that what the gypsy had said was all true and okay and could be used against me because her lies were in comparison with other liars of her age. Or what? From the other side, could I understand that all people of her age population were psychopath liars? Or should I understand that most people of her age population are mentally retarded, mainly in the moral field?

Here is the explanation by the author of that statement, Docent Stancak.

"That means that she assesses a situation for her self-advantage, even by using lies."

It would be so much better to say that in a way that even Demjan could understand it. In plain language, just the way it was—that she was a liar, so she could not be trusted—rather than by beating around the bushes.

Then the docent continued,

"The witness is flat emotionally, with the ability and tendency to blame others, especially to her own advantage. When she wants to damage or blame somebody, she is not choosy in means—any way she can, including lies."

How true. I agreed with that description, but in my opinion, it fits much better for Demjan and most of all the officials I was dealing with.

Docent Stancak continues: "Both women began full sexual activity a few years ago, from which came two children each. As for the fathers, they pointed to men from Germany. Neither of the chosen fathers admitted to being the fathers.

"According to psychological analysis, they are suspicious individuals in the direction of psychopaths with an acceleration of sexual instinct of the hedonistic type [self-gratifying type].

"Anna is capable of blackmailing, because she claims that she wants me to be punished because I did not pay, and she was young."

One of the items that Demjan requested was to find out what damage the time she spent with the defendant had caused to her mental development? The expert concluded that no damage had been caused by her time spent, because, after puberty, her sexual acceleration had ended up in multiple pregnancies.

My question on the subject is much more logical: "What damage did the police cause to Anna Demeterova's mental development when they slapped her around at her school, forcing her to falsely testify against me? She was just thirteen or fourteen and still a virgin when policemen dragged her to medical examination falsely claiming that she had sexual intercourse with me. Could it be that the abuse by the police had contributed to the fact that she had become a prostitute? I believe so.

I also have another question for Docent Stancak. After discovering that Anna Demeterova was psychopathic liar, capable of blackmailing and using lies to her advantage, he concluded that her testimony made in front of the investigator was truthful, except for the part about the money. How in hell could the testimony of that kind of person be truthful?

Docent Stancak should have had enough sense to notice that all gypsy's statements had been fabricated by Demjan. There were words that she could never understand. I did, and I proved it from my cell. But not Mr. Stancak.

After that, all my respect for him disappeared. He was still only a puppet for the police, the same as he had been all his life during communist times.

The last person in my case whom Mr. Stancak examined was Eva Pukiova. She was the best liar of all of them. If he seriously believed that her lies to Demjan were truthful, because she was able to repeat some of them, then he has to live with the knowledge for the rest of his life that this gypsy woman with very low mental abilities, as he wrote, had fooled him just like she would fool a stupid little boy.

He picked up this and that, claiming that this was a lie and this and that was the truth. What was he? A mind reader—to know that these few things are truthful, and those few are lies? It was absurd. When somebody is a psychopathic liar with the intention of lying, he is going to lie whenever it suits him. Some people can repeat the same lie twice, three times, or even more. These women said it differently every time they spoke. And it was the truth, as far as Mr. Stancak was concerned.

Mr. Stancak totally screwed up. On one side, he stated that I was totally truthful. On the other side, he named Anna Demeterova a psychopathic liar, and a liar, and even more of a liar with a tendency to blackmail. The problem was that she was claiming something that I was totally denying. To make it clear, the honest man was denying something that the psychopathic liar was claiming. But the liar's statement was truthful, as far as Mr. Stancak was concerned. How could that be? He signed his name under all of his findings. Only in communist heads could that be possible. A few decades of a communist system, and humans totally lost their common logic. That kind of Slovak outrageous specialty was to be found in many claims by Slovak officials.

An interesting fact was how Investigator Demjan formulated the requests for the examinations. He was warning experts that the law required them not to evaluate his evidence. In the same document, he was requesting them to do just that on the next page of the same document. He was requesting Stancak to state whether the answers of the witnesses were truthful and usable in the court process, another specialty for Slovaks.

It was not a question in my mind at all that these psychologist examinations were for one, and only one, purpose: to be used as collaboration of fabricated documents, which the officials had made up and could not find any proof for.

He had concluded that the gypsies were psychopathic liars with virtually nonfunctional memories. But he also wrote that their statements were truthful. How could that be? They were antagonistic claims and could not possibly be both correct. Shame on you, Mr. Stancak.

Demjan was avoiding anybody and anything that pointed to my innocence. He even avoided talking to the parents of the gypsies. He had written such absurd things in some statements that my hair stood up when I read it. He wrote in one statement that Anna Demeterova came to my place to get licked all over her body about twenty times a week. At the same time, Eva Pukiova was coming to get the same service about twice a week over a stretch of two years. My tongue must have been worn out completely.

Demjan kept his fabrications away from everybody, and he knew why. Later, when the television station Markiza asked the father of Anna and Alena Demeterova what his opinion was, he stated bluntly and publicly on television about his two daughters that "They are whores. Demcak is innocent. They would not go there if they did not want to."

Only on my insistence, through my lawyer, did Demjan finally interview Jana's family, which included Jana's two sisters, her mom, and her dad, who all stated that they had never heard anything like what he had fabricated. They have never heard it, and they did not believe that I would touch the child in any improper way. Her parents stated that they simply did not believe it, because they knew me well and Jana always wanted to visit me. Jan V. stated that, when he had talked to his daughter about what we did at my place, Jana had said that she only played there, and she had never hinted about any wrongdoing.

Her mom went even further to say that Jana could visit me anytime she wanted to.

"I trusted him then, and I trust him now," Jana's mother stated, and she continued about how her daughter had been abused at the police station. "A policeman came after me in person. I do not know his name. He had a moustache. He requested that I go with him to the police station where I found out that they had Mr. Demcak there and also that they were interrogating my daughter. I was not present for any of those questionings. My daughter was in the office in the presence of about five policemen, and there was smoke—cigarette smoke—in that room. I took my daughter home after policeman Stefanak questioned me.

"At home, my daughter told me that the policemen were asking her if Mr. Demcak had condoms, and she told me that they were forcing her to forcefully state against Mr. Demcak. She was also afraid of the policemen—for two days, she was unable to go to school—and she had also urinated herself."

The most cynical question I have ever heard in my life followed. You could guess that it could only come from Demjan, as he asked the child's mom, "For what reason did you not report to the superiors of those policemen, who were interrogating your daughter, and find out why they were proceeding with that kind of questioning?"

"I immediately reported it to the police, and the next day, I went to school to see the school principal, Ms. Ferkova, and I told her that the child would not attend school, because she was in shock from what the policemen had done to her."

Demjan knew very well that she had done that, but nobody had moved a finger. No investigation had ever been launched into the conduct of the police. I had even filed a complaint, and it had placed me in jail.

Helena Visokaiova continued, "I'm stating that a man approached me in town. He was short, fat, and had glasses, and he told me that he was an investigator and that he was asking about Mr. Demcak. He also went to see my daughter at school, because she told me about it."

A question from the lawyer, "How has the child behaved since this took place?"

"I'm giving her pills, brand Belaspon, because she is stressed and cannot sleep."

The question from the lawyer, "What kind of feeling did you have about your daughter meeting Mr. Demcak? Was the relationship friendly, fatherly, or as lovers?""Friend or father. Family friend."

A question from the investigator, "Tell us if your daughter ever cheated or lied or if she told you something and you later discovered that it was the truth or a lie?"

"Yes, my daughter is honest and will be honest. She cries if she tries to lie."

When I had received a letter from Jana's mom, mentioning a little, fat man with glasses who had approached her and introduced himself as an investigator from court, I knew right away who it was. It could only be the creep Danko. He had come to snoop and to see if he could persuade them to change their minds and testify against me.

Jana and her parents were suffering already for the same reason as I was—for telling the truth. But the worst was only to come for that family.

You just did not tell the truth in that country if it did not suit the police. Period. Or you were finished. Period.

Remember the subtitle of this chapter? "Only psychopathic liars are considered to be telling the truth." How true.

While all those totally corrupt activities were going on outside, I was locked in my cell, unable to do anything about it. Wondering where those kinds of people came from kept me from sleeping.

CHAPTER TWENTY-TWO

"We Are Not Stupid Cows Like Policemen." (Crook)

Where in the world can you blackmail by fax? In Slovakia.

A new prisoner was assigned to our cell. His name, or anything that could disclose his identity, I will not disclose for his own protection. I will just call him Mr. X. If there was a young man, whom you would think must be innocent, it would be him. But the opposite was true. He had had the kind of job before taking up residence in the gulag that he really knew what was going on, so he filled me in really well.

A photo of his girlfriend was his only reminder of life on the outside. Looking at her photo every night, he mopped tears from his chicks, while his head was turned to the wall, so we could not see his wet eyes. I knew what he was doing, because I was using the same cover-up, when I could not keep my tears inside.

I had not cried for at least forty years. When I escaped my old country, I lost everything. My country, my friends, and my family—everything was gone. I was all alone in a strange country without friends and with no knowledge of the language, but I did not cry.

After many years, I met Ed, who became my good friend and who was like a grandfather to me. We lived together for twelve years. He was 103 when he died. I was more than a thousand kilometres away, almost at the Canadian border with Alaska, touring with my show. That morning, two black crows were sitting on the back stairs of my bus that had been converted into a motor home. I felt something was wrong, so I called. And sure enough, Ed was dead. I loved that man like he was my own family. I was totally devastated that I was not with him in his last days. It was my first real cry; I cried with sadness. It was new feeling, the kind I'd never experienced before. After, there was a feeling of relief.

There in prison, under the mental and physical abuse, crying was different. It was crying with hopelessness, fear, and anger—all three at the same time. There was a fear for your life, a fear for the lives of your loved ones. It changed to a feeling of wanting revenge, and a feeling of hopelessness followed.

Each time, I received some mail and discovered other false acquisitions based on bona fide lies, broken laws, and forged documents, I would show it to Mr. X as if it was something big, a discovery that I could do something about.

"Don't be naive. This is completely normal," he assured me. "This is how they do things around here. Nobody will touch it at all. They would have to lock up the whole country, including themselves. Everybody is corrupt. People used to steal little by little during the communist system. Now, politicians steal by the millions. Some, even by the billions. That is why I did the stupid thing that got me here. All officials steal, so why not me? That was how I was thinking. The difference is that they are safe, protected by their immunities and the corrupt justice system. I have no immunity like officials have; that is why I'm here. They only want to steal by themselves; they don't like for other people to steal."

"This is your first act against the law, so maybe you will get less time," I speculated.

"Just the opposite, I will get more, because I was a —, and I have broken the trust."

"Look. I have all this evidence about how they are breaking the law. If I get out, I will file complaints against all those officials."

"No proof that you have will leave this prison. They will take everything from you when you get out. If you get out at all."

It was scary to listen to him. He was not the type, who would tell me bullshit.

I considered what he said and tried to find out some more.

"How could they do that?"

"Everybody who has money or some assets goes through it. This is how it works. First, they destroy your health. They know how to do it. They had many decades to learn from the Soviets. When you are almost finished, hardly alive, then they show you to your family. Your family will sell everything, just to save your life. That is how it goes here, and nobody can do anything about it."

It was chilling to listening to all those things, especially when, more and more, I was realizing that, in fact, it was happening to me.

Mr. X had done something bad, but he was a very nice guy. He was just the small fish; that was why he had ended up in there. I hope he will serve his time and get out without any serious damage to his mental and physical health. He kept reminding me not to think so much about injustice, because it might destroy me completely. He offered me food from a parcel he received from home when I was unable to eat the terrible prison grub.

"Everybody in justice is corrupt. Nobody can fight them and win. You can forget it."

"How do you know all this?"

"Come on. Everybody knows that you are a millionaire from Canada. They can hardly wait for you to break down and start paying."

"Well, they are not getting my money. I worked very hard for everything I have. I'd rather died here than pay those bastards. I also don't have the kind of money they are asking for."

"Do not repeat that anymore, because it may happen. Nothing stops them."

I thought about it very hard. As time went by, I realized how right he was.

It was so normal to extort money from prisoners. In a pub, policemen and justice officials talked about it openly. After a few drinks, they didn't even quiet their voices, like normal people do when talking about communists.

Voices in the pub were heard as saying, "How is Demcak doing? Is he paying yet?" That was a policeman to the judge. "No," the judge said. "Not yet. I wish Janko [Investigator Demjan] would give me something to sue him with. So far, I have nothing to sue him with at all."

"Hey Janko, you should move your skeleton. Christmas is coming. Do you know how many people are waiting for Demcak's money? And here the judge is saying that you've given him nothing to sue him with."

"Take it easy," Demjan said. "I'm working on it."

Everybody had a good laugh.

******

December arrived, snow fell, and I was still locked up. Demjan had applied to restrict my imprisonment by section 67b T.P.—that meant I would be moved to a different cell with more restrictions. He had completely changed Jana Visokaiova's testimony, lied to her mom, and twisted her answers as well—a real creep at work.

Any time, I could have been taken to B cell, which was for those with the most restrictions. I was hoping it would not happen before Bibiana and my brother came to visit, which was planned for the next day.

I was lucky, because I was called down to a visiting booth. Bibiana and my brother were there. She looked beautiful, wearing a white skirt. We had to be very careful, because it was obvious that the booth was bugged. I tried to hide how bad my situation was. I did not want to transfer my worries to her. The hour went very quickly, and I felt very sad and lonely when I returned to my cell.

Mr. X and I went out for our daily walk to the chicken coop that same afternoon. Downstairs in the locker room, we changed our sandals for big, ugly, work shoes, from which all shoestrings had been removed. Dark grey jackets were also there, and we put them on over our blue sweat suits. It had been snowing for the past few days, and there were small hills of snow piled up in the corners of the chicken coops.

I felt terrible; my head felt like a rock. My nose began bleeding from my left nostril. It had happened many times before, so I did not think much about it at first. I went to the corner, trying to stop the bleeding my usual way: pressing on my left nostril and wiping up the blood with toilet paper, which doubled as a handkerchief. I always carried it in my pocket, just in case. Usually, it stopped soon, but not that time. The bleeding was much more profuse, and I was unable to stop it as usual. I ran out of toilet paper, which had become all red. Blood had gotten all over the dark grey coat and was dripping down on the white snow, colouring it red.

Mr. X noticed that something was wrong and yelled to the guard, who was looking down from the watchtower. He did nothing at all, just looked down at us. It was the same thing as when I had almost died, when Janco G. had saved me. It was quite a while before the door opened and we were let out. By then, I was dizzy and shaky from the loss of blood.

Mr. X informed the guard that something was wrong and asked him to take me to the doctor. He said he would arrange it and ordered us back to our cell. Mr. X helped me as I wobbled back to our cell.

The bleeding continued. I bent over the sink, placing a cold towel on my neck while red drops coloured the white sink.

Zdeno pressed the red alarm button. A guard by the nickname of Mojo opened the little feeding window.

"Hey, he needs doctor," Zdeno said.

The guard slammed the little door without saying a word. After a while, Zdeno pressed the button again. The window opened.

"Stop pushing that button," the guard ordered and slammed the opening before Zdeno could say anything at all.

I was hanging onto the sink, and my knees caved in. Zdeno and Mr. X helped me to my bed.

"No lying on the bed," Mojo yelled through the opening. He was that big nasty, young *bachar, (bachar – nasty prison guard)* who always carried a big, T-shaped baton. His main role was to "fix" those prisoners who needed it.

"He needs a doctor," both cellmates yelled back.

"No lying on the bed," he repeated his order.

The bleeding slowed down, because there was not much blood left in my body. I lost consciousness. They placed four stools in a line, led me out of the bed, and placed me on them.

The feeding hole opened again.

"You are not allowed to move the stools. Put them back."

"He needs a doctor."

The little opening slammed again.

At 5:00 PM, they carried me and placed me on the bed. Mr. X. boiled some tea and forced me to drink.

"They want to break you down badly. It's because you are not paying and you are writing all those complaints," Mr. X explained. "Mojo and the others were watching you through the peephole to see how you were doing. Most likely, they will leave you to die. Tomorrow, we will all be transferred, and we will never see each other. That is what they do after every act of brutality to cover it up. That way, nobody can corroborate what is going on here. There will only be somebody telling something, which will be denied simultaneously by all the guards. Be very careful. Try not to get sick. They will not help you at all."

Mr. X was right. The next morning, they called him first and locked him up in the shaving and haircutting room. They locked me in an empty cell. They ordered Zdeno to pack his things. After he was gone, they brought me back and ordered me to do the same. I packed everything into my blanket. I had a few books and some food that Bibiana had mailed to me, as well as a lot of papers, which were copies of my complaints and copies of the documents that had been were delivered to me.

My strength was gone from the lost of blood the day before. I could not lift my bundle, so I dragged it on the cement floor. Two guards followed me down the long corridor. I dragged my bundle behind me. My knees were bending and letting me down from time to time. Neither of the guards gave me any help.

We reached the end of a hall. I looked at them, as if to ask where to go now.

"Oh, we made a mistake; it is the other way." The guards began to laugh.

I wobbled back, passing my cell (222), all the way to cell (217), which to be my new residence.

Nobody cleaned the bloody snow for weeks to come. Neither was the coat cleaned of dried blood. Each time I went for a walk, the coat was still hanging there, and I used it over and over again. It became my coat, because the other prisoners did not want to wear a coat with dried blood on it.

Two young prisoners were in my new cell: Peter M. from Poprad and Nemec J. from Michalovce. Both were small-time crooks. They were both also being held by section 67b T.P., because their accomplices were locked in different cells. They kept them separated so they could not talk to each other. That made no sense at all, because the whole investigative section of the prison was run so that you could not even see any other prisoners.

Nemec J. had been hired to drive a car to the neighbouring Ukraine. He had received all the necessary documents as proof that the car had been sold legally. They had promised him that he would get a thousand korun on completion of the delivery. He had had no idea that the car had been stolen and that he was, in fact, smuggling it over the border. His "employer" was a smuggler; he was outside and free. Nemec J. himself had no idea of the actual identity of his "employer." The officials would not believe him. They believed he was covering up for smuggler, so they kept him in the investigative prison to persuade him to talk. It would take a very long time before he would actually be convicted. I believed his story, because he was too young to be part of any serious car-smuggling ring.

A different story was that of Peter M. from Poprad. On the outside, he had been a gorilla *(gorilla – bodyguard in language of criminals)* for his boss, who was the real criminal, leading extortion, blackmail, and a so-called burning down organisation, which set businesses or cars on fire if owners did not pay extortion demands. It was happening under the mountains of High Tatra in the city of Poprad. His boss did not need any gorillas to protect him, because he was a big gorilla himself. But it was in style that every boss had to have at least two gorillas with him so it looks impressive and vicious, especially when they came to collect blood money from little business owners.

They proudly called themselves a mafia, but most of the time, they were poorly organized crooks, who extorted money from small businesses for a promise of providing protection. In reality, it was protection from them, the crooks. To make it clear, "If you pay, we will protect your car; we will not destroy it." If that friendly message did not work, there was a backup: "If you pay, we will watch your business to make sure that we will not burn it down." After that, there was still the ultimatum, "If you pay, we will not blow up your car up with you and your family in it." An offer like that was hard to refuse, and you sure felt "safe," after you paid your weekly or monthly protection fees.

Sometimes, they became very mean. If somebody reported extortion to the police, the policemen reported it back to the crooks. Businesses were burned down, cars were blown up, and businessmen were killed or went missing. One statistic showed that more than ninety cars had been blown up in one year. All was done in a primitive way, with a sea of evidence left behind. The only reason they could still operate was because they shared the loot with the corrupt policemen and other officials in the justice system.

Where in the world can you send your extortion demands by fax? How hard is it to trace, sender's fax number? It shows it right on the telephone bill. That happened when one gang took over the territory of the other. The whole gang had a meeting in a private section of a restaurant, in a room upstairs. A man with a machine gun walked in and killed them all, including an unimportant man, whose only function in the gang was as a "starter." His role was to start the boss' car first, in case a bomb had been wired to it. Does the mafia in Chicago during the Capone times come to mind? Not at all. It happened in a small city in Slovakia.

After that, the murderers faxed messages to all businesses, stating that they were taking over all the extortion "business," because all the previous crooks were dead.

By faxing the messages, not only did they send proof that they were extorting money but also evidence as to who had murdered the other gangsters.

The meanest cases were recorded when gangs fought over territories, in one case, when one crook, a boss, was required to get out of the way. His opponents had set up a Czech-made plastic explosive under his car. One kilogram of it would already have been overkill. But why fool around? It was estimated that about twenty kilograms of explosive were used. Only a hole about a meter deep was left in the place where car had been parked. Virtually no body parts were discovered, except the left arm, which had flown a hundred metres to a tennis court. It landed on the net, scaring to death the couple playing a game.

There were plenty of guns and explosives available; that was why the criminals did not fool around when counting their bills. When the Soviets were finally ordered home after sitting around for forty years, they sold machine guns and other weaponry from the train that took them home. The price was just a few bucks. Different explosives were also easily available.

"I'm innocent. The only reason I'm here is because I knew about the robbery and did not report it," Peter M. began his story. "I didn't do anything. I just did not rat them out. How could I? I would have had to prick my eyes and ears not to see or hear about the crime, because everybody I know is a criminal, breaking the law. I was just sitting in a car in front of the bank, but I did not go inside. How was I to know that they were robbing it? They told me 'wait here.' So I waited. Then they came running; they jumped in the car and said, 'drive fast.' So I did. They did it, not me. The money was in the other car anyway.

"All they got was forty thousand korun. Twelve million were supposed to be there according to the information we had. They went straight to the safe. All there was forty thousand in it. So they grabbed the forty thousand and ran. All twelve million were right there on the counter, packed nicely and ready to be transferred to a factory, and they didn't look. They sent a chopper after us, but the money was in the other car.

"Then they knocked on my door and asked me to come to the police station. They claimed we took twelve million. All we took was forty thousand. The police and the bank manager split the twelve million and placed the blame on us. I have been here for more than three years, and the boss is just a few doors down in another cell. The judges and investigators want their cut. They keep asking us where the twelve million is. How do I know where the police hid it?"

It was a very similar story to that of Giraffe. The officials thought that he had the money, so they kept him in, just like Peter. It made no difference how absurd the claim was. The police could do it and get away with it. I realized again that I was in a very bad situation. They also thought that I had big money—much more than I really had.

Peter and his friends had picked the wrong town to rob. The town sat among hills, and only one road crossed the town. It was easy for the police to track getaway cars, even though the cars went two different directions. The other disadvantage was that there were no clerks in the small-town bank, only a manager, who was everything—manager, clerk, and even caretaker. Twelve million was sitting behind the counter, ready to be transferred. A police chopper was to do the transferring. They were close by, heading to pick up the money; therefore, the crooks did not make it very far before being apprehended. The getaway car that went in the other direction was stopped by a police patrol. It was bad luck for the robbers, and good luck was on side of the police. It was easy for the bank manager to make the deal with the police. The police still transferred the money as planned—just to a different destination—and put the blame on the small-time crooks.

Before they had tried to make the big hit of twelve million, Peter, his boss, and some other bullies had been terrorizing small businesses in the city of Poprad and around it. The usual procedure went like this. The boss, who was the size of a gorilla himself, visited a small business with his two goons, who were the size of bulls in a bullfight amphitheatre in Spain.

"We need thirty thousand," the boss begins a friendly conversation.

"Sorry, I don't have it. The business is very slow," the owner tried to explain.

"Look, even a pig feeder," he pointed to one of his bullies, "and a cow manure mover came with me," he pointed to the other. "And do you know why they came with me? Because they want to get paid, and you say you have no money." While talking, he had closed in on the poor man, and his bullies followed. "You know who I am? I'm the boss." He was about to crack his head open with his forehead.

The poor man looked at him and his two bullies. He shat his pants, still claiming that he had no money. The smell of the production in his pants persuaded his visitors that he was telling the truth and really had no money. They gave him two weeks to get it.

As Peter said,

"We are not stupid cows like policemen. We are not going to hurt the man, if he really has no money. These bastards keep asking us where the money is after they took it. How should we know where they hid it?"

In his spare time between the hard work of blackmailing and extorting or robbing, the boss and his bulls spent time relaxing in a local casino. It was not cheap to loosen up in casinos these days that was why they had decided on a big-time score in the small-town bank with the big cash at the one destined time.

Usually the boss played, and the goons just watched and decorated him. Two goons stood behind him, making him look very important. Now and then, they gave him advice in a game, as they did one time when the boss was playing. Peter described the generosity of his boss.

"He [the boss] was playing roulette. I told him to put it on zero. He put one hundred korun on zero.

Trrrrrr ... zero. He won seventeen thousand. You know what he gave me? He bought me a beer. I was waiting for him to give me half, and he bought me a beer instead.

"Then he played a machine. I told him to set it on eight. *Blllll* ... eight. Eleven thousand. And you know what? He bought me half a shot of vodka. Twenty-eight thousand I won him, and he bought me a beer and half a shot, the dickhead. Now the big boss is in jail, and he is crying. The investigator was asking him questions, and I was showing him circles on my forehead, as if he was crazy, and he was saying, crying, 'look he is hitting his head.'"

He was tough and nasty on the outside and just the opposite on the inside. Jail changed people's personalities. Most likely, they had put me in a cell with Peter, hoping he would create fear in me; just the way, he and his goons had been doing around the city of Poprad. Just the opposite was the case. The same as the other prisoners, Peter was very polite to me. On top of that, he admitted to me that, as he noticed me facing the wall on my bed, crying, he himself was doing the same.

Nobody came to see him for over a year. His lawyer was demanding five thousand korun, just to come visit. After all, Peter was a rich man. He knew where twelve million was hidden. In reality, his family could not even afford the five thousand Korun for a lawyer to go to see him and get things moving. In the meantime, he was just waiting and waiting, just like so many other prisoners, for the miracle that his case would finally get to court.

Like almost everybody, Peter had also been taken to be examined by not one but two psychologists. When there was not much to go on in some cases, they used just psychologists as evidence against the defendants.

Here was the story of how Peter honestly described his encounter with the psychologists.

"I was with a psychologist—twice. One reminded me of someone stupid, and the other of someone stupid and ridiculous. He gave me a kind of 'haky-baky,' and asked what it reminded me of. There were some kinds of dots, so I said a crow or bat; he was so stupid. Then he gave me a bunch of kid's puzzle pieces so I could place them together. So are you crazy? What am I, some kind of kid that I'm going to play with these pieces? So I was placing those pieces and asking him, 'why did you give me pieces that do not fit? Can't you see that they do not fit?' He just flipped the pieces over, and they fit perfectly by themselves. I was looking at him as though at a stupid bull. Why did he ask me to place those pieces if he knew how to do it?"

Peter also had a message for the world, in case I ever got out of there: "I do admit that I have done many bad things but I swear that we took only forty thousand korun when we robbed that bank. We have never seen any of the twelve million that went missing, and the blame was placed on us. I swear that this is true."

CHAPTER TWENTY-THREE

If You Were an Honest Communist, You Suffered. If You Were Not a Communist, You Suffered Even More

Would a Slovak policeman jump in a sewer? Yes, if he was ordered by a communist.

Another month went by, and the time for a once a month visit approached. I was looking forward to seeing Bibka. I was shocked when I entered the visitor booth. Only my mom was sitting there. I had wanted to spare her the disgrace of visiting me in jail. I had not wanted her to see me like that. But Demjan had arranged it so that only my mom could visit me.

It was in line with what Mr. X and some other prisoners had told me. They would pick up the most vulnerable member of the family to see the poor prisoner when he was in bad shape. The prisoner would beg the family to pay whatever it took to get him out of the hell he was in. After something like that, the family would do anything it took to get its loved one out. Some would sell everything, including the house.

My mom was already prepared. A gypsy nicknamed Belavi (his real name was Milan Tancos) approached her and told her,

"Your son will not survive. He will not come out alive. But if you pay five million korun, Demjan will drop the charge. He sent me to let you know." Belavi had also approached another two members of my family with the same message.

In prison, my mom was wearing a dark blue, winter coat. She had owned it for many, many years. She took very good care of it, so it looked like it had when it was new if not better. When winter arrived, she took it out of the closet, where it had hung throughout the summer, and she spread it out nicely on the chesterfield to keep it free of wrinkles.

She could not hear as well as she could when she was younger, but she did not require a hearing aid, because she could hear us as long as we talked a little bit louder. But there in jail, through those little holes in the glass wall, it was very difficult for her to hear me. I had to scream full blast into those little holes for her to hear me. No doubt there was a bug in the booth, since there was already interest from officials to know what I was going to do next.

I was trying to hide my poor mental and physical condition.

"Hello, Mama. How are you?"

"Hi, Dodku, son." "Dodku" was my nickname. My mom had been calling me that all my life, but only when I was a good boy. When I was bad, she called me Dodu or Jozef.

"Why are you alone?"

"'B,'" she said. She was referring to the fact that I was being punished with more restrictions by

section 67b.

"But 'B' does not mean that only one person can come. It only means that they will listen to what we say."

"Investigator Demjan told me that only I could come."

"Demjan is a liar."

"I went to see him, and he told me that only I could come."

"He is a liar. What else did he tell you?"

"He told me that the court wants money. I want to ask you if we can sell your car and your house. I will also sell my house. I will go to live with Borca in Michalovce, and Nadka also told me that I can live with her. Milan can live at his work. They want five million."

"Do not pay them one halier [a halier was the Slovak penny]. They are crooks. They are liars."

"He told me that if you don't pay, you will not get out of here. I don't want you to die here. You look very poorly." Tears began rolling down her cheeks. She turned her face to the side to wipe them quickly, as if she was trying to hide them from me. She had always been a proud, respectable lady, but she was broken down this time.

"Please, Mama, do not pay them anything at all. I have done nothing wrong at all. They are all gypsies, prostitutes. The police talked them in to saying things about me. The police are even bigger liars than gypsies. Tell Milan to play you that tape, then you will see."

"What about Jana? Demjan told me—"

"Demjan is a stinky liar. He knows that it is not true. He is a liar and a crook."

I was very, very upset.

Imagine how my mom would have felt when he lied straight to her face that I had done something to that child. She knew the child and my fatherly feelings for her. My mom, Jana, and Bibiana—we had even gone to the circus together. We were like family for that child, and he lied to her face, saying that I had done something and that only money would get me out. Demjan himself found out that there was nothing wrong going on and the psychologist Stancak confirmed, my total innocence. And he went right ahead and lied to my mom's face. The man had no conscience at all. A total psychopathic liar. A man like that should never have been born.

I was screaming full blast so that she could hear me and also because I was very upset. My yelling echoed throughout the whole hall. All the visitors and prisoners looked my way from time to time.

"Demjan is a liar, and policemen are also liars" echoed throughout the room. The man in charge and a guard walked in to check on what was going on, why all the screaming.

"My mom cannot hear me well through these holes; that is why I must yell. Demjan sent only her on purpose, because he knew she would have difficulty hearing me."

"We could take them to booth one or two. There are telephones there, and they could talk through them," the guard suggested.

"But we are not set up there," the man in charge explained to his colleague. He got the message. I did too. The bug had not been arranged for those booths, so they would not be able to record our conversation. They decided to leave us there.

"I believe you, son. I also did before, but Demjan said it, so I had to ask. Stop writing those complaints, and tell Biba to stop. Demjan told me that it will only do you damage, if you complain."

"Do not listen to Demjan. He is a crook and a liar. He made up all of this against me. Tell Milan to play you that tape of the gypsies. You will see."

At the beginning, I had not wanted her to hear those tapes, because of the vulgarities that were also against her. Now, that Demjan had painted me with black, it was time that she knew what kind of partners he used against me.

"Dodku, son, you look very bad. I'm very worried about you. Are you going to be all right? Do you have enough food to eat?"

"Yes, momka. Bibka sends me sausages every month."

"Hang on, son. I will fight for you. Tomorrow, I will go after them again."

"Just do not pay them any money. Remember, they are all criminals, with Demjan in charge. Just listen to that tape. You will see who his partners are, and he is not any better. He is much worse."

I was very upset after we said good-bye. *Will I see her again?* crossed my mind. When you are in your eighties as she was, you never know. But I knew what a fighter she had been all her life. I was sure she was not going to die while her son was in disgrace, sitting in jail. She had something to do, and she would do it, even if it would be the last thing she did. She would not give up, until she was done. Later, I found out that that was exactly the way she did it. She had been a fighter all her life, which was not easy at all, because it was always a fight against mean, corrupt officials, like the one she was up against then. They had called themselves communists then, and now they claimed they were whoever. One things was for sure: they were corrupt all the way from the top to the bottom.

My mom, Maria, was born in 1916 in a very small village in eastern Slovakia called Senne. She lived through times when that part of Slovakia was under Hungarian government, so she also learned the Hungarian language fluently.

My dad, Michal, was born in 1906 in a very small village called Jesenov. He learned his trade by working for his brother Jozef (we called him Jovzi, read Jovzhi) in a small town called Secovce. My dad married his first wife, Alzbeta (read Alshbeta), and they had a daughter by the same name. We called her Bozena (read Bozhena). His first wife died of tuberculosis.

Later, he married my mom. I was their first child. I was born in our little, rented house.

After my dad finished learning his trade as a baker of sweets, they opened a business in the small town of Trebisov, which was just sixteen kilometres from Secovce. Both brothers produced sweet pies, different sweet cookies, wedding cakes, and of course, ice cream. They sold them in their own stores.

The beginning was not easy for my mom and dad. They rented a three-room house from Mr. Hospodar on a small street called Hodvabna. Just across the back property line, they rented a store on Main Street called T. G. Masarika. The landlord's name was Mr. Hruza. He produced cement products, like big bridge pipes, pig-feeding containers called *valovs*, different rain-catching containers, and other cement articles needed in construction and around dwellings.

In our rented house, my mom and dad slept on a large bed called the marriage bed. I, as a baby, slept between them on mom's side, and my sister, Bozena, slept on the couch that adjoined our bed where our feet were.

The live-in caretaker, Hanca, from the village of Cejkov slept on the sofa in the kitchen, which was the middle room. The back room was the bakery, which doubled as a bedroom for the apprentice, Jozko Klima, who was also from Cejkov. He slept on the fold-up bed, which had small wheels and was wheeled out into the kitchen during the daytime to make room in the bakery. Later, another apprentice from Cejkov joined in. His name was Jozko Koval. It was a tiny house, but we were close, and we were happy. Only an outhouse was available as the toilet for everybody.

My mom sold in her store whatever Dad produced in his bakery. Money was very short. All ingredients were bought on the so-called "book," which could be compared with today's credit card. That means that, for whatever Dad bought, Mr. Ivan, who was the owner of the neighbouring grocery store, marked in his book how much Dad owed. Once my folks made some money, they paid, and Mr. Ivan marked it off. No signatures or interest was necessary. My dad never looked in the "book." Everybody trusted everybody. Rent was done the same way.

"Pay when you can," Mr. Hospodar and Mr. Hruza told my mom. Not once did they ask any questions if my parents were late with paying when they were not able to do so.

It was a society you would just love to discover today. But it will never return again.

It had looked like everything would be all right, and it would have been, if Hitler had not decided to take over the world.

Soon Germans were passing through Slovakia on the way to Russia. The Second World War was here. I was born right in it. People were evacuating wherever they thought it would be safer. My parents chose Torona, a small little wine village close to the Hungarian border. Many people tried to escape the horrors of the war to wine-producing areas, because large wine cellars were available for people to hide in. I was one year old. My sister Bozena was five.

My dad asked a local farmer and soon, his two horses were pulling his farm buggy. They took whatever fit on it, mainly feather down blankets, some food, something to wear, and something to drink. All business equipment was left behind. My mom had me bundled in her arms. She sat in front beside the farmer. My older sister sat right behind them, facing back.

My dad and some other men walked behind, because there wasn't space on the buggy, which was fully loaded with the most needed, valuable belongings.

I was just over a year old, and I still remember turning my head to be able to see the horses. They were dark, almost black.

In Torona, we all occupied one basement room together with the family who owned the basement.

I remember white angora rabbits our hostesses were raising for valuable fur. People were sleeping all over in the basement room, some on makeshift beds made out of wooden fruit boxes, some on boxed benches called *safaren* (read shafaren).

I also remember heavy rain, and water filling the whole floor of the basement. I was the first to wake up in my baby bed, which was called a *koliska*, and the floor was not there anymore. It was covered with water. A big pot floating around the basement room stuck in my memory. I started to yell as if they were killing a pig. Everybody in the room jumped. My mom ran to save the most important thing in the room—me. Men grabbed pails and began splashing water out of the basement through the open door. Water was all over and was returning back into the basement. The water acted like the good soldier Svejk (read Shvejk). When they kicked him out of the pub through the front door, he returned through the back door and vice versa.

The river Ondava had caused a tremendous flood all over. Later, my dad took an old wooden washtub and used it as a boat, floating me around in the water where the yard once used to be before.

In the mean time, the German army passed through Slovakia all the way to the Soviet Union. It had seemed like it was a good idea to move to Torona, as it was very peaceful there. The Germans passed through eastern Slovakia easily with very little resistance, using main roads, which they paved as they went. They also used railroad transportation. On the way, Germans stopped in our rented house in Trebisov and felt at home, helping themselves to anything they needed.

It was a totally different story when the Red Army began pushing the Germans back home. The German soldiers chose country roads and forest areas where there was a better chance of hiding and surviving. That time, they also passed through small towns, including Torona, where we had hoped to hide from the war. The Soviets were following them and pushing the Germans in front of them.

The Germans ran through Torona first. They looked very young, tired, and afraid. They asked politely for some food. My mom was making potatoes pancakes called *loksa* (read loksha). She offered them some. They loved them with buttermilk. Hitler had left them without any supplies toward the end of the war.

"Dankeschön," they thanked her, before they left in a hurry.

Once Germans passed into the west from Torona, the Soviets dug in their makeshift rocket launchers called *katusa* (read cathusha) just east of the village. They were blasting nearby forests and fields with rockets, even though the Germans were long gone. *Katusa* rockets flew just over the village. Everybody ran to the basements to hide. I was getting old by then, reaching almost four years old. All my life so far, I had lived through war. Looking through the small basement window, it was a fantastic sight. The sky was lit by the Soviet rockets flying over.

Suddenly, my mom realized that I was missing. She looked out through the little window and froze. I was standing in the middle of the yard, enjoying the fireworks, not understanding why the people were running and hiding from such beauty. My mom ran out, grabbed me around the waist, and ran back into the basement. I received my first real licking and got the message that she really meant it. "No more watching fireworks outside."

Soon the Soviets, who were following the Germans, were in the village. They had different manners than the Germans.

"*Davaj casy*" (give me your watch) was something nobody would forget. The Soviets were mesmerized by the fact that the watch was so small, and it was ticking. Never mind that it also showed the time. There were happy, smiling faces as they listened to the sound of it. Only afterward did they look at what was on the stove and begin eating without saying "*bu*." After supper, they all crashed on whatever was available. The highest ranking soldier got the bed that my mom, my dad, and I were sharing. The officer didn't even take his muddy boots off. With all that mud and his dirty coat, he crashed on the white sheets that my mom often washed by hand in an old, wooden washtub outside. It was the same washtub my dad had used to boat me around during the flood.

We all spent the night in the barn, sleeping on the hay. Fortunately for us, our night guests could not spend more time visiting. In the early morning, they left, chasing their enemies, leaving muddy beds behind. My mom lost her wristwatch in the process, but Dad still had his pocket one, because the Soviets had not seen it. I still have that watch. It was a much prized gift from my dad.

Our house in Trebisov met a similar fate. The only difference was that there was nobody there at all. The Germans had helped themselves to anything they chose on the way to Russia, and then again, when they were running back home. After them, it was the Soviets who were following the Germans.

Returning back home after the war, we found the whole house had been ransacked, the windows were broken, and most of the equipment was gone. Starting again from the scratch was the only way to survive.

The apprentice Josko and the home helper, Hanca, both from Cejkov, were back to help. Things began to move ahead after the war.

Things were falling nicely into place. Even electricity was installed in the old house. No more oil lamps. And my dad bought a three-door electric oven. No more big, brick oven to be heated up by big pieces of wood called *shahovina* (read shadowing). Even a big, electric mixer to mix large quantities of dough was delivered.

My dad got himself a new bicycle, completed with a carrier. In Kosice, my mom bought me a little red car that was powered by my feet moving pedals back and forth. It was the only one of its kind in the town. All the kids in the neighbourhood were jealous. Only my best friends got to drive it.

I was suspicious when Josko, Dad's apprentice, asked me if I want him to give me a ride on my dad's new bicycle. All that time I had been begging him, and he had kept refusing. Suddenly, he came and asked me. I had no idea what the scoop was, but I did not worry about it. I was glad to be able to get a ride on the carrier of my dad's new bicycle. We went all around town, all the way around a large, beautiful park. He was not in a hurry to get back at all. In the past, when I managed to persuade him to give me a ride sometimes, he would have gone around the block, and that was it. Not this time. He took his time.

When we finally returned home, there was a baby's cry coming from the bedroom. My mom was in the bed, and baby Sona was lying beside her, already wrapped up in a white blanket. Later, it came to me why Josko offered to give me a ride. Baba, the midwife, was about to deliver my sister, so they needed me out of the house. I did not mind. I was glad, because I got a long ride on Dad's bicycle and a new sister in the process. The bad part about this was that it was the last time Jozko gave me such a long ride on Dad's bicycle.

The communists began snooping around after the war. People heard stories from the Soviet Republic about what they were all about. All we knew was that they hated everybody who was doing well. Suddenly, my uncle disappeared. He was Dad's brother Jovzi, the one from whom my dad learned his trade. He was the only one in the whole town of Secovce who had a two-story house. The store was in front, and the bedrooms were above it. That was a perfect setup for the local communists to be jealous of and for them to hate the owner. The buzz was that the local communists had requested that Soviets kidnap him in order to get him out of the way. All we knew was that Soviets knocked on his door in the middle of the night and took him away. My mom was worried about my dad. She thought he might be next. It did not happen. We did not own any property at the time. Everything was rented.

They took my uncle all over—apparently to Poland, the Ukraine, and Russia. There was a small chance that we would ever see him again.

But a miracle happened. One night, he simply walked in. His wife, Anna (we called her Anula), could not believe her eyes. He would not say where he had been or what had happened. He was not allowed to mention what he had gone through.

When my dad asked him about it, he only said,

"You do not want to know, because if you know about it, you may also be gone, and you may never come back."

Nobody knows if he ever told his wife, because she did not even tell it to her own children, my cousins. Recently, I asked Michal (we called him Miky), their son and my cousin, about it. His knowledge about it was very limited. He told me that his dad had not wanted to talk about it.

I have come to my own conclusion. The way I knew my uncle Jovzi, he was a hardworking but also highly pleasant, intelligent gentleman. Same as my dad. Both brothers were highly respected in the whole community. They were also very pleasant to be around; therefore, whatever the local communists had requested that the Soviets do with him, they had just refused to do it. They could not miss the fact that this is a man who would not hurt a fly. So they let him go, and he walked all the way back. Logically, they ordered him to keep his mouth shut. And he did. He was very lucky that he was not one of the forty million people that the dogma of Lenin and Stalin murdered.

Young people were getting married after the war. Wedding cakes were going like hotcakes. Children were born like the white mice. That made greater needs for birthday cakes. More than a hundred cakes were needed on some weekends. The cakes were all over our rooms. Ice cream was sold nonstop during long, hot summer days.

Mom was saving money. She ran a strict family budget.

One day, we moved to a large house. It used to be owned by a Jewish family that, unfortunately, did not make it back after the war. Three doors down the road, there was another nice house. A family with young twin girls used to live there. They were beautiful, well-dressed young children. Nobody, except their parents, could tell them apart from each other They disappeared with their parents. They were also Jewish. My dad told me they had left for Palestine. I sure hoped that they made it there safely. Now I know that they were taken by Nazis.

Our new house was a large, L-shaped building. Two rooms facing Main Street were my mom's store. Two big rooms in the back were my dad's bakery. There was a three-bedroom apartment in the middle for all of us.

There weren't flushing toilets yet, but we had two outhouses—one for our family only and one for the apprentices. Dad's brother Juraj lived with us, working for my dad. Mom also had help in her store. My grandma moved in with us and helped in the kitchen. Things were just like a good story in a book ... only with a bad end.

In the beginning of the 1950s, there were signs of another nightmare. The Slovak communists established themselves and began destroying everything that was functioning. They called it building socialism. In fact, they were robbing everybody who owned something and destroying everything in the process. They called it nationalization—meaning to bring everything under their control. They took everything from everybody. My parents were no exception.

Two policemen were at our door one morning. Both had been imported from small towns. They had some authorization stating that, in the name of the republic (meaning, at the wish of the communist party), they were to execute a search of the property. They were to look for anything the communists could use. My parents had been expecting it to come. The communists had done it already to other families.

The older policeman was a real bastard. He was vulgar to my dad, as you can imagine. My dad had to do all the dirty jobs, like shovelling coal that was piled outside or replacing firewood in the woodshed in order to see if there was something hidden underneath. They piled everything valuable in the front yard. All the equipment from Mom's store and from Dad's bakery was marked with numbers in white paint. They made an inventory of everything. My dad and mom were informed that everything marked had been nationalized and that it must not be moved.

It was a blow to the lives of my folks.

It was the first time that I had ever seen my dad upset and even mad. When the policeman gave him a pick and yelled at him to dig into the coal outside, I was standing beside my dad.

He asked me,

"Should I kill him?"

I was eleven years old and felt that there was something really wrong. Nobody since has ever been able to tell me that a good communist exists. That situation always comes to my mind when somebody mentions a communist.

There was my dad, a hardworking, respectable citizen, and there was this no-good bastard, imported from some village—a makeshift policeman, using his uniform to disgrace my dad. Demjan who was doing the same to me, sure reminded me of him. My dad had never sworn once, had never stolen anything, had never broken the law. He had never disciplined us as children. That was always my mom's job. Only once did my dad ever kick my ass. It was later, when I tried to tell him what I had just learned at school. He did not discuss it with me. He just opened the door, grabbed me by the collar of my jacket, and kicked my butt. It did not hurt at all, because I was always physically advanced. I flew out the door and landed on my feet as a cat would. But I got the message loud and clear, "Never try to tell Dad that there was anything good that communists had ever done."

My parents were devastated after the search of our property.

You wake up one morning, and you own your company and your home, and by sunset, you own nothing. The store and the sweets-producing company were now owned by communists. As well as all the equipment that my parents had worked for years to put together was ours no more. We were still in our house, but it wasn't ours anymore. Try to imagine how it could feel. We had been robbed of everything by people who had nothing, and they could steal from us just because they had signed on to be members of the party.

They had confiscated everything, except our personal clothing and some pots. But they had confiscated the basics, like sugar, flour, and even lard, which had been produced from our pork through an official permit issued by the communists themselves. The little typewriter that we as kids had been learning to type on was also confiscated.

My brother was just a baby, crying in my mom's arms as she ran around, trying to explain that they had no right to rob us like that. They loaded it all on a big cargo buggy that was pulled by a Zetor tractor.

To top it all off, they served us an order to clear out of our home, because they needed the place for a policeman. Most likely, it was the one who was doing the search. Nobody mentioned where we—a mom, dad, and four children—were to go. It looked like, besides our business, we were also losing the roof over our heads.

Right from the beginning, the communists believed that they could do anything they chose. Humans meant nothing to them, because they were not humans themselves. The Slovak people had to do what they were told. The mighty Soviets were behind all the dirty work. The sad thing was that it was the Slovaks who were committing atrocities against their own people. The Soviets were only backing them up, giving them an example, and providing them with confidence. The Soviets were declaring themselves freedom providers, because they had chased the Germans back home. They had chased the Germans, but they had brought Czechoslovakia, and other countries that they called Soviet satellites, too many decades of total communist suppression.

Some people had already obeyed similar orders and left their homes behind. But not my mom. She was not about to sit down and watch as everything disappeared into the hands of those bastards. She yelled over my brother's cries that she would take it to the court and show them. The policemen did not take it seriously, because nobody had tried it as yet.

But she did it. The court house for the whole district was in the town of Secovce. My mom represented herself. She had a list of everything the police had confiscated. She also described the arrogant way they had gone about the whole situation. People did not think that my mom had a chance.

The judge was older and still from the era of democracy. Not only did he cancel the eviction order, he also ordered the return of all the confiscated belongings and ordered an apology from the policemen and the officials involved.

"Is this the way you have done this? Is this the way you show respect to working people? What gives you right to have this kind of arrogance?" the judge asked the policeman who had done the search.

"I was only following the orders of the communist party." The policeman was surprised that there was still a law above the communists in the country.

"If they ordered you to jump in a sewer, would you still do it? Shame on you. Something like this is not going to happen as long as I'm sitting on this bench." And it did not happen, but not for very long.

Word spread around town about what my mom had done and what the judge in Secovce had dared to do. He had stood up to communists and to the police.

Soon, the communists realized their mistake. They had to replace the judge and create new laws if they wanted to continue their dirty work. Soon, they installed a judge who danced when they whistled. For more than forty years, the judges of Slovakia were just puppets dancing to the communist tune. Now the judges were dancing to their own whistle—the tune of money.

But really. Would a policeman jump into a sewer if ordered by a communist? Most likely yes. They brought all kinds of policemen from small villages to do the dirty work for them. They were so happy that they didn't have to shovel manure anymore that they would do anything to keep it that way.

Some people would jump into a sewer for an entirely different reason. But about that later.

My mom left the visiting booth, encouraging me to hang on, because she would fight for me.

CHAPTER TWENTY-FOUR

A Prisoner Hung Himself. Or Did He?

Where do they use proof that does not prove anything? In Slovakia.

It was a terrible time for me. Christmas arrived and New Year's. My intention had been to spend the holiday season with my mom and my family before returning home to Canada. I had been looking forward to eating my mom's sauerkraut and dried mushroom (*kozare*) soup, which was the best soup I had ever tasted. Instead, I was in cell with two prisoners, eating porch-style food from a beat-up aluminum pot. I was lucky Bibka had sent me some smoked sausages and some other goodies, like Turkish Honey and other food, to keep me alive.

To keep sane, I wrote one complaint after another and studied Slovak law. The more I learned, the more I was shocked. Nobody in the justice system went by the law. They could not even understand simple sentences. They were a bunch of primitives with academic titles or high police ranks. Take Investigator Demjan. He had the rank of mayor in front of his name. I was in the function of an officer, as the commander of a troop when I had been in the Czechoslovak compulsory military service. I considered Demjan a total disgrace to any rank of soldiers. In my troop, he could never have provided any responsible duty, other than washing the cement floors in the military washroom. And there he was, sitting as a mayor, using all illegal means to frame people and calling that an investigation. And for this, he was getting promoted in the ranks of officers. He was a disgrace to the human population, not to mention to the officers.

258

On January 7, 1999, I was escorted downstairs from my cell. My lawyer, JUDr. Fercakova, Investigator Demjan, and the typist Ms. Volochova were there waiting. It was to be a so-called study of the investigative file. It was done when an investigator finished his investigation. The prisoner had a chance to look over the file, and his objections were written down.

Amazingly, Demjan had put together almost three hundred pages. They all had holes in them and were tied together with a string. The cover was a little bit thicker with a stamp in the top left corner that reading "District Office of Investigation - Police Force 07501 TREBISOV." In the middle in bold letters was "INVESTIGATIVE FILE # VS:OUV - 600/10 - 98. At first glance, it appeared to be a normal document, but only if there were no laws or regulations. By law, every process, and every page of the file had to be registered in the book of the Office of Registration. None of the documents were numbered, stamped, or marked, when they were presented as having been filed in the book of registration. That made them all invalid and open to manipulation and falsification.

I was standing up, turning the pages and looking down at the documents, trying to remember as much as possible. Looking straight down helped me to remember pages, just like with a camera, without reading every word of it but recognizing the contents of the documents.

I was totally shocked when I discovered how many illegal changes Demjan had made. Wherever his name had been signed, there were illegal changes. I was shocked and pissed off, but I kept my mouth shut as much as possible. I had a good reason for it. Last time, I had yelled at him, bringing up all the illegal steps he had taken, and now I could see that he had fixed them up. Whatever I had said was missing, he had added it to the file, and what I had said was against the law, he had corrected. Those that he could not correct had been removed from the file, and the copies I had had were confiscated from me. What open corruption. He was able to do it in front of my eyes and then claim that it had never happened. A creature like that should never have been born.

The whole file had not been sealed, as was required by law. The strings hung free where the official seal should have been attached to them. Complete anarchy.

Not one single person stood the chance of receiving fair justice.

I was informed that the child Jana Visokaiova had been dropped from my case.

I noticed that all documents that were proof of my innocence were missing. I had requested in writing that the audio cassettes and their contents, which the investigator had conveniently dropped, be made part of the file as required by Slovak law.

Demjan had left out my written complaints and requests dated October 30 and December 13 and 30 of 1998, as well as November 16, 1998. Other documents, which had been mailed to the provincial court, had not been included. In other words, he had left out everything that was proof of my innocence or proof of his corruption and the corruption of the justice system as a whole. The audio recording, which was proof that I had been blackmailed by their so-called witnesses, had also been left out.

I had also requested that they bring the Book of Registry to the trial to point out that none of the documents had been registered; therefore, they were not valid and not admissible in court. The Book of Registry was never brought to court.

Again, I brought up the fact that the whole charge was false and primarily that my imprisonment was illegal, because it was over the time limit without any legal documents and had been done illegally.

When I noticed all those illegal steps, I had to decide how to go about it, because I knew that everything would be fixed up and denied, unless I had proof. I requested a copy of the whole investigative file. Demjan was shocked at first when I requested it. Most likely, nobody had done that before. He looked at my lawyer as if to ask what to do now. She also looked confused a little, but I had the law ready.

"Here is the law by which I have the right to obtain a copy of the whole file." I showed her the paragraph in the law book I had with me.

"He has the right to it by law," she translated for Demjan. Of course, I had to pay for it.

"I want it here by tomorrow," I added. I was thinking that it would give him less time to manipulate it. Whatever he might decide needed to be fixed, he would have one night to fix it.

I also requested that my first lawyer be present at the hearing. Not that I needed him. I noticed that his signature had also been forged by Demjan, together with mine and others, so I was going to ask him about it in court and have it recorded in the court document. That was the only reason I had requested that he be there.

Bibiana picked up the copy of the file to bring it to me. She went to the police station, where Demjan was all upset and making the copy of the file. He was all red in the face, threatening that I would see how they were going to get me.

That same evening (January 7, 1999), I wrote a two-page complaint, which I mailed to the office of the district prosecutor and the provincial prosecutor, in which I named all the laws broken by Demjan. I also requested another prosecutor, because, as I stated, all the broken laws had taken place under the watchful eyes of the so-called prosecutor mgr. Maros Sabo.

I mailed those complaints by registered mail. The registered stubs were not delivered back to me as they usually were. I inquire about them the next morning. The warden Mojo informed me that my mail was going by slow mail, so stubs were not available for now. I asked what he meant by slow mail. He could not explain what it meant. He just said something about that it had to be censored before it could be mailed. I reminded him that official letters were not allowed to be censored. He refused to explain further.

My lawyer, Ms. Fercakova, also filed a complaint, dated January 13, 1999, in which she pointed out the fact that Investigator Demjan had left out all my proof, promised to place them back in, and had not done so, even though he was required by the law to do it. He had also taken other illegal steps, promised to fix them up, and fail to do so. It was a nice way to say that he was a liar and a cheat.

Neither the district nor the provincial prosecutors' offices replied on our complaints and requests.

My letters were not mailed for weeks until the Canadian consul came to visit; I gave him copies of the letters that the prison officials had refused to mail.

Maros Sabo had signed the indictment. And an indictment it was. Oh my God. Idiots in a mental institution in Garani could have made it much better.

Investigator Demjan had dropped all allegations concerning the child Jana Visokaiova during the investigation, but they appeared again in the indictment. The law was broken. He had dropped them, because the whole family, including Jana, was testifying that I was innocent, and they pointed out police brutality and illegal activities.

Again, the whole indictment had been formulated, as if I had already been convicted. Whoever had written it had no idea about Slovak law, which forbade that kind of formulation. More laws were broken. No doubt, it had been written by the same person who had written other papers in the file. Demjan had signed all those documents. That person was totally out of his mind, as far as the law was concerned.

The false allegations that had been fabricated by Demjan and written in the first, original false charge had virtually disappeared and were replaced by other lies. Only the gypsies who had been blackmailing me were left, otherwise there was not a single one witness or piece of evidence against me. None!

In spite of the fact that the whole case connected with the child Jana had been dropped, later she had been written in as "not straight proof" in indictment. "Not straight proof" didn't even exist in the justice system. Demjan had not found any normal proof; therefore, he had listed something like "abnormal proof" or proof that did not prove anything.

There was not a single piece of evidence to collaborate anything that was written in the indictment. Somebody had just sat down and written total garbage. In order to not have an empty indictment, they had listed as evidence all those documents that had already been dropped by Demjan. The names of the dropped witnesses were listed against me, in spite of the fact that every one of them had testified that I had done nothing wrong. Of course, it was illegal.

How could somebody explain to anybody else this sentence, "His level of danger for society is established by the actions of the defendant who, by his conduct, grossly broke with the interests of society, consisting of protecting the moral development of underage persons, the life and health of citizens, and also their property. Where did that come from? Nobody knew. Whoever wrote it did not understand the meaning of sentences and did not remember what he had written in previous pages.

One sentence read that I was a danger to society, and the next sentence read that I was positively regarded by society and had never been charged before. The first page read that I was unemployed; the last (ninth page) read that I was employed as a freelance artist. My case was full of crap like this; it was beyond explanation.

All of the listed junk in the indictment was proof that I was totally innocent, and whoever had written it was a total idiot.

Signed under all of it was Mgr. Maros Sabo. I was suspicious that somebody had written those nuisances for him. It would take a total idiot to make up that kind of crap, and Sabo had not struck me as one. The only senseless, stupid idiot of that calibre that I could come up with was Jan Danko, former MP. He was definitely the biggest idiot in the district of Trebisov, and Jan Demjan, the investigator, could be right after him. While I had tons of proofs of Demjan's corruption, I had none of Danko's. It was only my intuition. He always hid behind somebody. Only if there was a normal investigation would somebody have named that Danko was really behind all of this.

The whole indictment amounted to nine pages, but in reality, it was only two pages. If you subtracted everything that was repeated twice, which they usually did when they had nothing to go on, and if you subtracted the first page, where there was just the name of prosecutor's office, my name, and my address, and if you took away those statements that had been officially dropped and were there illegally, you would end up with less than two pages.

The indictment had been dated January 7, 1999, and it had been delivered to the District court on January 18. After that, I was waiting for my hearing. A stretch of time followed. I received the official date of my hearing, which was set for February 18, 1999. It did not happen. The next one was to be March 4. It was also cancelled. Another was set for March 11. That one finally took place. It had taken them more than two months from the time of the indictment (the whole two legal pages of it) until I was taken to court.

All that waiting and all the postponements were very hard on me. Reading the false indictment and responses to my complaints had a disastrous effect on my mental health, which in turn had negative consequences on my health. When you realize that you are dealing with total creeps and that there is nobody who can control them, you really start to worry where it is going to lead.

My case was assigned to a new judge, JUDr. Milan Jurko, who was to be my presiding judge. I had no idea who he was, but I did not think that he could be any worse than the bloody brother, Jan Milko, who I had had until then. Another good sign that he might be little bit better was that his first name was not Jan, as were the names of the three stooges who had been involved in my case so far. They were bloody brothers Judge Jan Milko, Investigator Jan Demjan, and the former MP, Jan Danko.

I decided to apply for bail then. I was losing my health in there, and I knew that I could do more if I stayed alive.

The new judge, Milan Jurko, set the bail at 100,000 korun (about $4,000, which was about five years of a Slovak worker's salary in 1999.) My family raised the money, and my brother Milan deposited it with the court.

The presiding judge, Jurko, wrote the official release from prison, dated February 16, 1999. As of that date, I was officially released from prison but only on paper. In reality, they kept me in. Somebody (maybe Danko) had arranged, that I would not be let out.

When questions arose about why I was still in jail, since I had been officially released, somebody (Jan Danko) visited Judge Jan Popovec more than a month later (March 11, 1999). He wrote that he had a secret proceeding of the provincial court, where he had decided that I would be kept in. By secret proceeding, he meant that nobody was present, only him.

He used some already dropped, which meant nonexistent, accusations.

The question was why he took more than a month to come up with this masterpiece, when Slovak law prescribed that that kind of decision must be made immediately, without delay.

Right in his paperwork, it stated that the written objection to my release was nonexistent; the reason for objection was never given, and the name of the prosecutor who objected to my release was unknown. Not even the communists could come up with a more outrageous proceeding.

Slovak law section 148 paragraph 1c T.P. is quite clear that the superior organ should refuse a complaint when it is not reasoned. Provincial Judge Popovec accepted the nonexistent complaint completely.

Only they know what the judge received from Danko for that favour. Some claimed it was a fat envelope. The others said that a couple bottles of Vodka would do the trick, because the old drunk Popovec always had some bottles in the fridge in his office. Nobody knew for sure. The only one thing that was certain was that Judge Popovec had proceeded against the law. Another thing was for sure: the first name of Judge Popovec was Jan, and that tells it all. I no longer had three stooges in my head but four.

Can you imagine how I felt when I received that kind of crap?

I heard a story of how one prisoner hung himself on the gater. It happened overnight while his three cellmates were sleeping. It sounded very improbable to me. I knew that prisoners hung themselves from time to time, but not that way. In all the time I was in there, not a single night did I sleep normally. The stress would not allow you to sleep in the usual way. All night, guards came to the door, opened the peephole, turned the lights on, and looked inside. They turned the lights on and off, even though there were plenty of lights shining in from the outside, because the yard was brightly lit like a sunny day. Even when they were three or four doors away, I could hear them coming.

Every single prisoner I talked to said the same. None could sleep, and they could all hear everything that moved. How could the boy tear his bedsheets, make a rope out of it, hang himself on the gater, and have nobody in the cell notice it? I had my suspicions, and later, I discovered that I was right. I was talking to a prisoner who was very familiar with the situation. I will only adjust his story so it will be not possible to identify who he was. Otherwise, he would be a dead man. He begged me to make sure that nobody would recognize who he was.

"Of course, they (the cellmates) would hear him hang himself. But they could not. He himself did not notice that he was hanging himself. The guards had mixed so much sleeping medication in their food that they could not wake them up until noon the next day. The poor boy. He had no idea what happened to him. The guards hanged him while he was sound asleep."

"Why did they do it?" I wanted to know.

"Politics. Order from the outside. First, they used him to do their dirty job, and then they got rid of him and locked him in jail, so he could not talk. But he began talking anyway. They decided to shut him up permanently. The new government of Mr. Dzurinda had begun asking some questions. He was willing to testify against the old government of Meciar in connection with a kidnapping and murder. They arranged to murder him right in jail. The idea of murdering someone in jail did not go over well, in spite of the fact that it was labelled suicide. But during Meciar's rule anything went. All witnesses to the Remias murder are dead or missing. Now they let you out first and murder you out there. Be careful, if you ever get out of here. They will wait for you out there," my cellmate finished his story.

Ever since then, I never drank the tea that was served, and I always smelled the food for chemicals, just to be on the safe side.

Just when I was on the verge of total desperation, a little hope blinked at me.

"Get a clean shirt and pants; the consul is coming to visit," Mojo informed me.

Contact with the outside world was restricted, so I had no idea that Bibiana had informed the Canadian consulate in Prague, Czech Republic, about my sad situation.

The Canadian consul had requested a visit, but Judge Jurko had refused it. In Trebisov, they still lived with the belief that they could do anything they chose. It took some time before the Canadian consulate realized that it had the right to visit me anytime it chose according to international agreements the Slovaks had signed.

A date was set, and I could not wait to see him. Hopefully, I would be able to tell him what was going on there.

I had written a letter, dated January 31, 1999, to the Canadian consulate in Prague, Czech Republic. I knew I was taking big chances with my life, because I described what was going on. My physical and emotional situation was so bad that I did not care what would happen to me. If the letter got to them, then okay. If not, then there was nothing I could do. I also mailed a copy to Bibiana, with a request that she mail it to the consulate. Another copy, I tried to arrange another way. I cannot describe it, because I want that person to live.

Here are some of the most important sentences from the five-page letter:

Canadian Consulate, Mickiewiczova 6, Prague 125 33

Dear Consul,

I'm afraid for my life and even more for the life of my fiancee Bibiana Gombosova. Please ask Mr. Pitner, as I have asked him many times, to please arrange for our safety before it is too late. We are afraid of Trebisov's police. I have received threats. Please.

On Friday, January 29, 1999, I received a verbal message from the director of this institution that you may be coming. I cried all night and all day. I'm crying now too, so please forgive my mistakes as I can hardly see through my tears. Also my emotional state is, after four months of <u>mental torture,</u> in very bad shape, so I can't spell right anymore.

I'm going through a <u>hell</u> beyond imagination, because <u>the police and gypsies want my money.</u>

<u>The police</u> in Trebisov have <u>more power than the government</u> of Slovakia.

The whole prosecution is based on the fact that the gypsies are able to repeat <u>some sentences</u> that the police taught them. They even mixed those up. According to the statement of a court-appointed specialist, a psychologist, those gypsies are mentally retarded prostitutes, streetwalkers, hitchhikers, and blackmailers who can't read or write, and they are liars. Their families and friends are convicted criminals.

The police refuse evidence. My witnesses and pieces of evidence are simply refused. When I offered recordings from my answering machine that clearly show that the gypsies blackmailed me, the police arrested me, not the gypsies.

A child was molested by the police, and I was arrested for it.

The police took the eleven-year-old Jana V. from school to the police station and forced her to speak against me. They used words like condoms, cocks, blood from genitals, sticking a cock between the legs, and so on.

The child collapsed under pressure from the police. Little Jana collapsed and urinated in her pants, and while she was crying, they gave her a paper to sign; she had no idea what it was. This horrendous piece of paper was used against me for three months as the main reason for me being arrested, and then it was dropped as nonsense.

Next, I described all the illegal steps taken by the police and others involved in my case.

So far, I've had four months of emotional torture to break me down, so that my family would pay. This system worked so well that even hard criminals and multiple armed robbers cried, almost every day, watching what it was doing to me. I was falling down, fainting, bleeding heavily from my mouth and nose, lying on the cement floor, because I had no energy to sit on a stool.

I continued with the description of my sufferings, which is too hard for me to write about again.

Demjan cut off my visiting rights and also my mail. Letters go through him. If he likes it, he passes it on in a month. If he doesn't, it goes into the garbage.

> At Christmas and the New Year, I didn't know anything about Bibiana or about my family. He knows exactly what he is doing.

I also described most of the crap that Demjan had fabricated about me:

1. I was trying to escape to Canada. (in my car with no luggage)
2. I was mentally ill before or now. (all these years, nobody except Demjan noticed it, not even a court-appointed specialist)
3. I might not be able to recognize that my actions are a danger to society. (but I do recognize that Demjan's actions are a danger to society)
4. I might not be able to recognize what criminal activities are or what an investigation is. (in fact, it is Demjan and his associates who have broken virtually every law in the book)
5. I might be a sex maniac. (not me, but whoever abused Jana was a maniac for sure)
6. My presence on the outside might be a danger to society.
7. I might need preventive treatment. (the men who abused Jana should get one)
8. I might have taken some photos of child pornography. (only if they are invisible)
9. I could be a producer of pornographic videos of children. (only with a nonexistent camera)
10. I might have raped some children. (in his fantasy)
11. I could be an international drug trafficker. (without even an aspirin in my presence)
12. I might have murdered somebody. (with an old rusty gun that has never been fired)

Not a bad record, from a man who had never been in trouble with law at all. Mobster Al Capone would look small beside me and would have to learn how to be a criminal from me.

> I have proof for every single fact I'm writing. There is a hope that my country <u>Canada</u> will help me, and the fact that the consul is coming to visit gave me a little energy and a little hope.

Trebisov is a long way from Bratislava, and the law is getting here very slowly.

Prime Minister Dzurinda is still trying to break through.

Mr. Pitner (the minister of interior) and Mr. Carnogursky (the minister of justice) have sent some requests to Trebisov.

In the meantime, I'm suffering, and I'm cut off. My family knows nothing about me, and I know nothing about them.

I have really learned what democracy is—Trebisov style.

I made a few copies of the letter to the Canadian consul, with the intention that somehow I would be able to get at least one to him. There was no chance to get it to him by mail, because all my mail went through Demjan's hands. He had them translated, and nothing like that would ever get past him. I had one ready to hand to the consul if he came.

Even now, after so many I get sick to my stomach when I write about it. I imagine Demjan was just sitting there in his office and fabricating anything that came to his mind against me. My blood pressure went up just thinking about him and his accomplices, like Danko. I swear that, just thinking about them, my nose bled again, just like it did in jail.

The date for the consular visit was set for February 4, 1999. My luck was not with me. A huge snowstorm settled over Slovakia, and the airport in Kosice was closed. I was devastated. It was like expecting Jesus to save me, and he did not come.

The winds were strong, even down behind the prison's tall walls. Not one single prisoner went for a walk. I had too much stress in me, so I decided to go. The snow was about two feet (sixty centimetres) high in that chicken coop. The shoes had no strings in them, and the coat had no buttons. It was the same coat that was still stained with my blood. I began walking in the shape of the number eight, as usual. Soon there was a little walkway in the snow. My shoes were full of snow, but I did not care; I didn't feel much of the cold. I kept walking for the full hour. There was only one guard on the tower, because nobody else was walking. Dressed in a big, long army coat, the guard kept coming out to see if I was frozen enough to go in. Then he would run into the tower booth to warm up.

He could not understand how I could stand the cold, dressed so lightly. I had a lot of stress to get rid of, and the freezing temperature was doing just that.

My lawyer wrote a special request (6220233, dated February 4, 1999) to remind the prison officials about their duties by law to move me and to remove the restrictions, because Jana had been dropped from my case.

I was kept illegally with the restrictions for a few more weeks. Finally, I was moved to another cell, and two young gypsies were my new roommates.

On February 15, 1999, I was escorted downstairs to the office where I got official visitors. I sat down. Nobody was in the office, and nobody had told me who was coming. I was suspicious; it could be the Canadian consul, because they had not let me bring down any documents.

The door opened, and I was more than surprised. Bibka and a well-dressed man walked in. I knew he could be the consul. Dressed in a navy blue suit, white shirt, and dark tie, he had to be a Canadian man. The guard followed and sat on a chair by the door. Bibka ran to me first to give me a hug. I could not hold back the tears.

"Do not cry," she comforted me. "This is Mr. Tiefenbrunner, Canadian consul."

We shook hands.

"How did you manage to get in here?" I could not believe that they had let Bibka in.

"They do not have anybody who speaks English, so I'm the official translator."

"I have some papers, ready for you, but they do not let me to bring it here." I explained to the consul.

He turned to Bibka, pointed to the guard, and said,

"Tell him, I want to see the investigative file."

She told him in Slovak. The guard left the room to check with his superior.

I pointed to ceiling and whispered, "The room is bugged."

"I would not be surprised. They did not want to let me in to see you at all. What do they have here to hide?"

"You will never believe what is going on here. They torture me. And not only me. Nobody will think that that is possible these days. Prisoners cut themselves to pieces because they cannot stand this mental abuse. I'm completely destroyed." I was trying to tell him as much as possible while the guard was gone, whispering into his ear, hoping that the bug would not pick it up.

"You can show him your papers, but make sure that he does not take any out of here," the guard informed me after he returned.

He accompanied me to my cell. I took my shopping plastic bag full of documents. He checked it thoroughly.

"Make sure that everything comes back," he warned me one more time.

I took out one of my photos, when I was with Bibiana.

"Look. This was me not even a year ago. It was taken in Canada on my birthday. And look at me now. This is what they've done to me."

The guard ran out to inform his superiors that he could not understand the words we were saying. Nobody could speak English in the building, so they just sent him back to make sure that no papers would leave that room.

The consul was shocked when saw the difference between what he saw in the picture and what was left of me. Nobody would have recognized me anymore.

"What are they doing to you here?"

"It is ongoing abuse. I'm cut off from civilisation, cut off from everybody."

"But you are with the general prison population, aren't you?"

"There is no general population at all. Every cell is individual. The prisoners are divided, and nobody sees other prisoners. I only see the two gypsies with whom I'm in a cell now."

"Why do they keep you so isolated?"

"That way, the brutality is contained, and they don't have virtually any witnesses or just very few. Prisoners cut themselves to pieces. They destroy themselves. One guy cut his stomach open; his intestines all came out. It makes me sick just to think about it."

"Why do they do that?"

"It is a reaction to mental torture. The guards don't have to touch you. They drive you to do it by yourself. They make you suffer by intensifying your natural pain. They took almost all the blood out of me. My brain felt cold and hot; my heart began pounding; I thought I was a goner. Then they would not let me lie down. You really suffer, living in pain, and they just make it worse and worse. I'm allergic to cigarette smoke, so there are always smokers in my room. Each time, they light up cigarettes, my nose bleeds. How long can I last like this?"

I noticed tears in the consul's eyes. He did not say how he felt. He made some notes.

"I need a lawyer who will be on my side. This one is no good. She only does what I tell her, and even that is not very good. I have some money in the bank in Canada. Can you find me a lawyer who will really defend me?"

"I can only give you a list of Slovak lawyers."

"That is no good. I need a lawyer from the Czech Republic or some other country. I have already tried two Slovaks; they are no good at all."

"I realized that when your lawyer refused to meet me."

I was very disappointed that Canada had no access to lawyers to help Canadians, who get into trouble in foreign countries.

"Did you get any of my letters?"

"No, I did not."

"I mailed you two registered letters. I knew something was wrong when nobody replied. I have the copies of those letters and others I wrote to you recently, but they warned me to make sure nothing leaves this room."

"Give me those letters; I want to see how they are going to stop me. You hang on. I will do what I can to bring this to an end."

He took copies of the letters and some of the other documents that I had prepared for him. He lifted them up for the guard to see them.

"Here, I'm taking these papers," he mouthed. Then he folded them and placed them all in his inside jacket pocket.

Of course, the guard did not understand the words, but he got the message. Nobody attempted to take those documents from the consul, but it was clear to me that I was going to pay for it. It was not a matter of if, just of when they were going to get me for not obeying their orders. But I did not care. I decided that I was going to get as much information as I could about this gulag out.

That same afternoon, I finally received the postal stubs of the registered mail I had mailed to the consul long before, which the prison officials had refused to mail for me. I had mailed the on January 7. Now it was February 15.

It was very ironic when the Slovak minister of the interior, Mr. Pitner, returned from the United States, where the world's leaders had had meeting. The theme had been "Corruption in Justice." What a coincidence!

In Slovak media, he noted:

"The communists had it all corrupted—police, prosecutors, judges, and even prison officials and guards were together in abusing prisoners."

What a coincidence. Didn't he know that that corruption was blooming right under his nose? It was his police that had placed me illegally into the gulag, and it was a jail under his responsibility where guards were abusing prisoners.

He knew it, but he refused to recognize it. I had personally written to him a number of letters, describing it all. How could he not know?

CHAPTER TWENTY-FIVE

"When a Farmer Needs to Shit, Then Let the Dude Shit." (the most famous statement of a Soviet Politburo member)

Where was the automatic ass-wiper invented? In the Soviet Union.

Slovak policemen were not the only ones who were willing to jump into a sewer or septic tank if asked to by communists.

In British Columbia, Canada, there was also a known jumper, but he did not jump into a septic tank to please communists. He did it to please himself. As it appeared in Canadian media, the man unscrewed a toilet seat, climbed into the septic tank, replaced the seat from the inside, and waited. It happened in a rest area off a road, where there were still outhouses with septic tanks right under the toilet seats. He did it in the ladies' washroom for a reason. When the ladies came in to seat on the toilet. He then enjoyed the sight from the frog's view. Nobody, except him, knows, and he is not saying, how many enjoyable sights he had the pleasure of enjoying, before disaster kicked in.

One lady did something totally unexpected. After she did whatever she had came to the outhouse for, she turned around and looked inside the toilet seat. A pair of eyes were looking up at her. All four eyes froze, the same as both bodies. But only for a moment.

"Maaaan! Maaaan," she yelled as if somebody was cutting her fingers off with bolt cutters. She was running, yelling, and pointing at the outhouse.

Her husband did not hesitate at all. He began running toward the ladies' washroom, ready to kill. A few men who were standing nearby and talking, joined in.

The man down under wasn't going to just wait. As soon as the lady ran out, screaming, he began climbing out of his enclosure. As his head appeared above the toilet, he could see men raging toward the outhouse like a flock of mad buffalos down at Buffalo Jump in Canada. His survival instinct kicked in, and he did what most of us would have done in the same situation. He turned around and jumped back into his hiding place. His foot slipped off the edge, and he ended up where none of us would like to end up—right in the middle of everything. It was not a pleasant sight, but it saved his life.

The husband was ready for the kill. All they (the husband and his followers) could see was an empty room.

"What is the matter with you? Nobody here," he yelled out.

"Down there. Down under," the lady yelled at them.

All the men were pushing each other to the sides, trying to see down under. Nobody could believe his eyes. Only scared eyes looked up at them from the pile of s---. Nobody would dare to jump in and fight the man who had seen the private parts of the still upset lady in action.

"Come on out, you bastard," husband yelled into the hole.

The man underneath was scared to death, so he did not yell back what we would have in the same situation, "You come in here, if you dare."

The police had no choice. They had to deal with the stinky and brown-painted subject, and they did. The man was charged with mischief and damaging public property.

It was never published why that destined lady had looked down into a stinky septic tank after she relieved herself. Some said that it could be that she just intended to say good-bye to what she had just produced. Sounds stupid, doesn't it? There were those who said that he must have made some noises when rubbing his "gun." My speculation was that it could have been her extrasensory perception.

My wife Bibiana said that she did not like outhouses, because she was afraid that something might jump out of it. She always looked down there before she sat down to make sure that nothing would jump up and grab her "moon." When pressed by me to be more specific on the subject of what exactly she was afraid might jump out, she said,

"Something like a frog. But since this story, I also look down to make sure that no man's eyes are looking up at me from down there."

Nobody knows who was more shocked—the lady looking down, or the man looking up. Sometimes, the Royal Canadian Mounted Police missed very important points in their investigation, or they made a secret out of it.

No big conviction was expected for the man. There were a number of mitigating circumstances, like the stink of the enclosure, which prevented the man from opening his eyes all the way to see clearly, not to mention the poor lightning at the performance or that the man had also fulfilled a much-used request by women: "Look, but don't touch."

This was more proof that a man does everything he does just for a woman. Remember Brian Adams' "Everything I Do, I Do It for You"?

We never know what will save our lives. That man would have been a pancake, if he had been caught by the charging men. Instead, he ended up in a safe enclosure, surrounded by the contents that protected him and thus saved his life. That man wasn't the only one who was saved by stinking. But that is another story.

There were many other reasons why men ended up in sewers, having to deal with s---. The story that became legend in the Soviet Union and was denied by both the Soviet Union and the United States most likely happened as was told and was carried from generation to generation, because most legends are based on real facts.

It happened when the Soviet of the highest authority of politburo, President Nikita Khrushchev, visited President John Kennedy in 1961.

Mr. Khrushchev was the most open-minded of the other Soviet leaders, even though he labelled American-made cars "stinky chesterfields on wheels." He surrounded himself with the best secret agents to protect him and with spies to look for anything wrong with the dirty capitalist system.

There were anti-American slogans written all over the United Soviet Socialist Republic, and children in schools sang dirty, degrading songs about President Truman. No wonder adrenaline was high, and trust was at its lowest for that historic visit.

Mr. Khrushchev went to the washroom in the White House, after his agents checked it throughout, just before he entered. They were searching for bombs, hidden cameras, or signs of radiation. The Soviet agent almost fainted when the toilet flushed automatically. He stuck his hand into the toilet as far as he could reach to find out who had flushed the toilet. He could not understand it, and even more confusing was the fact that there was no string to pull in order to flush it.

Mr. Khrushchev entered the washroom, while agents stood right behind the door, just to be sure. They were defying strict orders of their superiors to not let Mr. Khrushchev out of their sight even for one second under any circumstances. They had forgotten to discuss what to do when Mr. Khrushchev was to go do his private chores, but no agent dared offer to go into the washroom with him. Soon they realized that they had made a big mistake. After a few minutes, the door flew open, and their boss ran out with his pants still just above his knees. His gorillas caught him in time, just before he fell to the floor. Some agents charged into the washroom, looking for the contraband that they assumed had attacked their boss. Nothing was found.

At the same time, Mr. Khrushchev tried to explain to his translator (who was also one of his agents), that he never pulled a string and the water began charging toward him, which he had taken as a sneaky assassination attempt on his life. The Soviet translator quickly translated his concern to the United States translator, who assured them that it was just an automatic flush, which was installed in all the top government washrooms.

The story was pronounced top secret, and nobody was allowed to talk about it in the Soviet Union. Only after Mr. Breznew pushed Mr Khrushchev out of his position to take his chair did the story became legend and get told in different variations over and over by different generations.

The politburo was full of old members, who simply refused to believe it, claiming that, "It is all bullshit. How could the water know when he was finished?"

Mr. Khrushchev wrote in his little notebook, in which he was making notes for his spies, "Find out how the water in the toilet knows when to flush or who pulls the string."

At the Kremlin in Moscow, they were still flushing toilets by pulling strings, letting water down through a pipe from a container that was attached to the wall, high up by the ceiling. The water came rushing down, occasionally over the edge of the toilet onto the floor. A drain hole was in the middle of the washroom floor to let the water out in case that happened.

That could be a little embarrassing for Mr. Khrushchev, who had decided to impress President Kennedy, who had been invited for a return visit to Moscow.

Soviet spies did not manage to figure out in time how self-flashing toilets worked in the United States. It was the main embarrassment for the KGB, the Soviet spy agency that was able to snoop out traitors in the

United States, from whom they bought secrets of the American-made nuclear bomb but not the secrets of self-flushing toilets.

At the time, the Soviets were working on the first Soviet computer, called "Pocitac." They had a lot of information in it, but it was big, like a football field. It worked on the basis that, if you required some information, you went to the window where the man called "control" was sitting. He then passed your request on to a connecting hall, where a number of men called runners were sitting and waiting. The selected runner would run to the place where the requested information was stored. He then grabbed it and ran back to "control," who would make copies of the requested information and pass it out through the window.

It was working pretty well, but how it worked was a secret. The size of it was the main setback. Since it was a known fact that American computers were much smaller—just the size of average living room. The Soviets decided to shave off as much of their computer as possible. They managed it by using midgets for runners, because they took up less space than a full-size man took. But there was an apparent setback with the speed of retrieving information, because midgets were usually slower runners than full-size people. It was concluded by Politburo that, with midgets as runners, it would be hard to fulfil the slogans that were all over the Soviet Union. Those slogans read: "To catch up and overtake the USA."

President Khrushchev had a much more serious problem on his hands. It actually developed into a big crisis—the second largest crisis, right after the blockade of Cuba.

Whoever visited Eastern European countries' washrooms around those times will never forget the stink in them. There were no individual urinals but a large cement wall with a little creek underneath and a hole in the middle of it. You could say good-bye and watch the foam go down the creek until it disappeared into the hole. The cement wall was about eight feet high, as it was believed that no man could pee higher. Nobody had counted on our invention at the high school, when we managed to hit the ceiling.

Mr. Khrushchev was a man of action, and he did not give up. He remembered the embarrassing moment in the United States when he asked the gentleman where the washroom was when he was standing in the middle of it. The washroom was so clean and brightly lit, and the stink was nowhere to be found. How could he know where he was?

He ordered the repainting of all toilets in the Kremlin, along with the replacement of all flushing strings with bright new ones. The floors of the washrooms were washed repeatedly with a bleach disinfectant, which stank like chlorine but did the job. The smell of chlorine overpowered the usual stink of the Soviet toilets. Nobody was allowed to use any washrooms at all until after Kennedy's visit. All members of the Politburo and all employees were ordered to use the washroom in the basement. Signs in English were attached to the wall with the instruction, "To flush, stand to the side of the toilet and pull the string. If the water fails to come, shake the string and pull again. If the water keeps on coming, shake the string repeatedly while pulling until the water stops." The reason to stand on the side was as a preventive measure to keep your pants dry in case the flushing water splashed over the edge of the toilet.

A total disaster came out when the toilets in the army barracks got onto the agenda of the Politburo. It seemed that nothing could be done with that situation to improve it.

Mr. Khrushchev had toured the army complex at the Pentagon, and all the toilets had functioned just like in the White House.

"You get up, and it flushes automatically after you. Can you believe it? How does that water know that you are done?" He was talking to members of the Politburo. Those members who were not sleeping were listening with their mouths open. Some were suspicious that the old man was making things up. Those who could think concluded that somebody was watching through a hole in the ceiling and pulled the string when the man was finished.

The Soviet army was impressive, if only it were not for the latrines and those outhouses. There were only outdoor latrines for regular soldiers and outhouses with big septic tanks under them. Those were strictly for army officers with the rank of captain and higher. All soldiers of lower rank sat on a long pole, called the "sitting pole," on the edge of a big hole dug into the ground. The whole complex of latrines was situated in the back part of the barracks, with trees and bushes around it, providing privacy for the soldiers relieving themselves. The long horizontal sitting pole was long enough to provide enough comfortable space for fifteen soldiers to relieve themselves simultaneously. Of course, there was another pole in front of them that was not as thick and that was called the "hang on pole"; it was a safety measure. The soldiers were instructed to hang on, at least with one hand, while doing their business to prevent them from falling into the hole full of s--- with their pants down.

The open space provided great ventilation, especially if the wind was blowing from a favourable direction. The only setback was during the hot summer when mosquitoes as big as bulls and horseflies the size of horses sat down in the hole—you know on what—waiting. As soon as some soldier approached, the horseflies sounded the alarm of celebration. Everybody got ready, and when the pants went down, the mosquitoes and horseflies attacked fiercely. The "moon" of every soldier was marked with stars, which were the colour of the Soviet flag. At times like that, soldiers wished that it was possible to do the job with their pants on.

The Politburo came up with a solution. It should be explained to Mr. Kennedy that the latrines and outhouses had been installed on purpose to fulfil a known slogan in the Soviet army: "Hard in training, easy in a fight."

Most of the men of the Politburo were old farts from Stalin's times and could not understand what all the fuss was about. At meetings, those who were not sleeping were snoozing. Those who weren't snoozing were napping. The only time they woke up was when it was time to lift their hands for voting. It was always 100 percent, because nobody would dare to have an opposite opinion from the boss, and nobody cared anyway. The important thing was to wake up, because right after voting was the time for the Vodka break.

"*Shto eto za problema? Kogda chozjaj nado sraka, togda nuzno davolna muziku sraka. Vy ponimajete?*" (What is the problem? When a farmer needs to shit, then you must let the dude shit. Do you understand?) an old member suggested. Those who were awake applauded right away, and the rest, who were awakened by the applause, joined in. That meant the motion was approved. The bell rang, and everybody lifted their hands again to be sure that their votes were counted, got up, and began moving out for the break—and a few glasses of vodka with smoked bacon and black Russian bread.

Mr. Khrushchev was disappointed and mad. He knew that, as usual, all their problems, even important ones like this one, he had to solve by himself. The Politburo did not realize that there was a real problem facing the mighty Soviet Union, which was on the verge of a national crisis. But Mr. Khrushchev solved the problem by himself.

During the visit to the Kremlin by President Kennedy, Mr. Kennedy went to the washroom and managed to pull the string of the flusher without needing any assistance. The toilet functioned perfectly, did not overflow, and the United States' president's pants stayed dry. He could not understand why all the Soviets were looking at his feet when he got out.

"*Suche, suche,*" (Dry, dry) the Soviets were whispering to each other with great relief. Members of the United States delegation looked at each other like they were stupid, not understanding where the happiness had come from or what it was all about.

It was a success beyond expectation, and Mr. Khrushchev was content that he will be re-elected in the next election.

He was also prepared for the visit of United States delegation to the barracks of the mighty Soviet Red Army. He believed it would be an even greater success than the visit to the washroom in the Kremlin.

The idea of the procedure in the Kremlin washroom was his, but it had been voted for in Politburo by those who had been awake at the special meeting. They might even try to take credit for it. But this one in the army barracks was totally his. None of the Politburo members knew about it, and nobody could take the glory for it. He had decided to do it on his own and to keep it top secret and a surprise. It would catch up and even surpass the smart American water. He could hardly sleep well at night because of the excitement.

"*Shto mokre to ciste,*" (What is wet is clean) an old proverb, was on everybody's mind. Soviet soldiers were scrubbing their halls, over and over.

The outhouses were repainted over and over again. Only a special one was selected for the United States president, should he decide to use the toilet.

The visit was to show the United States delegation and the president of the United States the usual, typical day of Red Army soldiers. They looked a little strange, dressed in their bright new uniforms, still smelling of Naftalin, the usual pest control deterrent to prevent damage by moles. The marching outside was just perfect.

All the Soviets were happy, and everybody forgot about the outhouses, except Mr. Khrushchev. It looked like his idea and all that preparation might have been done for nothing. Lunch was great, and—no and no! Mr. Kennedy was not asking where the washroom was. Mr. Khrushchev wanted to remind the president of the United States that he should go and do what everybody must do sooner or later, but he couldn't find the words to say it. He himself already had, but he decided to do it again.

"*Skazi mu, ja idem sraka,*" (Tell him I'm going to shit) he finally ordered his translator. Mr. Khrushchev hoped that it would also raise the appetite of his compatriot. The translator looked at him confused.

"*Skazi, skazi,*" (Say it, say it) Khrushchew ordered again.

"President Khrushchev is excusing himself; he must go to the washroom," the translator finally explained with hesitation in his voice.

"Okay. See you in a while." Mr. Kennedy smiled at Mr. Khrushchev.

"*Eto charaso!*" (It is great!) Mr. Khrushchev tapped his stomach after returning from the outhouse. The gesture worked like magic. Not long after that, Mr. Kennedy excused himself, and Mr. Khrushchev could not wait until he returned. He was sure the president of the United States would be highly impressed. But he was very wrong. You can expect that something might go wrong with every invention, no matter how great it is, especially when it is complicated like this one, but you would not expect this kind of disaster.

First, there was a screaming, coming out of the outhouse. All the secret agents rushed toward it. The door opened, and the president of the United States ran out. He was trying to pull up his pants with his right hand and wipe his face with his left. By the smell, it was clear what the brown stuff on his face was, but only Mr. Khrushchev knew how it had gotten there.

Not being able to discover how self-flushing toilets worked in the United States, he had decided to even top that invention. He had arranged for one soldier of the Soviet Army to be sitting down in the septic tank, where Mr. Kennedy was destined to go.

The instruction was very simple:

"After the president of the United States finishes his business, with a mop-style soft brush, you wipe his ass back to front and then the opposite way—front to back."

Simple, right? Anybody could do it. The soldier down underneath did his part exactly as ordered. If only Mr. Kennedy had not spoiled the whole thing. After the first wipe from back to front, he had jumped up, turned around, and looked inside to see what was going on. It was perfect timing for when the man underneath was doing his second wipe from front to back. He did not mean to, but the second wipe ended up on Mr. Kennedy's face.

The president had not been surprised that there was no toilet paper. It was a widely known fact that toilet paper was a rare commodity in Eastern Europe and an even rarer one in the Soviet Union. Everybody, including the president of the United States had some in his pocket, just in case. But who could expect that there was a fully automatic ass-wiper? It turned out to be a tragic one.

Under threat of the death penalty, nobody dared to talk about it publicly. But the story travelled by whisper for many generations to come and is still going.

After this, Mr. Khrushchev was abruptly pushed out of the Soviet political field. All he received for his lifelong service to his country was an apartment in Moscow and Dacca, a cottage in the country, and a pension. He was very lucky that he was pushed out alive. The man whose favourite statement was about American cars, which he called "stinky chesterfields on wheels" was eventually replaced by a ruthless, Stalin-type ruler—Breznew. He had objections against all of the American lifestyle, except for American cars. After Breznew's death, the Soviet people were shocked when they discovered that he owned a whole fleet of American-made cars and limousines, while most people were still riding bicycles.

All of the above stories are not my fantasy or fiction. Every one comes from legend and survived through many generations.

When I was at school in Czechoslovakia, I learned that virtually all the world-class inventions had been invented in the Soviet Union. I learned about Puskin, Lomonosov, Mendelejev, and of course Lenin, Stalin, and their gulags.

The last one was my biggest problem, because I was sitting right in it.

CHAPTER TWENTY-SIX

Who Is Building a Latrine of Bullshit in Court? Four Retarded Gypsies.

Where in the world can those who can't read write? In Slovakia.

At first, I was shocked when heard that my lawyer had simply refused to meet with my Canadian consul. She was acting like it would be disaster if she had met him.

"No, no, no. I cannot do it," she repeated to Bibiana, when she was told that the consul would like to talk to her. I noticed that, after she had taken my case, she had filed a few complaints, and it had seemed that she was defending me. But after a while, she had stopped. I was thinking that maybe evil Danko had brought some fat envelope to cool her enthusiasm down. But, knowing what a despicable bastard he was, it would be most likely that he used the old line the communists used:

"We know everything about you, so you'd better remember what side you should be on." A threat like that usually worked miracles.

She had also lived most of her life in a country where it was crime to keep in touch with your own brother who lived in a western country. My sister, who had graduated from a philosophical university with 100 percent marks and was high school teacher, had been dismissed from teaching, because I escaped to Canada. Her five years of study had gone down the drain.

The consul was very offended, because it had never happened to him before. I was also very disappointed, especially because she never gave the reason for that kind of degrading behaviour.

******

The big, heavy door opened, and my name was called.

"Demcak. Court," the guard yelled in.

It was March 11, 1999. I had been in jail for five months already. I was more worried about the journey to Trebisov than about court itself. If they had decided to get rid of me, that would probably be the right time for them to do it. I had received a few warnings to stop writing complaints, or else ... Scenarios like "the prisoner was shot, trying to escape" were going through my mind. I had written a few letters to different Slovak officials, listing my concerns and hoping that nothing would happen.

It was nice to wear my own stuff after five months.

Outside, we passed a huge pile of onions. About ten gypsies were sitting around them, cleaning them.

There were some other prisoners going to the same court in Trebisov and also some going to a court in Michalovce.

We were warned that talking was strictly prohibited and would be enforced by all means available, including the use of a gun. There were bars dividing us prisoners from the guards. We were outnumbered by the guards by at least two to one. They were armed with handguns and batons.

All that time since morning, we had all had handcuffs on.

It took about an hour before I was taken into court. Members of my family sat on the right side. I noticed my two sisters and their families. My brother Milan was also sitting there. There were some reporters sitting in a back row on the left side. I remember two young girls who were from the national magazine *Plus 7 Days*. They stood out from the others, because they were dressed in a really western style. About three rows in front of them, which was just about in the middle of the left rows, was Bibiana. She was all alone and looking very good, but the movie *Lone Soldier in a Field* came to my mind. The picture of her sitting there alone is still in my mind, and I still cannot believe that it was real.

This young girl whose life had barely begun, and she had started it fighting for my freedom, fighting those corrupt monsters, who were willing to do anything to get what they wanted. They were monsters that were used to destroying everything and everybody who got in their way. Monsters who made you sick just to think about them. Monsters who repulsed you when you had to talk to them. And there was this young girl, trying to fight them. My goodness!

In times like that, I only wished that I had done more to deserve her. This was the time I was promising God that, if I got out of this, I would do my best to be better than I was, to pay him back for sending me somebody like Bibiana. This was the time when I learned what love really was and how much I loved her. It took me a long time to learn what love really was, but I did discover it, and I'm grateful to God that I did. I learned about real love in my advanced age. But later is much better than never. I'm grateful for it. It took me so long to find somebody like her, and I had to be locked in jail to realize it.

On the left side of the court was the puppet prosecutor mgr. Maros Sabo. On the right were my two lawyers, JUDr. Fercakova and JUDr. Hajdu. Presiding Judge JUDr. Milan Jurko sat in the middle on a higher podium, and two ladies were seated on both sides of him. They were JUDr. Valeria Havrilkova and Agnesa Cernakova. Because Ms. Cernakova did not have an academic title, it meant that she had not studied law or she had not completed university. How she ended up in the chair of judge beats me. Prosecutor Maros Sabo only had a pedagogy education. How he became a prosecutor also beats me. Ms. Maria Dolobacova was the typist. Trials by jury were nonexistent in Slovakia, so you were stuck with a corrupted system, whether you liked it or not.

None of the so-called witnesses against me had shown up. Policeman Stefanak and his partner got busy, looking for those gypsies.

In the meantime, I had time to talk to my lawyers. First of all, I took two copies of some documents to Mr. Hajdu. His signature had been visibly forged on them by Investigator Demjan.

"Is this your signature?" I asked him, pointing right at the place where his name was signed. He looked at it with obvious surprise and then looked again, as if he had a hard time deciding what to say. Then after a while of thinking, he said, not reassuring me at all,

"Yes." Then he thought again.

"Are you sure? Because my signature was forged. Look at it."

You could see from ten miles that his signature had been forged. He knew it was forged, but he was not about to admit it and get his friend Demjan in trouble.

"I would like to look at the investigating file," I informed my two lawyers.

"No, you don't need it. I already checked it, and everything is all right," Ms. Fercakova jumped in.

"But by law, I have the right to read that file."

"If you ask to see it, I'm quitting your case and leaving right now."

No doubt she had seen the file and knew all the illegal steps in it, because I had told her about it. There were a few reporters, and they would witness all the illegal things in that file. I had not trusted her since she had refused to meet my consul, and this only confirmed my belief. I would let her go, but I was well prepared for this trial and wanted to get it on with it. That is why I did not tell her to screw off.

My side of the story was heard while the police were looking for the so-called witnesses who had not shown up.

"I have never been in court before, so I don't even know how to call you, sir judge and lady judges," I began my opening speech.

"We have read your psychological evaluation and were impressed; who knows how it would turn out if we were examined." The judge pointed at himself and his two sidekicks. It was a nice gesture for him to be honest like that.

I explained to the court the whole situation and all the proof I had that none of the gypsies were underage.

The young prosecutor Sabo even tried to ask me some questions. I was very pissed off at him, because his name had been signed under all those documents that had kept me in jail.

"The damaged girls claim that you took them from a disco club to a dance in Michalany. How did you happen to be in a gypsy disco club?" he asked, and the formulation of the question pissed me off even more.

"First of all, Mr. Sabo, those are not damaged girls. None of them ever said that they were damaged. That is why they are not present here right now, because they do not feel they have been damaged in any way. It was the police who were telling them that they were damaged and what they should say. Secondly, they are not girls anymore; now they are grownup women with very bad reputations. And to answer your question, I never went to the disco club. I was talking to a friend across the street from the disco when those, now so-called, witnesses came running and talked me into driving them to the other dance. I never denied it, but this is only more proof that I did not break any law, because every one of them had a citizen's ID, which means that none of them were underage. They could never have gotten into the disco club or the dance without ID. By Slovak law, you justice people should investigate mainly if the law was broken, not if somebody has done something stupid. I now realize that it was stupid of me to let them talk me into giving them a ride to Michalany, but I was not familiar with the situation in a small town. It was stupid of me, but I did not break any law. That is the bottom line. I'm denying all accusations that are in the indictment concerning sexual accusations. It was all made up by Policeman Stefanak and Investigator Demjan."

I also brought up an absurd claim in the investigative file.

"Did you study this file? According to it, I was told twenty-five times that those girls were fourteen, and I did not get the message. Have you read the psychological examination by Docent Stancak, where he concluded that your witnesses are psychopathic liars, and I'm an intelligent and honest man? Wouldn't an intelligent man recognize, at least once out of twenty-five times, that the age of fourteen was underage and that acts like the described would have been against the law?

"How did you feel when you read that they were all fourteen at the same time, even though there is four years of difference in their ages? Isn't it the prosecutor's job to get rid of this kind of nonsense? You and Investigator Demjan threw away all proof of my innocence. They did not interest you, because you were only interested in smearing my name. Even the recordings that proved that I was blackmailed were ignored. This is all illegal, and if it ever comes to justice, somebody may ask you why you broke those laws like this."

I had requested in writing that they present the file called *Ntv*, as well as the Book of Registry and the control diary of the prosecutor, to point at other illegal steps in those. None were ever produced. None were ever properly done. Everything had been done illegally.

"How did the witnesses manage to get your phone number and address?" Sabo pushed further.

"So far, I have organized the four largest cultural and entertainment productions in Trebisov. Many thousands of spectators attended. Thousands of fliers were handed out with information about the services my company offers. My telephone number and address were printed on them. I have also written scripts for the owner of the disco, where those women hang out; my contact info was also on that script, and apparently, the disco owner sent them to my place to rent some clothes for his production."

"Do you let anybody in, and how many times did they visit your place?"

"My place was also my business, for which I have a business licence. They knocked on my door four times. They always had something about the beauty contest they were getting ready to attend. On the first visit, one of them stole a bodysuit from me. Then they brought it back the next time. Anna D. wanted 100 korun that she claimed she had paid for it to her friend, who had stolen it from me. Then they came and wanted me to take photos of them. I took one photo of one who had a citizen ID on her, and I refused to photograph the rest of them, because they did not have the IDs with them. The next day, they showed up with IDs. They did have ID; therefore, they were not underage, and I have done nothing against the law. They blackmailed me; they broke the law."

"Did you report it to police that they were blackmailing you?"

"I did report the fact that I was being blackmailed by those gypsies to a policeman who I knew. I thought it would be dealt with normally. Later, he warned me that I should beware of them, because they were spreading nonsense about me. He also told me that Anna Demeterova had been examined at a gynaecological clinic after the police bit her when they were trying to force her to testify against me. It all happened at her school. It was confirmed at the examination that she was a virgin, so they could not use her against me, and nothing was done with my complaint. The police only wanted me behind bars.

"Afterward, they picked up the child Jana Visokaiova and forced her to testify against me. They escorted her from school to the police station and abused her there, using words like condoms and piss dicks and comparing batons to penises. The police blew smoke in her face. Her parents had no idea what was going on. Imagine if this happened to your daughter." I was talking as fast as I could before the judge could stop me. I knew he will not let me bring it all out. And I was right.

"This is not a matter for this court; Jana's occurrence has already been dropped from this case by the investigator and is not a subject for this indictment," Judge Jurko jumped into my speech.

"No, your honour, she is."

He looked at me as if I was stupid, then he repeated to me loudly and slowly,

"She was dropped by the investigator; she can't be in this indictment."

"I'm aware that her case must not be in the indictment, but it is. Please check the indictment. I know it is against the law, but they list her and all her family."

The judge was mad. He grabbed the investigative file, looking for the indictment. He turned the pages, but he was unable to see where

Jana's case was listed. He knew that it should not be there, because it was dropped. I guess he did not study the indictment very well, and to make it even harder, the so-called witnesses were not listed by name but only by initials. I would understand that he missed those, but how could he miss two where the last name Visokaiova of Jana's mom and dad were written in full? I decided to help him.

"Page four of the indictment, your honour. Articles 127 to 138, also 150 to 154 and 176 to 186. Those are all concerning the child Jana, and they are there illegally. They placed those in the indictment, because they do not have any other witnesses or proof. They are there just for numbers, so that indictment is not empty. But the one that is most important, which is proof that Jana was abused, is on page eight, dated October 2, 1998."

Judge checked and could not believe his eyes. Now he was furious, not just at me but also at whoever had written the indictment. Hopefully, he was also mad at himself for not studying that piece of crap a little more before he entered the court. There was nothing he could say, unless he would like to say that some idiot had written the indictment, and it could be the one who was sitting in the court, Mr. Sabo, because he had signed it. I personally believe that it was Jan Danko who had put that crap together. Sabo had only signed it.

The judge moved on without saying anything about it all.

It was a lucky day for the police. They managed to find two sets of two sisters—Demeterova and Pukiova—and escorted them to court.

Anna Demeterova was the first called to the witness stand. She had no ID, so it was not possible to confirm her identity, but it was okay anyway. She was the one who had been slapped around by the police at school when she was fourteen. Now, she was grown up, having had two children. Judge Milko led her like a goat. She told the court another story. She agreed with the judge's suggestion that she was bathing in a massage bathtub and that she had informed me that she was fourteen years old.

The judge wanted to know if she could describe the situation in my house. He knew that she should know, because I had filed a few complaints against the police for taking them illegally into my house to see it. But she confused it all anyway.

"From the room where the bathtub is, you walk to the kitchen, and from the kitchen, you walk to the stairs, upstairs to where the bedroom is."

There was no way from my washrooms to the kitchen, unless you went through the long living room and the dining room. And there were no stairs from my kitchen leading upstairs at all. The stairs were clearly from the hallway.

"The massage bathtub was installed at the end of 1995, when you were already over fifteen." The judge wanted to know about the discrepancy in age.

"No. I know I was fourteen then."

"When did you finish elementary school?" my lawyer asked.

"I finished when I was fifteen in the seventh grade, but I have no idea what year it was."

"When were you fourteen?"

"I don't know."

"Then how can you know how old you were when you met Mr. Demcak, when you don't know when it was?"

"I cannot explain when I was fourteen. I only know that, when I was with Mr. Demcak, I was fourteen."

"By what fact can you claim this?"

"I don't know by what I'm claiming it."

"When were you fifteen?"

"I don't know when I was fifteen. I only know that it was in June."

Judge Jurko was trained and used to crap like that in court, so he managed to keep a straight face, but his two ladies (the side judges) had difficulty keeping from laughing at this kind of reasoning, but they were managing fairly well.

Ms. Fercakova, my lawyer, was looking in the investigative file.

"At the confrontation in front of the investigator, you said that the defendant did not know how old you were, and now you are saying that he did. When did you lie? Then or now?"

"I don't know what I said then, but if I said it, it was because he waved his hand to tell me not to tell it all."

"Did the defendant ever take a photo of you, and did he ask you to see your citizen's ID?"

"No. He never took any photos of me, because I never asked him to, and I never showed him my ID." In the original charge, it was written that "after he took photos, he had sexual intercourse with her" a fabrication of Investigator Demjan's.

"It is written here that you said that you showed him ID when you were fifteen." My lawyer pointed at the record from the investigative file.

"I told him that I was fifteen, and he told me that I must show him a citizen's ID. Then I did show it to him."

"You just said that you never showed ID to him. Are you lying again? When did you call him and tell him that you were fifteen, and why did he insist that you must show him ID?"

"I don't know when I called him. I asked him to take a photo of me, and he told me that he would not take a photo of me if I was not fifteen so that I had to prove it and show him ID."

"You just claimed that you never asked the defendant to take a photo of you, and now you are admitting that you did. You must be lying again. When did you borrow a bathing suit from the defendant?"

"When I was fifteen and wanted to go to the Miss contest."

It was one lie after another. The psychologist was right when he concluded that she was a psychopathic liar.

I got a chance to ask questions. I concentrated only on proving that, when we met for the first time, she was already at least fifteen. It would be enough proof that I had not broken any laws. I asked the question that I was hoping would prove just that and hoping that I would get satisfying answers to.

"Do you remember where we met for the first time? Was it by the disco?"

"At the disco by the overpass we met for the second time," she said and then continued, "The first time we met was about two weeks before at the bus station."

"Who asked me to take you to the dance in Michalany?"

"I don't know who. We did."

"How many times did you come to my place?"

"Every week for two years."

That was a huge lie. I realized that everything was getting bigger. Soon after they visited me, they began to blackmail me, and then I left for Canada, where I stayed for two years. If that was true, she had to be visiting me in Canada. I opened the investigative file to a page I had marked with a page marker.

"You told the psychological examiner that you visited me four times altogether."

"No, I was there every week for two years."

I should have been mad that she was lying straight to my face, but I was not. The more crap she said, the better it was for me. It would be easy to see that it was just a clear lie.

"It is recorded here that you said to examiner four times."

"If it is there, I didn't say it. I was there four times alone and then every week for two years with Eva Pukiova."

"If you didn't say it, then the psychologist must be a liar. Right?

She nodded her head.

Now the two side judges were covering their faces, because they could not hold back the laughter anymore. The presiding judge still kept his serious posture. He would have to judge this ridiculous situation. He was used to dealing with a lot of crap, but my family was present, and even the press was there.

Ms. Fercakova finally joined in. She was also looking in the investigative file.

"At the confrontation on November 26, 1998, you claimed that you were at the defendant's place twenty times, which is not even enough for one year. Now you are saying that you were there every week. Why did you claim it that way?"

"It is not true that I said at the confrontation that I was at the defendant's place twenty times during two years. I was there every week for two years."

"It is written here what you said," my lawyer kept at it.

"I did not say what is written in the protocol of the confrontation." Now, she had made the investigator liar, because he has written that protocol. That time, she was right; Demjan was a liar.

The presiding judge was also interested in something.

"You were claiming before that the first time you were at the defendant's place with Eva Pukiova. And now you are saying that you were there the first four times alone. Explain the discrepancy."

"I was telling it until now."

The judge did not attempt to continue, I hope because he realized that it was a hopeless situation. But I had some more in my notebook.

"Did a policeman—tall with a moustache—came after you and ask you to falsely testify against me?"

"Yes, they took me to the police station."

"What happened after?"

"The second time, I was interrogated by Investigator Demjan at the hospital."

"Was anybody with him?"

"No. He was there alone."

"What about a typist. Was anybody there with a typewriter?"

"No. Nobody was there. Only Demjan was there alone."

"Did he give you some papers to sign?"

"Yes. He gave me something to sign."

"What was it that you signed?"

"I don't know."

"Didn't you read it, or did he read it to you?"

"No. Nobody read it to me, and I did not read it."

"So you have no idea what you signed, right?"

"No."

"Was it this document that you signed?" I took the record—the one that Demjan had made up from the top to the bottom. It was the one with more than two hundred mistakes.

"Here is your signature. Sign it one more time for me." I wanted to have it signed, in case they decided to manipulate it more and try to deny that it was in court all. She signed it once more under her previous signature.

"Please read it for us. Here. Anywhere you want."

She kept looking and looking. Not a single word was coming from her mouth.

The judge stepped in,

"We know she can't read. We've read the report."

I knew that she could not read, but I needed it in an official document, especially for the following reason:

"Please notice that the witness cannot read the page on which is her signature under a statement that she had read it and agreed with it. How could she agree to something that she could not read and that nobody had read to her? This is forgery, deception, sham."

Can you even imagine? It is proven in court that a woman cannot read. She testified that Policeman Demjan had not read it to her, but the document he made her sign read that she had read it herself. The document and whatever was on it were still part of the proceedings. Something like this could only be done in Trebisov - Slovakia.

Anna was blamed for discrepancies, which were fabricated by Demjan, not by her.

My biggest problem is that the Canadian government still defended or at least excused that kind of outrageous action.

There was a little whispering from the present public. The judge was already uptight. I was showing everybody that the whole case was a total sham and that his friend Demjan was a crook.

"Are you finished with this witness?" The judge was getting very nervous.

"Just one more question, your honour."

He agreed very reluctantly.

"Tell us what a transparent dress looks like."

"Like the one she is wearing." Anna pointed to my lawyer, Ms. Fercakova. Almost everybody laughed a little, including the two side judges. I'm not sure if the presiding judge laughed or not, but if he did, it was very short, because I'm sure that he knew that I was not asking that question just for fun. He must have known that I had a good reason for it. And I did.

"Please note that, in the same document she signed, it is written several times that she claimed that I took photos of her in a transparent bathing suit, while it is proven here that she has no idea what the word transparent means. She could never say something when she has no idea what it is. She has also repeatedly in the past, and also now, denied that I took any photo of her at all. It is proof that the whole charge was false and that this record, the same as the others, was fabricated by Demjan."

The problem is that not everything is written in a Slovak court just as it is said. From time to time, the judge dictates to the typist what to write. The law orders the typist to write very close to what was said, but judges change sentences, and if they want, they can leave out anything they choose. But even with what was recorded, I had enough proof that the case against me had all been made up.

Natasa Pukiova was next. She was the one who was eighteen when they knocked on my door, but Demjan had made her fourteen.

"Upon questioning, you claimed to the investigator that the defendant never asked you how old you were. Now you are saying that he did. Explain the discrepancy," my lawyer was looking at the records and wanted to know.

"I don't know. I don't remember."

"You also said that you were in the defendant's place twice. Now you said that it was three times. Is any of this true?"

"I did say that I was there three times."

The lawyer just nodded her head in disbelief.

"When were you fifteen years old?"

"I'm not sure. Maybe in 1992 or in 1993."

"How old are you now?"

"I think twenty."

It was my turn to ask questions. It was clear that her intention was to lie, so I decided to do the part that the investigator should have done long ago.

"Do you remember when I played you a recording tape? You told me the name of the man who was talking on the tape. Who was it? What is his name?"

"I think it was Milan Tancos."

"Could you please record the name of Milan Tancos? He is the man who was blackmailing me with those who are used now against me as witnesses. I would like to have him in court for questioning."

He was never brought into court. If they did bring him in, he could confirm that the policemen were blackmailing me as well. Milan Tancos, nicknamed Belavi, had approached three members of my family, claiming that the policemen had sent him to request 5,000,000 korun for my freedom. He had also said,

"You don't have to pay now. Just promise to, and Demjan will drop the case in one week. Otherwise, Jozef will not survive and will never get out alive."

That is why they kept Belavi out of jailand out of court. I wanted to have it on paper. I was doing the investigation, and I had managed it much better from my cell than the policemen had from the outside. Belavi was never brought to court, because he was just an extended hand for the police.

"Why didn't you report me to the police then, when I was causing you that hardship?" I was taking chances with that question, but I was willing to take the risk, hoping that she would tell the truth, and she did.

"I never reported it then or now. I don't feel to be damaged in any way."

"Did I rub anything on you?"

"No, you did not."

I was puzzled why she had agreed to lie to policemen before and now in court she was trying to tell the truth. Most likely, she was dupped by her sister and her friends.

Eva Pukiova, Natasa's sister, was next. She had the best memory of all four of them, and she was willing to say anything at all. Like her sister, she had been brought onto my case later, after it was clear that the whole charge was false and that Anna and her sister Alena were kind of ridiculous witnesses, who had little interest in participating in the scam.

Everything she said was in contradiction to what she had said before.

Even during the court appearance, she was adjusting her statements. She said that she came to my place alone in 1992 and 1993, and she took baths in both bathtubs, including the blue massage tub. When the presiding judge informed her that the massage bathtub was installed at the end of 1995 and at the beginning of 1996, she said that she didn't remember when it was but agreed that it could have happened in those years. Prosecutor Sabo noticed that his case was collapsing, because, in those years, they all were of age, so he tried to bring it back.

"Are you sure that the massage tub was finished then?"

I could have killed the son of a bitch, because he was just trying to get her to say what he needed. Even someone stupid would know what to say, so she did.

"The defendant was just making the tub at that time."

Just a minute before, she had claimed that she bathed in both tubs, and now she was saying that I was just making one of them.

"When I was alone with him, he told me that he would marry me when I was fifteen, if I let him fuck me."

What can you say to something like that? I wanted to slap her as hard as I could, but I could not, because I was in a "respectable" court. Seeing two side judges having a hard time holding back laughter helped me not to run and give her one across the face.

"What grade did you finish of elementary school?" my lawyer asked.

"Grade four in 1995." She did not even know that she had never attended grade four.

"An official statement that the principal has written on request of the investigator reads that *Eva*

Pukiova repeated grades one, two, and three a few times. In 1994 [not in 1995 as she claims], she finished attendance in grade three," I read from the document.

"Where was the bathtub you said you took a bath in?" the lawyer wanted to know.

"After you get in the house, there is a big room. Then you go into the dining hall, and there is that white tub." She was totally wrong. From the dining area, where she said the bathtub was, you had to go out to the hall, then right into the living room and right again through a special door into the bathroom. If she was there taking a bath, she would remember it. I knew that she had only been in my place once. Now she was saying that she had visited me many times and that I almost married her.

I lifted my hand up, asking to speak. The judge complied.

"Listen, love, how many times were you in my house alone, since I almost married you?"

"I was in the defendant's house alone many times." She knew she was lying, because she was not answering to my face but looking away from me.

"Hey love, look at me when I'm talking to you." I opened the investigative file to a page I had marked. "On December 2, 1998, you told Docent Stancak that you were visiting me alone three times a week for a stretch of five months. I guess that was when we were getting married, because you practically lived with me. Just six days before, that was November 26 at the confrontation, you told Investigator Demjan and me that you were with me alone only once. That is how I remember it. Now, you are saying that you were alone with me many times. This amounts to false testimony. They should,"—I pointed to the judges—"arrest you, because you are lying in court. Explain this to us."

"I'm staying with my claim that I was alone with you many times, because you wanted only a virgin." Now the side judges tried to hide their laughter again.

"You lied then, or you are lying now; there is no other way. Which one is it?"

"I was there more times."

"Why did you tell us at the confrontation that you were there only once?"

"I don't know why I said so."

"Because you are lying, and you cannot remember your own lies. I'm objecting to this witness, who has said different lies on November 18 and 26 and December 11 of 1998 and today at this hearing."

I decided that it was proven enough that she was a pure liar and it was time to show that she was not underage when we first met.

"What did you do with the photo I took of you when you were naked?"

She looked surprised at the word "naked."

"I mailed it to the convict Gejza Tancos, and I was not naked. I was wearing a blue, full body bathing suit." I knew that she was not naked, and I knew that she had mailed it, but I wanted it recorded.

"Please record these facts," I said to the judge. He dictated his version to the typist. I guess he realized my reason for it, because he asked Eva the question I was going to ask next.

"Where was Gejza Tancos at the time the photo was taken?"

"Gejza was serving his sentence in jail." That was a very good answer, because, just by this fact and the dates when Gejza was in jail, it was clear that all these false witnesses were not underage when I met them for the first time. I needed to have it confirmed that Eva had also met me at the same time as all the others, because she was saying anything that came to her mind. She had a little bit better memory than her friends, but she could not remember all the many lies she had told in this process.

"When did we meet for the very first time?"

"It was at the disco at the overpass, where, before you gave us a ride to Michalany, we were at your place and you were touching us and licking our pussies."

"Did I vomit?" She looked at me very strangely, as if she did not understand.

"Did I puke while licking all those pussies? There were three of you." I noticed that the judge was getting restless, so I did not insist on the answer. If you saw those women, you would agree that I could not have been able to survive without passing away or at least passing out.

Looking in my notes, I had another point to clear up.

"You told Investigator Demjan that you met me when attending grade four at the elementary school Komenskeho. Is that correct?"

"Yes, it was then."

"I have here a report signed by Demjan that is proof that Demjan went to your school to verify your statement, and the school principal reported that you had never attended grade four, because you repeatedly failed grade one and two and finished school in grade three, not in grade four. There is only one possibility: either the school principal or you lied. Who do you think is a liar? "

"I did not lie."

I could hear noise in the court, and the two side judges were trying to keep serious faces.

They brought four retarded gypsies into the court. They were openly building a castle out of bullcrap, naming the psychologist, the school principal, the investigator, me, and others liars, and everything was hunky-dory. Nobody was kicking them out of court; nobody was charging them with contempt or for false testimony; and only I was pointing out their lies. They called them respectable court proceedings, and I was sitting in jail, not them. The judge was doing what the prosecutor should have been doing, and I was doing what my two lawyers should have been doing.

I took my notebook and read to her the part of the recording that she said when they were blackmailing me:

"'Jozef, don't be mad, but I must report you, and do you know why? Because when I want to meet you, you don't want to meet me.' Do you remember saying this?"

"I don't remember."

"What about this? 'I will place my pussy on your mouth; also Kuka with her naked ass, she will sit on your head.' Do you remember this?"

"Yes, those were my words."

Now everybody was trying to but having difficulty holding back the laughter.

I had proven enough. It was recorded that she was a liar, that she was of age, and that she was one of the blackmailers. She had come to court and told us crap openly. She had admitted to blackmailing. In a normal court, she would have been arrested, but not there. This was not a normal court. This was a Slovak sham. A shame of the human race. A sham and a shame. It didn't come close to justice.

The last so-called witness was Alena Demeterova, the sister of Anna. The psychologist had described her as the most retarded of all four, and I have to agree. But she also surprised me and everybody present.

Judge Jurko was trying very hard to find at least one little thing to convict me, and so far he had nothing. She could be the one, because she was, in fact, underage at the time; therefore, she was the judge's biggest hope. I did not remember her from those times. She could have been the one who had come once with her sister, when Anna had come to return the jumpsuit. I remember that somebody came with her, but I did not register her, mainly because she was not involved with them when they were blackmailing me. That fact told me that she had been pulled into my case by Stefanak and Demjan, which could have been on the suggestion of her sister Anna, who, as the psychologist had written, had organized consummate sex for both of them. So Anna could have helped to pull Alena into this scam.

Her answers had been so terrible that Policeman Demjan had rewritten all of her statements, in which he made up that famous statement that, after she had informed me that she was fourteen, I had replied, "It is okay, but I want to try you out." That was the document on which he had also forged those signatures.

I was going to bring that insane sentence into the court as proof that not even a retarded person, like Alena, would say anything like that and that only Demjan or another idiot like him could make up something as senseless and stupid as that. I had the line ready, because I was still upset that somebody would even make up a sentence with me saying "I want to try you out" after I had been informed that she was underage.

I was going to say:

"Only a person who is more retarded than she is could say something so stupid. She could never make up anything like this on her own."

But a total horror happened. I was completely stunned.

Alena's Shock Number One

As she passed by me on her way to the witness stand, I heard her repeating that incredible sentence. Head down, she was just repeating it to herself, so as not to forget it. "He wanted to try me out. He wanted to try me out. He wanted …"

I thought I was going to fall down. It could only have been Policeman Stefanak who had been purring this one sentence, as though through a funnel into her ears, while escorting her to the court. I was sure that, even as he opened the door to the court for her, he was telling her that magical sentence. There was no other possibility. Now she was repeating it to herself so she wouldn't forget it, and she was going to say it in front of everybody in court.

It was a total disgrace for me.

I'm finished, I said to myself. *It looks like she is willing to do as they said.* I felt like hitting her head on the wall. All previous three so-called witnesses had gone all right, because I had proven that they were of age and that they were liars, and now this disaster. I could not prove that she was of age, because she was, in fact, underage. I had counted it, and she was two to three weeks underage at the time.

She would have no trouble describing sexual intercourse. Some years in the shoes of a prostitute had given her enough experience. The judge would help her, with his questions, to make some lines fit with what Demjan had made up in his statement. That was exactly what Judge Jurko was doing. He had the crap that Demjan had written in front of him, and he needed only one yes from Alena, and then I would be a goner. Kaput.

"Why did you voluntarily listen to the defendant, take your clothes off, and do what he wanted," The presiding judge asked.

It was a very dangerous question for me, as well as an illegal one. Slovak law prohibits giving the answers while questioning. Judge Jurko was aiming for the rape of a minor, and I would be in jail for many years to come. He knew that she was the only one who was underage at the time, and after all the others had failed, she was the last and only one hope for him to put me away. Section 241 paragraph 2b T.Z. of Slovak law states that, for the rape of a person under the age of fifteen, the minimum punishment was five years and up to twelve years. If she said that she had not agreed, I was finished. He would sentence me to twelve years, and then they would ask me if I was willing to pay for my freedom or not. I was standing as though on hot nails, waiting for the answer.

"I was afraid, because he had snakes there."

It was going the judge's way. She was afraid; that was a good sign for him. All she needed to say was that she did not wish to do it, and I would have been done.

The judge tried for just that:

"Did the defendant force you or insist in any way that you take your clothes off and that you do as he wished?"

Judge Jurko was doing the prosecutor's job. And I was shaking in my boots, waiting for the answer. The judge had outlined the whole answer for her; all she needed to say was yes, and I would have been done. She surprised me.

Alena's Shock Number Two

"No, he did not force me in any way to take my clothes off or to do as he wished." I had expected anything but that. The judge was shocked and disappointed, but he was not as shocked as I was. I was sure that she would say yes or at least give some indication of some little force from my side that the judge was expecting, and I would have been burned, like the toast on the stove when my wife smoulders it in the morning.

Alena had just saved my life. The judge would have given me at least twelve years. My guarding angel was with me, standing there with his hands open. That was the only thing I was sure about.

But the judge was not about to give up. Rape was out, but there was still sexual abuse of a minor on the line:

."Did defendant ask you how old you were, and did you tell him, that you were underage?"

It was another tricky, illegal question, and answer was just in it. That was exactly what Demjan had been doing. In the Slovak law book, it is written very clearly that you do not ask a witness a question in which the answer is outlined. But this court was just as far from justice as it was possible to be. All she needed to say yes. All of them had been trained to say yes. It had been written in investigative file twenty-five times by Demjan. They had all been thoroughly prepared just to say yes to this one crucial question. And the judge had just asked it. Would anybody expect her to say no when she had been well trained to say yes? I knew that was it. I was finished; I was done.

Alena's Shock Number Three

The answer was such a blow to my ears that I do not believe it even today.

"No, the defendant never asked me how old I was, and I never told him how old I was."

The judge and Prosecutor Sabo were stunned, and I was even more stunned. *What is going on*, I thought, *after the mountains of lies I've heard today, the woman is telling the truth. Something is wrong here.* But the judge was in charge, and to him, she was just a stupid little girl. She had to say what she was required to say.

"But your sister Anna said that she was there when the defendant asked you how old you were, and she heard you tell him that you were fourteen." *That should remind the little bitch,* I imagined the judge said to himself, *what she should say.* If she said yes, they would write that she had forgotten it and that then she remembered that I had asked her and she had told me. That way they would have me where they wanted me.

But there was another surprise.

Alena's Shock Number Four

"No, it was when we were going away that my sister asked me if the defendant had asked me how old I was, and I told her that he had never asked me and that I had never told him."

I was very surprised, and it looked like there was nothing that could be used against me. From this, it should have been clear that I hadn't raped her—I didn't insist in any way—and I had no idea how old she was; therefore, I had committed no crime.

But the judge used another trick.

"How did you know that all this took place at the beginning of 1995, as it was written in your statement?" the judge kept on asking. If she had some reasonable explanation that she knew it by some point, there could still be some case against me. Again, it was a question with the answer right in it. What could I do? Could I yell an objection to the judge who was going to sentenc me? Could I sue the judge for breaking the law? Could

I at least kick his face? Not likely. All I could do was wait for the answer, hoping for the best, and see what he was going to try next.

Alena's Shock Number Five

"I have no idea what is in my questioning statement, because nobody read it to me and I don't know how to read. I only know how to write."

Again, a quiet laugh was heard in court. It was another honest answer and a lifesaver for me. You would expect that this would be enough. Not quite yet. The prosecutor, who had been quiet until then, decided to step in and help the struggling judge.

"Are you sure that the defendant did not know how old you were?"

It would have been nice if one of my lawyers had objected, because she had already answered the same question a few times. Were they going to keep asking it over and over until she finally said yes? But nothing. Everything was okay as far as my lawyers were concerned. I just had to wait for the answer, and it seemed too long coming.

Alena's Shock Number Six

"The defendant did not know that I was not fifteen."

If this wasn't clear enough, what could be? Finally, my lawyer spoke. It was a question that everybody knew the answer to, but at least it took away the pressure from the judge and the prosecutor to make her say yes and thus put me in jail.

"Do you know when you were fifteen? In what year? And how old you are now?"

"I have no idea when I was fifteen. Now, I think, I'm seventeen."

"Do you have any children, and how old are they?"

"It is true that I have two babies. One's father is a German *gadzo* [a farmer in gypsy slang] who has already died. I don't know who the father of my other child is. One baby was born on November 28; I don't know what year. It is two years old already."

"How long were you in the Czech Republic before the baby was born?"

"I don't know how long I was there before the baby was born, and I don't know what time of the year it was."

Even though it was so clear that she had no idea about time, if she said yes at least once, they would have locked me up for a very long time. I was walking a very thin line between life and death, when the judge and the prosecutor were trying to make her say that one magic word—"yes."

On that one word, my whole future hung. I was in such bad shape that I don't think I could last those years that they were planning for me in that gulag.

I would really like to know why Alena decided to stand up and tell the truth. I was shocked, because I did not expect it after her sister and the other two had bluntly agreed with the lies that the policemen Demjan and Stefanak had told them to say. All three were buddies with the same pimp. Alena D., on the other hand, was an individual on her own. That could have had something to do with her refusal to lie. It looked like Anna and Eva were competing for who could tell more lies. Natasa P. was just tagging along after them, and Alena all alone had refused to lie.

I believe that she is not retarded like the psychologist had concluded. A totally retarded person would have just said yes under pressure like that, but not her. I believe that her natural, honest conscience overtook her feelings, and she simply refused to lie as forced to by the police, the judge, and the prosecutor. She had refused to lie and had stood up for the truth. It was incredible to see. I do not have the answer for this. I'm still shocked.

Remember when Anna Demeterova was in elementary school and the police were trying to persuade her with slaps to testify against me? Remember how she shocked everybody when she saved me from gulag then by telling the truth and, mainly, by being a virgin? Alena was her sister. It looked like the truth ran in the family.

Their father did not stay far behind his two daughters. When the television show Markyza approached him and asked him what his opinion about my case was, he said publicly and bluntly, "Demcak is innocent. They [the gypsies, including his two daughters] are whores; if they did not want to, they would not go there." That was an honest answer. The father called his own daughters whores and named me not guilty.

What about their mother? I cannot leave her out, alone, like an orphan. When the police claimed that I had slept with her daughter, and it was revealed that she was still a virgin, she had yelled at the policemen, beside others obscenities, "You fucking, lying dickheads." It seemed an honest enough statement to me.

The whole had family shocked me over and over.

But the court and the judge, who was trying to frame me on the basis that Investigator Demjan had fabricated, were something else. Having retarded gypsies come to court and say these kinds of absurdities should be just too much, even for a town like Trebisov.

I requested to call three of my witnesses to testify, because Demjan had written that all the women had taken a bath in my massage tub. Virtually all of my neighbours knew when I finished it, because I had invited them to see it. I had decided to call four of them, but Mrs. O., my neighbour from across the street, got so terrified about being punished for testifying on my behalf that I dropped her.

Mr. Jozef Biro, a friend of mine, was called first. He stated that, in the spring of 1996, I had requested that he paint something in English on my trailer, because I was leaving on my tour of Canada. At the same time, we were rushing with the installation of the bathtub in order to be finished before we left.

My other neighbour from across the street, Michal Kundrat, testified that, at the beginning of 1996 when his son returned from the United States, I had invited him to my place and shown him that massage tub. It was there in place, but it wasn't working as yet.

Doctor Ondrej Bobik, my neighbour to the side, could not attend the proceeding, because he had broken his leg, but he wrote a note, confirming what the previous witnesses had said. His statement was filed in the court file.

The proceedings were adjourned. A new date was set for March 18, 1999, at 10:30 AM.

CHAPTER TWENTY-SEVEN

Human Garbage, Rectum Disposal: But They Think They Are Humans Because They Can Walk and Talk

Where in hell do they tell "You are free" just as they handcuff you? In Slovakia.

Court, part two.

On March 18,1999, the heavy door opened, and my name was yelled.

It was a different bus that transferred us. The prisoner's section was divided by heavy bars from section for guards. The prisoners section was just big enough to hold four seats, which faced each other. The vehicle was designed to transfer dangerous criminals, so the section where the guards were sitting was much larger. It was not me who was being considered dangerous.

Two huge guys were brought in. They had handcuffs on their hands, and they were also handcuffed together. Shackles with chains were also decorating their feet. They both could have passed for professional wrestlers. One was heavily built, with a neck thicker than his head and a body wrapped in pure muscle. The other was big, but some fat was mixed in with the muscles around his body.

There were big, heavily armed guards—two for each of those prisoners—hanging onto them from both sides, and four followed them at a safe distance, a few steps behind. Those two looked like criminals, and I was like a guardian angel beside them.

There was one more prisoner, but he, I guess, did not impress me, because I do not remember him much.

Those two were too big to sit beside each other, because the seats had been built for normal-size people like me. The guards had to remove the chains that kept them together so they could sit opposite each other.

The big guys were talking openly, in spite of the fact that we had been warned at the beginning that talking was strictly prohibited and would be enforced by any means, including guns.

"No talking," one guard yelled at them.

"Come here and tell me to my face," the one with a neck larger than his head said and then continued talking as if nothing had happened.

This regulation of no talking had been put in place so that the atrocities that were happening in the prison did not spread around.

"No talking," the guard yelled even louder.

"Why don't you come here? You should come in here to try to stop us from talking. Are you going to shoot me or what?"

There were about ten guards and only two talking prisoners, but they wouldn't dare open the bars.

The two kept talking, just as if there was no ban on talking at all. From their conversation, I noticed that they were in for double murder. Allegedly, they had been running an extortion ring in southeast Slovakia, where Mr. Muska was what they called a mafia boss. He was the one with the neck larger than his head. His brother had been killed by a competing gang. Mr. Muska had taken the law into his own hands. He allegedly managed to kill two members of the gang that had killed his brother. It was a similar circumstance to that of Mr. Holub, the one who was with me my first day in jail.

"There are no witnesses," he said, "because they all left the country. They are apparently hiding in Bulgaria, afraid to come back. They don't want to testify. So they keep us in jail. From time to time, we come to court. The witnesses don't show up, so they put it off for another year, and they try it again. That bastard investigator made up stories, and all mail goes through his hands. He forged an investigative file, that cocksucker."

He did not mention his name, but I knew right away who that bastard investigator was.

"It was Demjan right?" I whispered. I was hiding behind his large body, so I could say something without the guards noticing it.

"Yes, that dickhead."

They brought us to the same holding cell I had been in a week before. The two big men kept talking, and the guards kept yelling, "no talking." Those were new guards who had been assigned to court duties. After a while, about five or six guards took one of them out of the holding cell. I later saw him handcuffed to a steel pipe down the hall. That was the only way they could halt their talking.

Mr. Muska stayed behind and began talking to me. I pointed toward the guards, as they were watching.

"It's okay. I will talk, and you just listen, and you can nod your head." I was sitting facing him, with my back toward the guards, so I could whisper something without the guards noticing.

"How did you know it was Demjan who screwed with my case?" Mr. Muska asked.

"That pig made up stories about me and forged whole pages of documents. You have no chance with him. He is twenty-four–karat prick. Try to see your investigative file. You will be very surprised."

"You see how things change. Just a while ago, you had all those beautiful women, and now they keep you in this hole." – Muska said.

I asked him how he knew all of that. He told me, but for a very good reason, I cannot write about it as well as other details of our conversation, because it could be harmful for him and for other prisoners. In spite of the fact that they kept prisoners separated, without being able to see each other, the stories and messages go through the whole prison anyway. I'm not about to reveal how it was done. The prison officials would make arrangements to stop it, and I don't want to be the one to help it happen.

Mr. Muska was familiar with my case, and he knew some details, including the main one, which was that I had been framed by the Trebisov police for ransom.

It was a long wait in that holding cell. I felt tired, because I had not slept well the night before. I was kind of leaning sideways on the long bench. The guard began yelling,

"Sit up."

"Can't you see the poor old man is sick? He is innocent and sick, and you pricks keep the poor man in jail. He needs a doctor. This is police brutality. Open those bars, and come here; I will show you. Torturing an old man like this," Mr. Muska let the guards have it.

"Are you sick? Do you want some water?" The guard wanted to know.

"I think I will be okay. I just have to lie down."

"Yeah, he needs a doctor. Let him lie down. Can't you see the old man is sick?"

"Okay, you can lie down," the guard finally gave in.

I smiled and twitched with my left eye. "Thanks," I whispered. He smiled.

I talked to him only one more time. I was walking in the chicken coop. He was in his cell across but sideways from me, looking through the window from behind the gater. He was on the ground floor, where all murder suspects were. It was a one-way conversation again, because the guards were watching from the two towers. I pointed to them to say that I couldn't talk.

"It is okay. I will talk. I'm not afraid of them." He told me that his case was still dragging on, because they didn't have any witnesses.

"Do you want a candy?" He finally asked. He was quite a way to the side. I could not see how he could pass it to me. He threw the candy straight into the chicken coop that was in front of him. He told the prisoner who was there to pass it two sections over. He tried a few times and managed to aim it through the hole in the chicken wire and over the wall to the next section. The prisoner in there did the same, and the wrapped candy got all the way to me. The strange thing was that all involved were risking severe punishment if spotted by any guards. You were searched before you went for a walk, because you were not allowed to bring out any objects at all. Even a single match in your pocket could get you strict punishment. Passing candy would give you a few days in the hole. It made no sense to take a risk like that over candy, but they all were willing to do it. It could be because your mind was so uninspired from doing nothing, and you welcomed any activity at all, just to have something to do. This could also have been peppered with the challenge of not getting caught.

My time was up. We waved.

"See you on the outside," he yelled.

It is not my business to consider him guilty or not or good or bad. There were no witnesses, but if Demjan was handling his case, he would invent some, like he had invented mine. I also knew that I would not mind meeting Muska again on the outside and talking some more. I would have liked to hear more about what illegal steps Investigator Demjan had taken in his case. I could only spit in Demjan's face, if I had a chance. On the other hand, I would not have minded having a drink with this man, and I didn't care what he had done. There were some others like him. For example, Jan Gore, who saved my life when I was passing away in that chicken coop. I would like to see him again. Those were the people who, most likely, I would not have liked to talk to before my imprisonment. But after I felt and saw the cruelty they were put through or punished with for whatever they had done or even what they had not done, my attitude shifted. I guess jail or "times they are the changing" *(Bob Dylan)*.

It was already almost 11:00 AM when I was escorted to court. My family was seated just like before. *The Lone Soldier in a Field*, Bibka was again sitting in the middle of the left rows. I was pleasantly surprised to see her mom also sitting about two rows back.

If you have ever heard about sham proceedings, this one beats them all. First of all, prosecutor Sabo had been replaced by JUDr. Bicko. I learned that Sabo had realized that he was being used to convict an innocent man, so he had quit.

In the section of the proceedings where proof or evidence was to be read and I was to give my side of the story, the judge only turned over the pages and read the titles of the documents and file numbers. From time to time, my lawyer Fercakova nodded."Yes, we know it. Yes, we are familiar with it."

The judge went through it from front to back and then from back to front, reading just the titles. I was not allowed to say one single word about any of those documents. The file NTV, which I had requested, was never presented. The witnesses, like Ms. Volochova, who was a witness of when Demjan had been "schooling the gypsies how to testify," was not invited to court. Milan Tancos Belavi who had been blackmailing me, was also not escorted to court. He could also say that the police were his partners in that scam. That's why they left him out.

The two psychiatrists who examined me were also left out. They could have testified that Demjan had manipulated the file as he pleased and gave them only those pages from the file that suited him. He did that to cause me more damage.

The psychologist, Stancak, came, because I invited him through my lawyer and Bibiana.

He confirmed that Anna D. had most likely visited my place four times, just like she told him and like I claimed. The claim that she had been to my place twenty times or twice a week for the length of two years, like she had said, he considered doubtful."

I only wished that he said things the proper ways, so that everybody— even the judges and prosecutors in Trebisov—could understand him.

Instead of saying that "the witnesses are not able to place their dates of birth, and they are not informed about the usual facts of life, because they don't have an exact point of their age, their estimation is enteric, purposive."

He could have just said it bluntly: "The witnesses have no idea about their age, so all claims concerning time are simple fabrications or lies." How could Docent Stancak expect a judge in Trebisov to understand the meaning of words like enteric and purposive?

It took some more questions to get him to say that the "claims of those witnesses are not credible when concerned with time orientation or time positioning of certain events."

With further questioning, he finally confirmed that these findings could be generalized for all four witnesses—Anna D., Alena D., Natasa P., and Eva P.

He confirmed that, as far as I was concerned, I'm highly developed intellectual. No disorder of any kind was diagnosed; there was only the fact that I oriented around younger age groups.

I got a chance to ask him questions.

"You and the other two court experts already confirmed that I practise normal sexual activity. Those so-called witnesses described their version of their sexual encounters with me. Would you say that what they said was normal sexual activity?"

"In the case of the defendant, it was proven that he practises normal sexual activities, and other methods that precede that actual sexual act, for example teasing with the tongue, are not a sign of any sexual disorder in this circumstance."

He did not get my point, so I decided to make it more blunt.

"It was written in their records that they said that I only licked their bodies and sexual organs and never had sexual intercourse. It all was to have happened after I rubbed some kind of emulsion, and in one case, I provided licking four times with three different women in a stretch of approximately thirty to forty minutes. Would you consider this kind of claim to be normal sexual activity or the imagination of some pervert himself, who has written those statements?"

"I forbid answering this question, because it is suggestive," the judge stepped in. He could not let this answer be heard, because it would prove that Demjan and his partners had fabricated all that nonsense.

"I will rephrase the question. Most men who pay for sex want sex and not to be cleaning some gypsies' bodies." I saw that the judge was getting restless, so I got to the point. "Would you say, Mr. Docent, that these so-called witnesses would be able to reproduce sexual encounters if somebody described them to them?

"Yes, they would be able to do that."

"Now that you know much more about the case, do you still claim that the answers of those witnesses are objective?"

"The answers only as written in my report are theoretically objective, but it is necessary to verify them."

"Would you agree that somebody prepared those witnesses, so they would know what to say?"

"Yes, I agree with the suggestion that somebody prepared the witnesses for the answers, but in repeated questioning, those discrepancies would be hanging in the air. That fact could be proven by repeated questioning."

There were so many discrepancies in their answers that it would not be possible to fit in more. I knew I would not get any more straight answers, and I had enough, under the circumstances, but I had one more point to clear.

"Mr. Docent, you have a former student here in town. His name is Jan Danko. Did he come after you to influence you about my case?"

"I have had so many students over the years; I can't remember all of them," He got red in the face, and I saw how upset he got. I was sure that Danko had come after him, and I knew it would be confirmed if the docent denied knowing him. How could he not remember the one who was known as the biggest ass in the province? Impossible.

The presiding judge stated that the examination of evidence was finished.

"When am I going to be able to tell my side against false evidence?" I asked JUDr. Hajdu, one of my lawyers.

"Later," he said. I had more than twenty pages of notes prepared, and it looked like the court proceedings were winding down, and no chance had been given to me to address those issues.

The new prosecutor, Bicko, his face red as though he had just finished a few drinks in a pub, asked to drop Anna Demeterova from the case, because it was proven that she was not underage when she met me. The judge was granting his request. *Good*, I thought. If they dropped Anna, then Alena, her sister, was useless for them, because she had refused to lie and had kept claiming that she had never discussed her age with me. They had only two liars left. But imagine this.

My lawyer JUDr. Fercakova, in her closing statement, reminded the judge and prosecutor that they had made a mistake by dropping Anna and that they should have dropped Alena, because she was useless. *What side are you on, bitch?* I thought to myself. *If they are stupid, let them be dumb. Especially if it is good for my case.*" But not her. She had to spoil it. After court, they wrote in the court record that they had made a mistake, and Anna Demeterova was back on my case.

Finally, they even let me say something. Apparently, it was to be my final speech.

I opened my book and was ready to start. The judge, looking at my notes, warned me,

"We are all hungry, because we have not eaten since morning, and it is already noon. Can you speed it up?"

"I have quite a few objections, your honour, that I would like to point out. I would prefer, if we could continue after the lunch break."

"Do not think that this is UN meeting and that you will read this entire book, like they do there."

"I would like to say that all these allegations against me were fabricated by Investigator Demjan and Policeman Stefanak. It would be absurd and illogical that I would go with those women after they had been blackmailing me. Everybody in town knew the reputation of those girls— that is, that they make a living by prostitution—and it is absurd to suggest that I would do what is written in the document and risk being infected by sexually transmitted diseases.

"All this evidence points clearly to it all being fabricated by the police. It is in the investigative file that is in front of you. Whole pages were made up by Demjan, and—"

"Your objections concerning evidence will not be recorded in protocol, because only the court has the right to evaluate evidence," the judge jumped into my sentence. He must have been hibernating and had not noticed that the good old communist ways should have been on the way out.

"By Slovak law, I have a right to evaluate every single piece of evidence that is used against me."

"Evaluation of evidence belongs to the court only."

I was devastated that the judge had no idea that there was a new law in the country.

"Your honour, I would like you to acknowledge that I was escorted to the court late by a few hours, which amounts to illegal apprehension and disregard for the Slovak law, Slovak constitution, and the international agreement that Slovakia signed."

"You are wrong. The police have twenty-four hours, and the court has twenty-four, which amounts to forty-eight hours."

"No, your honour. The police have twenty-four hours, after which point, I should have been released from custody."

"I just told you that we have forty-eight hours," the judge insisted on his communist way of thinking, where the law was only in the books but not in the court.

"I'm in a very regretful situation, when I have to disagree with the judge who will be sentencing me."

Judge Jurko was very mad, and he nodded his head, but I had my knowledge of the law, and I was not about to let him think that he was right.

"All Slovak paragraphs are clear on one point: that, if the police are not able to bring the apprehended person in front of a judge within twenty-four hours, they must let him go free."

"You have read it wrong. Is there anything else?"

He was clearly wrong. How could I talk to somebody like to a normal person, when he did not understand a plain and simple sentence? There were three straight paragraphs concerning police apprehension of a suspect. Every one stated clearly that the police had twenty-four hours to bring the suspect in front of a judge or he must be released. A while before, my lawyer, Ms. Fercakova, had also been surprised when I had pointed the law out to her, and I had had to show her what the paragraphs said.

I decided to drop the subject and move on.

"Please note my disgust at the fact that the child Jana Visokaiova was brutally abused at the police station and forced to falsely testify against me."

"This is not a matter for these proceedings. Is there anything else? I told you that we are hungry."

It was obvious that the judge was losing his temper, so I decided to bring out at least one fact that I thought was the most important.

"I have a large amount of evidence in this investigative file that is proof that Investigator Demjan fabricated whole pages, which amounts to false charges, including falsification of signatures."

"This is not a matter for this court," Judge Jurko insisted. I realized that he would not let me prove anything that had been done illegally against me.

"In that case, I would like it to be recorded in the protocol that facts concerning illegal steps taken by the police and the investigator were not allowed to be proven in this court. If not, I'm requesting that the senate vote on it."

The judge was getting furious. It would not matter how his two side judges voted. Even if they voted that they would not allow it, their result and my objection would be recorded in protocol, and that was all I needed.

The judge dictated,

"The defendant, in his closing statement, requested the opportunity to prove during his closing statement that the interrogating records were falsified, but the senate did not allow him to do so."

In every situation, they knew how to screw the defendants. Did you notice? Twice, he used "closing statement." He would be covered in that case. You do not usually request to prove anything during a closing statement if you had a chance to do it when evidence was being dealt with. But that chance had been denied to me, because the evaluation of proof was not done at all—other than that the judge had named them while turning pages forward and backward.

I was never allowed to present my proof of the illegal acts of the police and the investigator or other important proof of my innocence. I had evidence that Investigator Demjan had requested keys to my house and let the so-called witnesses walk freely in it in order to get familiar with the situation in my home so they could falsely testify against me. Afterward, Demjan lied about it when he was questioned by the investigator of the ministry of the interior, which amounted to contempt of justice.

"I'm requesting to have this written in the protocol as required by Slovak law." I was sweating, and the judge was furious.

Somebody should have asked, "What about your two lawyers? Why are they not helping you?" They knew very well what I was going to do. They both left the courtroom as soon as I got a chance to talk. They all knew that the laws were being broken, and they did not want to hear about it, so they left me in court alone, thus my lawyers broke laws of their own. The court proceeded without my lawyers present. Only in Trebisov could it have been possible.

Bibiana, watching me fighting evil alone, ran out to the hallway where my lawyers were standing and talking.

"Please go in. He is struggling there alone," she begged Ms. Fercakova.

She came in and asked the judge for permission to talk to me. The judge was visibly relieved and glad to do it.

"He does not want to hear anything concerning my defence."

"Just give them your notes; they will have to read them."

I had my doubts, but I did not have much choice. I gave them my notes. After all, I had a copy of it all. They all left the court.

I was totally drained from fighting that wall of garbage. It was worse than talking to a hollow tree. It was a total disaster, facing that example of human garbage, that rectum disposal that was a disgrace to the human race. Creatures like that still believed that they were human beings, because they could walk and talk. But they were wrong. Inside, they were dead souls who would do anything out of jealousy and for money. This judge, who just a week ago had tried to frame me for rape and had been willing to jail me for years, was still using all kinds of manoeuvring to stop me from bringing out the truth, using tricks, while dictating what was going into the protocol, hoping that I would not notice it.

If you ever go to Trebisov, try to avoid everybody who has anything to do with justice. They are creating a hell on earth.

I feel so sorry for everybody—guilty or innocent—who faces that kind of corrupt system, where not one single person has the faintest hope of justice in that injustice full of horrors.

It took a very short time before the judge, his two side judges, and the prosecutor returned. My hope for justice was very slim.

I was very surprised when the judge read his decision. On points 1, 2, 3, and 4, concerning Anna D. by section 226b T.P., the court frees the defendant from the indictment in full.

Dropping the case concerning Alena Demeterova.

> On point 5 (concerning the shotgun), the defendant is found guilty. The fine for this act is set at 10,000 korun [about $300].

Section 226b T.P. read: "The court frees the defendant when his act is not illegal."

I was surprised, but also suspicious of this verdict.

"If I knew that your decision would be so fair, I would not have given you such a hard time before." As soon as I finished my words, I received another surprise.

Prosecutor Bicko so far had spoken only one sentence during the whole proceeding—when he requested to drop the wrong person, Anna Demeterova. He had finally spoken again. It was just a mumble under his breath that nobody could hear. The only reason I noticed it was because

I was expecting it. He objected to the judge's decision. As soon as he mumbled his words, he beat it from the court through the back door. He gave no reason whatsoever, and he never put anything in writing. There was another prosecutor, JUDr. Frantisek Bicko, who openly broke the law in court, and there was no problem at all. Slovak law was very clear that an objection had to have the reason stated, and of course, it had to be in writing. No reason was ever given, and no written objection was ever presented. What was that? Crazy country.

My sister, her husband, Bibiana, and others came down to me to congratulate me for winning the case.

"It is not over yet," I told them. "It is over only when I'm out."As my family were around me, I managed to pass a bundle of documents to Bibiana.

Soon after the judge read his decision, stating that I had been freed, handcuffs were placed on my hands, and I was escorted back to my cell.

FORGERIES of SIGNATURES.
MAROS SABO - young man with no education in Law
was used against me as Prosecutor. When he realized
that he was being used illegally against me, he quit.
But they kept forging his signatures and using his name
in other illegal documents. All resulting in illegal
imprisonment.
In another case they simply signed instead of him as "Bos"-
Next page.

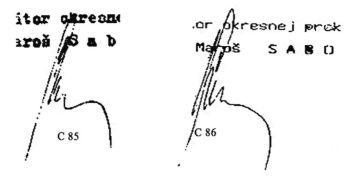

Two REAL SIGNATURES of Sabo on different documents:

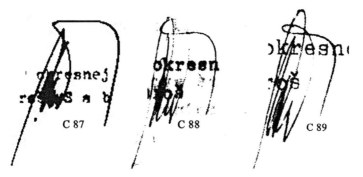

Three FORGED SIGNATURES of Sabo on different
documents:

They fabricate illegal document under the name of any prosecutor and sign
it "instead" of him/her. In this case, *(top document)* they used PUPPET
PROSECUTOR Sabo's name and signed "istead" of him. *(circled)*
In another example they used Prosecutor Pacutova's name. *(bottom document)*
Both documents were fabricated in order to cause grave damage to Mr. Demcak.
(The author)
Chances are that Ms Pacutova and Mr Sabo have no idea that their names
were illegally misused to damage innocent person.

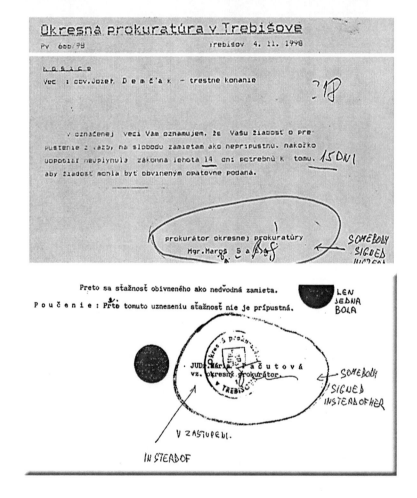

Forgeries of Psychologist PhDr Stancak. All signed on different documents, within one month.

First three signatures are his real signatures. Any expert will confirm that two bottom signatures were forged. All of them were signed when corrupted investigator Demjan was manipulating investigative file. All forgeries were in order to fabricate some damaging claims to hurt Mr. Demcak.

pečiatka   podpis

pečiatka   podpis

pečiatka   podpis

Two Forged signatures of PhDr. Stancak

Znalec psychológ:
Doc. PhDr. Stančák Andrej CSc

(18. NOV. 1998)

Znalec: Doc PhDr. Stančák

(18 NOV. 1998)

Lawyer Stefan Hajdu's SIGNATURES were also FORGED.
I did bring it to his attention, but he declined to take
any action. Policeman Demjan who was forging was
Hajdu's friend.

Two real Hajdu's signatures from different documents:

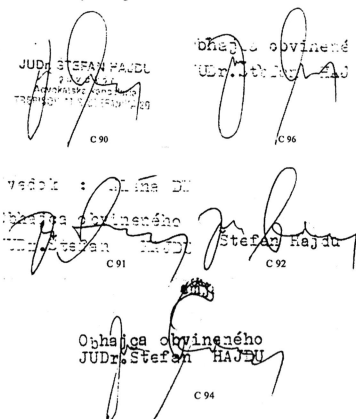

Three FORGED SIGNATURES from different documents:

CHAPTER TWENTY-EIGHT

"This Is My Place, the Place Where I Want to Die." (my dad)

What happened to honest communists? They became very poor.
What about crooked ones? They became very rich.

"He is going to run this company, because he has nothing. That means he is a good man."

Owning nothing was the greatest asset to becoming a good communist in the 1950s, when the communist system was establishing roots in Czechoslovakia. The problem was that most of those who had nothing were lazy and drunk for most of their lives. Their heads were empty, just like their pockets. Heads whose brains were floating in alcohol began running politics, companies, and offices in Czechoslovakia.

The communists let my mom work in the store that used to be hers. They also let my dad work in the company that he had put together with his own two hands. We had to fight in court to be able stay in our own house. Nobody owned any land anymore.

Even the man who had a small shop where he repaired shoes was called a capitalist by Slovak communists. They closed down his shop and confiscated his equipment. They called it nationalization.

We stayed in the middle part of our house, but the three front rooms, where my mom's store was, and the two large back rooms, where my father's production bakery was, were used by the communists.

Soon, they decided that they wanted our garden to build a panelled apartment building. Our garden was adjoined to our property. My dad had planted about forty fruit trees there. Every spring, my mom and my grandmother planted vegetables for our family. All that work was bulldozed. About half of our property was taken away from us—no more garden, no more trees. But the communists were not finished yet. There was a tiny piece of land left, on which our house was located. Mom was growing a little bit of vegetables there, and dad had planted two apricot trees and some other fruit trees on it.

Just when the trees had grown to adult size, the communists decided that another pay-up time was due. That time, our house and whatever land was left were on their list. My family was served a notice that our home would be demolished. The price of the home was set up by them, of course, and it was not negotiable.

The bill of sale was signed by all neighbours but not by my mom. She had decided that she would never sign away the home that she had worked for all of her life. Those who signed received some money. My mom received none. It looked like all would be lost. She still did not sign.

In March 1977, an official from town delivered a notice that our home had been expropriated. In other words, we did not own it anymore to be able to reconsider and sign the agreement.

"You can take it, but I'm not signing my life's work away to anybody," was my mom's answer.

In the official document (C.j.Vyst.1174/76-539), which my mom kept all of her life as proof that she had been robbed, it was clearly stated that it was done against her will. The reason for the expropriation was stated as being that town had the intention of building apartment units under the name of Complex Centre. It had been signed by Vasil Dano. Twenty years later, our property was still empty, but our building, which had included the store, home, bakery, workshop, and other adjoining buildings, had been demolished.

My mom rented a one-bedroom apartment in a panel complex across the street, where she moved with her mom, my grandmother. My dad almost lost his mind. He could not absorb how anybody could come and take your home away. How could people be so cruel? Exactly the same thing happened to his brother just fifteen kilometres away in the town of Secovce. That was Mr. Jovzi Demcak, from whom my dad had learned his trade as a baker of sweets. Jovzi did not survive the cruelty. He died an early death after the communists took everything from him, just like they had taken everything from my dad and mom.

After my mom and my grandmother moved to the one-bedroom apartment, my dad stayed in the kitchen of our home. The kitchen was approximately in the middle of the long L-shaped building. They began demolishing it from the front, while my dad watched with tears in his eyes.

"Why are you doing this? It is good house." He repeated that every day. They were demolishing it the old communist way. Meaning, they took a long time while the gypsies took everything they wanted. Each time a wall fell, part of my dad fell as well.

"Please, Mr. Demcak. We have to demolish your kitchen," one worker pled. My dad was sitting on his couch, which was also his bed. Tears were running down his cheeks and dropping onto the linoleum floor. A once dignified man who had been respected by everybody had become a completely broken man who didn't understand the cruelty of the communists. He was a man who had never hurt anybody. Why did he have to suffer so much? Where was the justice? Where was God? God was there; he was still looking out for him. Nobody had the nerve to come face-to-face and ask him to go. Some policemen refused to do it as well.

So they let him stay in his kitchen and began demolishing from the rear. Besides the couch, there was only a woodstove, one chair, and a wooden table in the kitchen. And just some pots, one tin cup, in which he made himself white coffee. One tablespoon was also there. There were only candles for light, because the electricity had been off for a long time.

The demolition continued from the rear of the house. The pig pens and chicken coops came down. Then our large, wood shed, which was later used as garage as well when we finally bought a car, a Skoda MBX. Then Dad's workshop and the two large rooms that used to be my dad's bakery. The summer kitchen, the veranda went down; it had all been made out of glass, with grapevines providing a nice shadow all around it.

Everything was gone. Only the kitchen with my dad, his tears, and his broken heart, was left standing. Winter arrived; snow had fallen. He kept warm by burning some wood in his kitchen stove. It was hard to imagine that saddest sight: an old man who could not leave his home, even though it was almost all gone. All of the neighbouring buildings were long gone. Only the old man and his kitchen were left standing in the middle of a large empty property, right in the middle of the downtown. Broken walls were all around, as adjoining rooms had been removed. Doors were on each side and to the front. All were doors that used to lead to adjoining rooms before; therefore, none of them could be locked.

Our family members tried to talk to my dad, offering him places to live to no avail.

"Why would I go? This is my place. I lived here all my life. This is where I belong. This is the place where I want to die." His answers were always the same.

The town deposited some money into my parents' account in the National Bank of Slovakia. It was for compensation for our family property. It was under the condition of "take it or leave it." In approximately 1977, according to the exchange rate, it was as follows:

For the land (size 1888 m²) at 8 korun/m² (22¢/m²)

The total for the land: 15,104 korun ($431)

For the investments (buildings): 313,337 korun ($8,952)
For the trees: 7,477 korun ($213)

Total: 335,918 korun ($9,596.-)

No comment is needed. The numbers tell it all.

A lot of land (1,888 m²), a three-room store, a six-room home, a large two-room bakery, a fully built workshop and garage, and adjoining buildings for domestic animals—all for under $10,000. Not a thousand years ago but in 1977.

My mom was sixty-one, and my dad was seventy-one when everything they had been working for was gone again.

My grandmother, who had lived with us for many years, could not take it anymore. She just lay down and died. My mom was devastated. How many times can you lose everything and start again?

But she did not give up. At sixty-one, she decided to rebuild her life once again and live the rest of her life with dignity. It was that or die like her mother had. She chose life. Life with dignity, life that she knew she deserved.

With the little money they received from the town, her and Dad's savings, and money that she borrowed from relatives, she bought a little, old house on a quiet street. There was a tiny garden for her to plant some vegetables.

It was a heart-wrenching situation, when they finally decided to remove my dad from his kitchen. The kitchen was standing like a sore thumb in the middle of a large empty property right downtown. He was seventy-one when two policemen came and informed him that he had been there long enough and it was time to move on. They loaded him into their police car like a common criminal and took him to the house my mom had bought. He kept turning his head back to where his kitchen was; tears ran down his cheeks. In an hour, he was back in his beloved kitchen.

The next time, the communists were better prepared. They took him to the police station for questioning. It took a few hours. The gypsies had already been on standby, and they worked hard that time. After the police released him, he walked straight to his kitchen. It was gone—demolished. Everything was gone. His stove, his couch, and all his personal possessions had been taken by the gypsies. He just dropped face down into the dust and passed out. He was taken to the local hospital.

My family persuaded my dad to come to what was the new home. He missed his kitchen, but when he saw five trees standing there for him to take care of, he got used to it and accepted his new home.

My younger brother built a little workshop for my dad, where he produced some cream pies for whoever placed an order. Soon, word spread around about where you could buy the best cream pies in town, and orders came in.

My mom was taking seasonal jobs in a local sugar factory and, later, in a coat deposit booth in the local Hotel Tokaj.

It was another beginning in her sixties for my mom and his seventies for my dad.

Ten years later, their debts were paid off, and they had saved 30,000 korun each (about $1,000) for their funerals, as they said.

The communists were falling out of power by then, and I was finally able to visit the town where I had been born. It was great to taste my mom's soup, which everybody said was the best in the world. We had a lot to catch up on.

She was so glad when the communists fell and I could visit regularly.

Now it was another disaster. She was visiting me in jail and telling me that the ex communists wanted five million korun for my freedom. There would not be enough, even if she sold my and her house.

I asked her not to pay one halier (one penny) to those bastards. She left prison worried about my health. I had been trying not to show her how much I was suffering, but I could not fool her. As every mom would, she felt my terrible mental and physical state. She left that prison and decided to fight for my freedom.

At home, she asked my brother to play her the tape of the gypsies, as I had asked her to do. She got really mad, because now she had proof in her hands that it was all just the dirty, stinky work of gypsies and the corrupt work of policemen and other officials in Trebisov. My dad was dead. She was eighty-two then, but she decided to put up one more fight against those communist creeps.

Inevitably, somebody could ask the simple question, "Is there an honest communist at all?"

My natural answer would be, "Yes, but I have not met one."

I like this answer best, but I cannot say it, because I have in fact met some honest communists. I have also met some didn't have any choice, because it was the only way they could improve their position and provide solid support for their families. I do not expect everybody to sacrifice everything just to admit that they do not believe in the communist system. Many were destroyed just for doing that.

The most honest communist I have ever met was my uncle Andrej Milovcik from Secovce. We called him Andris *(read Andrish)*. He was my mom's brother and also my godfather. He was an ideal candidate for the communist party, with only a basic education and no trade skills. In spite of our huge differences of opinion on the subject, I had and still have very high respect for him. He was also a typical example of what happened to honest communists in those times.

He had a very good job, in which he could have gotten very rich if only he wasn't honest. He was a director of a coal warehouse, which was a wholesaler and retailer of coal for the whole district. Coal was the only source of heat, besides wood, in those days. That meant that truckloads, cargo trailers pulled by Zetor tractors, and farmer trailers pulled by horses for private people were loading coal all day long. His job was to scale the loads and collect all the money in cash, as cheques were not a known commodity in those days. There was only one secretary, who helped with the paperwork, and one tractor driver, who delivered the coal.

Andris could have made millions if he had not had that terrible handicap that kept him from getting rich—he was honest. All he needed to do was sign for a few more kilos here and there and then sell the difference to some private person and take home a few thousand korun every day. But not him. He had to be honest.

No customer ever went in to check what the scale, which was inside the office, read. No control was possible, as trains of coal were unloaded, and it was in huge piles outside, and the weight of coal fluctuated by rain and sun. No person would be hurt, and the big state-owned company would never feel any damage. It would be the perfect way to help his family but not him. He did not believe in the well-known proverb in those days: "If you don't steal, you are stealing from your family."

He was so honest that nobody would believe that it was possible to be so. One man learned the hard way. Like everybody else, he could not believe that somebody who was a party member could, in fact, be honest. A company trailer was loaded with two tons of coal, weighed as usual by Andris, and pulled by Zetor tractor, as ordered by a customer, to a nearby village. Andris followed the trailer on his Manet scooter to make sure the Zetor driver would not stop at his home, which was on the way, and throw a few shovelfuls of coal into his yard for his personal use during the winter. Once the driver had passed his house, it was safe to return back to the office, which he did.

At the customer's home, the owner shovelled the coal through a little window into his basement. The Zetor driver was helping him for a bottle of homemade vodka called Slivovica.

The coal was almost all in the basement, when the owner asked the Zetor driver,

"It does not look like two tons of coal. What do you think?" It was a big mistake. He should not have asked that question.

"What did you say? Shovel it all back onto the trailer," a voice came like a storm from the outside through the little window. And sure enough, it was Andris. He had come on his Manet scooter to see why it was taking so long for the driver to return.

It just so happened that Andris had been looking down through the little window to give his driver shit for taking so long when the customer had asked that destined question. Talk about bad timing.

Nothing helped. No apology or plea that he had not meant it nor excuse that he had only been asking. The coal had to be shovelled back through the little basement window, loaded back onto the trailer and hauled back onto the scale—every little piece, including the coal dust. This time the customer had to come to the office and see it for himself. It was exactly two tons, not a gram more or less.

No apology was accepted after that at all. That was an offence that could not be tolerated at all by a man who had been weighing coal honestly all his life.

I'm not saying this because he was my mother's brother, my uncle, and my godfather. Neither am I saying this because he gave me a Flexaret camera that inspired me to lifelong hobby or because he took me hunting when I was a young boy. I'm saying this because it has to be recognized that there were communists who were also honest communists. He was one of those honest ones.

Andris had lost his two brothers (my uncles), who were fighting for freedom of Slovak people, in the war. He honestly believed that socialism was what freedom was.

Would I be that honest? No way. I have to be honest and admit it. I have good reason not to be that honest. And the reason is actually Andris himself.

All the party members who were not that honest built themselves big two-story houses with full basements. They moved out of Andris' neighbourhood to new, lucrative locations. Andris lived off the salary he received from selling coal all of his life. He could not afford to build a new house. Andris and his wife Piroska lived in the back part of a small house, which had been inherited from their family. The front part of the house was occupied by their relatives.

When Andris' communist party colleagues built big houses and moved away from the old street, they just abandoned their old houses. Inevitably gypsies moved into his neighbourhood. I felt sorry for him when I visited him the last time. Gypsies were living on both sides of his home. The communist system had officially fallen, but he was still a member of his party and hoping that the ideology he believed in would spread all over the world. When I told him how it was in Canada, he did not believe me. He told me that tall buildings were not real but only painted pictures. I invited him to see it with his own eyes, but he refused.

I still have respect for a man who followed what he believed. He died, while I was in prison because his former party members had placed me there.

Andris was an honest communist, and he suffered for it.

His sister, my mom, was an honest non-communist, and she also suffered for it.

His two brothers died in war.

His two brothers-in-law (one was my father), suffered, because they learned their trades and wanted to work hard. None of Andris' relatives could ever understand how he could join such a terrible party that had destroyed so many people's lives.

When I brought up the atrocities that communists had caused for so many people, he had only one answer, "Those were that kind of times."

The times when you suffered when you were an honest communist. If you were not a communist, you suffered even more.

CHAPTER TWENTY-NINE

"Do You Think I'm Going to Die If I Drink This?"

Where in the world do they reward adultery? In Slovakia. (Where else?)

Miro Horvath was a big, young gypsy from a town called Valaliky, which was almost a suburb of the city of Kosice.

His nose was running, and he was pulling the snot back into his mouth and swallowing it. It was a typical noise, as if a bulldog was snoring and snarling. He was walking back and forth nonstop, producing that noise each time he passed from the window toward the door. At first, I felt disgusted, but because it was not his fault, I got used to it.

Being locked in a small area for twenty-four hours a day, most prisoners walked back and forth between the gater and the door for hours.

At first, I thought that I would never walk like that, but in time, it came naturally, and it gave me some kind of relief, Time passed a little bit faster. I walked across, and Miro walked lengthwise.

Being locked in a small area had a very negative effect on his gypsy-nature psyche, on top of his young age.

He had done a lot of walking the length of the cell. You could hear and feel his steps, which were like the steps of a miniature elephant. It was his first encounter with adult prison, because he had just reached eighteen. On the outside, Miro had been committing crimes with his uncle, dad, and other family members and friends.

The first time, he spent six months in a youth detention center for a crime he actually did not commit. His family members had committed theft and robbery on a bigger scale. Because he was just a young boy with no criminal record, it was his duty to the family members who had actually committed the crime to take the blame on himself. As a youth and with a clean record, he would spend only six months in jail. His uncle and other family members would have received at least three to five years, because they were all convicts with mile-long records. It was routine in gypsy families that children took the blame for crimes committed by other members of their families.

Stealing and cheating was completely in his blood, inherited from his predecessors for many generations back.

He told me of many encounters and close calls with the police when he was "working" mainly with his uncle.

"We were stealing potatoes from the fields, as usual, but the police showed up as if from nowhere. My uncle was driving like crazy, right through the cornfield and straight to our yard. They [the police] would not dare cross our gate. Our family members were there; everybody had axes and shovels in their hands. All we managed to take was half a bag of potatoes. We had some rotten potatoes at home, so we put them in the bottom of the bag, together with some rocks to make it heavier. We sold it to our friend, who had a junkyard and bought all our stolen stuff. He was a good friend. The next day, he asked, 'What kind of potatoes did you sell me?' But we gave him no money back. No way. He was good friend. He even came to court to testify. The judge asked him, 'How many times did he sell you stuff?' He said, 'Only once.' He didn't say, 'All the time.' He was a good friend."

Stealing and cheating were totally normal. There was no place he would have been and not stolen something. There were the different electronics at elementary schools, aluminum crosses and decorations at the cemeteries, canned fruits and vegetables in summer cottages and homes, different items in soccer stadium buildings and local grocery stores—potato bags full of live chicken, pigs from collective agriculture, parts of railroad trucks, including cables.

They went through it all.

But what do you do when you are locked up in a prison cell and you can't steal from your cellmates, because you are never alone? How do you satisfy your cravings? No problem.

Another gypsy was in a cell on the third floor, right above us.

"You have some cigarettes?" he yelled to Miro.

"Sure, I do. What do you have to trade?"

"Very good American shampoo."

"Send it down. I will send you a package of cigarettes."

Remember, there was no trading allowed, and you could not reach the window, because the gater was in front of it. If there was a will, there was a way. The gypsy upstairs took a bedsheet and tore it into thin lines, which became a string. Then he rolled magazines, which became a pole. He placed the bottle of shampoo in a little bag that he also made out of the bedsheet and tied it to the string and to the end of his made-up pole, on which he had rolled the string. Then he stuck it out the window, unrolled the string, and lowered the contraband down to the window below. Miro also has his handmade pole ready, which was bent on the end, forming a little hook. He pulled it in and fetched his shampoo. All he needed now was to place the cigarettes in the bag, and his friend could pull it up. He could, but the problem was that Miro had no cigarettes. He was not a smoker, because his respiratory condition did not allow him to puff. He knew what to do. He took his shampoo, tore the empty bag, and dropped it on the ground outside.

"It tore off and fallen down," he yelled upstairs. His trading partner realized that he was screwed. All he could do was yell a few obscenities and learn from his stupidity. In the meantime, Miro had a great feeling of satisfaction and felt that the day worth living for had finally arrived.

It did not bother him that he had just screwed another gupsy or that he did not need any shampoo—he had very short hair, and I had given him a big bottle, because Bibiana had sent me too much.

You would think that this boy or that gypsies in general had no ethics, but that was not so.

I was very surprised when I visited a friend, named Lado, who lived in the town of Hriadky. His friend lived right next door to a gypsy village, not far from a city called Vranov in eastern Slovakia. He had a huge fruit orchard, full of all kinds of fruits. They were delicious apples; we went there to get some. I could hear the noise of the gypsies right behind his very low fence.

"How do you keep them [the gypsies] from stealing your fruit?" I wondered.

"I have no problem at all," he said. "These are the ethics of gypsies: never steal from your neighbours. But beware if you are not a neighbour." Again, I had learned something new.

The same as his family, the only thing Miro knew to do to survive was to steal, and now he had graduated to robbing as well.

"We stole diesel from a semitruck. Fifty litres. We added water into it—fifty fifty—and sold it to another trucker. It was a hundred litres. Then we stole oil, diluted it with water, and sold it as diesel.

"This time, I got assault and robbery," he told me. "I hit him. He got a black eye, and I got his credit card. He said in court that he saw me only from behind. My family told him to drop the charge. Maybe he will, because he is afraid now. He can't even speak right. I had his card on me. I told the police I'd found it. There were no witnesses. The policeman had big arms, like this. He hit me so hard that I got dizzy. He grabbed me by the neck and lifted me up. I was bleeding from my neck. They took me to the doctor. The policeman wrote that it was an old wound. I was still bleeding.

"I took a crowbar and broke the doors of cottages. We went downstairs. There was a big padlock on the door. I stuck the bar under the door and stepped on it. The door just went up. Inside, the basement was full of canned fruit. We broke every one of them. All I took was full bags of potatoes, because I can sell them. My friend took some vegetables home. Stupid. I just broke all the cans of fruit. We were going to cottages like going home. I will show them when I get out. I will burn them all down. I will cut all the tires on police cars. I will show them."

I personally hated vandals, so I interrupted.

"Next time you break in somewhere, you just take what you need, but don't do any damage, because you may need something later. It is also not nice to damage things for no reason."

He thought about it, but it was a big question as to whether it would have any impact on his wild nature.

There was also some "artistic" talent in him. One day, he placed a white pillowcase on his face and, with black marker, drew what was supposed to be his portrait. He followed the curves of his face with the marker. It didn't come out very pretty and did not resemble his portrait at all. So he added a devil's horns on it and wrote "Guard" under it. Each time he got mad, he picked up the pillow, screamed obscenities in the guard's face, and began hitting it wildly.

He must have noticed that I was a wise man, because he kept asking me many hard questions, and I had to think hard to get the right answers. There were too many, but just to mention some:

"Is Czechoslovakia smaller than Slovakia?"

"No, Slovakia was part of Czechoslovakia, so Czechoslovakia must be larger."

"What is a fascist?"

"Fascists were fighting the world and were killing Jews and gypsies."

"What is the president for if he gives no amnesty?" This was after Mr. Schuster became president and gave no pardons to anybody. Schuster disappointed even me.–

"Presidents who give no amnesty are good for nothing."

"Can snakes have babies?"

"Yes. Some hatch from eggs, and others are born like you."

"What language do they speak in France?"

"French."

"Is French the same as English?"

"No"

"Are England and the United States the same thing?"

"No, but they speak the same language."

"If Havel was trying to be president, he would get more than a hundred voices, right?"

"Yes."

"Isn't Zirinovsky a Slovak?" (*Zirinovsky was a controversial, drunk, Russian leftist who was hoping to bring the Soviet era back.*)

"No, he was a Soviet."

As you see, I had to answer many "hard" questions. But Miro did not just ask; he also told his opinions: "If we could kill those guards, we could get out. We could do it with a knife, when they peep through the peephole. *Peef* through the hole in his head."

When the guards placed obstacles in the sink pipes so prisoners could not pass any objects through them to neighbouring cells, water went down the sink drain much more slowly. Miro told me why: "The water is going slower, because they installed bigger pipes there yesterday." Then he continued, "If I could change to water, I would go nicely downstairs through the pipes and then out. The guards would have no chance with me."

There were, of course, more questions from Miro.

"Is Europe in Slovakia?"

"No, Slovakia is in Europe."

"But America is also Europe, right?"

"No, America is on the other side of the earth. Now, it is night there."

"Is it dark in America at night?"

"Yes."

"How can it be that it is dark in America now?"

"Because when the sun is here, the moon is there."

"Europe is the same as America, right?"

"No, we are in Europe."

"So Europe is farther than America? Right?"

"No, America is farther. We are in the middle of Europe."

"Is London and Paris the same thing?"

"No, London is London, and Paris is Paris."

"The capital city of Bratislava is Prague, right?"

"No, Bratislava is the capital of Slovakia."

"So, Czech is the capital city of Prague, right?"

"No, Prague is the capital of Czech."

"Isn't it the same thing?"

"No, it is … I guess it is." I felt that he had learned enough, so I let it go. I did not want him to get too smart in one day.

That was what I got when Miro discovered that I might be smarter than him. It could have been too much for him—all those answers—because he hit his forehead with his palm as hard as he could. Then he slapped his right cheek. The slap echoed through the whole cell. He was doing that kind of self-punishment from time to time, so I did not pay attention to it. But when he hit his collarbone with his fist, it sounded like a sledgehammer, he screamed in pain, it got my attention, so I looked at him, with a question in my eyes.

"What are they going to do if I break it?" he wanted to know.

"They are going to slap some cloth or some cement on you, hang your arm on your neck, and bring you right back here. No, they will not take you to the hospital, if that is what you think."

"Is it going to hurt if I cut myself with razor blade?" -

"It will, you can be sure."

This conversation put me to sleep.

As you've noticed, I "learned" a lot in that jail. But I also paid something back. I was writing many complaints to the Slovak government by hand, so my handwriting improved very much. Arpy, another young gypsy in my cell, noticed what beautiful writing it was. He was from Roznava, about seventy-five kilometres west of Kosice, and had been charged with robbery. He was writing many letters in his terrible style to his family and his girlfriend.

"Sure, I can teach you to write nicely, like me," I told him, after he asked me if I could teach him. I took one of my writing books with lines in it and ordered him to write the same letter of the alphabet for the length of a whole line and then for the length of the whole page. Of course, I outlined samples for him. It took about a month, he passed my test, and I gave him the green light to write home in bright, new, beautiful style. The reaction from home was incredible.

"What happened to your writing? Nobody can read it anymore."

We played cards and checkers. Miro and Arpy tried to cheat a lot. After we finished playing, I told them about every time they cheated. They were embarrassed and wanted to know why I let them do it for a long time.

"Just to make little boys happy," I said. After that, they tried to play without cheating. I also tried to teach them chess, but it was too complicated of a game for them.

They had some misunderstanding one day and ended up in a little fight. They both received ten days in the hole. Everybody was really afraid of the hole.

"I'm really afraid of that hole," Arpy told me one evening, just one night before he was due for his punishment.

"Do you think I will die if I drink this? He had been peeling paint from the cell walls for a long time that day. He had a glass full of the paint dust, which he was getting ready to drink.

"I only want to get sick, because I don't want to go into that hole, but I don't want to die," he explained.

"I can tell you one thing. If you don't want to die then don't drink it. It will get you nowhere. If you survive, they will put you in the hole anyway, after you get better."

It looked like he took my advice, because he placed the glass to the side. But soon after bedtime, he went to the corner where the toilet was, mixed the paint dust with water, and drank it. Huge convulsions followed. We pushed the panic button. He looked like he was having an epileptic seizure. We kept pressing the red button. I lifted him by his stomach, trying to make him vomit. Finally, the guards came and took him away. We never saw Arpy again.

The worst part about the whole situation was that we didn't know what happened afterward. We wondered if he survived and if he was all right. It just added to our stresses. But that was the way they ran that gulag full of horrors.

The next day, Miro went to serve his ten days in the hole.

Time went by, and I had no idea what was going on. I had been released, but only on paper. Not knowing what was going and knowing that I was in the hands of atrocious monsters had a terrible effect on my mental and physical health.

Hearing and witnessing other prisoners suffer terrible abuse only added to my own hardship.

Imagine the story of another Arpy, and he also happened to be from Roznava. This Arpy was not a little, gypsy crook but a decorated army officer who had committed all his life to serving the Czechoslovakian army. Now he had been placed in my cell, charged with armed robbery, uttering threats, and endangering lives with a weapon while under the influence of alcohol. Why would an army officer have done something like that? That was the first thing that crossed my mind. It was shocking when I finally got the answers. It became obvious that he had never committed any of the above crimes at all.

His right foot was like that of a full-grown Hippopotamus, swollen in size all the way up to his knee. You could not see the foot at all. He was still in the function of a hall boy, limping and serving food to prisoners.

"I accidentally spilled a cap of tea," he explained about his swollen foot. It had to have been a lot of tea to inflict that kind of wound, I thought with my suspicions, and I was right. I also find out about his crime—"terrible robbery," beyond the human imagination.

The most recent field exercise was to have lasted six weeks. The field manoeuvring was shortened by five days. Arpy rushed home to see his loving wife whom he had missed for over five weeks. He came too early and at the wrong time, because he discovered another man in his bed with his wife. He was too proud to make a scene and too smart to kill his wife and her lover with his nine-millimetre gun, which he kept in his strongbox. He took his money from the box and stashed it in the right pocket of his army jacket. About 10,000 korun ($300) was there. He broke a gold necklace and placed the pieces in his outside pocket.

"Here. it was for you for our twentieth wedding anniversary." It crossed his mind to shoot them both when he grabbed his gun, but being an army officer, he was able to control his feelings.

If I kill them, nothing will happen to them. They will both be happy and dead, and I will suffer for the rest of my life in jail. I will just punish myself and reward them.

"When I come back tomorrow, I don't want to see you here," he addressed mainly his wife. He waved his gun and placed it in the left inside jacket pocket.

He returned to his office in the military complex. He was pissed off and could not sleep, because he could not believe it could happen after their long years of marriage. He pulled a bottle of Vodka that he had in his office closet, which was a must for every officer in the Slovak army, in case higher ranked officers visited. Arpy treat himself to few shots, hoping it would help him to get some sleep. But he did not get any sleep at all.

Four armed military policemen entered his office without knocking. They placed him in a military jail. After scrambling and jumbling, he was transferred to a civilian prison, because his dangerous conduct had happened after duty in his private residence.

How could that happen? After he left his loving wife, she, on the advice of her lover, ran to the police station, reporting that her husband had come home drunk while she was sleeping alone in her bed, threatened her with his gun, raped her, and robbed her of her life savings, including her jewellery, which was a gift from her mother.

Her story fit very well. Arpy was arrested, smelling of alcohol. In his army jacket was gun, money, and also pieces of jewellery. The city police discovered the empty strongbox. They did not look for the man in Arpy's bed. He was long gone anyway, and the city police had not talked to Arpy as yet, so they only knew his wife's side of the story. Only the DNA of the lover was left in the bed, but nobody was looking for it.

In a normal country, he would have been out on bail the next day or never even apprehended. But this was not a normal country, and there was a big obstacle in the way. Because of this incident, Arpy was discharged from the army, but because he had served for more than twenty years, he was entitled to his army pension, and he was getting it. It was deposited into his jail account and, through his lawyer, divided among the justice officials, who were always willing to be involved when a steady stream of money was coming. Nobody had the smallest interest in helping him out, which would stop the solid income of cash into their pockets.

Even after his side of the story was clearly proven to be truthful, he was kept in and was destroyed piece by piece. You could feel how the old guards enjoyed abusing him, because he was a real officer, not like them, who had only so-called, borrowed army ranks.

One blow to his psyche followed after another. The lover of his wife—the one he had discovered in his bed—moved promptly into his bed. His wife filed for divorce. She claimed all the lies that she had made up. The divorce was granted. Then she applied for the apartment to be transferred to her name. It was situated in a military complex, and it was transferred to her. But the rental fees and monthly utilities payments were still Arpy's responsibility. She also applied for alimony, which would have virtually eaten his military pension. The request was granted but postponed or placed on hold until further notice. It was understandable, because his pension was going to the justice officials. If he got out of jail, most of his pension would be going to her and her lover, and he would still owe backpayments for alimony and utility payments that his wife and her new lover enjoyed. When he came out, he would be a totally destroyed man with no place to live. That was the future that was waiting for him. Nobody was interested in bringing his case to a hearing. When they were destroying somebody, they did not fool around. They did it right.

In more than two years of an investigation, there was not one piece of evidence to corroborate his wife's claims. The investigator collected such absurd evidence, like his fingerprints on his strongbox and his gun. Did they expect something else? And what did it prove? That he held his box and his gun? How stupid can you get?

After more than twenty years of serving his country, his life was already destroyed, and he had not reached court yet. Everything was decided in his absence.

He was getting one piece of bad news after the other, just like me. A totally innocent man. His energy left him as a result of the stress. To top it off, they made him a hall boy, and he had no energy to do the extra work that was required. It was almost three years before his soul could not take it anymore.

That was when he had that "accident" with a hot cup of tea. It was a little bit different from the way he described it. I found out the truth some time later, after I was moved and Igor Gregor was assigned to my cell. He was there in the cell, when the "accident" took place.

Igor told me the way he had witnessed it. "Arpy was a hall boy, so he brought in a pail of hot water from the shaving room. The water was pretty hot already, but he still dipped the tea boiler in it. We did not pay any attention to it, because he was always doing *rajony* [washing and cleaning of the halls]. That is until he began pouring steaming, boiling water on his leg. He was screaming like a black monkey, but he kept pouring the water from his knee down. I ran and knocked the pail from his hands, but the damage was already done. Then I pressed the emergency button. He fell down and rolled in pain on the cement floor. The guards took him down, and I have never seen him again." Igor had never seen him again, because Arpy had been assigned to my cell. His foot was swollen, and he had a temperature, but he was not allowed to lie down and still had to do his duty as a hall boy.

He was in my cell for quite a while. Eventually, his foot shrank to a smaller size. The grossest part of it was the smell of boiled skin and when he began to peal dead parts of it off. My stomach turns when I think about it, even now.

I do understand why he did it. I know the feeling firsthand. You suffered more when you were innocent, and you suffered even more when you had been somebody on the outside. He was an army officer, and I was a high school professor. Suddenly, we were less than nobodies, living in a small room with convicts and recidivist criminals. The primitive guards were always on our cases. Those empty-headed guards were always the worst.

I told Arpy that, if we lived, we could still do something to turn our lives around. Maybe the new government would care more about what was going on in the justice system. That was when he began to exercise. As soon as his leg got better, he was running in the little square in the chicken coop outside while I was walking in the shape of the number eight. He could never stop thinking about the system that had rewarded his wife for committing adultery and punished him after more than twenty years of loyal service to his country. It would be nice to know how he ended up, if he ended up at all, by now. There was no limit to how long he was entitled to his pension, so the justice officials may still be collecting it.

That was the system in Slovak prisons. You could only witness limited numbers of horrors, and you hardly knew how they ended up. And horrors were all over there.

Take the story of the gypsy who was sick, and they would not let him lie down. The lady doctor told him that he was not sick enough to get permission to lie down. He was drained of energy and knew that the lady doctor was wrong.

They brought him back to his cell, and something snapped in him. He took a blade out of the razor and ran it across his stomach. The cut was better than he expected. He was overweight, and his intestines began to push themselves out through the cut. He began to panic and grabbed the nearest object. It was his slipper. He pressed it against his stomach to keep his insides in. His cellmates began screaming, "Help." In the panic, it took them a while to remember to push the panic button, but they finally did.

Guards wrapped a blanket around him and took him down to the clinic. The same lady doctor and nurse were still there on duty.

"What now, more?" the doctor asked.

"I lost my slipper. Can you find it for me?" he opened the blanket.

The horrible sight of the bloody slipper pressed against his stomach and intestines protruding around it appeared. It was too much even for the young lady doctor. I guess she was not a surgeon. Both the doctor and the nurse fainted. The nurse fell on the floor, vomiting, and the doctor bent over the chair, holding her stomach.

They called an ambulance, and he was taken to the army hospital, and his wish came true. They finally let him lie down.

This is not a bedtime story. This is a true story, exactly the way I was told by more than one prisoner.

The guard who once told me that you had to be dead before they let you lie down there was wrong. This gypsy was proof that, if you are lucky, they let you lie down even before death. But you must be very close to it and only as an exception.

It does not matter who I talked to; everybody had some horror story to tell. Slovaks who had money or assets were targets, but foreigners were prime ones. At the time I was in, they could keep anybody before conviction for three years. The more stubborn prisoners decided that they would suffer through it, rather than pay for their freedom. The officials did not like it, so they adjusted the law. Now they could keep you in without a conviction for five years. Most of the time, they ignored even that law. If they decided to keep you longer, no problem. Nobody cared about the law anyway.

It was no secret that German "tourists" loved Slovak girls. Slovak girls were pretty, well dressed, and, mainly, inexpensive. German customers traveled all the way to Slovakia, where assortments were much larger than by the Czech-German border. Some wished they never had.

The case of the German and French tourists was known around the whole prison. As soon as you crossed the Czech or Austrian border to Slovakia, there were pretty hitchhikers available to welcome you. A young German man picked up two of them in a suburb of the Slovak capital of Bratislava. He noticed in his mirror that they were examining his belongings, which he had behind the backseat of his black Mercedes. He stopped promptly and ordered them out of his car. They already had his camera and other items in their bags. After a short scuffle outside when he tried to get his things back, the girls began screaming, "Help. Rape."

Some lights came on in nearby windows, so he decided he'd better forget the things they had just stolen from him, and he left the scene.

The poor girls reported the rape to the police. Nothing was more welcome for corrupt officials than a westerner and two willing witnesses. It made no difference how absurd their claim was. I'm not an expert on rape, but I'm sure that those who are will agree that it is not exactly an easy task to rape two girls simultaneously in your car, unless you had a machine gun. But that was the claim; this man had raped those two women. First, he had raped one, and the other had witnessed it, and then he had raped the second, and the first had witnessed it. Sound familiar? You bet. Remember Demjan's stories about when I was "cleaning up" those gypsies with my tongue? There was always another witnessing it. These absurd claims were normal in Slovakia, and the pathetic judges listened to them, and with a serious face, convicted innocent people without blinking an eye.

There was no other proof than that the women could describe the car inside and knew the licence plate number. No medical examination of any kind was performed, and no signs of any struggle were ever mentioned. The technique or description of how he managed to rape two women was never explained. Just the claims of those two were enough to keep him in jail and to destroy his life. He lost his job, his reputation, all of his money, his assets, and years of his life. Almost everybody—all the way up to the highest official—knew that it was a setup, made in Slovakia, but nobody lifted a finger to help him. Slovaks called it independent justice.

Another unfortunate man was from France. He arrived in Slovakia by air, rented a car, and travelled around. He decided to also visit Uzhorod, which was a large city in the Ukraine near the Slovak border. His rental car was stolen there. Nothing new. Thousands of cars were stolen in the Ukraine every year, especially from tourists. But this was a big chance for Slovak justice officials. They jailed him and accused him of selling the car in the Ukraine. There was never ever any evidence to support this claim. He was a westerner, and the officials envisioned big money coming their way.

He was a young, strong Frenchman, when he was brought to the same prison I was in.

He knew he was innocent, and he had no idea what they were able and willing to do. Two guards brought him in. Not knowing the language, he was suspicious, but he was not sure what was going on. Once he spotted the heavy, steel cell doors, he realized he was being arrested. He grabbed the office door, trying to refuse to go in a cell. He yelled in French, asking what was going on and that he wished to see the consul, but nobody could understand him. The two guards who had brought him in were trying to tear him off the door, but they were unable to, because he was too strong. Another two who were on duty in the ward ran to help. Four guards were pulling him off, but the Frenchman was holding onto the handle of the door with all the power he had in him, and the fact that he was angry even added to his strength. The four guards pulled with all their might; one even braced his legs against the wall. Suddenly, the door let go and crashed down with part of the wall, burying them underneath. Dust filled the corridor. Everybody ended up with various, non–life-threatening injuries.

He had fallen in badly with most of the guards, especially the older ones. The usual long process of abuse began.

After a long time without a trial or a lawyer who spoke French, he realized that there was no end to it and decided to shorten his suffering. He refused food or water. No officials were worried.

One guard, who was friendly with me, explained,

"It is much worse now than during the last years of communist times. When somebody was starving himself then, everybody ran around, because some superior communists could ask some questions. Now they made a law that suits them. If a prisoner inflicts some wounds on himself or kills himself, nobody worries. They made a law, according to which it is only his problem."

The Frenchman was out of luck. As usual, they placed him in cell alone, so that other prisoners could not witness his suffering. The cell was located next to the prison health clinic. The prison doctor came by every day, telling him that he should eat, because starving could hurt his health. Weeks went by, and he became just a shadow of the man he used to be. His bottom lip cracked. He was unable to get up.

A young guard who was witnessing it could not take it anymore. He called the French consulate. It was anonymous call. The French consul insisted that he wanted to see his man right away. He was shocked. The man was starved and dehydrated, almost dead. The French consul insisted that he would not leave the prison until his man was taken to a hospital.

He was taken to a hospital and brought back to life by intravenous nutrition. He suffered permanent liver and kidney damage, as well as other physical and mental complications. With the help of the French government, he sued the Slovak government in a European court and won some compensation, but his health would never be the same.

Nobody was ever legally held responsible for these cruel examples of what went on in the Slovak justice system.

Like in many other cases, the Slovaks simply pay whatever the European court ordered, and the abuse keeps going, like the water in Danube River.

I wonder if the Canadian government will still defend Slovak justice after reading this. Or will they tell me that it never happened, because I cannot prove it? Remember, I'm not writer, and I can't write fiction.

CHAPTER THIRTY

The Judge Has Not Finished His Crime Yet; We Must Wait Until He Is Done

How do Slovak top officials present their diplomatic lies? "With profound honour."

On March 18, 1999, I was found not guilty by the senate of the district court in the town of Trebisov. The presiding judge was JUDr. Milan Jurko. The judges sitting to the sides were JUDr. Valeria Havrilkova and Agnesa Cernakova.

The not guilty verdict was pronounced according to section 226b, which applies when the act committed is not illegal. In other words, I had not done anything illegal in all four major accusations. The not guilty verdict was announced at the court proceedings and was also written in the proceedings. It also stated that I was released from prison. The presiding judge had also written the Sentencing Judgement in the name of the Slovak Republic, which was also dated March 18, 1999, and reads that I was found not guilty, because I had not committed any crime; therefore, I was released from jail.

The question is "Why then was I escorted in handcuffs back to prison?"

Prosecutor JUDr. Bicko mumbled his objection, but he did not state the reason. Slovak law is very clear that a prosecutor must state the reason if objecting a judge's decision. But that is not all. Bicko had not even written down anything. He clearly ignored section 249 paragraph 1 T.P.

According to this law, the complaint or appeal had to be clear about for what reasons it was filed.

Before him, another prosecutor in my case, mgr. Sabo, who had apparently objected to judge's decision to let me out on bail, had proceeded in the same way. Nobody heard him object, and nobody has seen the objection in writing, because it never happened. Neither of them actually legally objected to my release. All of that was just fabricated.

The question is: can a man break any law without any consequences?

Judge Jurko, had also written a separate decision, which stated that I was released from prison also according to section 72 paragraph 2 T.R., because according to this paragraph, the reasons for imprisonment had expired.

The question is: why was I kept in prison even after that?

Both documents—the Sentencing Judgment and the Decision of Release—were dated March 18, 1999.

The question is; why did Judge Jurko not give me any of those documents at sentencing? If he did, I would have been released right then.

The question is: why were those documents delivered to me only May 7, 1999. All documents that were delivered to me in jail were stamped by the date stamp of the prison administration, which was May 7, 1999.

The question is: where were those documents for almost two months? Did Judge Jurko keep them in his desk, or did somebody else arrange that they be kept out of my sight and out of the prison officials' sight; therefore, I was kept illegally in prison. Or the documents were delivered to the prison, but somebody arranged that the prison officials ignore them to keep me in illegally?

On the same day (May 7, 1999), I also received a third decision. It was from Judge JUDr. Jan Popovec. It was dated April 15, 1999. If he made the decision on April 15, where were the documents for three weeks? This decision stated, and the fact was, that he was somewhere alone. Nobody was there. No prosecutor, no lawyer, not me as the defendant, and not even a typist. But he still named himself the provincial court and acted on a nonexistent appeal or nonexistent complaint. Can anybody top that? How can anybody invent a more anarchistic example of events? Nobody even knew where he created that idiotic masterpiece, through which he cancelled the district court's decision and kept me in jail. He called it a secret proceeding, in spite of the fact that, by law, it must be done at a public hearing. He had no problem knowing that he had done it alone without a prosecutor, because the prosecutor de facto had not even filed any documents. Logically, he could not have been there. My lawyer wasn't invited, and I, as the defendant, was not there either. The law could not be clearer on the point that the defendant who is imprisoned must be in court, unless he gave up his right to be there. That way, nobody could ask Judge Popovec any questions.

The question is: can a judge break all laws and have it be normal in Slovakia?

But when the whole story reached the general prosecutor's office in Bratislava, they—JUDr. Dorica under the watchful eye of General Prosecutor JUDr. Hanzel—saw no broken laws.

The broken laws were sitting in front of them, and they claimed that they were not there.

They were all breaking laws as if on assembly lines, and they kept me in jail.

It was total and complete anarchy.

The question is: who arranged that all those documents be kept hidden, and who and how was it arranged with Judge Popovec to write that illegal document that kept me in jail?

Breaking the law wasn't anything new for Judge Popovec. He was the one who had illegally cancelled my bail after it was accepted and paid for. He had done it on the basis of a nonexistent complaint and by a virtually nonexistent prosecutor. Judge Popovec was an example of a totally corrupt judge.

Unknown to me, Bibiana had written complaints to different government officials, including the president of Slovakia, Mr. Schuster. She also called upon my Notary Public and my travel agency in Vancouver, Canada. She also let my friend David Chandler in Duncan, British Columbia, Canada, know. David requested assistance from the Honourable Lloyd Axworthy, who was Canada's Minister of Foreign Affairs at the time. There was never any indication that he ever moved his finger with any assistance.

The Canadian consul stationed in Prague, Czech Republic, had visited me on February 15, 1999, on the request of Bibiana. He had requested assistance from the Slovak Ministry of Foreign Affairs, and on February 22, 1999, faxed a diplomatic note to the Slovak Ministry of Foreign Affairs, as well as to the Ministry of the Interior and to Judge JUDr. Milan Jurko.

In his diplomatic note, the consul objects to Sabo's objection against my bail, which the consul called "an irregular motion as per legal requirements of Slovak law." Then note how he continued:

"As the Canadian embassy is greatly concerned for the health and well-being of Mr. Demcak, we would greatly appreciate your immediate investigation and assistance in rectifying this highly irregular procedure filed by the district general prosecutor.

"The Embassy of Canada avails itself of this opportunity to renew to the Ministry of Foreign Affairs of the Slovak Republic the assurance of its highest consideration."

To make it blunt, the Canadian consulate informed the Slovak government that laws were being broken and an innocent man is in jail. He was requesting an investigation with the highest consideration.

And the highest consideration it was, but Slovak style.

On April 22, the Ministry of Foreign Affairs was the first to react on the Canadian note from February 22. It took them two whole months to inform them that the Canadian diplomatic note had been passed on from the general prosecutor to the Ministry of Justice.

On April 26, General Prosecutor Milan Hanzel informed them that everything was going on according to law in my case. He also noted that I had filed a complaint, which would be settled by the criminal section of their office. The investigation results would be given to the consul. No indication that any investigation was ever conducted ever appeared. All these lies were confirmed with profound honour. The name of the general prosecutor was written, and his signature was also there.

On April 28, the provincial prosecutor in Kosice also assured the Canadian consul that everything was going absolutely and completely according to the law, and it would continue the same way from then on. Even the fact that, being allergic to cigarette smoke, I was in a cell with three gypsy smokers was not their fault, because they had no idea about it. It was signed by Provincial Prosecutor JUDr. Jan Pernat and was another note full of lies and no mention of broken laws or the illegal procedures used by everybody involved, including the provincial judge, Jan Popovec.

On April 30, even the Minister of the Interior Ladislav Pitner was writing, "the fact that the investigative document was not returned back to the investigator by the district prosecutor or the judge for correction was proof that there were no mistakes or broken laws committed by the police. After indictment, only the Ministry of Justice and the general prosecutor are competent to answer the questions contained in your note (10714)."

Ladislav Pitner was a man whom even I had trusted. There were so many people in Slovakia who trusted him, and he washes his hands

of it just like that. Shame on you, Mr. Pitner. It was policemen who
abused Anna D. and Jana V. It was policemen who illegally apprehended
Bibiana and me. It was Investigator Demjan who falsified documents and
signatures, and it was Investigator JUDr. Zurcaninova who investigated
the illegal steps taken by Demjan and refused to see them. It was you to
whom I wrote a number of letters, informing you about what was going
on. It was you who came to the prison in Kosice where I was abused, but
you avoided me, because you did not want to face the truth. It was also you
who, after all of this, even denied knowing anything about my case when
Bibiana asked you about it when you came to Trebisov to see what was
going on there. You disappointed me greatly, and in note KM-1412/1999,
you even lied to the Canadian consul, and then you assured the Canadian
embassy of your profound honour. Is this the legacy you want in history?
A liar? My case was in national magazines, in newspapers, on television
(Markyza). I and the Canadian consul wrote a number of letters to you,
and you claimed that you had never heard anything about my case.

On May 1, the Slovak Ministry of Foreign Affairs simply wrote a
chronological record of events from the beginning. As the new reason for
my prolonged incarceration, it was noted that the judge in Trebisov had
made a mistake.

On May 12, the Slovak Ministry of Foreign Affairs assured the
Canadian embassy that everything that was going on in jail was in
accordance with Slovak laws and regulations. An interesting claim was
that I had been placed in the general prison population. The fact was that
there was no general population in the investigative section at all. Every
cell was individual, and the prisoners were completely isolated from each
other. Besides their own cellmates, they did not get to see anybody else
at all. Not even during the daily walk. The question is how they knew
anything about my situation. No outside officials ever came to see me to
check or ask any questions. It was another clear diplomatic lie, together
with profound honour.

We were dealing with arrogant, corrupt bastards, and nobody
controlled them. That was fact. I talked to the consul afterward, and I
cannot repeat what he said about dealing with Slovaks, because he told
me his opinion privately, and I promised to keep it that way. I can assure
you that his opinion was in line with that of mine.

The atrocities kept going on, and the officials in Slovakia had only one
line to address it: "Denied, denied, and then denied again."

I was cut off from the outside world. My mail was under the control of the prison officials, and telephone calls are unthinkable there at all.

I wrote around eighty complaints. It was pathetic to read their replies. You would have great difficulty finding something that primitive in any part of the world. Every complaint went from the top right to the bottom. In other words, the culprits were asked to investigate themselves. Could anybody expect that they would find themselves guilty of any wrong-doing? That was the Slovak way.

I would need another book to be able to mention all of the mountains of stupidity that they were able to come up with. I will mention only some of the best answers that only Slovak officials could make up, like something brainless like this in official document Pn 20 19/99, dated April 12, 1999.

The general prosecutor and the Ministry of Justice in Bratislava requested that the provincial prosecutor in Kosice investigate my case. The provincial prosecutor, in turn, requested that the district prosecutor in Trebisov investigate illegal activities committed by Trebisov's officials.

The district prosecutor in Trebisov refused to do it. As a reason, he stated that it had been requested by unauthorised person. He also stated that an objection against his (genius) decision was not possible. That was signed by mgr. Maros Sabo, district prosecutor of Trebisov.

What that meant was that the general prosecutor and the Ministry of Justice were unauthorised people and had no rights to request that the district prosecutor in Trebisov investigate. How can you explain this?

Mr. Sabo should not feel bad, because I suspect that his name was used by some stupid idiot who forged Sabo's signature.

Here is another example of how one investigator investigated another.

pplk. JUDr. Dzurcanicova Alzbeta from the Ministry of the Interior was sent to Trebisov to investigate Demjan. All of the illegal activities, including interfering with the investigation and the lies Demjan gave her, were written in the statement she wrote. But at the end of the same document, she wrote that she did not notice them. I do not blame her. Many of the heroes who acted against policemen were dead, and she had decided to live.

That was official document K-307/03-st'98, dated February 22, 1999.

The office of the Ministry of the Interior, on my suggestion, investigated the lousy job of his previous investigator, Mrs. Dzurcaninova, who had turned a blind eye to evidence that was proof that Investigator Demjan was lying to her and thus was obstructing the investigation and thus braking the law. Both investigators, Demjan and Dzurcaninova, had proceeded against the law, and there was a third one, who was investigating them.

I'm letting you know that according to section 20/1#152/98, I have again reviewed your previous complaint and found out that it was inspected properly.

With this, I'm considering your repeated complaint resolved.

There was no sign of what he had done, and he never asked to see the evidence I was offering. He had done nothing but cover it up, just like everybody else. It was signed by the chief of the control office of the Ministry of the Interior. Unreadable signature.

Official document IV Pz 385/99-11, dated June 25, 1999 was one from the office of the general prosecutor of Mr. Milan Hanzel, the one who promised the Canadian consul they would monitor my case closely.

The proceedings in the highest court of Slovakia were guaranteed by Slovak laws. But it was turned down by the general prosecutor; listen to those reasons. I'm writing according to the meaning: The provincial judge has not finished his illegal activities yet; we must wait until he is done. We can use the highest court only in cases were correction can't be achieved another way. The Supreme Court does not deal with normal cases. I did not see any broken laws by the provincial court, so I'm placing down this without further action. It was signed by a prosecutor from the office of the general prosecutor, JUDr. Igor Dorica.

There were others—kpt. Ing. Jozef Kuba, Ing. Viera Carnanska from the Ministry of the Interior, JUDr. Jana Pirselova, JUDr. Ivan Brierer, JUDr. Lubos Masaryk from the office of the general prosecutor, JUDr. Zdenka Strbkova, JUDr. Stefan Minarik from the Ministry of Justice, JUDr. Zuzana Hlinkova from the office of the provincial prosecutor, and even JUDr. Viera Dvorska, the president's office of Slovakia—just to add to those listed before. None of them noticed anything wrong or illegal at all.

Take Mrs. Jarmila Trnovska from the office of the prime minister of Slovakia, Mr. Dzurinda. I wrote a few letters requesting action. In the end, she realized that it was a losing battle and that not even the office of the prime minister would be able to do anything about it. Her last sentence in our correspondence was:

"We are honestly sorry, that we cannot provide you with a more favourable answer, but we believe that you will accept our message with understanding about the limited competencies of our government office."

She is not the only one who is sorry. All honest Slovaks are sorry as well.

Anyway, I would like to thank Mrs. Trnovska for what she did and for being honest.

CHAPTER THIRTY-ONE

His Blood Stank Like the Worst Septic Tank, and It Tasted Like Rotten Fish Oil.

When will communists stop hurting people? After they are dead.

My situation was turning from bad to worse. But in spite of the fact that all the officials in Trebisov and Kosice who were involved in my case were covering up for each other, they became less sure of themselves. The new government of Mr. Dzurinda was settling in after winning the election, and it was asking more and more questions. Now and then, somebody from the top even visited the cursed eastern Slovakia and asked some questions.

The new minister of justice, Mr. Carnogursky, and the minister of the interior, Mr. Pitner, even showed up in prison. I had written many complaints to them, and unknown to me, the Canadian consul had written some as well. My mom, my sister, and Bibiana had also been writing complaints. So they paid a visit to see what was going on. The inspection was even done at the provincial court in Kosice. The justice people of eastern Slovakia were blaming my case for mixing the muddy water and spoiling their comfortable, corrupt lives. They all lived like roosters on piles of manure, and I was spoiling it all for them.

Pitner and Carnogursky came to jail, but they avoided visiting me. Why?

The answer was very obvious, and it goes far back to the communist system. Let's say Mr. Pitner, or any other top official, calls and announces a visit to prison. His intention, in fact, is to find out what is going on. But when he arrives, there is a welcome table set up, just like at the best wedding in the country—The best food, the best drinks, and the best gifts are all ready and waiting on a white tablecloth. After a great meal and a few drinks, the real reason for the visit to prison is long forgotten. It went on that way for generations, everywhere from schools and hospitals to pubs and wherever government inspections were conducted. I have no doubt that, in my case, the repulsive Danko was involved everywhere, presenting extra bonuses to officials trying to conduct inspections. He had extra interest to cover it up, because he was in it up to his ears.

Somebody (most likely Danko) wrote about my case to a provincial newspaper in order to smear a little more dirt on my name. The media got interested in my case and approached Bibiana, requesting our side of the story. The provincial newspapers and national magazines ran my case as a feature story. All of them were afraid to point at the police or other officials, so they mostly pointed their fingers at gypsies. Imrich Javorsky for *Novy Cas*, Anka Lucaiova for *Plus 7 Dni*, Marcela Galova for *Korzar*, and others were afraid to point out the real criminals—the police and the rest of the gang, who called themselves justice officials.

Some reporters, like Mr. Verlik from the daily newspaper *Novy Cas* or Mr. Angelovic from *Pravda* were interested in the story, but when they realized that the police and Danko were involved, they became afraid and declined. Meciar's government politicians were still suing anybody who had written or said anything negative about them.

I do not blame the reporters for being careful not to point out the real criminals, hidden behind justice titles and in justice functions, because they wanted to live. Look at what happened to me for writing the truth in my complaints. There was one reporter who took a chance, not a big one, but he did it anyway. Mr. Karoliy was a reporter at a national but private television station Markyza. Markyza had a program called *Palba*, which focused on corruption in Slovak justice.

No reporter was ever allowed to see me, so Bibiana was trying to get the truth out on my behalf. Bibiana described in detail many corrupt procedures in my case. Most of the blame went the gypsies' way, but *Palba* also broadcast Bibiana's statement that Investigator Demjan was very much involved in a scam to extort money from me.

That stirred a lot of dust. An investigation was launched against Markyza and Bibiana. Nobody was interested in knowing the truth. They began to plan for how to get Bibiana of the way. The only question was how they were going to do it. Were they going to jail her? Were they going to hurt her? Those were the questions going through my mind. I was hoping that they would not make her "disappear" completely, like some witnesses in some other cases, who disappeared or were blown up in their cars.

I received another letter from Bibiana. It had been written right after the cameraman and reporter from Markyza left the house.

"Hi, Darling! 31.3.1999

So it is after the visit. They [the television crew] came at 9:00 AM and left at 12 noon. I was quoting facts from your letters. I played them the cassette of the blackmailers. I told them enough. I kept strictly to the facts. Now they want to see the gypsies and the investigator. I told them that he [the investigator] had asked for money from you. The whole base of this case is hate, jealousy, and money. It is going to be sharp.[…] I was pointing mainly at the investigator who broke laws. I denied (your) sex with those monsters. I also told them about the prosecutor and your closing statement. Now we just have to wait until it is broadcast.[…] It will be a shock for everybody, but mainly for the investigator!!!

Darling, I would like to disappear right now. It will only be a matter of time before the whole world of Trebisov crashes onto me.

Okay darling, somehow I will live through it. But now really, you should pray for my safety. So far, I'm fine, because it is only in the developing state.

Okay, I won't cry any more, if I've pulled through so far, I will pull through to the end. I'm counting on violence against myself.

So darling, I do not care for this kind of fame. I do not care for any fame at all, because only problems will come of it.

Okay darling, I'm nervous about what will happen to me as a result of this … so I'm ending.

Your love, Bibka

All up until then, I was worried about my safety, but not anymore. Suddenly, I felt safe, like sitting in an egg full of cotton balls compared with Bibka's safety. There were a large number of corrupt officials who kept breaking laws, as if on an assembly line. There were the policemen who abused Anna Demeterova and Jana Visokaiova. Then there were Stefanak and Dziak, the policemen who had illegally arrested us. Also Investigator Demjan, the liar, the forger, who had fabricated the whole indictment and had prosecutor Sabo sign it. Not to mention the judges, Milko and Jurko, who had proceeded illegally based on different illegal and invalid documents to keep me in prison. Then there was a whole lineup of prosecutors, who had just showed up and illegally objected to my release without giving any reasons—prosecutors like Serecin and Bicko from Trebisov or Masarik from the office of the general prosecutor in Bratislava—as well as judges Popovec, Liska, and Brdarsky from Kosice. There were some more involved. All of them proceeded illegally, and none of them wanted the truth to come out. Then there was Danko, that ruthless former MP who, in my opinion, was directing it all.

On the other side, there was just Bibiana fighting for justice. One young, little lady against what felt like a whole army of corrupt officials. Some of them had cement instead of brain cells in their heads.

I was devastated when I realized all that, being locked in and unable to help. Bibiana was like a hot rock that had been blown out of a volcano sitting in my head.

They had just murdered young Remias. He was supposed to be a witness to the kidnapping of the president's son. Murders of witnesses in that case followed one after another.

After I was found not guilty, nothing was going on with my case at all.

I was worried mainly about Bibka. She knew about the danger she was in and went ahead with it anyway.

"Our God, who art in heaven, please do not just look at us. Please do something. Take me but protect my Bibka. I have done some bad things in my life, so I deserve this, but she is just beginning her life. What has she done to deserve this? Please God, forget about me and instead protect her. Please, we need not one but ten guardian angels. You can send all ten to guard Bibka. But if you decide to protect me as well, just send me one angel and send Bibka nine. One is enough for me, but she needs at least nine. Thank you, Lord. If I get out of here, I will fight against evil and for justice, just like it is in the Bible, even if it takes the rest of my life. Thank you, Lord."

A few times a day, I prayed like that to God. The first time was in the morning, the second was at noon. And then, I prayed during my walk in the chicken coop and once or twice before night. I was not the greatest man, and I admit it. I lied, I cheated, and I was unfaithful. I had even stolen some things—nothing big, but small little things. But bad things and unfair things also happened to me. One thing I had never done was abandon God. I was always faithful to God. All the way since I was an altar boy until today.

******

"Stop your complaining, if you want to live." I had received some warnings and threats.

Instead of stopping, I wrote more complaints to the top Slovak ministries. In each of them, I informed top Slovak officials about the danger Bibka and the rest of my family faced. I requested protection for Bibka and for the rest of my family. I tried to be one step ahead of policemen, hoping that, even if somebody from the top just asked some questions, it would make them think twice about doing something to her. I also described all the new and old broken laws and my continued imprisonment after I was found not guilty.

I described all the broken laws—very serious ones—so that there would be nothing new for Bibka to say. After my consul complained about prison officials manipulating with my mail, there was a better chance that at least some of my mail would get to the address.

My suffering was getting worse and worse. My worries about Bibka were getting unbearable. I was trying to reach my subconscious mind to have it show me what was next and to have it give me a sign of what to do.

Then, suddenly, I was released from prison. They just opened the door, and I walked. I had no money—not even the change to make a phone call. I decided to walk home to Trebisov. I estimated it would take me about ten hours to walk. I passed the city limit and walked next to a corn field. It was a cold, drizzly, and foggy night.

I spotted three men chasing some girl, who was running across the field. From far away, she looked like Anna Demeterova, the gypsy who had been abused by the police when in her last year of elementary school.

I did not clearly recognize the men until they caught the girl. Two of them were big men and had only white shirts and black underarm holsters with big guns in them. The third one was an ugly, little, fat man with black-rimmed glasses. He had no gun, but he was swinging a big baton in the shape of an L.

Then I heard one of them screaming in the girl's face,

"You slept with Demcak." That was when I recognized that it was Stefanak, the policeman who had been present when Jana was abused at the police station. And later, he had arrested Bibiana and me at the border crossing to prevent me from proceeding with my complaint.

"No, I did not," the girl screamed back.

"I will teach you how to listen, you little bitch. Demcak pushed his dick in you, big like this baton." It was the little, ugly, fat man, who was yelling at the girl that time. He was waving the big baton in the shape of an L. His glasses fell down. That was when I recognized who he was. It was that creep Danko. He had been behind all that illegal imprisonment. He had been the one who was making up all those filthy stories.

I came closer, still hiding in that cornfield, and noticed that it was not the gypsy girl. It looked more like the little child, Jana. She was the one who was abused at the police station. Danko had a gigantic cigar in his mouth, and he blew smoke right in the little girl's face. I recognized her cry right away. I almost ran out to help her, but common sense stopped me. I was not a match for three men—one with a big baton and two with big guns. I looked around in panic, trying to decide what to do. Helplessness was unbearable.

There was an old, rusty, wire fence, partly standing and partly laying on the grass. They had torn the fence down and had begun wrapping the poor girl in the fence wire. They were rolling the wire on the ground with the crying child in it. When the whole fence had been rolled around the poor girl, they stood it up with the poor child upside down. It was a horrible sight. The worst part about it was how helpless I was. I knew I had to do something, but I was alone, hiding in a cornfield, and nobody was close by to help me.

"Now you can complain to Lamparna," the little, ugly man was screaming at the girl, as she hung wrapped up in the rusty fence wire. Danko was trying to stick his baton through holes in the fence to hurt the poor girl, and his companions were laughing. Her cries were going through my heart like swords in the Roman wars.

"Help!" I recognized the voice right away, and I almost fainted. The voice belonged not to Janna but to my Bibka. There was no mistake about it.

Nothing could hold me back any longer. I rushed toward the ugly, fat man like a German express train. My intention was to kill the bastard as fast as possible, before other two would be able to shoot me. I knocked him down, like a bull when hitting a matador in a Spanish arena. The fat man fell down like a bag of rotten potatoes. I began tearing his neck apart with my teeth, like a tiger munching on a stinky pig. I was missing four top front teeth, so the number three teeth on both sides went into his neck, like the fangs of the vampires from Romania. Blood squirted from his neck, like from a natural fountain in Herlany, East Slovakia.

I was expecting gunshots at any time from the two policemen, but none came. So I kept tearing at his neck, making roaring noises, like a lioness tearing apart a water buffalo. Danko had caused me and so many people so much damage that I kept tearing at him, even after he was long dead and his head had been almost severed. It was like payback for all the lives he had destroyed. Then a terrible feeling came over me. All that blood everywhere. The ugly, fat man was dead, and his partners were standing over us, laughing. They had really enjoyed the sight.

"Are you finished?" one of them finally spoke, after I had fallen down, exhausted. There was treason and real happiness in his voice.

"You have done us a favour. You helped us get rid of this creep," he pointed at the bloody Danko

"And now we can put you back where you came from forever—this time for murder. Unroll her," he ordered his partner. Stefanak began unrolling Bibka. I realized it had all been a setup.

Only then did I recognize who the third man was.

It was Investigator Demjan, the man who had done everything illegally to put me in prison and keep me in prison.

All three of the main, corrupt partners had gotten together and invented the clever setup, and I had fallen for it. On top of it all, they had used me to get rid of the man everybody in town hated—the *shpicel* (snitch) Danko. The plan had worked out perfectly for them. It was too smart to be true. I could not believe that these primitive men could come up with such a smart setup as that. I kept asking myself how and could not come up with the answer. But I did not care, and I did not mind going back to prison, from which, most likely, I would never come out. The main thing was that Bibka had been saved. The fact that I had paid back the man who had caused my suffering was just a bonus. Danko would never hurt anybody else.

His blood stank like the worst septic tank and tasted like rotten fish oil. It was making me sick. I could not stand it anymore. I fell on my back and began to vomit. It began to choke me. I could not breathe anymore. I got dizzy, and I felt I was going to die.

Then, I heard a voice,

"*Bachi, bachi,* wake up." *(Bachi —good man in Slovak slang)*

I open my eyes, the terrible stink and the taste of blood still in my mouth. It was actually my vomit. Miro Horvat was shaking me and kept yelling, "*Bachi.*" He helped me to the sink, where I washed my whole body. I still had the terrible taste in my mouth. The taste of that evil Danko's blood hunted me for a long time. I get that terrible taste in my mouth each time I think about the creep.

It was another nightmare. But this one was different. I had had many other nightmares in that prison.

Once, I was in an SS bunker. Hitler and his top Nazis were there in their uniforms. I do not know why I was there, dressed up casually and even with long hair, just like I used to have in the 1970s. I was kind of out of place in front of those well-groomed, tall SS officers. All I knew was that, for some reason, I was trying to prove that Hitler had only one testicle. The way Hitler and his officers were looking at me was a clear indication that, that time, they would tear me apart with their teeth, and they would do it much better than I did with Danko. Most likely, they would even eat me, and no pieces of my body would ever get out of the bunker. It was a total horror. I will never forget the looks on their faces when they approached me. I was very relieved when I did wake up just before they began eating me alive. That kind of dream, in which my situation was totally hopeless, I had plenty of while in that prison. It was instigated by my actual situation.

But the nightmare with Trebisov's policemen was different. I felt sick from the terrible taste in my mouth from the blood of Danko, but at the same time, I was sorry that it was just a nightmare. If it was true, there would be one less bastard in the world, and it would have been a favour to the human population. Instead, I was still in prison, Bibka was still facing danger on the outside, and the creep was still free to do anything he wanted.

The worst nightmares were those in which I relived the many different ways they hurt Bibiana. I felt that the only way I could save her life would be I was no longer around.

I wrote my will. The gypsy Miro Horvat signed it as a witness. Most of my estate, including the whole magic show and the savings that I had in a Canadian bank, I left for Bibiana. Some savings that were in Slovakia I willed to my brother, my mother, and two of my sisters. One copy of my will I mailed to Bibiana, one I handed to my lawyer Ms. Fercakova, and I kept one.

Bibiana was shocked when she received the will, from which she concluded that I was giving up. She was right. It did not look like the suffering was going to end, so I was thinking of making it shorter and, at the same time, saving her life. I could never forgive myself if anything happened to her because of me.

The prison authorities read my will, which I sent to Bibiana, and they decided to help me. From a container about the size of one gallon, the doctor gave me some cream on a piece of a plastic sheet. The cream looked exactly like the grease I use on the wheel bearings of my trailer. I still have a sample of it. It was to help with my skin problem. For my sore back, the doctor handed me a box of one hundred pills of veral. Fifty milligrams, *Entersolventne Tabletky*, made by *Slovakofarma Hlohovec*, to be taken twice a day." For my irregular heartbeat, the doctor gave me another box of one hundred pills of vasocardin. Fifty milligrams, also made by Slovakofarma Hlohovec, to be taken once a day.

The interesting fact was that the doctor gave me all two hundred pills at once, including the boxes. That was against prison regulations. All pills went to the hall warden's office directly. Prisoners did not even see the boxes of them. Prisoners had not the slightest idea what the pills were. Every day, on special wooden tray that was nicely divided and marked, the medicines were passed to prisoners, but only whatever was prescribed for that particular day. Why then such a special privilege just for me? It had to be just the "kindness" of the prison representatives, who were trying to help me with what I intended to do when I wrote my will.

In case they tried to deny giving me all those pills at once, I had some witnesses, and I also could never have been familiar with the names of those pills if I did not have their boxes. They gave me two hundred pills at once, because they really wanted me dead. A completely innocent man. What kinds of people were these?

I began to have doubts about my decision to kill myself, but I was going to do it for my Bibka. Once I was gone, all focus would leave my case, and they would leave Bibka alone. I wrote a suicide note, in which I listed the government failures to investigate my case and the inhuman conditions of the prison. The failure of the government to arrange for protection for Bibiana was a main reason for my decision. I also mentioned how the prison officials had handed me all two hundred pills at once. All my personal belongings that I had in jail, including three kilos of smoked sausage, I left for Miro, the gypsy who was with me in my cell for a long time. I also requested a thorough investigation into my case, based on my complaints and investigative file, but that they leave Bibiana and my family out of it. I clearly named Jan Danko and Jan Demjan as the main criminals in my case.

I wrote four copies of it. One, sealed in an envelope, I gave to Miro; one I addressed to Prime Minister Dzurinda, and one I addressed to the Canadian consulate in Prague.

I was not really counting on any real investigation. These corrupt creeps would be happy that they had gotten away with another scam.

I sat down to write a last letter to my mom.

> Dear Mamka,
>
> This will be my last letter to you. Tomorrow, I believe, I will be in a better place. It must be better, because this one is hell on earth. I want to thank you for everything you have done for me. You supported me through school. Without your support, I could never have graduated from university. Without your influence, who knows what kind of man I would be today. I will never forget how you made me take the marble back to where I found it. It was a big influence on my life. I do not have to tell you that all of my case is just fake, because you know it better than anybody else. I know I could have been a better son than I was, if I had tried a little more. Sorry for whatever I have done wrong.
>
> Now, I cannot take this anymore

It stopped me right there. How could I write to my mom that I was taking my life because I couldn't take it anymore? This was the mom who had lost everything over and over and over and kept on fighting back. She had lost everything in the Second World War. Then she lost our family business to the communists. Later, she lost her home, also to communists. But never did she give up without a fight. She did fight the communists, even when the fight seemed to be totally helpless. Sometimes, it took a long time, but in the end, she won. To top it all off, she was fighting for me even then, and she was in her eighties. And here I was trying to write something that was not in our family nature. I was trying to write it, but my hand refused to move. That was not in the Demcak family nature.

I placed the letter to the side and pulled out a new piece of paper. Now, for the hard part. I sat down to write my last letter to Bibiana.

Dear Bibka,

That was all I managed to write. Tears filled my eyes, and I could not see anymore. Thoughts were going through my mind. How could I write that I was doing this for her safety? It would be like placing the blame on her. Then she would blame herself for it. It would be stupid to write something like this. My subconscious mind told me that she would never agree with my decision.

That young girl was running all over, talking to and begging people who had cement in their heads. She was trying to save my life, and she was taking risks, and she was not about to give up. I was having doubts about my decision to end my life. The two most important women in my life were my mom and Bibiana. My mom would be confused and even mad. She would never agree with giving up, because she never had. Bibiana would be very sad and disappointed. Did I really want to be remembered like that? I did not like the way the prison had changed me. Communists would even claim that I did it because I was guilty.

And then, I received a letter.

Hi darling,

Darling, you must not give up. I love you very much. I want you alive! Honey, the will is secondary. You are FIRST. Next week is court. Please, please don't give up for me. I want <u>you.</u>

I received your letter today, Tuesday, February 19. I will try everything, but the hierarchy is unbelievable. I have it all full teeth. *(I'm fed up)* I'm on the end of my strength, but we cannot give up. A lot of love, and God is with us.

Don't worry, I have very bright dreams, so I'm still hoping. Honey, we have each other, and we have us.

Darling, I need you to survive. We have a great show, and without you, it will not work. You have to be by my side. I'm your follower. WE CANNOT GIVE UP! And *punktum. Basta figli na bicygli.* Darling, I'm serious. Honey, I'm sending you a big heart, which is only for you. Because of him, you must not end it in jail. I want to go to your hearing, not to your funeral. Honey, you must not do this to me. <u>Do you understand?</u>

Pink is love; yellow is the sun; green is hope. Please keep these colours in your heart.

Your love, Bibka

A three-colour heart was nicely sketched. It was pink on the outside; yellow followed, then green, and then pink again in the middle. It was like a miracle energy going through my body. I began to feel the idea that to take my life would be stupid. I had not written to her what I was planning to do, but she had felt it and followed her intuition.

I took those two boxes of pills and threw them in the little closet. So far in my life, I had never taken any pills, and I decided not to start then. I decided to take a completely different approach to the whole situation. For that, I needed to stay alive.

In two days, I received another letter from Bibka. In the first part, she stated her disturbance because of how the officials illegally continued with my case.

I'm declaring war. Darling, love, you cannot give up.

Darling, please do not destroy yourself mentally. Do you understand? Okay, love, I will try to do what I can. It will be very hard; I felt a sharp pain in my heart. It is terrible crap. I know that it is very hard for you, but you must not give up. I'm begging you. Do not force yourself into the darkness. You are my only sun on earth. And I will not let it go away. You must stay to shine for me. Darling, I only want you and your love. So please, do not give up. Do not give in to this mental pressure. I know it is heavy.

Tomorrow, I will make a few phone calls, and I will go to Kosice in the afternoon.

It is a terrible war. I never thought that it would happen to me. I must fight for my man. It should all have been the other way around. This world is standing upside down. But, please, do not destroy yourself mentally. Be patient. Try to imagine how much pain and disgrace Jesus must have gone through—suffering, disgrace, and being nailed to the cross. You are carrying your cross now, and I know that you are strong enough, and we will get out of this war as winners. Darling, you must not give up.

On the other side was a drawing of a big heart made out of six colours. It took up almost the whole page (size A4), with colours so heavy that it gave an almost three-dimensional image. On the bottom right side was writing in red. "So this is my, your, and God's heart—Bibka."

I never, ever felt such love in my whole, long life. At the same time, I felt so much hate. The love I felt was coming my way from Bibka, and some love I felt was going the other way—from me to her. I still feel that love; I hope it will never stop. Can you imagine: "I'm declaring war." One young, little lady on one side, and all those old corrupt policemen with guns and the rest of the corrupt judges and prosecutors on the other side, with Danko in the lead.

Hate was going one way—from me to all those who were keeping me there, who were in between Bibka and me. I decided there and then that only God could take my life. And if anything happened to Bibka and I got out, I would do it by myself. I would personally kill them all, starting with Danko and Demjan. Then I would continue to kill them, one by one, until they killed me. At least, they would not be able to hurt anybody else.

I felt better about my decision, because it gave me a reason to live. But I wanted to be sure that it was okay with God. I pulled out my Bible and began turning pages. I remembered reading it before, but I wanted to confirm and be sure. I had it marked, so it did not take me long to find it. It reads:

"We shall not let evil have a free ride. We should stand in evil's way and try to prevent it."

That was good enough for me. I was absolutely sure.

I realized that the only possible way those old communist bastards would stop hurting and killing people was if they were dead.

Jozef Demcak

My previous requests did something good. Some top officials sent somebody, who came to Trebisov and began to ask questions concerning the safety of Bibiana and other members of my family. That put the brake on any drastic plans that they could have had to stop Bibka in her war against them.

Every single day, I wrote a letter to Bibka. I have a whole pile of her answers to me. Those letters from my family and Bibka helped me to survive.

CHAPTER THIRTY-TWO

Without a Bribe, They Will Even Let Him Lose His Hand.

Is English language complete? No. The words to describe some Slovak creeps are missing.

After my mom visited me in jail, she went home a broken old lady. Everybody who came to visit me noticed that I was going through tremendous suffering. My front teeth were missing, my hair had turned grey, my back was sore, and I could not stand straight. I was just a shadow of the man I used to be.

My older sister B. just sat behind the glass of the visiting booth, saying nothing at all, her tears just rolled down her cheeks. I received a letter from her. Here is a part of it.

Dear Dodo,

I'm not even able to express my honest sorrow at your suffering, which you are living through for stupid, little excuses. I would love to help you, as well as your whole family, but it is beyond our possibilities. You can see yourself that they are just stretching and stretching it …

I have not written to you so far, but that does not mean that I did not feel with you. All of my family is with you and wishing that you will get out of this labyrinth of horror soon.

I'm praying to dear God to help you, so that he will give you the power and patience to live through these hardest times of your life. I believe that God will help you. And you also believe, and do not let negative thoughts in, and you will see that it will end positively. Just hang on.

You will come, and we'll celebrate your homecoming.

All the best, mainly strong health, endurance, and optimistic thoughts

Wishing, your sister B.

My younger sister S. was also shocked, when she visited. She was more in a fighting mood.

Dear Dodo,

Do not be afraid. We have it all under control. We understand what is going on.

"[Devil will punish them]"

We need to wait until court so that they will "colour" themselves. Afterward, we will hit them step-by-step as needed.

Even that stupid bail they turned over, so they could stretch the time. That is why I did not want you to do anything, so they would not have the excuse to put off court.

Do not let them destroy you; don't give them that kind of pleasure.

Do not get upset at court, let it end the way it wants. We will watch what kind of job they do, so we can react to it and then make justice take over.

I will not waste words, because not words but work is what counts.

Your sister S.

I'm adding best regards from the family and Robert, who is suffering with his studies of law.

P.S. I decided to write without accent marks and "Y," because Slovak spelling should look like that in the future.

We decided to wait until court so we will not give them any excuses, from our side, to postpone the court date. What do you say? Just one more week without our interference, so they have no excuses for anything.

I'm standing by you. Your sister S.

[…] I have written to the president. I got an answer. He wrote that it is not in his competency. Your sister S.

My two sisters and our mom kept meeting at my mom's house to decide how they could help. At first, my mom believed that there was some justice in the system. It was felt in her first few letters.

Dear son Jozef!

At first, I'm sending you greetings and wishing you a lot of good health to live through these hard days, to which those bad people, ill-wishers, speculators, and blackmailers, who don't work and just bum around, creating evil got you.

Jozef, take it easy. Hang in there in peace. I think that the truth will succeed. Just peace and calm.

Jozef, you did not come to your father's funeral, but you came to see your sick mother, who was eighty-two in August. On November 10, my brother died, so this is how I live last days of my life. I'm content, because I know that I gave all my children a good education in life—be good, work, never hurt anybody.

Jozef, I'm asking you one more time, please, to hang in there with peace. It will be all right. I understand that you are innocent and in prison. I did calm down, and I'm waiting, hoping that soon you will be at home. I'm hoping, and I have this kind of feeling that it will be all right. Just peace and calm. Hang in there. We are working on it.

Greetings, and kisses

Mama

But she was waiting for justice to no avail. My mom and my brother M. put together 100,000 korun for my bail, just to be pulled by their noses by corrupt prosecutors and judges. Times were changing but for the worse.

Dear Jozef!

First of all, I'm sending you greetings from my heart and wishing you a lot of health and patience, while you are waiting for that "just" court. They are stretching and putting it off from one week to the next. I do not know where they are taking this kind of law from which they are putting off this court for the third time. What did I pay that bail for? I believed in the laws and the court. The whole family is disappointed by this kind of manipulation. They appoint the court date, and last minute, they put it off and then again.

Dodo, please be patient and wait in peace, calmly. Believe that it will end up okay.

Best regards. We will wait. Hang in there.

Mom and the whole family

In her old age, my mom was not about to give up. She kept fighting the only way she knew how, and she kept writing letters to me to keep me from destroying myself. She was not feeling well, and this only added to her suffering. She had lost two of her brothers at the end of the Second World War. They died as heroes for peace and justice. And this kind of justice she received in her old age. The corrupt representatives were keeping her son in jail. She knew better than anybody else that her son was innocent. She even knew that those who were keeping him in jail knew that he was innocent, but they did it anyway. To top it off even more, her only living brother had just died. How much of a beating could one person take?

She was totally broken on the inside. My mom did something that she did not believe in. She has done something like that only once before. It did not matter to her that my brother, my sisters, and I told her not to do it.

Her whole life, she worked hard, taking care of her family and trying to save some money, just in case. With four children and a communist system, it was hard to save some money. But she kept 30,000 korun (about $1,000). That money she would not touch for anything in the world, because she had saved that money for her own funeral.

Tears ran down her cheeks as she lifted the mattress in her bedroom and pulled out the old brown envelope. She counted the money for the last time. Exactly 30,000 korun in bills. The bills were straight and hard, like a starched shirt lapel, from sitting under her mattress. Now her funeral wasn't important any more. This money, she thought, would end the suffering of her son.

She remembered the only time she had ever done something like this. It was still during communist rule, when my dad accidentally cut his hand on his scythe. It was quite a deep cut, stretching across his palm to his index finger, and needed to be sewn. My dad was in and out of the hospital for three days, and doctors were just wrapping his hand, which kept bleeding and was getting more and more infected. They just slapped more wrappings onto his hand. My dad was in terrible pain. My mom had no idea what was going on until my brother came home. He had been out of town.

"Just take ten thousand korun, and give it to the doctors. Without a bribe, the doctors will even let him lose his hand," my brother advised. Mom was quite surprised and disappointed, because the communists claimed that medical services were free. Only sick people knew about bribes, and they only whispered about it. She had no idea about it, because, thanks to God, we were a generally healthy family.

That was the only time my mom let herself down and did something against her dignity. But what would you not do when your family member is suffering? She took an envelope and took it to the hospital. My dad's hand was sewn after all, but it was done too late and done so badly that he could never move his index finger again. It was red and pointed straight forward for the rest of his life. He had to take extra precautions in winter, because his finger had a tendency to freeze very easily.

Now it was her son who was suffering, so she took the brown envelope and took it to the office of the judge. She did not tell anybody at the time, because she knew that nobody in our family would agree with her decision. They would also explain to her that her life savings were just peanuts for those judges. To her, it was all the money in the world. To them, it was just peanuts. They were counting on millions for my freedom. It was the kind of money that even I did not have. They were dealing with hundreds of thousands of korun in bribes. But they took the brown envelope anyway and did what they usually do when they took bribes—nothing.

When a prisoner's family pays a few hundred thousand korun, all he could hope for was that he would be convicted a little bit earlier and moved from the inhuman conditions of the investigative prison to the jail of convicted criminals. There, conditions were more humane. At the time I was imprisoned, by Slovak law, they could keep you in prison without a conviction for three years. Even that law was not honoured by many judges, because many innocent prisoners, who had no money for bribes or refused to pay it (like me), decided to suffer through three years of abuse. To accommodate the judges' and the prosecutors' lust for money, they raised the limit of investigative imprisonment to five years. Now it was more likely that prisoners and their families would pay a bribe, when facing the possibility of five years in a terrible prison without a conviction.

At first, my mom had been hoping for justice. When it failed, she thought that her life savings would help. They did not. She decided to try to deal with the top officials. It was a move that I was making already, and she had been against it at first. Now that she realized how corrupt the system was down there, she was hoping to get help from the top.

Dear Dodo,

Today, I received an answer from the Ministry of the Interior. This is what they write:

"Your request from 10.5.1999, we passed on to the Ministry of Justice, because they are competent to deal with the courts. The Ministry of the Interior cannot interfere with the courts."

They take care of the police. I also wrote a request to the Ministry of Justice. Then I sent a letter to the government of Mr. Dzurinda. Now I will wait. Dodo, now I will work even better. Just calm down, and do not say anything. You can see that they do not know how to close your case. Papers are flying from Trebisov to the province, from the province to Trebisov, and months are running, and they keep you in investigative prison [...]

With regards and kisses,Mama

It was a typical, cynical example of the office of the Ministry of the Interior to wash its hands of something that they were directly responsible for. It was Policemen Demjan who had fabricated whole investigative documents on which basis I was kept in prison. It was the Ministry of the Interior's moral responsibility to clear my name and to investigate and jail Demjan. To make it even worse, it was the office of Minister of the Interior Pitner, who so many people in Slovakia trusted, and he simply turned his back on an eighty-two-year-old lady who was crying for help. Later, Mr. Pitner even denied ever hearing about my case.

I knew that my mom's desperate attempt to get me out was going to go the same futile way that my, Bibiana's, and the Canadian consul's requests had all gone—all the way back to corrupt local representatives, so they could investigate their own illegal activities. But it was an encouraging feeling to know that the whole family and Bibiana were trying and cared.

Dear Jozef!

I sent you a letter June 8. I hope you received it. Now I'm writing again. They began an investigation of the blackmailing of the gypsies. Finally, they requested the recording, and they will send it to Bratislava for examination to confirm the gypsies' voices. The recording is very good proof—a clear witness of their threats against you. They even threatened me, and I don't know them at all.

The recordings should have been used right in the investigation. Why were they waiting for that? Whatever office I go to, I mentioned that clear proof that you have that nobody can deny. Too late, I found out about the recording. It should have been used during the investigation. Not television or newspaper but reality—a tape.

I do understand why they are hurting you who are innocent and those who are guilty are free. I don't understand it.

Dodo, be patient, on good behaviour. Take it easy. Wait. I think it will work now, just do not say anything. I will

write wherever is needed, so that you will be at home soon.
It will begin to move.

With regards and kisses,Mama

She was very upset and mad, when she was told that it was Investigator
Demjan who had kept the tape out of everybody's sight. She remembered
how he had lied to her face about little Jana when she had talked to him
for the first time. She realized that the judge was trying to frame me after
he had promised that he would proceed honestly. She also noticed that her
life savings, which she had given to the judge, had done nothing good.

Dear Dodo,

I received your letter. I don't have to write how I feel.
I would like to live until the day when you will come
home healthy and soon. I'm trying; I cannot sit down in
peace, without thinking about them keeping you there
innocently. This are times when criminals go against weak
people. The criminals are free, and the government is
feeding them. It is going very slowly [...]

Dodo, I understand you. We think of every way, and
you see no and no. But I began, so I will continue until
the end. I cannot work, because I don't know why that
prosecutor appealed or what reason he gave. I went to see
your lawyer to get some advice. On Monday, I wrote to
the ministry. I got sick from all of this. It was my health
problem; I could not walk, because I'm not healthy yet.

With best regards and kisses,

Your mom

It was so sad to imagine my old mom going from office to office to
talk to those corrupt officials, who were lying strait to her face. She was
getting sick from it and feeling sorry that she could not do more. Nobody
had mentioned to her that it was Investigator Demjan's responsibility to
accept the tape, which had been delivered to him right at the beginning of
the investigation. He had simply kept it and returned it back to my family,
without even mentioning it in his file.

After repeated requests to take the tape into consideration, a suggestion
finally came down to the provincial prosecutor, who sent the request to

Trebisov, with a suggestion that the tape, which was proof that I was blackmailed by the gypsies, should be investigated.

That was when the Trebisov police began to pretend that they were investigating it. This is how it went. They waited a few weeks and came to me to ask where the tape was. Noticing that they were writing on only one paper, I requested if I could have a copy. They said no and, if I don't like it, I could refuse to tell them. They actually wanted me to refuse to tell them. I told them that Demjan had had it all the time and then returned it to my family. Why didn't they ask him? It was clear to me that they were just stretching time.

After they waited for another few weeks, they went to my family and got the tape. After another few weeks, they claimed that they had sent it to Bratislava for expert examination. Nobody ever knew if they really did it, because no statement of any kind was presented to me or to my lawyer. We never heard about the tape again.

The examination of the tape was not necessary anyway, because the gypsies' voices were clearly recognizable. They called themselves by their names in the actual recordings, and they had admitted in court that it was they who had called. Even the name of their pimp, who had also called, was revealed in court. Everything was written down in the court documents.

This was another example of how corrupt police were able to do whatever they chose, and nobody would do anything about it. They refused to investigate the gypsies, because they were just tools for the police, and the police were the main players in blackmailing and abusing me.

My mom could not know that it was the police who were keeping the tape out of sight to cover their own illegal acts. It was totally sick to lie to the face of an eighty-two–year-old lady.

Dear Dodo!

[…] July 8 should be the hearing. Please take it easy. Do not say anything, because even if you say the truth, they will keep you in jail. The main thing is that you will be out and will be suffering no longer. If court should finish, then it will be finished. If, by any chance, it will not finish, we will go after the president. When he was taking office, he showed the citizens and the whole world on TV that it is the power of the people, and every person can open his door, and it would be helpful for him. It is the

government key. We should believe in it and the promise
of Mr. President. We helped him with our votes.

Mama

And so, sick with sore legs, she walked from office to office, talking,
begging for mercy for her son. It makes me sick just to think about the
kind of people she had to face. When I was still out and needed to get
something done with local officials, I hired Mr. Ivan to do it on my behalf,
so I would not have to face those assholes. But my mom had no choice,
because she wanted to help me.

She was writing all over. I kept receiving many letters from her, and
my heart was bleeding because of how much she suffered. I really admired
her consistency and her dedication to getting me out. I also realized from
whom I had inherited that drive to fight for justice. I inherited a good
memory from her. I also remembered what politicians said, and it upset
me when they didn't keep their promises. It was all from my mom. God,
please bless her heart.

Those corrupt bastards who jailed innocent people to beat money out
of them should realize that they were not punishing just those whom they
imprisoned illegally. They also punished their loved ones. Now, when I
read letters from my family, I realize how much they suffered with me. It
is incredible, and you can only understand it if you live through it.

I cannot sleep at night or sit without thinking about you. I got sick
from all of this. I could not walk. I'm not healthy yet [...] Your mom.
I'm very sad. My heart is sore from all of this [...] Your sister S.

I cannot describe the sorrow that I feel [...] Your sister
B.

I got a sharp pain in my heart from this [...] Your Bibka

Didn't those assholes know how much pain they were causing to all
those innocent victims? Had they lost their human feelings completely?
Can we call them humans at all? The English language is very poor,
because there are no words in it that could describe that kind of creep.
The Slovak language has a word. We call it *zadubeni*, meaning that their
brains are hard like the wood of an oak tree.

How many of them noticed that an eighty-two–year-old lady was
breaking down? She could hardly walk anymore. But they just kept on
pounding on her with lies. They were ready to let her die, confused by
their slurs.

That is why I still fight for justice. I want to do what I can to at least lower the number of those who are suffering because some corrupt officials want their money.

I could not understand why the Canadian government would not help me fight these terrible people. The government even defended their actions.

Remember, this is a true story.

CHAPTER THIRTY-THREE

"For a Thousand Dollars, My Friends Will Kill Anybody." (Igor Gregor)

What is most the impossible dream in a Slovak prison? To take a peaceful shit.

In my prayers to God, I pled with the Lord for nine guardian angels for Bibiana and one for me. I prayed for her safety most of all and was willing to sacrifice mine as long as she was safe. Soon, I heard that two of my sisters, my mom, the Canadian consul, and Bibiana were all trying to help me. That was five people.

After receiving that supportive letter with big heart from Bibiana, I made my decision that I was going to try to get out of there alive. I also decided that I would get as many documents out as possible, to have proof of what was going on in there. It was not an easy task, because the guards were making sure that no incriminating documents ever get out.

All documents that were proof of brutality, mental torture, or other acts of intimidation were taken from prisoners, and they would never see them again. That way, justice officials were free to do anything they wanted, and the of having to take responsibility for illegal acts was next to none. If somebody dared to fight them, he would end up back in jail for a long time, until he lost the desire to fight for justice.

The only way I could ever bring the abuse to light was to get some proof out, before I was released or convicted and transferred to another prison. Getting documents out would be a difficult task. Getting me out of the prison alive would be even harder. I realized that the only way to fight those corrupt officials would be from outside of Slovakia. Witnesses to police brutality or other crimes committed by the police were jailed or disappeared. Cars were blown up with witnesses in them. Bodies were discovered buried in forests or in the bottoms of rivers. Some were never found.

Justice representatives were aware that trouble would come their way if I got out; therefore, they had a lot of interest in me not getting out at all. That was when they handed me those two hundred pills after I had written my will. It was only a matter of time before I would be gone, and they were waiting for it. My lawyer stopped visiting me.

When they realized that I was taking my time with those pills, they decided that I need a push to make up my mind. My conditions went from bad to worst.

Instead of taking all two hundred pills at once—what they were hoping for—I took three a day as the doctor had prescribed, but instead of eating them, I kept flushing them down the toilet.

Two boys were assigned to my cell. Igor Gregor and Zdeno Vidlicka. As usual both cellmates described what brought them in. Zdeno was first:

" We had nothing to do so we decided to fill in some of the empty space in our lives. All we were hoping was some fight."

To make the fight fair and even, they pick on a boy who was walking alone down the street Of Kosice. Zdeno and his two friends felt that three on one would be a fairly even fight. As a climax, they did not forget to take the poor boy's wallet and what was in it.

The three boys became three suspects the same night. They even forgot that they were friends. Zdeno claimed that it was the other two who beat up the boy, and he had just turned the street corner; therefore, he could not see what the other two were doing. The problem was that the other two friends were claiming the same story in reverse.

Zdeno was a nice boy all the way to the core. He told me that he would try to join the Legion Army, because he wanted to see how it felt to kill somebody. After talking to him for a while, - psychopath who should be treated in a psychiatric clinic was my personal diagnosis for him. Later, he showed me the record made by Docent Stancak, the same court specialist who had also examined me some time before.

"Look how stupid that psychologist is," Zdeno told me. "He wrote here that I need treatment. I think that he should get some." I gues my diagnosis was correct.

Igor, my other new cellmate, had come to Slovakia from Russia. Like many other Russians and Ukrainians, he had intended to go farther west, but he was stopped at Czech border. Czechs noticed that "nice guys" were coming from the former Soviet Union, so they closed their border fast. Meciar's government was so busy stealing that it did not pay any attention to the eastern border across which Russian-speaking boys were coming. They were really "peaceful boys," and those big guns they brought with them were only "souvenirs" from their mother country. Those with real love for the late Soviet Union packed in hand grenades, mines, missiles, plastic explosives, and other peaceful devices.

To hire some of those nice boys to make a bomb in somebody's car or on somebody's head became very easy and dirt cheap. That was the time when more than ninety cars went flying through the air in one year in Slovakia. Store owners and other businesses owners also went missing, because they could not afford to pay the money that was demanded by extortionists.

And Meciar, who was by and large responsible for the situation and for breaking up Czechoslovakia, said to Slovakia's citizens, "I did not hurt you." He said it with tears in his eyes when finally leaving the office of the prime minister after losing the election. He could blame the Czech for that situation. Had the Czechs let them go into their country, the "nice boys" would have kept going.

Being stuck in Slovakia, Igor had married a Slovak girl. He did not make it a secret that he had married her only in order to be able to stay in Slovakia.

"I don't care. Tell her I only married her to be able to stay here," he yelled at his wife's lawyer, who had come to jail to inform him that she was filing for divorce.

Igor had lived a peaceful life, the same as the other Russian-speaking boys who had gotten stuck in Slovakia. He had always carried a big gun under his jacket. During the summer, he carried it in what looked like a document folder, because it was too hot to wear a jacket.

Igor used his gun only on special occasions for self-defence, like when he was trying to make an honest living by robbing some businesses. He also used his gun to protect the good name of his mother country, the Soviet Union.

Once, he was having a peaceful meal when the restaurant owner said to his friend,

"All Russians should be deported back to where they came from." It just so happened that Igor heard him say those offending words.

"Did you forget who freed you in the Second World War?" he yelled at the restaurant owner, getting up from his chair. The restaurant owner also got up and backed off with his hands up. To preserve his Soviet pride, Igor opened the black document folder. He was looking for a book of Marx-Lenin philosophy to read a chapter to the restaurant owner. That was spoiled, because he discovered that there was no book by Marx but a more realistic sign of Lenin's philosophy—a big gun. It was higher calibre than a nine-millimetre Magnum, the same size ammunition that fit into the famous Russian machine gun, the Khalashnikov.

Disappointed that he had forgotten his Marx-Lenin book, Igor decided to use his gun in line with the main communist ideology: "Who is not with us is against us." He aimed at the poor restaurant owner, who was backing off with his hands up. It was a shot that sounded like thunder, and it was in "self-defence," as Igor put it. The kickback of the huge gun knocked him back into his seat.

The restaurant owner fell on his back. People in the restaurant did not need a rehearsal at all. All of them ran out of the restaurant, as though they were being chased by a bunch of bulldogs. Igor also knew what to do. Maybe he saw it on TV. He ran to the man he had just shot dead with the intention of collecting the projectile in the man's head, so it could not be traced to his beloved gun. At first, it scared him, and then it surprised him when the restaurant owner opened his eyes. The man was also stunned when he noticed that he was still alive. It was never cleared by the Slovak police whether he was not moving because his pants were full. In the moment when he thought that he was shot dead, he let it all out, because he thought that he would not be getting up again.

Igor ran to where light was shining through the wall. He looked through the hole and saw the kitchen. He ran into the kitchen and found a broken mirror on the wall. The bullet had passed across the kitchen and was stuck in the wall where the mirror used to be. Igor grabbed a pointy kitchen knife, dug the projectile out, and ran like a rabbit chased by a greyhound dog.

He ended up in jail, charged with attempted murder and some other "self-defences" that he had committed before with his mascot, which just happened to be a gun.

In jail, Igor dreamed about the good old times his father told him about when everybody was a Soviet. They had had special methods to persuade everyone. The most common method was to press a machine gun against somebody's head and ask, "Are you a friend?"

"Yes, yes, yes," most people knew what to say. That way, the Soviets made tons of friends in all countries they occupied around the world.

In jail, Igor decided to do his best as well, by becoming an informer or a snitch. First, he proudly transferred his life savings to his jail account. It amounted to more than 200,000 korun. He had earned that money through honest work with his gun. The justice representatives had two choices. They could confiscate the money as the gains of a crime. They knew it would be an honest but stupid thing to do. The money would have gone to a government account and then to Meciar or his ass-kissers. They decided on a much smarter procedure. By the time, I met Igor, there was only 20,000 korun left. It took almost three years, but the money had gone nicely to his lawyer, investigator, prosecutor, and judge—or kept "all in the family." Igor was also useful in jail. That was why he was placed in my cell.

"You know, I'm different," he told me with his Russian accent. "If I had been framed like you were, I would have killed them all. I know guys who would teach them how to frame innocent people. I even know the guy who killed Ducky" *(Ducky a federal politician who was shot dead by a Russian-speaking man)* "For a thousand dollars, I can arrange it for you. My friends will kill anybody you choose for a thousand dollars."

"No thanks," I said. "All my life, I have been honest, and I'm too old to change now."

Later, I found out that Igor was sent from cell to cell, wherever they needed somebody to frame. He would pull some incriminating sentences from prisoners, which would be used against them. My cell was bugged; there was no doubt about it. If I had told him, "Okay, do it," arrange the payback, they would have gotten me for attempted murder. He only went for a walk once, and he sat behind a wall hiding. Somebody could see him and yelled, "Informer!" He got some little favours for his services like a shirt that fit, while other prisoners had to take whatever they received.

His main problem was his stupidity. I even gave him the numbers of paragraphs from my law book, according to which he should have been released at the three-year point after his arrest, because an extension of imprisonment was not requested by the prosecutor.

"Did you ask them about the three-year request from the prosecutor?" I asked Igor after he returned from court.

"Oh yes, I did. The judge had no idea what I was talking about. After I told him the paragraphs, they looked in the law book, and then the judge said, "Yes, it was done."

"But did he show you a record of it?"

"No, the judge said they will send it to me."

"You idiot, you know what they are doing now? They are writing the document now. This document should have been delivered to you before the three-year deadline expired."

Igor was hitting his head about the fact that he could have been out, if he had insisted on seeing that document.

Igor was not pleased that, after three years of faithful service (as a snitch) to the justice system of Slovakia, they had done this to him. He got even more furious when I told him where his "hard-earned" almost 200,000 korun went.

"As long as there is money in your account, do not even dream about being convicted." I explained. "Why would they throw your money away? If you are convicted or released, that money is gone from them. As long you are here, the money keeps on going into their pockets."

After he got the idea, he changed sides. We began to exercise. Four stools lined up were used for a bench press. The steel double bunk bed was the bar and the weights. When a heavier bar was needed, somebody climbed up and sat on the bed. The desk, with the stools hooked onto it, was used for other types of body-building exercises.

There was a speaker on the wall. During the night, messages were yelled and passed from cell to cell all over the prison. The dogs barked all night long. There was never a quiet moment at all. On Sunday mornings, they played a live worship broadcast from a church. I listened to it every Sunday, but there was the problem with that as well. While I was trying to pray, my three cellmates were hanging on the gater, looking down to the chicken coop, yelling at other prisoners, and swearing like on an assembly line. It was next to impossible to nourish my soul.

The radio: "Lord be with you—"

My cellmates: "Look at that whore; she is that prick next door's girlfriend."

The radio: "And also with you—"

My cellmates: "Hey, you cunt, you robbed your own grandmother."

The radio: "Let us pray—"

My cellmates: "Aren't you and your cunt-sucker ashamed of yourselves?"

The radio: "Our—

My cellmates: "You and your dickface should be hanged, robbing your own grandmother …"

Believe me, it was much worse, but my conscious does not allow me to repeat those words as they sounded against the background of prayer coming from the radio.

A peaceful shit was a dream in that prison. The toilet was in the corner just by the door. I sat on it, hoping that whatever I was expecting would finally appear. Miro was walking back and forth as usual. Each time he made his turn, which was about three feet from where I was pushing, he sucked his snot back into his throat with the sound of a Zetor tractor. I was used to it, but in that situation, it was disturbing my concentration. Zdeno and Igor were horsing around about one metre from me. It was their own kind of Sumo wrestling. Only now and then, and only by accident, did they wrestle themselves into my territory, at which time I gave them a good push, so they would not knock me off my throne.

The guard opened the peephole, and now he was looking at me. It was mitigated by the fact that at least I couldn't see him; only he could see me. I was trying to concentrate on what I was sitting there for, but it was not over yet. Then the feeding window opened—"Demcak. Mail. Sign here." Then I could also see the guard's face. What should I do? I was sitting with my pants down.

Igor ran to the feeding window to offer to take the post record book to me to sign. His offer was abruptly refused by the guard. Regulation did not allow him to let his book out of his hands. Of course, I had to get up off my throne, pull my blue pants up, and sign the book. Then I received my envelope. By then, it was too late, because what I was trying to achieve had already retreated. Better luck next time.

It is a world where you don't want to be. I had psychopaths, informers, and gypsies as my roommates. What more could I ask for? But after a while, they all showed respect to me, which was easier to take than dealing with the Canadian government.

All four of us filed a few complaints and requested a visit of the prison warden. We made a list of our objections, like no sitting on the bed and no suitable chairs in the cells, no typewriters, or that the shower towels were the size of kitchen towels, and so on. Next thing, Zdeno and Igor were transferred to different cells. Only Miro and I were in the cell when the warden came. It was clear to me that splitting us up had been done to make it impossible for us to file a complaint as a group. They had noticed that we had become a team, so they had decided to break us apart. It was useless to even file a complaint.

CHAPTER THIRTY-FOUR

Physical Torture That Inflicts Invisible Marks

Is there a way to stop corruption in Slovakia? Yes. Arrest all the policemen, and close all the courts and prisons.

I was alone in the cell, because Arpy was gone, and Miro was in the hole. It was nice to be alone for the first time since my detention, but I was also worried, because the guards could do anything to me, and nobody would know about it.

Most likely, Igor had informed the prison representatives that I had begun exercising, so they would have realized that their dream of me being gone forever was not likely coming soon. They began watching me and yelling at me for virtually no reason.

The head guard, Mojo, was always on my case to make my life as hard as possible. It began the time he asked me how I could lie on eleven nails, which was the world record. He was very disappointed when I told him that the secret was in psychical and mental fitness and, mainly, a positive state of mind, which amounted to being a good, honest person. I suppose "good, honest person" was most discouraging for him.

It was about midnight. I was trying to sleep when the little feeding window opened, and the guard yelled,

"Why are those clothes lying on the bed? Fold them into chimneys." Overnight, I had been spreading my blue day clothes on an empty bed to give it some air. It had always been okay. Suddenly, there was a problem with it. I knew it was just to harass me on orders of Mojo. I threw my clothes in the little closet and slammed the door. The next day, Mojo asked me how come I had refused the order of the guard. I told him that I had been the commander of a troop, so I had never learned how to build chimneys out of clothes. He realized that the order of the overnight guard was ridiculous, because he dropped the subject. But he marked it in my report card, without even telling me. My report card was not spotless anymore.

It was time to change the bedsheets the next day. My back was in pain in those days. I leaned over the bed while tucking the sheets into the far side of the bed. The feeding window opened with a big bang.

"Demcak, why are you lying on the bed?"

"I'm not lying down; I'm just changing the bedsheet."

"You were lying on the bed." Mojo slammed the feeding window. I knew I was in trouble, and I was right.

The next day, I was escorted to the office. Mojo handed me an official document to read. I was to be punished with three days in the hole for lying on the bed, which was prohibited by prison regulations. Mojo handed me a pen and pointed to the bottom of the document to have me sign it. I noticed that there was a space on the document, which read "Comment of the prisoner:" I began to write: "This is a false accusation, because I was not lying on the bed at all; I was leaning against the bed while changing the bedsheets—"

"What are you doing? You just write yes or no, you agree or you don't agree, and sign it like the others do," Mojo began yelling.

"It reads here 'Comment of the prisoner,' and I'm the prisoner here, so I should decide what I write."

He was really furious, but he let me continue.

"I request to speak to the chief warden before being committed to this punishment."

"Are you going to cry again on the warden's shoulder?" This was Mojo's favourite line to use to put me down. I did not react to the malicious, stupid remark of an individual, who was tall, strong, and far behind average in his mental abilities. That was why he got satisfaction from abusing anybody he felt was smarter than him.

The chief warden did show up. This time, he was wearing his full army uniform. In army ranks, he was only one step below a general. I explained to him that I wasn't lying on the bed, just changing the bedsheets. I requested to be moved to a different hall, because Mojo was always on my case, provoking me and looking for any little excuse to get me in trouble. The chief warden said that he would see to moving me to a different guard, but he had no power to cancel three days in the hole. No doubt, he was lying. Mojo was just a regular guard in charge of the ward. The chief warden was responsible for everything that went on in the whole prison.

The first time I had talked to the chief warden, he had been a different man. He had given me some advice that would help me live through those obviously hard times for me. He had introduced himself as Mr. Nagy and even told me that I used to teach him when he was a kid in a town called Novosad. I remembered that little boy who arrived at school on the bus from an even smaller village than Novosad.

I wondered how this boy from a little tiny village in eastern Slovakia came to be in charge of a large prison in the second largest city of the country. The answer came to me. It was very common during communist times. All dirty jobs had been filled with men from small towns, because the local men did not want to do the dirty work.

Most likely, that creep Danko had appointed Nagy to be his puppet in the prison. Nagy was so thankful and would do just about anything for the boss, who had given him such a lucrative job. That could be the reason why Nagy had become one of the liars and did not cancel Mojo's punishment, even though it was clear that it was totally wrong, especially because I was in bad shape, as far as my health was concerned. I felt like something bad was coming my way.

I was lucky that the next day was the monthly visiting day. I was able to tell Bibiana and my brother what they were preparing for me. That was a real lifesaver for me. I told Bibiana and my brother that this was it. Unless somebody from the outside came, I would not come out alive.

I knew that, while in the hole, they cut off even that little contact that you might have with the world. No monthly visit, no mail, no daily walk, no lawyer, because my lawyer had stopped visiting me at the time anyway.

Had the visit not taken place, nobody would have known what was happening with me. Who knows if I would have come out alive?

Miro had been taken to the hole to serve his punishment. That was after he had a little fight with another gypsy, Arpy. I still remember how relaxing it was to pray, when only God was in the room with me

It was after midnight. I was trying to sleep. A guard walked in. He had a big baton attached to his side. He was not a regular guard. I had only seen him twice before. Once, when he had strip-searched me in the haircutting room, and a second time, when he had been going through my official documents. He had seized important documents that were proof of many illegal actions of Policeman Demjan. Fortunately, I already managed to get some documents out of jail; therefore, I have proof of that.

Now I knew that this guard had a special duty in the prison. One of them was to snoop through documents and destroy incriminating ones, and the second was to break prisoners who needed to be broken. Unfortunately, that was me.

I knew something bad was next, because there was nobody standing outside the door as usual.

"Give me your pills, and come with me," he ordered.

"Where are we going?"

"To see your warden, so you can cry on his shoulder."

It was obvious he was lying.

I was escorted down the hall to the lift. The lift went up and down a few times. I got the idea that it was in order to confuse me so I would not know what floor I was going to.

All the halls were the same, so when the lift door opened, it was hard to guess what floor I was on, but I had some idea of where we were.

We did not go far. We turned left. There was door on the right. We turned left again. There was a wide door in front of us. He opened a door on the right side. It was not an ordinary cell. The room was divided by bars lengthwise, as well as across with the gater. The lengthwise bars prevent you from getting to the door, and the gater prevented you from walking to the window. The window had been completely painted over with dark yellow, the same as the wall. That was it. I was in the hole.

"What about the medical examination?" I knew that prison regulations stated that, before a prisoner is to be punished in the hole, a prison physician had to examine the prisoner in order to verify that the inmate was physically fit to undergo that kind of cruel punishment.

"You just had an examination; here are your pills. Now you can cry on the warden's shoulder here." The guard pulled out my two boxes of pills, dropped them on the floor, and slammed the heavy steel door.

The light went out. I was in total darkness. Slowly, my eyes got used to the darkness, and I began to see a little bit. There was nothing in the room at all. On the wall, there was a board about two feet wide. It was on hinges and locked against the wall with a big padlock. This was going to be my bed, if they unlocked it and opened it up.

In the middle of the room, there was what looked like a square, cement block about sixteen by sixteen inches and about three inches high. There were four little holes in it that were leftovers from the stool that used to be there, but it had either been cut off by the guards or broken off by an inmate who was in there before. To make it complete, there was a hole in the floor about five or six inches in diameter. It was kind of set into the floor, and two marks in the shape of a shoe were set a little bit up from the hole. You guessed right. You stepped on the marks with your pants down, and if you aimed properly, you might be able to hit the target—the hole. And do not worry, in time you would get used to stink that is coming out of the hole, which was connected to the sewer. The hole in cement floor was always open, so the stink had free passage to get to your nose.

Suddenly, I was in a stinky cell with no ventilation in darkness in a totally empty room that was approximately five or six feet wide from the wall to the bars. All I had done was lean against the bed when changing bedsheets.

My back was sore. I was missing four front teeth, and a few of those still in my mouth were wobbling. My mouth felt like it was getting infected. My skin problem was getting worse, because even the cream that looked like wheel grease and had been given to me by the doctor on a piece of plastic had stayed in the cell. The worst feeling was the feeling that my heart was experiencing an irregular beat.

Because they had bypassed the doctor's examination, it was clear that they were doing this against regulations, and not many people knew where I was. They could do anything they wanted with me. The feeling of total helplessness had a destructive effect on my mental state. The pain that I felt from my health problems and conditions was speeding up and multiplying my suffering. Huge stress just overwhelmed me.

It is not easy to pinpoint the actual location of the hole. It was either on the ground floor or in the basement. I had only seen two faces; that meant that no regular guards were on duty in the area. There was no indication that other prisoners were walking by; therefore, the location of the hole must have been out-of-bounds to other prisoners.

I was in constant suffering. There was no break in pain.

This torture had been invented in Russia by people close to Lenin. They had simply sped up and inflamed natural pain and illness. It would kill you if you did not break down and do what they wanted you to do. Once you broke down, you would confess to anything and everything, even if you had done nothing. That was how they broke Mr. Slansky after the war. In those days, those who broke down sold everything they owned, and the money went to corrupt justice representatives.

If you died from an unthreatened, sped-up illness, there was no problem at all. Even an independent autopsy report (if there was one) would read "Death of natural causes or illness." In other words, the perfect murders. There would be not one single mark of abuse on the corpse. They caused you unbearable pain and suffering without touching you.

"Torture" was clarified by Amnesty International as pain that is purposely inflicted on humans or other living things.

This mental and physical torture was more effective than the primitive torture practised in Syria, Iran, and other countries alike. They simply beat and raped you. The pain was on and off, according to the actions of the torturer who was inflicting it. The victim got some breaks. The Soviets invented torture when the pain never stopped. They acted in such a way to keep it going and to keep increasing it.

Millions died from pain, and virtually nobody had slashed them with electric cables or had pressed cigarette butts against their skin.

It was done under the slogan: "Who is not with us is against us."

Once they realized, how nice the procedure was, the Soviet scientists studied and kept improving it for years to come. They began mixing inmates who were infected with contagious diseases with healthy prisoners so the sickness spread faster. Soon, they discovered that mental torture could do miracles for speeding up different sicknesses, and physical discomfort finished victims off. All Eastern communist countries more or less followed Big Brother, the Soviet Union.

It is a mystery to me why the world almost ignores these atrocities, while much more attention was focused on the Holocaust. Both mayhems caused unimaginable suffering to the human population. It is beyond comprehension how those who invented it, those who ordered it, and those who practised it can be called human beings. If we can call them humans, then I do not want to be in the human race. Both atrocities slaughtered millions, and it seems to me that the holocaust stole the show.

The only difference is that the suffering and slaughtering during the Holocaust was concentrated in concentration camps, and in the Soviet Union, it was spread all over as well as far out in Siberia, so it was less visible. But more than forty million people were murdered by Soviet communists. They achieved these horrible results without building costly gas chambers and wasting expensive poison gases.

The Holocaust is over and done with, but the Big Brother invention keeps going even today. All we hear now is that Russians jails are infected with tuberculosis and other diseases. The prison facilities are infested with rats, fleas, and other pests. The suffering of those infected is not a secret any more. Some prisoners intentionally infect themselves with tuberculosis, because their conditions are unbearable, and they hope to shorten their suffering or go to a hospital, where conditions would be better. The world is covering its eyes against what is very much known.

Who was going to ask Mr. Putin questions when he came clean shaven and dressed like all other politicians? Did everybody forget that he was a high-ranking member of KGB? Was it not the KGB that was the main hand in the suffering and slaughtering of those millions of innocent people? Was a member of the KGB going to do his best to investigate his own organization for the atrocities it caused? Was he going to try to stop their corrupt minds to prevent it from happening now?

Exactly the opposite was the case. Just ask Khodorowsky these questions. He is absolute proof that those atrocities have been active in the communist and former communist countries until today. He is only one example of a political prisoner of new times. Just recently, he was sent to a uranium labour camp, the one that is known to be one were nobody got out alive. And his crime? He was attempting to run against Putin in a Russian election. He was swept out of the way by good, old communist ways.

It is duty of all humans to try to stop all those atrocities.

The worst part of me being locked in the hole was the feeling that they could do anything they wanted to me, and nobody would know about it. Soon, I got to know why the cell was also divided lengthwise. The bars across, the gater, were obvious. They restrict you from going to the window. But the bars dividing the cell lengthwise?

I discover the hard way. I was in pain and felt sick. The cell was completely empty and dark. I slid down against the wall and sat on the cement floor. The door flew open.

"No sitting," a guard yelled. I had never seen him before, but his face told me that he meant it.

I got up. The darkness, pain, and tiredness were taking over. My strength was leaving me. I leaned against the wall with my shoulder. The door opened again.

"No sleeping."

No doubt there was the camera in the ceiling or the guard was watching through a peep hole. They kept me on my feet for hours.

I was in constant pain, and they kept me on my feet. When there was no more energy in me to keep standing, I passed out on the floor. I heard the guard yelling, but it sounded like it came from the grave. Then I felt pain in my ribs. The guard was hitting me with a broomstick, demanding that I stand up.

It went on and on. Each time I passed out and fell to the cement floor, the guard pushed me on the floor with his broom. I was unable to get up all the way. I was on my knees and elbows. I felt a sharp pain in my left side. I realized that he had walked in and was kicking me with his boots. It was a very sharp pain. I think he broke my ribs. I could not take deep breaths anymore.

There was no way I could know how long it all went on. There must have been some light behind the painted window, because the little light that came in was always the same.

With all that pain and no sleep, it felt like forever.

I tried to walk and pray. At first, I kept praying, pleading with the Lord to help me get through this alive, asking why it was me who had to suffer so much.

"Lord, why it is me? I have done some bad things in my life, but I'm really sorry for them. Please forgive me and reward all those I've ever done any damage to."

Afterward, I was pleading with him to let me die, so that it would all be over.

Later, I was arguing with God because he was not letting me die to take me away from all the suffering.

I was standing but falling asleep. Then I saw Janco yelling in my face. I smelled his stinky tobacco smell from his mouth: "If you die, they win." Then Lubo Mrazik from Bardejov was telling me, while offering me a smoked sausage he had just received from home: "If you get out of here, run like crazy to Canada and tell the world what is going on in here." Then my sisters were writing to the president, and my dear old mom was limping, taking an envelope with her life savings to the judge, hoping it would save my life.

A big colourful heart suddenly opened up in the middle of it and yelled straight into my face, "You must not give up. I don't want you dead in that hole. Do you understand me?" I could not miss that voice. It was coming from the heart that she had mailed to me, and it was the voice of my Bibka. The voice came again and again. Once from the heart, and then it was her unforgiving face, "I don't want you dead. Do you understand?" I took those two boxes of pills and dropped them into the hole in the floor. I heard the splash when they hit the water in the sewer. Now only God could take my life or the guards would have to kill me if they wanted me dead.

I had to step over the stinky hole in the floor to get my food, because it was given to me through the feeding hole in the steel door, which was right behind the bars and over the hole in the floor. Sometimes, I received some tea and bread. Later, there was some soup and some mixed food that tasted terrible. There was no sink, and the lack of liquids caused the dehydration of my body. They refused to give me water. I felt very dry on the inside.

My life was going through my mind, just like in a movie theatre with a foggy picture:

I was at Michal Kundrat's place, which was across the street from my summer house, trying to cross back to my place, but I could not make it, because there was a deep canal full of mud in the middle of the road. In other dream, I was stuck in the mud with my trailer, trying to get out. I had to unhook the trailer and leave it in the mud. Then the house was on fire, and I tried to put the fire out. There was a whole bunch of cages with rats in them. Somebody opened the cages. Rats were running all over, but in one cage, the dead mother rat was lying on her back. Her tits were all red from baby rats sucking on them. To make the sight even worse, somebody had bitten off her tail, so there was only a little stub left on her. I decided to bury her, so I grabbed her by whatever was left of her tail. Suddenly, she began shaking and turning. It scared me, so I dropped her on the floor. I was going to check whether she was alive, but I came awake.

I was shaking and felt scared like never before.

It was a feeling of horror, because it reminded me of the situation that I was in. Being stuck in the mud, my house on fire, rats all over, a dead mother rat—nothing that you would like to really dream about.

All the nightmares were happening while I was standing up, because I was not allowed to sit or lie down.

My mama, Bibiana, and my sisters were in my dreams a lot as well. It must have been, because they began to really fight for my life. As soon as Bibiana and my brother left the visiting booth after I told them what was being prepared for me, they visited my lawyer, Viera Fercakova, in Kosice and asked for help. Bibiana called the Canadian consulate in Prague and traveled to Bratislava to the office of the minister of the interior, Mr. Pitner. My mom went from office to office in Trebisov.

One of my sisters wrote a letter to the minister of the interior on behalf of my mom; the other wrote to the Slovak president.

I only wish the Canadian consul had come to see me. Even if he sent somebody with a diplomatic passport, my situation would have changed immediately. My family was not allowed to visit, but they could not refuse a visit from the Canadian diplomat. Slovaks abused prisoners if they could cover it up. Prime Minister Dzurinda and his government did not support abuse in any way. Nobody showed up, and the torture was ongoing.

Everybody in my family was raising hell. I only wish I knew about it all. Being in the dark, deprived of sleep, and in constant pain, I had no idea what was going on out there. If I had known about it, I would have felt some hope, which could have given me energy and helped me cope with the worst days of my life.

In the chronology of events of my case that was recorded at the Canadian embassy in Prague, it was written on this subject that "The Canadian Embassy has now been informed that Mr. Demcak was transferred to another cell and that his bed and chair are removed from the cell each morning, forcing Mr. Demcak to sit on the floor. No reason for this cruel and unusual punishment was given."

After my release, Canadian Foreign Affairs claimed that they had doubts about the abuse the Slovaks committed. They even claimed that they were not aware of the abuse at all.

My lawyer Ms. Fercakova had the right to see me. Either she avoided coming so that she would not be a witness to the torture or they refused the visit.

She wrote the following complaint:

KE 140/98-Fa   10.6.1999

JUDr. Fercakova

Prison System

To the hands of the chief, Kosice

As the defence lawyer of the defendant Jozef Demcak, born July 20, 1941 and presently incarcerated there, I'm asking that you please arrange a medical examination, because he and his family are complaining to me that he is sick, that he has heart and back pain. Because this is the case of an older person, he needs to lie down, because his imprisonment is stretching unreasonably.

I'm sure that it is known to you that he is complaining about different organs, so I'm asking that you please transfer him to a different cell, because he is very much complaining about the present situation of his imprisonment. He claims that he has no window and no ventilation and that they remove his bed during the day, and his imprisonment is stretching unreasonably, in my opinion, without any reason.

Thank you.

Registered mail Stamp and signature.

That is proof that abuse was going on. I took chances there to let people know what was going on in that prison. The situation was so bad that I did not care, if they would punish me more. I believed that Dzurinda's government, including Minister of Interior Pitner, had no interest in that kind of corruption. Mr. Pitner kept away from the subject and even denied knowing anything about it. What could he do? Could he fire all the policemen and close all the courts and prisons? That would be the only way to stop corruption in the justice system of Slovakia.

This is where the Slovak government needed help from Canada. If anybody from the Canadian government had come to visit, the torture would have been discovered and could not have continued. If the Canadian government had protested torture on the highest level, improvement would have taken place. I believe so.

A message about the torture reached the Canadian government, but nobody came to see me.

CHAPTER THIRTY-FIVE

Not Only Did They Talk Stupidly, They Also Looked Brainless

Why did my brain threaten to quit? It could not take so much stupidity.

You can check the internet. Visit any official report on Slovakia, and you will find out that they have one major problem: corruption in the justice system. It is probably one of the best criminal organisations in the world. It includes plain, simple crooks, policemen, investigators, prosecutors, lawyers, and judges. All hand in hand to extort money from the innocent and guilty alike. In communist times, nobody, absolutely nobody, had the smallest chance for justice. One more time—absolutely nobody. No one!

After the velvet revolution, when Meciar became the prime minister of Slovakia, he let the communists regroup and function again. That time, they got one more reason to continue with their dirty work: money. As in my case, the police could use official cars to kidnap and jails to keep kidnap victims. They even made written records of it, because everybody was involved, everybody got a reward, and nobody was afraid of being punished.

Records show that they used such primitive excuses to arrest people that the normal brain must collapse, because it was unable to absorb that kind of idiocy.

Take the situation of the Slovak gentleman who claimed that one of Meciar's ministers was a member of a youth Nazi SS organisation. Of course, it was denied, and the minister sued the gentleman in the court, challenging him to prove the accusation. Meciar and all citizens were stunned when a document was produced with the accused minister's signature on it. In fact he had signed a document to become a member of that terrible Nazis SS organisation. Now he was sitting in Meciar's cabinet. Can it get any worse? Of course! The district court confirmed that there was proof that confirmed that the named minister was a Nazi member. The media and Slovak citizens were delighted that justice in Slovakia was finally approaching. Some people suggested that the lady judge should get a bouquet of flowers for daring to rule against one of Meciar's puppets. You would think that it would be enough for a former Nazi member to resign or be fired by Meciar, and life would go on. Not in Meciar's Slovakia.

Instead, the case was appealed to the highest court, and the former Nazi won. The poor gentleman was fined 200,000 korun for telling the truth and having proof of it. The legitimacy or validity of the proof was not even challenged in court. The former Nazi claimed that he had signed the membership but that he was not a member. How far could you go with stupidity? The highest court sided with the former Nazi and punished a completely innocent person. The gentleman did not have the money for the fine, and it looked like he would spend time in prison. But there was a Good Samaritan who was so outraged by this idiotic decision of the court that he paid the fine to spare the innocent man from jail. Sorry, I forgot the names in this case, but the story is true and nothing but the truth. I'm sure that all people with good memories in Slovakia remember it, because the case was published in most Slovak media.

When I watched and listened to Meciar and his ministers talking on television, my stomach turned, and my brain threatened to quit, because it could not take so much stupidity. Not only they were talking stupid; some of them also looked retarded and brainless. The average intelligent person would have to go to a sanatorium to recover from the stupidity they were throwing at Slovak citizens. My mom would switch the channel as soon as Meciar or some of his goofs appeared on TV. She said that she could never survive listening to them. "Human stupidity has no limit," said Jan Verich.

Now I was in the hole, trying to survive the abuse of those monsters.

They did not let me sit; they didn't let me sleep; and they didn't let me drink. Lying down was totally out of the question. I was in the dark, but my eyes could see shadows, because they were used to the darkness. I was feeling very sick and had no energy to stand, but I knew that if I sat on the cement floor or leaned against the wall, the guard would run in and push me around with the broom or kick me with his boots. I already had had the left side of my ribs kicked, and I could not take deep breaths. I think that at least two ribs were broken by the kicks from that guard.

All my family begged me not to complain about anything. I also realized that by complaining, I only made things worse. If I complained about broken ribs, I would give them one more reason not to let me out of the hole.

I had a vision that I was doing my Floating Lady routine. Long before, when I was practising that magical routine, my biggest worries were what would happen if I failed to stop her from going up. I learned the hard way. Everything was going fine, except that my partner kept going up. At the time, I was trying to learn how to control the floating. The ceiling wasn't very high, because I was practising in my living room. She touched it gently, which awakened her, and she fell down like a rock. Fortunately, I was right under her; she hit me right in the face, which, together with my arms, cushioned her fall as she hit the floor. She was okay, but my nose was damaged and bleeding. Ever since, I have had nose bleeds when breathing cigarette smoke or paint fumes. I'm allergic to both irritants.

I have done that routine many times since, and I still have the same worries and the same exciting feeling when I perform it. I worry when the stage has a low ceiling and even more when the ceiling is high.

I was performing this routine outside. It was a beautiful night with a sky full of stars and a full moon. She wasn't wearing her usual gold bikini-style suit. Instead, she had on a very light, white dress, which flowed in the breeze. Everything was going as usual until I attempted to stop her from floating up. My mind kept sending her signals to stop and return back to her sword, but she just kept going up like a balloon. She was already above the trees.

Horror went through my mind when three ravens were about to sit on her body. I knew that if any of them touched her, she would fall down like a rock. From that height, it would be the end of her. They were black ravens, but they had human heads. I recognized all of them with horror. It was hard to miss the fat, ugly face with glasses of that monster, Jan Danko. He was behind all my suffering. He was almost touching Bibiana. Behind him was the sneaky Investigator Jan Demjan. The black circles around his eyes were clearly visible. Judge Jan Milko was the third one. Three stooges all together again.

I was panicking, not knowing what to do. Bibiana turned her head sideways and yelled down,

"Use your mind. Use your mind. Use ..." I got the message. I packed energy in my right hand and tossed it straight at that evil Danko. The energy went straight to him, like lightning during a storm in the Saskatchewan. It hit him right in his ugly, fat face, and he fell down like a wet chicken, flipping his wings, and kicking his ugly, fat legs. I repeated the gesture twice more, and they all fell down just in front of me.

Bibiana smiled at me and said,

"You see, you can do it. Just use your mind." She just floated happily away. All three ravens were wet and stunk terribly, just as if they had gotten out of the sewer. The stink was hard to take. I opened my eyes and realized that it was the stink that was coming out of the sewer hole, not wet ravens.

But the message was clear. I had to use my subconscious mind to help me survive this and thus beat those ravens, who hoped I would not get out of the hole alive.

That girl was helping me even in my dreams. I knew I had some powers, but I had forgotten to use them.

As is common in most martial arts where mind over matter is engaged, before you can achieve that ability, you must make peace with your conscience. It is important to remember that even a small achievement in which the subconscious mind is used consumes a lot of inner energy, which burns up a lot of outer energy. It showed as though it was general tiredness—sore muscles, headache, or other symptoms.

For years, I had been building my inner powers, which I had practised every day but used no more than twice a week on stage in my "Bed of Nails" demonstration and "Hypnotic" in the "Floating Lady" routine. I got used to the routine and was able to reenergize my lost energy quite quickly. Now that it had become a matter of survival, it was the best reason to try to get some help from my subconscious mind.

On the stage, during our "Floating Lady" routine, I sent my energy to Bibiana, which made her lighter and enabled her to float like a balloon. In the final stage of the floating routine, I collected my energy back. We were able to pass the energy back and forth.

Now I had not the smallest doubt that it was happening in the reverse direction. I had no doubt that that girl was trying to send me energy. I had no doubt that, every night and day, she was concentrating on helping me survive. I was failing to accept it. As soon as I began to accept this help, I had extra power to survive.

I felt so stupid not to have thought of it earlier. She had to send me a message through my dreams to make me realize it.

As soon as I realized it, I felt so much better. I felt that I could do something, even in the stinky, dark hole.

First, it was important to deal with my pain, which was caused by my health problems, by being kept on my feet, and by sleep deprivation.

Pain was a natural signal to let a person know that something was wrong and needed to be treated. Without pain, we would have no idea that something was giving up in our body. If you decide to "kill" the pain with the power of your subconscious mind, the pain is still there, you were just blocking it from your brain so you would not feel it. I decided to "kill" the pain, because it was depriving me of rest, which was essential for healing. I decide to temporarily block the pain so I could get some much needed rest. The hard part was resting while standing up. Since I had a lot of practise in killing pain (I used it in my "Bed of Nails" routine), it came quite easily. Resting while standing up was a different matter. Our leg muscles are the strongest of all our body's physique, but they are still not strong enough to be able to stand up without rest for so many hours. Horses or deer are able to do it, but their bodies were design for that purpose. They also have four legs. Humans have only two legs, and after few hours, our legs must rest, or they will get tired and consequently sore to the point that the knees will give up, and we will fall down.

I also had to deal with the lack of water, because I was getting dehydrated. When you are ill, you need more liquids, and they were giving me almost none.

Once I reached my subconscious mind with my conscious, I tried to reach a point of total balance. That allowed me to stand, without wasting energy, to keep the balance. That should also keep me upright in case I fell asleep. Dealing with the leg muscles was next. I applied self-hypnotic signals to my body and mind. I tried to slow down all of my body's functions to the minimum, and the energy I saved there I transferred to my legs.

I was afraid when I tried it for the first time. I wasn't sure what would happen if I didn't get the signal to get out of the self-induced hypnotic state. I was worried that I might die in it. In the past, when I had hypnotized others, I was able to make people achieve things that they could never have dreamed of doing without being in a hypnotic state. But I always had to give them clear signals to get out of the hypnotic state or what is generally known as "to wake up."

"Who is going to wake me up?" I kept asking myself. I'd never tried self-hypnosis before, and I had never met anybody who had. But I'd heard that somebody had done it, so I decided to take the risk. After all, I knew that it was the only way to survive.

I stood about two feet from the wall, facing it. I got my dead point of balance and began applying the hypnotic signals to myself, just like I did for others. I got a kind of dreamy feeling in my head, and the soreness in my legs vanished. I knew it had begun to work. Frantically, I kept repeating, "I must wake up when I hear the door unlock sound."

I have no idea how many times I repeated that order. All I knew was that I was very afraid.

In that jail, each time a guard walked by the door, he looked through the peephole, and then he pulled out and pushed on the big door latch. That was another check that the door was locked. A totally unnecessary action, because the door was also locked with a key-operated lock. The whole procedure was in order to make prisoners more miserable. The latch made a loud noise, which disturbed you from whatever you are doing. Whether you were thinking, dreaming, or sleeping, it would remind you that you were locked in, and your mental state would go all the way down again. The guards walked around all night long, turning the lights on in cells, looking through the peepholes, and wiggling the latch. You could be sure that your sleep would be lousy, and that was what it was all about. That was why every prisoner had black circles around his eyes. That was the sound that prisoners would hear for a long time after they were released from prison.

My system worked well. Each time the lock sounded, I was brought out of my self-induced hypnotic state. After a few tries, it was easier to do it, because my body and mind got used to the whole procedure. It helped me rest in a standing up position and helped me deal with the unending time of total inactivity.

The problem was that I knew that, from an anatomical and physiological point of view, my legs would not be able to take that kind of punishment for too long. Then I thought about horses. How was it that horses were able to stand all their lives? I remembered watching horses stand, and one leg was always slightly bent. That was exactly when the leg rested, because the weight was not on it. The mystery of the horses was solved. If I could apply it like horses did, I could get my legs some rest and survive. My problem was that I had only two legs.

But I tried it, and it worked well. As I stood there, I caught my balance on one leg and took the weight off the other. It was still touching the floor, but there was a little bend in the knee. That way my legs received some minimal rest, which was very important.

I needed some liquids badly.

One guard came and brought me an aluminum container full of water. I cannot describe him, because I don't want him to get in trouble. It must have been during a time when he was alone. He told me not to tell anybody about it. He could not stomach what they were doing, so he had decided to help me on his own initiative. It was like life returning back through my veins. I imagined what it would be like to be in the desert without water and then to find water … He also told me that he might show me something if the situation made it possible. He walked in when he passed me the water, so I did not have to step over the latrine as I was forced to do when receiving food from the other guards.

It was impossible for me to know how long I was in the hole, because it was always dark. It felt like forever. In a written statement, the chief warden wrote that it was three days. Because, he wrote down other lies in the same statement, I don't see any reason why he would write the truth about that. It could be more but definitely not less.

All I knew was that my mom, my sisters, Bibiana, and my lawyer Ms. Fercakova were fighting on the outside. I believe that the Canadian consul was also involved. The media wrote about it. Everybody in the government—from President Schuster and Prime Minister Dzurinda to Minister of the Interior Pitner, Minister of Justice Carnogursky, and General Prosecutor Hanzel to everybody all the way down at the bottom— were informed about me being abused. They began asking questions. Pitner and Carnogursky even came to jail, but they avoided seeing me. They did not want to be firsthand witnesses to what was going on. If they acted according to Slovak law, many officials would have had to be charged and sent to prison. Everybody involved was breaking the law.

But just because of the questions and raised eyebrows, the chief warden most likely decided that he'd better not go through with it all the way to the end. Most likely, he owed Danko a favour for giving him his lucrative job. But everything had a limit. He realized that if he went through with it and I died in the hole, Danko would not have been able to save him. Meciar's government had lost the election, and Danko had been his puppet. Power was shifting away from them a little.

All my family prayed for my safe return. Bibiana joined a young Christian group. Every night, they got together and prayed as group for my survival.

All I know is that the door latch sounded, and I heard keys opening the lock. The light went on. One guard unlocked the door and than the bars. I knew he was taking me somewhere. A feeling of worry went thorough me, because I had no idea where he was taking me.

I was taken to the shower and then a cell. It was just like a regular cell. Nobody was there. I noticed that my stuff was on one of the beds. I felt that my time in the hole was over, and I had lived through it.

Thanks to God.

CHAPTER THIRTY-SIX

Balls Like an Elephant, and the Penis Was Nowhere.

When do your neighbours look at you like you're stupid? When your ass is naked.

I was left alone in the cell. It was nice to see daylight and a bed. I felt like throwing myself on it after such a long time, but I remembered the rule very well: no touching the bed during the day. I noticed it was very hot in the room. I thought it was natural reaction, after being locked up for days in a dark, cold room with no blankets or bed.

I was alone in that cell for a few days. No guards came in. They passed me food through the opening on the door.

That elaborate system for destroying people sat in my mind. The combination of mental and physical torture leads to death and makes no marks on the body, because it destroyed you from the inside. Conclusion of any coroner would be – the death of natural causes. Nobody is responsible for obvious murder. How many prisoners died like this? It is still in my mind.

Mental torture affects part of brain, which then destroys the functions of the inner organs. The visual damage on the outside of the body is minimal, and it is the last damage to appear. That is the reason why it is overlooked by diplomats visiting prisoners in foreign jails.

After torture is over, healing takes place in the reverse order, meaning that the visible marks disappear first and then the healing of the inner organs comes next. All that is done by a subconscious function of the brain. Any damage to brain function is the most serious, and it takes the longest to heal. In most cases, the victim will never be well again.

Without Bibiana's help, I'm not sure if I would be sitting here today, writing. Their system to destroy people worked very well. No wonder so many prisoners inflicted horrible wounds on themselves. They are desperate for help, which is not coming.

I was thinking about Robo Kovac story. He was from Roznava. Robo requested that he be placed in a cell alone; he had nightmares, because his previous cellmate had cut his Achilles tendons on both legs. He had cut one first, but because they would not let him lay down, he had also cut the second one.

Robo had been arrested for breaking and entering, which he did with his friend. His friend was hiding in caves close to Roznava, which were left over from abandoned uranium mines. Those mines were occupied by soviets occupants while they were "robbing" Slovaks off all Uranium that was in them. Robo had no idea where his accomplice hid the money. It was a big amount, because they had broken into the house of a lawyer. Corrupted lawyers had already tons of money.

As the police were closing in on Robo's accomplice in the caves, he apparently committed suicide. At least, that was what police claimed. There was also a suspicion that the police had tortured and murdered him, trying to get information from him about where the money was. Most likely nobody will ever know the truth, because Robo was charged with murdering his friend. It did not matter that he was already in jail at the time of the murder. Robo was transferred down stairs to where all murderers are jailed. Police keep on asking where the money is. Just try to understand that.

***

Because I was alone and I stop writing complaints, I had a lot of time to think. I could not understand that the most effective torture had been invented by the same people who later invented the automatic ass-wiper or the computer that was as big as two football fields.It made me really wonder about where the human race had come from and what had happened to it. An even creepier question was where was it heading.

I spend few days alone after I was taken out of the hole. I made sure not to touch the bed. I kept drinking water and wetting my face and neck for hours. They passed me supper through the feeding opening. No guards came into the cell at all. I knew that it was safe to touch my bed after supper. I took the top bunk to get more exercise by climbing up and going down. You could not imagine how a bed felt after such a long time.

After a few days, I was taken all the way up to the top floor. It was a sunny summer day. From my top bunk, I was able to look out the window. I was terrified. Everything was blurry. I could see roofs and chimneys of houses, but they were not sharp at all. For almost eight months, I had been on the second floor, which gave me no chance to look farther than the prison walls. Even during my daily walk, I had been surrounded by the walls of the chicken coop. It had destroyed the ability of my eyes to focus on objects that were farther. I'm sure that those days in the dark hole had not helped either. To think that beside my teeth also my eyes had been damaged. It was very depressing. How many prisoners went home without teeth and with their eyes damaged? Those thoughts were going through my mind.

I could see the silhouette of a church that was in downtown Kosice. It was a huge and beautiful building. I knew that there were gold decorations on its main towers, but I could not see them at all. I began to focus on those towers to try to see those gold lines. I was hoping to improve my sight. I also tried to focus on adjoining roofs and chimneys to see some details on them.

The new hall warden was a reasonable man. He never tried to put me down like Mojo had done. It signalled to me that they had abandoned their attempt to destroy me in jail, and the time when I was alone in cell had been in order to fix whatever visible marks my ordeal in the hole had left on my body.

The new warden said an intriguing sentence,

"You will never go into the hole. Don't worry." It hit me, because just few days ago I gotten out of one. I was going to tell him, but I got the message. They did not advertise when they were trying to destroy somebody. Only the few trusted guards were involved in the abuse. In fact, while in the hole, it had been dark. The guards had no name tags or numbers on them at all. How could anybody prove who had abused him? That was why Chief Warden Nagy had told me bluntly,

"Stop the complaints. You cannot prove anything. All your complaints just come back to us." How true. Nagy told me this a few months back when I was writing all those letters.

Even today, I believe that my new hall warden really did not know about me being in the hole. He was one guard with humanity in him. He did not pass mail or anything through the hole in the door. He walked in, said good morning gentlemen, even shook hands and acted like a normal person. It was a huge relief. I didn't tell him about being in the hole. I didn't tell him about my broken ribs. I did not want to start any problem, which could result in more abuse and another hole for me. He could be even fired if he began asking questions about it. I was glad to be out of the hole and to do my best to get out of the prison. I would like to thank that guard who was a human being. I hope that one day when time will change, he will be rewarded for it. I do not know his name. All I can say that he was a young man and at the time when I was there, he was a warden on the top floor of investigative part of the prison. Most likely he could be recognised by the fact that he was limping a little.

I decided to try to get as many documents out of the prison as possible. I was warned by other prisoners that all incriminating documents would be confiscated from me just before I would be released.

I signed a request to see the doctor one morning. With a copy of the request from my lawyer, which stated that I needed to lie down, the doctor obliged and prescribed two hours of bed from 11:00 AM to 1:00 PM. How "nice." It really helped. I could lie down at 11:00 and in few minutes I had to get up to get my lunch. By the time I ate it it was almost 1 PM and my time for resting on bed was up. If I fell asleep and went over time, I would be punished. For every situation, they had a trick. In reality, the doctor had done nothing for me, but he had fulfilled my and my lawyer's request. Thank you, doctor. I noticed your dirty trick right away.

I used many different tricks to get some documents out of jail. I'm sorry I cannot describe them. I would get some people in trouble. It would also destroy the possibility for other prisoners to use the same ways to get documents out. The fact was that I managed to get out about four hundred pages of documents; therefore, I have proof of everything I'm writing.

Feeding pigeons was my favourite pastime.

It was about 3:00 PM, when I returned from my hour-long walk. About six pigeons came in through the open window. Some of them ate from my hands. My favourite pigeon, which I named Holub, came to get his petting and sat on my shoulder.

It was very nice.

Time was moving much faster than before. I was exercising to get back into shape.

A few days passed.

"Demcak, pack your things," A guard yelled through the little feeding window. I thought they were transferring me to another cell. They took me to the shaving room, strip-searched me, and went through my belongings piece by piece. They also checked my documents page by page and took whatever was incriminating.

They kept me in the shaving room for a few hours. Then they took me back to my cell. It was already after supper. When I entered, I was pleasantly surprised. Miro Horvat was sitting behind the table. After his punishment in the hole they had placed him with me again. He was starving, dehydrated, and very tired.

I new what the hole does to a person.

Miro told me that they had also kept him on his feet all day long, but they had opened the board for him to lie on for what he thought was the night. For him, they had kept a small light on all twenty-four hours. I guess they took it easier on him than on me. He had also had no health problems, like I had had. But he was dehydrated and kept on drinking, just like I had before.

I wrote to the Canadian prime minister and the Canadian consul again. I noticed that my mail was going through much better than before. I also sent copies of my letters to Bibiana, and she mailed them to the addresses.

The next day, another prisoner was assigned to our cell. He was an old, fat man from Cierna nad Tisou. His name was Jouska *(not his real name)*. He was only the second inmate who could have been older than me. I tried to be as polite to him as I could, which was not easy, considering a few obstacles. For one, he told me that, on the outside, he got up at 4:00 every morning. At 5:00 AM, he was already with his partners at the park, waiting for the store to open, which was at 6:00 AM. All that rush, because they could not wait for the store to open so they could buy Choochoo *(the cheapest wine, which was a favourite drink of Slovak hobos)*. That's how interesting his days had been on the outside.

The fact that he had been charged for babysitting his sister's infant kid did not help. The babysitting was not the problem. The problem was that, when his sister returned, she caught him with his pants down, lying too close to the baby's face. She came to her own conclusion, and the policemen went ahead in their own usual way. They arrested the old man first and then began asking questions. It did not matter that the baby was not hurt in any way or that Jouska denied all accusations to the whole extent. Actually, he claimed that he could prove his innocence without any doubt at all.

As I got to know him a little better, I had no choice but to transfer myself onto his side a little.

For one thing, I knew by then that most policemen were crooked in Slovakia, and I did not trust them.

For another thing, I could not blame Jouska for living his life in a way that, in Canada would be considered hobo style, because, in Slovakia, it was a way of life for so many people. How many men woke up in the morning, had two or three shots of vodka to kill bad breath, and then stopped in a tavern on the way to work to warm up with one or two glasses? By the time they made it to work, it was lunchtime, which could not go without some shots, and on the way home, it would go the same way as on the way to work. It was a lifestyle during communist times. Jouska just lived the usual way.

He told me some interesting stories. The best days of his life were when Meciar had visited town and drinks were free. Jouska was from the town Cierna nad Tisou. It was a town close to the Hungarian border, and many people spoke Hungarian. When they tried to speak Slovak, it was a mixture of both languages.

Jouska told me,

"She was before voting. Meciar say vote me; all drinks free. Me and everybody say HURRAH. Voting day, she say goulash and drinks free. Vote Meciar. Me, we say HURRAH. We all drunk vote Meciar. More free drink; me, we say HURRAH."

No wonder Meciar had won the election then. Later drinks didn't work that well anymore. Meciar had managed to get only about 7 percent of voters in his last election. In 2010 Meciar did not even make it to parliament. People finally got to senses.

Jouska claimed, in his defence, that he was unable to commit the crime as charged, even if he had wanted to. His sister had reported to the police that she had found Jouska lying next to her child with his pants down, from which she had concluded that he was attempting to stick his penis somewhere illegal. Sick! The police did not waste any time asking her any more questions. They went HURRAH-style to arrest Jouska.

Once he was in jail, "secret agent" Igor Gregor was sent to find evidence that Jouska was lying when he denied the accusation.

I knew about Igor Gregor, because he was the same guy who was sent to me to get me to incriminate myself. He was a "lovable" guy who was sent from cell to cell to snoop information and then to snitch to officials so it could be used against prisoners. People like Igor were called informers or snitches. No doubt he was sent to Jouska, which could amount to Igor's most intriguing, James Bond–style secret mission; he carried it out in a "professional manner", like all his other "dangerous" and "fascinating" assignments in the past.

Jouska claimed that all charges were false; he could prove it, and he even had a witness. His witness was—who else—Igor himself.

"Ask Igor," he told me "Me unable not do even if I wanted to. Igor, she see it when me in shower. And you know what she Igor say me? She say me 'You balls like elephant and cock nowhere.'" Jouska continued, "It is right. She must happened because of my drinking or because my cock no say hi to pussy for more than thirty years. First, me prick crooked like paragraph, then shrinking and shrinking. Now I look for she with flashlight, and she nowhere. Today me need magnifying glass to find she. Tomorrow, I need microscope. Me could no; how I do that kid?"

Not that I was interested much, but I didn't want to jump to a conclusion before I made my final opinion. I used the same danger and sophisticated method of spying that Igor Gregor had used during his assignment. On shower day, I glanced under Jouska's fat stomach. I discovered … nothing! And that nothing was the proof that Jouska was not lying. I had great difficulty seeing what I was trying to see. It looked no bigger than the button on my shirt. I had seen many little "peepees" when I was a swimming instructor at Broadway the YMCA in Toronto, but I'd never seen anything like that. I've seen wine bottle cork length and hummingbird size, but shirt button size? Never!

But balls? My goodness! I think Igor was wrong about an elephant. But a bull? Have you ever seen a bull's balls? They hang down about a foot and are larger than tennis balls. In Canada (Alberta, Saskatchewan, and Manitoba), they cooked bull testicles and served them as a delicacy. They called them "prairie oysters." I did not attempt to taste them, but they were quite a popular delicacy at some Prairie Exhibitions.

And that was what Jouska had hanging under his stomach. I can imagine when he has to prove his point in Slovak court.

Jouska also had an explanation for his pants. He explained, of course, in his Hungarian jargon,

"Me drink bottle of Choochoo. Room, she hot like oven. Me pants off to winter down. Me pass out. Baby sleep next me. Me wake up, me sister scream, hitting me head with roller, kicking me out. Me sister, he push me out door corridor, hitting me head no head. Me look, all neighbours look me like stupid. Why me neighbours see like she never see me before? What I done? Then me look, me see me ass is naked. Me no pants. I bounce sister door. Give me me pants. Sister, he open door, throw me pants on me head. I run and pull she pants on I. Neighbours look stupid, like she never see before."

The first time I heard about the charge, I thought, *Another creep.* After my discovery in the shower, I was moving slowly over to Jouska's side. After hearing his side, I moved even farther over to his side.

I would not want to be the judge when that case would be heard and proof will be presented.

Jouska had another surprise for me at the bedtime. Suddenly, there was blast, as if an old tire had busted. I thought that ceiling would crack.

Now that's the champion! went through my mind. In my times at the university farting competition, I had witnessed a lot of blasts, but Jouska beat them all. Too bad the communist system destroyed that valuable competition. Otherwise, Jouska could have signed up to show university students what a real champion could achieve. That all went through my mind, but I did not tell him, because I did not want to encourage him. I also did not want to reveal what we had been doing at university. Later, when Jouska told us his life story, I find out that his achievement would not be legal and therefore would be inadmissible at the university contest. Unbeknownst to me, Jouska used what would be considered as an illegal achievement enhancement substance.

He told us,

"Me life no easy one. When old, no even dog bark on you. I walk drunk to tavern yard to piss. Man saying, 'look at him, not even dog barks at she.' It is because, when drunk, you no more human, and dog feels that. Now I old nothing function. I no see on ears and no hear on legs." He noticed that we were laughing, so he corrected himself, "I mean I no hear on eye. Here sore, there sore; cock no more stand. It was crooked like paragraph, now she gone, bye, bye. This jail no worth shit. Eyes jump out my head, that how hard me push. And you know how much me push? Five gram. No even five gram of shit. Me eyes out, but no shit. Me have medication for shit, but I no take. I no want to wake you up at night."

That was when I realized that the blast he had accomplished on his first night was not legal, because Jouska was still on medication. It would have been considered doping.

I was relieved a little, because for a while, I was under impression that, after all that practise, suddenly an uneducated, untrained man had shown up from the middle of nowhere and beaten all the university students. It would have been really degrading to all of us trying for university degrees.

On the other hand, it's too bad that I did not know about that medicine in those days. I could have snuck it to Shooler, the competitor from our room in the dormitory, or even made a champion out of me. What a medication!

There was one more situation that could underline Jouska's story. The sun came out, and we realized that the roof of the jail was not insulated. It was hot like an attic under a tin roof. It reminded me of the Arizona desert. We all took all our clothes off, except our green shorts. It was impossible to keep anything on in that horrible heat. Fortunately, there was a sink, so we were able to keep wetting our bodies to cool down. That kind of made sense for Jouska's claim that he had taken his pants off because it was very hot. There were no air conditioners in Slovakia.

CHAPTER THIRTY-SEVEN

The most disturbing sight.
I Will Take a Lie Detector Anytime
to Prove It Is All True

Is the European Convention for the Protection of Human Rights and Fundamental Freedoms suitable to be used in a Russian latrine? No. The paper is too thick.

I received my monthly parcel from Bibiana. There was a lot of smoked sausage, which should take care of my protein supply. There was also one litre of honey in a jar and Turkish Honey. There were also some apples and oranges for vitamins. All of that was so important for my body, which needed the energy of which I was deprived in the hole.

I tried some exercising. There were no smokers in my cell anymore. I used the stools, the table, and the bed as weights. I tried to do handstands, push-ups within handstands, and regular push-ups. In the chicken coop, I tried to run for an hour in the shape of an eight. After the run, I did balance exercises in my cell. Because I had been in good shape before I was jailed, my strength returned.

It was also an asset that the hall warden was a normal, reasonable man, who was not on my case, like Mojo had been. After 6:00 PM, I was allowed to go onto the bed from where I could see the roofs of buildings and the downtown church. For a full hour, I exercised my eyes to be able to see a farther distance. My efforts paid off. In time, I was able to recognize the shingles on roofs and, later, even the gold decorations on the downtown

416

church. I was also able to jog for almost an hour. It was a slow jog, because the space of the chicken coop was very small. It was not easy, because my ribs hurt if I took a deep breath. In the cell, I continued with my eastern karate kata routine. I was a far cry from when I could break boards with my fist, but I improved day by day. Noticing improvements in my physical and physiological functions had a positive effect on my mental state. Finally, I could straighten my back and almost keep my head up. I began to believe that, one day, I would leave that terrible place in good health.

I decided … no more complaints. I needed to get out of prison first. Mail from Bibiana and my family was coming on time from day to day. It was a sign that the prison officials had stopped cooperation with Trebisov's corrupt crooks. Most likely, Danko had lost his influence on the prison warden. It gave me a kind of peace of mind, and I could concentrate on getting some documents out and taking care of my health.

I had some books that Bibiana had sent me. The special one hundredth anniversary book from when I was teaching at a high school in Brandford, Ontario, Canada, was among them. As was a yearbook from my teaching times at Central Technical School in Toronto. They were the size of A4 paper, which was larger than regular books. I decided to use them to get the most important documents out. The record from when Jana Visokaiova was abused at the police was one of them. I strongly believed that the former member of the Slovak parliament, Jan Danko, was part of it. My whole case had started right then. I knew that they would make sure that that record will not get out and into the public's attention. I cut the edges of that document to make it smaller and glued empty pages of the book over the documents. I made my glue by mixing flour and water. It worked well. You would have had to look very closely to notice that something was hidden between the hard covers of the books.

It was already June of 1999. In March, I had been found not guilty but not released. Ever since, corrupt justice representatives had been doing nothing but breaking laws. Prosecutor Bicko had not stated any reason for his objection and had not put it in writing. He had broken the law. Judge Jurko, who had found me not guilty, had written that he had released me from prison, but he had not given me the official release form. He had broken the law. Somebody ask the provincial judge to do something, so on May 7, they had delivered a decision to me from Judge Popovec, without any hearing and made on the basis of a nonexistent objection, that I would be held in prison. He had broken the law. JUDr. Igor Dorica from the office of the general prosecutor must have been blind, because he had written that he could not see any broken laws, even though large numbers of broken laws were sitting right in front of him. He had refused my request to have my case heard in the Supreme Court. He had broken the law. His decision was delivered to me on July 2.

In the meantime, Bibiana, my mom, my family, the media, the Canadian consul, and even some top Slovak representatives wanted to know when my case would be heard. It was clear that too many people in the country were raising their eyebrows, and my case would be heard sooner or later.

Finally, I received a trial date: July 8. And the trial was beyond the human imagination.

Just like before, I was escorted to the district court in Trebisov. My lawyer Ms. Fercakova came to talk to me just before I entered the courtroom.

"You are going home," she told me. "But there is one condition: you must not say one word inside there." I gave her a strange look, so she explained, "You want to go home or not? If you say one word, the prosecutor will object, and you will go back to prison. The summer holiday is next. That means the next hearing would be at the end of September, if you are lucky. Let me do all the talking, and you will go home. Remember, even if you don't like it, be quiet. If you say one word, you are back in jail. Do I have your word that you will be quiet?"

"I don't like it, but I agree. I'll be quiet from now on." I already knew that I could do much more from the outside. I was told by my brother and many other prisoners that "it never ever happened that somebody who was in investigative prison was found not guilty in the end. Every single person was convicted."

Great, the communists had invented a perfect system. They pointed a finger at you and arrested you. Then they had a few years to look for a false witness, even if it was somebody retarded who could not remember his name. If that somebody was dead, I do not think there was a problem with it. They could always forge his signature. In more than fifty years, it had never failed. Why would I be the first one to spoil that perfect record?

In court, Milan Jurko was still the presiding judge. Sitting to the side were the same ladies JUDr. Havrilkova and Cernakova. In the prosecutor's chair somebody I have never seen before was sitting. He was not very old and had brown hair and a beard. Nobody ever mentioned his name, and in the documents I received afterward, his name was not written. At every single procedure of mine, there was a different prosecutor.

It was the fastest hearing you could imagine. None of the gypsies—so-called witnesses—showed up. Nobody had asked him, but Policeman Stefanak had heard that the court case was coming up and taken action on his own initiative. He was hoarding gypsies, but he managed to find only Eva and Natasa Pukiova. Anna and Alena Demetorova refused to come and went into hiding. Even Alena had no idea that she had been dropped from my case on the request of Prosecutor Bicko at the previous hearing. Stefanak escorted the Pukiova sisters to court.

The hearing had already begun when he opened the door and shoved them inside. Everybody looked at each other like they were stupid. The judge looked at the lawyer. She nodded her head that she had not requested them. Judge Jurko had not requested them either, so he was confused and was not sure what to do with the two gypsies standing by the door. It had been a catastrophe each time they had spoken before. They had given different answers all the time. It had been a disaster to hear them the first time in court. All Judge Jurko needed was another line of idiotic stupidity. He looked completely lost.

My lawyer Ms. Fercakova saved the situation.

"Are you still saying what you said before?" she asked the two gypsies still standing by the door.

"What?" Eva did not understand what she meant.

"Are you still telling us what you did the last time you were here?"

"Yes."

"Then you can go."

The gypsies looked around, as if they were not sure what to do.

"Go, go, good-bye. Go." Fercakova was gesturing her hands. The gypsies left. The judge continued reading from his paper. He was mumbling so quietly that nobody could hear him. He raised his voice to read that I was released from prison. Good enough; I was hoping for it.

The door opened, and two gypsies' heads appeared in the door.

"Are we finished? Can we go?" Even the gypsies realized that it had been kind of meaningless for them to have been escorted to court in a police car by Stefanak just to say one yes.

"Yes, yes. Go with God," Fercakova yelled at them.

"You are released from prison," The judge addressed me, and that time, we could hear him. "Are you giving up your right to object to this decision and confirming that you do not want anybody to object on your behalf?"

"When am I going to be released?" I wanted to know if I was going to be released the same way I had been the last time, when I had been thrown back into my cell, but my lawyer jumped in. She pushed me as a reminder of what I had promised her.

"Yes, yes. He is not objecting to your decision, and he does not want anybody to do it on his behalf." I could not agree more. Anything to get me out.

"Do you give up your right to object to this decision?" The judge also asked the prosecutor.

"Yes," said the unknown man, who was sitting in the prosecutor's chair. Whoever he was did not matter, because it looked like I would be released after all.

The judge handed me the release form, and they did not place handcuffs on my hands on the way back to prison. If the judge had given me the release form like that after the first hearing, I would have been out many months before. Whatever documents I had with me I handed to Bibiana. My brother and Bibiana were to come and wait until I was released officially from prison.

I had been given the release form, which was taken away from me as soon as I entered the prison.

Otherwise, I had no documents from that last hearing. I kept requesting it.

Finally, after repeated requests, somebody wrote the document in 2003.

Imagine this to be the official sentencing document from my last court appearance. The date on the document was September 8, 1999. But it is stated on it that it was validated on September 3, 1999. How could that be? How could anybody validate a nonexistent document, and why was it delivered to me after four years and only after my repeated requests? Even after my release, somebody was fabricating documents and had mixed up the dates.

I have no idea who wrote that document, which was supposed to be the sentencing document. All I know is that it was another disaster of justice. It was to be a sentencing document, but the judge never signed it. Only the person who had written it made a little mark on it by the stamp reading "If correct complete:" It was a little mark that was an unreadable signature of somebody, but there was no name. On the opposite side, there was Jurko's name but no signature. Where did these people come from? Could it be valid? Had Judge Jurko seen it? If he had, why hadn't he signed it? Who in the world would make up the following crap?

This totally ridiculous document states that I was convicted, because the witnesses had confuted my defence. The so-called witnesses were listed only by initials, at first. Not by names.

A. D. (Alena Demeterova) was never a subject of that court proceeding at all. She had been dropped from my case after she had claimed in the first court that I had never committed any crime. Dropped from my case, never brought back, claimed that I was innocent—but used as a witness against me. It was totally illegal and outrageous.

Even more despicable was listing A. K. (Anna Karickova) as a witness. Policeman Demjan had tried to use her against me. He had even fabricated a false statement for her. But she had refused to go along with it. She had never been part of the indictment, had never appeared in any proceedings. No statement of hers was ever presented in court, but she was listed as a witness against me. How could she be used against me if she had never been present anywhere, never part of anything, and not part of the indictment?

What kind of idiot had written the sentencing? These questions should have been answered. Jurko's name was on it, but he had not signed it. Not one single name as to who had written the document was on it. Was that justice Slovak style—using nonexistent witnesses and sentencing documents without any signatures on it? Shit!

This was not the only example of crap that flew from one justice official to another. Every one of them simply ate crap instead of flushing it down the toilet. Provincial Judge Popovec had used Jana Visokaiova as a reason to keep me in jail. She was the one who had been abused by the policemen, dropped from my case, and reinserted in the indictment, without ever being brought back to my case. JUDr. Dorica from the office of the general prosecutor had not see any of that as broken law. Didn't he understand that using somebody who was not in the case at all must be against the law? How had he gotten all the way up to the office of the general prosecutor with a brain like that? Had he simply kissed Meciar's ass and been appointed?

I have a pile of official documents. You can pick up any of them. Absolutely any. There will be broken laws on them. I guarantee it. From the simple Policeman Stefanak, Investigator Demjan, and the prosecutor with no law education (Sabo) to the other prosecutors (like Bicko and Dorica) and the judges (Milko, Jurko, Popovec, Brdarsky, and others), everybody, absolutely every one of them, was corrupt, because they acted against the law.

To top it all off, Prime Minister Dzurinda, Minister of Justice Carnogursky, Minister of the Interior Pitner, President Schuster, and General Prosecutor Hanzel had been informed about the fact that I had been illegally imprisoned and abused by the named corrupt machinery, and they were not willing or able to do anything about it.

Can anybody imagine or comprehend my situation or the general situation in that country's justice system? These were the people who were paid to protect the citizens. Instead, they were the actual criminals in the country. They did anything they wanted, and they protected each other. One of the best organized mafia in the world was there, and they used official vehicles to kidnap people and jails to keep them in, and they tortured them using official documents, blackmailed them using investigators, and charged them using mentally retarded and nonexistent witnesses. All of the above without a possibility of being punished.

A short time before I was released, I was a witness to the most disturbing sight of all. I cannot describe the exact circumstances or the exact time it happened, in order to protect the guard who let me see it. The guard had told me before that he was going to show me something he would like the world to know about, and he kept his word. In certain situations, when we were allowed to buy groceries in the prison store, we had to wait for our turns. As you already know, nobody was allowed to talk or to see anybody else. In that situation, the guard took me to a heavy, steel door where I heard some commotion. Guard opened the door just enough for me to see behind it. There were also bars behind the door.

It was shocking. It felt like I was in one of the Milos Forman movies. There were prisoners marching in a formation of three lines, which were about ten men long. That meant there were about thirty prisoners marching. A guard was yelling "One. Two. One. Two. Straighten the line. One. Two. One. Two ..." That would have been normal, except for the fact that every single prisoner was injured in one way or another; some were even injured in more than one way. Some had crutches, some canes, and some had long sticks with legs wrapped around them and limping. Every single one of them had some part of his body wrapped up in white bandages; others had casts over broken bones.

"That is humanity the Slovak way. It is a result of torture," the guard who brought me there whispered into my ear. We heard the elevator door open around the corner. The guard pretended that he was yelling at me and pushed me toward the elevator. He could not answer the questions that were in my mind, like

"How did they break their bones?"; "Did the guards break them like they broke my ribs?"; "Or were the prisoners driven by mental torture to do it to themselves?"

All I knew for sure was that the prison system in the city of Kosice systematically caused pain and suffering that was beyond comprehension.

"What about that marching?"

Later, I learned the answers.

"They punish them for inflicting wounds on themselves. They also believe that, if they suffer like this, it will discourage them from doing it again and persuade them to pay."

SHIT, SHIT, SHIT! Who is going to believe me about this? I was shocked. I had heard of and even personally met some prisoners who had cut themselves with razor blades, burned themselves with boiling water, and ate paint dust, but broken bones? It was too much. I had also thought that they were isolated circumstances. I had no idea there were so many of them. Those with the most serious wounds like these were kept out of sight of the other prisoners and made to suffer even more by making them march around corridor.

It was a feeling that spectators have when attending my magic show: "You see it, but you don't believe it."

This was not a circumstance in the dark communist era. This was in the year 1999. The communist system in Eastern Europe collapsed in 1989. For ten years, they had been claiming that they were building human democracy. Slovakia is a member of the European Union. The government signed the Convention for the Protection of Human Rights and Fundamental Freedoms, in which paragraph three reads

"Torture is forbidden" and

"Nobody can be tortured or forced to be the subject of inhuman or degrading treatment or punishment."

WHAT THE HELL WAS THIS???

Was it not torture by European standards? If not, then was it not inhuman treatment? If not, then was it not at least degrading treatment? Aren't prisoners included in the human population? Are they not somebodies?

Canadian government, are you still defending Slovak actions?

While in prison and all these years, after I was released I have been informing the Canadian government about the inhuman suffering that was taking place in Slovakia. I have been begging them to help me do something about it. Instead of helping me, Canadian Foreign affairs kept degrading me. Canadian Foreign Affairs asked me to forget about those suffering prisoners in Kosice. I tried, but I cannot forget.

That is the reason why I'm writing this story.

If this is how the Council of Europe recognizes the meaning of the Convention for the Protection of Human Rights and Fundamental Freedoms, I suggest using a different type of paper the next time they print it. It is not even suitable for being used instead of toilet paper in a Russian latrine, because the paper is too hard! They are happy using newspaper, because it is much softer.

Most likely, European officials will deny knowing about it, but I did inform them. Or they will claim that it is not true, because maybe I'm writing fiction. But I will take a polygraph test (lie detector test) anytime to prove that this story is the truth and nothing but the truth.

If they keep looking the other way that does not mean that torture and abuse is not there any more.

I knew that if I was in fact released, I had to be extra careful. The communists would not just let it go, and the European Union would do nothing to stop these horrors. I had not paid the ransom, and I had filed many complaints against them. Bibiana had done many media interviews, in which some facts about illegal acts were publicized. The dirty ways of the Slovak police and the rest of what they called justice officials had been brought to light. It would have been naive to even think that now they would release me and leave us alone. They had never spared anybody who had done something against them. I knew they would come after us, one way or another.

***

In the meantime, it was kind of nice to be taken from court back to prison without handcuffs. Before I returned to my cell, they went through my documents. It did not matter, because most of the documents that I wanted were already out.

Back in the cell, I had a lot of smoked sausage and other goodies left, because I had received a parcel from Bibiana. I gave it all to Miro with the understanding that he would share it with old man Jouska. He was really happy that I also gave him a heavy knife and fork. I apologized to old man

Jouska for when I had said something offending to him. He said that he had no bad feelings.

The only things I took with me were my spoon because it was gift from my mom. I still eat with that spoon. I took the rest of my documents and my books. Two of them were the most important, because very important documents were hiding, glued between the hard covers.

I shook hands with Jouska first. Miro had been with me the longest of all of the prisoners. He was a small-time gipsy criminal. I had gotten used to him. Never once had he said anything nasty to me. He had always been polite to me, calling me *baci*.

"Take care of my pigeon," I told him, shaking his hand. I knew I would never see him again, because the situation was unfavourable. I was kind of sad because of it, but the sadness was overshadowed by the fact that I was finally getting out of that hole. I saw little tears in his eyes.

"See you, *baci*. I will write to you."

Miro did write me. I received a letter from him in two days. I was very occupied with my plans, so I could not answer. I'm sure he was disappointed, but I was really unable to do it. No doubt that I would like to write to him now, but I have no address. I'm sure he was released, and he is out or even back in again. All I know is that he was from the village of Valaliky in the district of Kosice.

I pressed the red emergency button to let the guard know that I was ready. Finally, the door opened, and I could breathe air as a free person.

I had been arrested on October 11, 1998, and I was released on July 8, 1999. That was three days shy of nine months.

CHAPTER THIRTY-EIGHT

Welcome to Czech Hospitality

Did the Japanese invent anything at all? Yes, the fake toilet sound.

It was an unbelievable feeling. I was actually out on the stairs behind the door of jail, facing the parking lot. Only about five or six stairs were above the blacktop of the parking lot. I looked around, hoping there would not be any policemen to arrest me again, like they sometimes did with some Slovaks when three years of investigative prison did not break them down and they still owned some assets that they could sell to pay money for their freedom. That way, justice officials had another three years to persuade the poor prisoner and his loved ones to be more cooperative and pay. Now they have raised it to five years.

Nobody was out there to arrest me, so they must have had a different plan for how to get me. No doubt Bibiana was also on their list. She had been fighting for my freedom and, in the process, had told the truth about corruption publicly. It was something that not many people had courage to do in former communist countries, where the old communists and the old ways were still in place.

I took a deep breath. It was my first free breath after nine months. My brother Milan stopped his Toyota Camry right by the stairs. I noticed a dark blue car leave the parking lot after us; it was following us.

The first stop was at Ms. Fercakova's office. It was located on a big street that was the main drag to Roznava. It was a little office on the second floor of an old building. In jail, she had requested some pages from the investigative file from me. I had given them to her with the understanding that she would return them to me when I got out. She pointed to all the files.

"Look how many documents there are. It would take me hours to find them."

It was a poor excuse, I thought. I let it go. Freedom was more important to me than another argument.

Now I even feel some sympathy toward her. She still had to dance when the communists played. The only difference was that she had the chance to charge her clients a lot of money. Then, she took my case, and I was able to see all the stinky corruption, and I saw all those broken laws. I kept asking her to do something about it. Each time she visited me, I pointed out more and more broken laws, and she knew there was virtually nothing she could do about it, because she wanted to live or at least be left alone.

No doubt she had read the story about the lawyer, JUDr. Havlat, from Bratislava who actually tried to defend defendants even against policemen or judges—something unheard of for the past fifty years. His young lawyers were on the sides of their clients. They even objected to broken laws committed by justice officials. He was young and naive.

I had written to Bibiana to hire him as soon as I had read about him in the magazine.

"Sorry," she wrote "Didn't you hear? He was just murdered." Over, and over, I realized what chances I took by fighting those monsters. To murder somebody was like eating bread for them.

Our next stop was in a deli right in downtown Kosice. I used to visit that deli even way back while studying at university. It was located not far from the library, where I used to go to study. I ordered my favourite meal—ham in jelly and a fish salad called "Trieska." In all those years in America, I had not come across those kinds of goodies. I really enjoyed that meal, which was my first normal food in nine months.

We noticed one man who was not even trying to hide the fact that he was watching us. He was not eating, just sitting and looking our way. When we looked at him, he turned his head down. One thing was for sure in that country: when you were under surveillance, everybody could see it. No wonder, when the SIS was following Mr. Remias before they blew him up in his car, all the neighbours noticed that he was under surveillance and even marked the car licence plates.

The same car followed us all the way to Trebisov. I knew they were preparing something; I was just not sure what. The best part was that, after we reached my summer house, which was located on Safarikova 18. The street was very quiet. Those who had cars kept them in the garage. Even the visitors parked their cars in the driveways. Cars had a lot of value there, and people did not like parking them on the street. Suddenly, there was the same car that had been following us parked on the south end of the street, which was about a hundred metres from my house. Two men were sitting in it. Would anybody consider it suspicious? Almost everybody in my neighbourhood warned me that the police were watching me. They were also really great at other types of surveillance. I picked up the phone and heard somebody breathing.

It was easy to tell that they were preparing a trap and waiting for the right situation.

It would have been stupid of me, if I had stepped in the same trap twice.

I was sure that they were going to go after Bibiana this time. She was not a Canadian citizen; therefore, there would be no consul sticking his nose in the case.

They had already sent her notice to appear while I was still in jail. They had accused her of publicly insulting Investigator Demjan. Everything pointed to a similarity with my case. There was no doubt in my mind that they had already arranged to stop Bibiana's travels but had not told her about it. Now they were waiting for her to attempt to leave the country; they would grab her at the border, claim that she was trying to escape, and use it as an excuse to keep her in jail—exactly as it was used against me. Later, I found out that I was absolutely right.

I knew that we had to leave that country but without stepping into the same trap.

In 1968, when the Soviets invaded Czechoslovakia, I was escaping the communist system for the first time. It was a dangerous move, because the Soviets were also occupying all the border crossings.

Many years later, I was in my mom's place with Bibiana, trying to find a way to tell my mom that she was going to lose me for the second time and most likely forever. It was very hard for me, because it was obvious that that was our final meeting. She was already in her eighties, and there was no chance that the corruption would disappear and I would be able to visit anytime soon.

I didn't have to say anything. She was always a smart lady who understood everything around her, and even in her eighties, her mind was very clear and alert.

I pulled the curtains on her windows. She was already prepared. Two little boxes were sitting in front of her. She opened one, pulled a gold chain with a cross on it out, and told me with tears in her eyes,

"Be good, my son. Take care of Bibka, and may God protect you from bad people, like those who caused you all that terrible suffering."

Then, she opened the other little box.

"Bibka, take care of my son. I hope love will go with you two to that faraway country." She pulled out a diamond ring and gave it to Bibiana. It was a moment filled with emotion, and it was so hard to keep the tears inside. Nobody had to tell her. She knew that the only safe way for us was to leave that country. We talked about my first German shepherd dog Strela and how Strela escorted me to school every morning, returning home and then going back at the end of school to wait for me. That was about fifty years before, and she still remembered it. I knew that it was Mom from whom I had inherited such a great memory.

She told me how she had taken her 30,000 korun—the money she had saved for her own funeral—to the judge. I told her about how he had been trying to frame me in court. I promised to send her money as soon as I got to Canada. She told me not to, but I had some savings and mailed her $1,000, which was a little over 30,000 in Slovak currency at the time. She put the money in the same old envelope under the bedsheet where her pillow was—the same place where she had kept it for so many years, before she took it to the judge.

"I would tell you to go back to Canada and forget about it all, but I know you will not give up. You are too much like me. But we must believe that truth will win in the end. Sometimes, it just takes too long."

It was a nice talk until late into the night, but it was also very sad, because it kept crossing my mind that this was it. This was my last talk with my dear mom. She was crying very hard when it was time to say good-bye. In the past, she had cried when I came home from Canada or when I left. This time, it was a much heartier sob that I could not keep inside me either. We did not say "See you soon," like we used to. We would only have been lying to ourselves. We both felt that this was our last time together.

It was already getting light outside when Bibiana and I drove three blocks back to our place. The dark blue car had been parked down the road from my mom's place, had followed us, and had parked again on the south end of Safarikova Street. They kept watching us.

The next day, I went to visit my best friend, Vilo Biro. We only talk for a while at his front gate. I could see that he knew that I must depart and it was in the hands of God, if we would ever see each other. He also had to try to keep his tears inside. It was a terrible feeling that some bastards had the power to destroy family ties, friendships, and even lives. Vilo was the only person outside of my family to whom I indicated that I was going to escape again.

I packed all the things that were dear to me in an old trunk. I also packed two big hockey bags. Bibiana also packed two big hockey bags. We were hoping to take them to Canada, if we managed to get out. The old trunk was to be taken by my brother to my mom's place after we were gone. The four big hockey bags were to be delivered to us once we are out of Slovakia.

Bibiana went to her mom's place so as not to raise suspicions in those who were sitting in the car. She, her mom, and her brother went to visit their family. She told her grandmother, aunt, and a number of her cousins that we were going to a man-made lake called Sirava to spend a few days breathing fresh air. Only Bibiana knew that it could be her final goodbyes when she left. She also went to visit her young Christian friends. When I was jailed, they had been praying together for my safe return. They had no idea that it was the last time they would see Bibiana. Only one man knew what was obvious. He advised her that she'd better leave the country fast.

I made some calls to my family to let them know that I was going to Sirava to get some fresh air and to forget about it all. It was actually a message for the police who were listening to our phone. Bibiana did the same from her mom's phone. That way, they would not get suspicious about us getting ready to leave.

Under darkness of night, we jumped the fence of my garden into my back neighbour's yard.

Somebody had bought us two tickets from Kosice to Prague for a late-night train. In order to not raise any suspicions, we had bought return tickets. Our reservations were for the sleeping section of the train. The car had a bunk bed for two people.

We had whole day before the night train was to leave. For lunch, we went to my favourite deli across from the hotel Slovan. I had my ham in jelly and fish salad Trieska. For supper, we visited a very nice restaurant, which was upstairs in an old building. I had chicken paprikash. It was Hungarian style and a favourite meal of mine.

I had a detailed plan for how to escape from Slovakia to the Czech Republic. Sorry, I cannot describe it, to protect those who helped us.

Once in the Czech Republic, breathing was easier. The feeling that I was out of the country that had totally betrayed me was one of relief but also sadness. After all, it was my old country, the place where I was born, the country where all my family lives, and where I cannot return.

I visited Prague right after the Soviets invaded my old country, and I will never forget the holes in the buildings around the statute of Vaclav. Then, it was still Czechoslovakia.

Czech hospitality is very famous, but it had been tainted by more than forty years of communist rule, so they still had to learn a little.

Some time before, we had visited Prague as regular tourists. Bibiana's mom, my mother-in-law-to-be was also with us, as well as Bibiana's brother Rado. My brother Milan and my friend Nada were also there. I treated them all to one of the best restaurants in Prague for supper. It was a little attempt to impress them all. And impressing it was. Really …

As I do every day, I needed to go to the toilet. The washroom was located on the left side, behind the entrance door of the large restaurant. The tables were just a few feet from the washroom, which made it feel like you were sitting in the middle of the restaurant when you were sitting on your throne. You could hear everybody talking. Common sense told you that they could hear you if, by accident, your behind said something. As was normal in many former communist European countries, the lady who was the washroom attendant sat right in front of the washroom door. I paid my admission, and instead of tickets, I received an exact amount of toilet paper. How do I know that it was an exact amount? Because the toilet paper sat nicely in line on the table next to the lady. Every little pile had the same amount of toilet paper, which had been counted by hand piece by piece to make sure that no one piece was over the Czech norm. It was a far cry from enough by Canadian standards. The quality was also a little behind, so you had to be careful, because it was very fragile and your finger might end up … you know where.

No problem. I was prepared. While in Europe, I always carried a little bag with me, and inside it was a toothpick, a comb, and most importantly, a roll of toilet paper that would be approved by Canadian standards. I strongly suggest to everybody who is spoiled like me to do the same, because that way you will be also prepared for those washrooms that do not have toilet paper at all.

In Japan, they dealt with this problem, well, you could call it the

Japanese way. There is no problem with toilet paper there. It is that the Japanese people try to fool everybody, including themselves. They do not want anybody to know what they are doing while sitting on that throne. They have a special button, located conveniently right next to where you are sitting.

"Don't just sit there, do something," the old proverb says. Here is an explanation of what that means in Japan. When the Japanese sit on the toilet and feel that their behind might make some noise, which would reveal the secret of what they were doing, they do something about it to keep it a secret. They reach for the button and push it. The button activates a sound system through a speaker that is installed above you in the ceiling. The noise is an exact replica of the sound that a toilet makes when it is flashing. That sound will camouflage and hopefully overpower the sound their behinds make.

If you, as a tourist, decide to take advantage of this unique invention, be sure to synchronise your push with the push of the button. That way, nobody will guess (at least according to Japanese logic) what you are doing when sitting on that toilet. If you miss, and push the button prematurely, do not panic. You can push the button again, because there is no limit on the amount of pushing the button, and there is no extra charge for the extra push. A much worse scenario is if you push the button too late, because nobody will be able to help you, and everybody will know what you did sitting on that toilet.

Nobody can claim that the Japanese have not invented anything at all. This is a proof that this invention was invented and even made in Japan, and nobody can take it away from them. I have travelled the world, and I have never seen anything as sophisticated as this.

Some people claim that this invention is just as ingenious as the Soviet computer the size of two football fields or the automatic ass-wiper, which was also invented in the Soviet Union. But there was a good reason for the Japanese to invent that fake flushing toilet sound. For generations, the Japanese were trying to fool each other by flushing the real toilet repeatedly, each time their behind was about to produce that unwelcome noise, which would reveal what they were doing while sitting on the toilet. It was wasting tons of water. Now, they are able to keep on fooling each other and save valuable water.

The Soviet invention of their first computer is another story. They could have invented a computer smaller than two football fields, but why bother? Russia is the largest country in the world. So, largest country, largest computer. It makes sense.

It was a different story in the washroom in Prague, where I learned about real Czech hospitality. I was sitting on the toilet, minding my own business, pushing gently in order to not spoil the appetites of diners behind the door, when suddenly a loud knock disturbed my concentration.

"What are you doing there?" a lady's voice was yelling, while she was knocking loudly on the door. It was easy to guess that it was the washroom attendant. Her voice echoed through the whole restaurant.

"I will call the police on you," she continued. I had known there was a limit to the amount of toilet paper, but I had had no idea that there was a time limit on how long you could sit on the throne. I wasn't timing it, but it had hardly been two minutes since I had locked the door behind me. It was very annoying when some small-minded idiot knocked on the washroom door while you were pushing, but this time it was much different. I was in a restaurant full of people, and she was threatening to call the police if you didn't get out. Everybody stopped chewing and began watching what was going to happen next. On top of that, my present and future family was also there. I could deal with my fiancée and her brother, but what about my future mother-in-law? I knew it would be embarrassing to come out, but I also knew that I would have to get out sooner or later, and the best would be sooner, before she started her second round of yelling.

Then I heard that nice lady telling somebody, "We have all kinds of junkies here, using our washrooms to use drugs."

"What do you think people do in washrooms in the Czech Republic?" I asked when I opened the door. I was going to give it to her, but I put a brake on my mouth when I noticed that all the guests in the restaurant were looking my way.

All those faces are still in my memory, but they were hard to read at the time. Some seemed like they were broadcasting, "Hey you, tourist, you'd better learn how to do it fast, before you go on your next trip." Another looked like it was saying, "Go home and come back after you learn how to do it." Still another said, "In the Czech Republic, you do it the Czech way, you ----." Some faces had no message on them, just that self-satisfied look from which it was obvious that they enjoyed every second of it.

My family and my family-to-be were all pretending that they had not noticed anything at all.

At the time of our escape from Slovakia after I was released from prison Bibiana and I stayed in a friend's cottage in Czech Republic, while I called my travel agent in Canada to arrange flight reservations and tickets.

We walked through the forests and fields enjoying the hot summer weather. It was sad because of the feeling that, a few years back, it had been one country called Czechoslovakia. Meciar managed to destroy it by splitting it in two, and in the part called Slovakia, he created anarchy, where those whose job it was to implement justice were worse criminals, from whom we were running.

The Slovaks had no power to interfere in the Czech Republic; therefore, it was safe to board a plane to Canada.

Only when we were in the air, sitting on the airplane, were we sure that we were totally free.

CHAPTER THIRTY-NINE

We Are All Taken Care of by God

What is the European Court of Human Rights? A cheap trick for the stupid.

Arriving at Vancouver International Airport brought another feeling of relief. It did not last for a long time. Soon, reality kicked in. I found out that almost everything I had been working toward for most of my life had been destroyed. We had been gone for more than a year. Our plan had been to return to Canada in three to four months.

My big motor home that had been home away from home had been stolen. My business was virtually in ruins. A tour for our show had been booked, but instead of attending to it, I had been sitting in jail. I had been unable to even cancel the bookings from the gulag, because I had not been allowed to make any phone calls. That ruined my reputation. In art, something like that was damage beyond repair. How could I explain to my clients that I had missed my engagements because I was in jail? Who was going to believe that I was innocent? Who would believe me that I had been framed? Starting again from the beginning was the only way.

To make things even worse, most of my animals were also gone. The person who was taking care of them thought that I had just dumped them on him and left. I couldn't blame him. I was supposed to have picked them up eight months before. When he had not heard from me, he gave them away or sold them for next to nothing. My beloved reptiles were gone. Only the boa constrictor, Jean Pierre Senior, and the Indian python, Big Foot,

435

were still there. I was glad that at least some had been returned to me. The rat, Houdini, was dead.

Worst of all was my mental and physical state. After I was released from prison, escaping from Slovakia had been the most important action to survive. That fact had given me energy.

Afterward, the realization kicked in.

The torture had destroyed my mental state more than I had realized. I was experiencing nightmares and waking up in the middle of the night, feeling like I was still in jail.

Whenever I looked in the mirror, I was totally terrified. I wasn't me anymore. Some old man with grey hair was looking at me. Just nine months before I had looked twenty years younger than my age. Now I looked twenty years older. That meant I had gained forty years in just nine months.

I lost a few teeth, which had gotten loose in jail. I also developed skin problems. There was a hissing sound in my ears even until today. An irregular heartbeat was scary. I had pain in the knees and other joints and problems with my stomach. All that from the mental and physical torture, bad nutrition, and stress.

Slovakia had done terrible damage to me, but I was determined to start again and rebuild my life. There was Bibiana, still young and willing to help.

My mom and dad were another push for me. I thought of how my mom and dad had lost everything over and over and repeatedly kept rebuilding their lives. It was like a pulling power not to give up.

A good friend of mine once told me something. His name was Mandrake, and he was a famous magician. We had been performing in the Crazy Horse Club at the same time. I was a struggling artist, telling him how hard it was to make ends meet.

"Do not ever worry," he told me. "We are all taken care of."

"What do you mean 'taken care of'?" I inquired.

"By God," he explained. "Whatever situations you get into, somebody will appear, just like an angel." And it was happening, just as he had told me.

Once, I had been sleeping in my big bus, which had been converted into a motor home, on a backroad in Vancouver on the Canadian West Coast. I was in a desperate situation, because I had offered to perform in Kamloops, but I had no money for gas to drive there. In the early morning, somebody knocked on my bus door. I got up fast, because I thought it was the police. No camping was allowed on city streets, and sleeping in a vehicle was considered camping by a city bylaw.

It was not the police. An old man, maybe in his eighties, was knocking on my door with his cane.

"What is this?" he asked, addressing all those paintings on my bus.

"The Magic Show. They gave my space to somebody else in the campground."

"You don't need to go to campground, park here on my property. A lot of room here." He pointed to his land. I was, in fact, parked behind the back of his garden.

"I'm sorry, but I have no money to pay you right away."

"I don't want your money; just park there, and don't worry about it."

It was like help from heaven. I thought I would park for few days until I could get out of that hard situation as a struggling artist. I had never applied for welfare or any other assistance, and I was not about to start then. The next morning, I saw the old man digging a ditch toward my motor home. Some pipes were already lying on the ground.

"What are you digging for? Gold?" I asked him, ready to help.

"I'm setting up water pipes for you."

I realized that my stay would be much longer than I was planning. We finished digging and became best friends for many years to come. He pulled out $200 when he learned that I had offered to perform for two weeks in Kamloops and had no money to get there.

"Is it enough to get you there?"

"Oh, one hundred is plenty."

"Keep the other hundred in case of emergency."

"Are you sure? I will pay you back as soon as I return."

"Just go, and drive carefully."

It was a very emotional situation, which it still is today. I bought gas, went to Kamloops, and made some money. After I returned, I tried to pay him back the money he had given me, but he would not hear about it.

"I told you to keep the money in case of emergency."

He was an old man, but I learned over and over that that man meant what he said. I decided to keep that hundred-dollar bill and spend it only in case of a real emergency. On the front of the bill, I wrote "G.L. SUNDAY APR. 19/87" with a black marker. On the back, I wrote "G.L.F. EDDY APRIL 19/87," which stood for "gift lent from Eddy, April 19/87." The bill had been printed in 1975, and I still carry it in my little wallet, as he said, in case of emergency. I thank God that I have never had to use it.

In time, I felt like Eddy was my grandfather. He became my only family, which I was missing because all my family was far away beyond the big sea. He died when he was 103. It was a huge blow to my mind, which was multiplied because I was far up north doing my job when he died. I cried and cried. It was the first time I had cried since I was a child. I discovered, for the first time in my life, what a relief cry can be to a human being.

We had spent a lot of time together, but I'm still sorry that I did not spend more time with him, and now it is too late. His full name was Edward Broderick, and I loved him very much. He came into my life when I was struggling to survive and helped me. He also gave me half of his property. It was the first real break in my whole life. I would like to dedicate this book to him and to all men and women who are or were good-hearted like Eddy—

people who appear when you need them most, just as if God sent them; people like Mrs. Cahoy or Mr. Bell, who appeared when my trailer caught fire on a major highway in Cabazon, California. Then there were David from Duncan and Michele, Raspal, from Richmond, British Columbia, as well as the Visokaiova family from Trebisov, Slovakia, and some others.

And at last but not least, I would like to remember my adopted grandmother, Mrs. Varsova from Hriadky, eastern Slovakia. She was one of the kindest grandmas I have ever met. It is hard to name all people I'm thankful to God for meeting.

I have been blessed to have people like that cross my path. I remember them when I see somebody else who is down.

After returning to Canada, I was very sad. I sat for hours, without signs of knowing what was going on around me, where I was, or why I was there. My mind was slow. I was afraid of falling asleep, because I had nightmares. I dreamed about being abused in jail again. Waking up screaming was an almost nightly occurrence.

We had tried to perform our magic routine in Jasper, Alberta. That was when Bibiana was floating in the air and fell down on eleven Swedish bayonets. It was our performance in front of a sold-out crowd in Legion Hall. The horrors of the times in the Slovak gulag went through my mind, and I lost concentration, which was the reason for the accident. That was when I recognized that jail had caused more damage to my mental state than I had realized. I needed more time and some therapy.

That was when I turned up for help at the Vancouver Association for Survivors of Torture (VAST). Bit by bit, I was fixing my health—family doctor, skin doctor, heart specialist, hearing specialist, dentist. Those were new people in my life, because, before jail, I had been completely healthy, Thank God.

I went biking in the morning and walking and running in the evening. The little gym in my backyard was for rainy days. It was under overhang roof.

Common sense told me that we could not just sit and wait for God to help us. The Bible also told me that we should not let evil have a free ride. In other words, we should help God wherever we could.

As soon as I was ready, I took the first steps to fulfilling the promises I made to those in jail. They had requested that I help bring the atrocities that were happening in that Slovak jail out in the open. We who are human must do what we can to bring it to an end.

******

Following are real facts from my case and other cases that happened at the time of my tragedy.

The Visokaiova family was destroyed.

Jana Visokaiova was just over ten -year-old child when the policemen abused her at her school and at the police station. She did not even understand why the policemen wanted her to lie. She was evicted onto the street with her parents. For three months, she was locked up in a mental institution and then placed in another institution. Her life as a young child was totally destroyed by repeated interrogations and abuse. After her release from the institution, she could not take the humiliation and left her hometown and Slovakia for UK. She still suffers from the damage the police caused her through the abuse and the bad reputation that was falsely created by the police.

Helena and Jan Visokaiova, Jana's parents, also refused to falsely testify. They were harassed by the police and other townspeople. They were evicted from their home and became homeless. For three years, they lived in the storage area of a basement in an apartment building with no water, no heat, no hydro, no window, and no enclosure, just open space. All that mental and physical abuse and losing their daughter created unbearable stress for the family. The family was denied financial assistance, which is guaranteed by the Slovak constitution. They survived off of handouts from friends. The father, Jan, died an early death, physically and mentally broken. The mom, Helena, attempted suicide with a butcher knife. Jana discovered her mom covered with blood and called an ambulance. All this because they had refused falsely testify. Until the police had stepped into their lives, they had been an average family, living a normal life. Their lives were totally ruined. They moved out of Trebisov.

Anna Demeterova was a fourteen-year-old child when she was abused at her school by the police because she refused to falsely testify. She became a prostitute.

Three other children were also negatively affected by Policeman Demjan asking them sexual questions when they were eleven or twelve years old. They were Anna Lukacova, Lucia Barancikova, and Marek Mazurkovic.

It is very shocking that the abuse of both Jana and Anna began at their schools without the knowledge of their parents and that the principals and teachers gave the policemen free reign to abuse the children.

Can this be acceptable in civilised society? I'm sure that the Council of Europe or the Slovak government or even the Canadian government believe that it is not. I must ask why they failed to do something about it when I informed them of it.

Maria Demcakova, my mom, spent her last years fighting for my release. Policeman Demjan and his goons lied to her face and created agonizing stories, which were impossible to take. Gypsies had threatened her, using the most vulgar words possible. The police would not touch the gypsies. They were their partners. She moved out of her hometown to Michalovce. Always a proud and hardworking lady, she died a broken woman with a feeling of humiliation and injustice as she was unble to see her son on her deathbed.

Bibiana Demcakova, my wife, also fought for my freedom. She suffers still today. A secret warrant for her arrest was filed in Trebisov on the request of Demjan, the policeman who fabricated the whole case and forged all those documents. For years, her mom was harassed by the police, asking questions. Bibiana can never visit her hometown and see her family, because the Trebisov police would like her behind bars to keep her from revealing the truth. On April 1, 2010, she received another false accusation for revealing the truth. More false accusations keep on coming.

Jozef Demcak—that is me—filed a complaint on the request of the

Visokaiova family against police brutality, concerning child Jana. I was arrested, jailed, blackmailed, and abused through physical and mental torture. I almost died there.

Policeman Demjan fabricated the charge. It was proven during the court process that the charge was completely false and illegal.

For his method of mental abuse, Policeman Demjan fabricated the following accusations:

1. I was apprehended trying to escape to Canada.
2. I was mentally ill. If not during the crime then before.
3. I might not be able to recognize that my actions were dangers to society.
4. I might not be able to recognize what criminal activities or an investigation were.
5. I might be a sex maniac.
6. My presence on the outside might be dangerous for people.
7. I might need preventive treatment.
8. I might have taken some photos of child pornography.
9. I might be the producer of pornographic videos of children.
10. I might have raped some children.
11. I might be an international drug trafficker.
12. I might have murdered somebody.
13. I should be locked up in a mental institution.
14. I licked the whole bodies, including the sex organs, of the dirtiest prostitutes in town.

There were more. None of the accusations were ever collaborated by anything at all. It wasn't even stated where the ideas had come from. All had been made up in corrupt, Slovak heads.

At the end of this book are real names and summaries of officials and other people who were duped, employed, tricked, used, damaged, or otherwise involved in this case by policemen on their way to frame me.

Other outrageous cases in Slovakia are proof of corruption in the justice system of that country.

Mrs. Ruzena Jancova of the Velke Kapusany region of eastern Slovakia was beaten almost to death by a police baton, because she complained against the police. She lost her home and lived in hiding, afraid of the police.

Brano Ruza of Malacky in western Slovakia shot Lukas Selc with a gun. In nine months of investigation, Brano was never charged. The policemen interrogated only him, the shooter. They did not talk to the man who was shot and survived.

Milos Bajus of Kosice (the city where I was jailed) in eastern Slovakia lent $30,000 US to Jaroslav F. Jaroslav visited Milos with an old revolver. Iveta Zajacova was also there. Jaroslav cocked his old gun, aimed, and attempted to place two bullets in each host's head. Each time, he had to cock the gun and pull the trigger. One bullet missed Iveta. The second ended up in the poor girl's head, killing her. The third and fourth bullets landed in Milos' neck and skull. He was extremely lucky, because he survived.

Provincial Judge Tomcovcik concluded that all four shootings, which had been cocked separately and aimed at the heads of two people, were accidental and careless.

Even after a higher court returned the case to be reconsidered, Judge Tomcovcik still ruled that all four shootings had been accidental.

Do we need any more proof of corruption in the justice system of Slovakia?

Do we need Canadian Foreign Affairs to defend them and offend us Canadians?

******

Once I had some energy, I filed a Complaint with the European Court of Human Rights.

Slovakia is a member of the European Union. They signed the European Convention for the Protection of Human Rights and Fundamental Freedoms. If you read it, your first impression will be that it is not bad. But if you look at it closely, you will be surprised.

Article 10 gives everybody the right to expression and free speech. Great, but does it? You think that, if you go to Europe, you can talk. Not so fast. Read it further. Free speech "may be subject to such formalities, conditions, restrictions, or penalties." Whoops. Free speech can be subject to formalities in Europe. Formalities is a very interesting word in the article. From this, it is clear that there is free speech in Europe, but only if you keep your mouth shut. Bibiana told the truth, and she is persecuted by Slovaks till today. Persecuted because she said one truthful sentence. The officials in Slovakia refused to find out if what she said was the truth, but they want to lock her up first. The European Court of Human Rights has been informed about it, but it does nothing.

The European Court of Human Rights is a completely lost cause. It is so busy that it deals with less than 10 percent of submitted cases. There are so many technical obstacles that more than 90 percent of cases are rejected just on those. If you count those victims who do not even try to file a court action because they are afraid for their safety and those who know that it is a lost cause, you can see how hopeless the situation in the European Union is.

The European Court of Human Rights will reject all applications if they do not go through all the local stages first. The local courts know that; therefore, they take forever with proceedings. In Slovakia and other countries, they can keep you in prison for five years while they try to see if you have committed any crimes at all.

I attempted to a file complaint, and I was very much surprised. Imagine this. They call it the European Court of Human Rights, but you have no right to be present in court when the court deals with your case.

Judges M. Pellonpaa, R. Maruste, E. Fura-Sandstrom, and Ombudsman P. Nikiforos Diamandouros were informed about the atrocities that were committed in Slovakia, but they could not do anything, because they had not seen any article broken.

All my complaints to the European Court of Human Rights were rejected based on formalities and technicalities.

Amnesty International of British Columbia acts like all political organisations do. Occasionally, the organisation makes a list of already known countries that practise torture. When asked, the organisation makes some public comment. It is happy that the public still sends the organisation money.

Amnesty International at the University of British Columbia, in Canada honestly tries to make the Canadian government do something. The organisation invited me to lecture to them about my case. Students listened.

These were young students who were upset that the Canadian government does next to nothing to help Canadians who are arrested and abused in foreign countries. They are honestly trying. The students learn very early in life what it is like to deal with Canadian politicians. Stretching time when replying works miracles with young people. By the time something gets to any point, the students have already graduated and gotten busy looking for a job. Others quit dealing with the Canadian government in disgust and disappointment.

At least eighty complaints were sent to the Slovak government. Sometimes, the government did not respond or it did, but the person who wrote back avoided the subject. The Slovaks did not deny the abuse. They refused to hear about it or to see proof. The Slovaks claim that I can't prove it. It is impossible to prove anything to someone who does not see or hear. The Slovak government is against torture when talking publicly, but it does nothing to investigate torture in order to stop it.

Dealing with the Canadian government was another disaster.

I was devastated just talking to them. It was like talking to a brick wall.

Canadians have done an even better job than Slovaks defending the torture and abuse that took place in Slovakia.

The Canadian government is against torture when talking publicly, and I believe it, so therefore, I'm demanding that Canadian Foreign Affairs stop defending foreign torturers and murderers!

Years of shocking dealings with Canadian Government are described in the next chapter.

CHAPTER FORTY

I Refuse to Believe in My Dealings with the Canadian Government

What did the Canadian government do when it learned about me being tortured? The government said that it appreciated being made aware of it. Then, it did nothing.

My dealings with the Canadian government were big disappointments. After a number of attempts by mail and telephone, I was unable to get the Canadian government to act honestly.

It all began when Mr. Chretien was prime minister of Canada and the head of the liberal government. Mr. Hiseler held my case from the beginning, as an officer for Canadian Foreign Affairs. He flatly failed me and other Canadians. Now it is 2010. It is the third government, and as far as I know he is still handling my case. He is still defending illegal Slovak actions; he is still offending us Canadians; he is still fooling his superiors; and nobody is doing anything about it.

Canadian Foreign Affairs are a disgrace to humanity. The way they treated me and other Canadians is a complete tragedy. The findings of my research hit me like a horror movie.

> "I don't want to be Canadian anymore," Samson stated publicly after the failure of Canadian Foreign Affairs to assist him properly when he was tortured in Saudi Arabia. *(Canadian Media)*

"Canadian politicians are the scum of lowest possible nature," Samson's father, after dealing with Canadian Foreign Affairs. (Global TV 16:9)

"It is like I am talking to the air. I feel my words are not being heard by the Canadian government," Stephan Hachemi said, after dealing with Canadian Foreign Affairs concerning torture and murder of his mother in Iran. (Canadian Media)

"Hiseler is worst human being I have ever met in my life," Michael Kapoustin said, after dealing with Canadian Foreign Affairs in connection to his abuse in a Bulgarian jail. (Personal contact with Michae)

"It is like listening to a Slovak abuser and talking to the brick wall," I, Jozef Demcak, said, after dealing with Mr. Hiseler in connection to torture I endured in a Slovak jail.

There are many more who claim that Canada failed them when they needed help most, while Canadian Foreign Affairs claims that Canada is doing it right.

How can Canada defend the interests of the torturers and murderers and, at the same time, tell us that Canada is against all forms of torture? That is exactly what was going on in a Montreal court when Mr. Hachemi was trying for justice in connection with his mother situation; she was tortured, raped, and murdered in Iran.

Maybe I'm too stupid to understand how somebody can be against torture but support the interests of those who practise it.

Isn't it Canada against Canadians for the interests of killers?

For months, the Canadian opposition was trying to discover if Taliban insurgents were abused by Afghanistan prison authorities. That would be fine. But the Canadian opposition was not looking into it in order to punish the Afghans who had possibly abused Taliban prisoners. They want our soldiers to be investigated and punished. Same time they want to smear mud on our present government. Canadian opposition wanted our government and our soldiers to be responsible, in case somebody else abused somebody. The Canadian opposition sided with the interests of the Taliban killers who were ready to destroy everything and blow themselves up just to kill many innocent citizens. On the other side were our heroes whom we sent to risk their lives to protect foreigners.

Maybe I'm not as intelligent as the Harvard professor, Mr. Ignatieff, who is the opposition leader, but I saw that as Canada against Canadians for the interests of killers. The Canadian liberals would do anything just to get some votes.

I was tortured in Slovakia, and Canadian Foreign Affairs defended Slovaks in all ways and every way possible, even claiming that the torture had never happened. Even the Slovaks didn't deny the abuse. They even admitted it in writing. Than claiming that I couldn't prove it.

In my opinion, Canadian Foreign Affairs defends different sick and evil regimes.

"The most fundamental duty of the state is to protect its people," former Prime Minister Chretien said publicly. But when informed about the abuse that was committed against me, he did nothing.

This hypocrisy must stop. What you say means absolutely nothing. Only what you do counts.

I refuse to believe that Honourable Mr. Harper approves of this kind of hypocritical attitude of Canadian Foreign Affairs, and I will refuse to believe it until he personally confirms his stance to us Canadians.

On January 31, 2010, I mailed a letter to Canadian Foreign Affairs As last attempt to avoid Court action against Canadian government for failure to protect and assist me in time of need.

On April 15, 2010, I forwarded a copy of the letter to the prime minister of Canada, Mr. Harper, because Canadian Foreign Affairs did not reply. That is an indication that they will spend our tax money to defend their rights to fail Canadians in need and to be arrogant to us afterward.

Copy of my letter to Canadian Government:

Jozef Demcak Box 32066, Richmond BC, V6X 3R9

Tel. 604 214 0738 E-mail: jozefmagic@yahoo.ca

www.justiceisdead.info

April 15, 2010

Honourable Mr. Harper

Prime Minister of Canada

Dear Mr. Prime Minister,

On January 31, 2010, I mailed a letter to Canadian Foreign Affairs and International Trade

(CFAIT).

By April 15, CFAIT has not replied; therefore, I'm forwarding a copy of the letter to you, the prime minister of Canada, because it is an indication that CFAIT may spend our tax money to defend its rights to fail Canadians in need and to treat us maliciously afterward.

Unless you confirm it personally, I will never believe that this is the kind of Canada you are trying to build and represent. I simply do not believe it.

I feel that the way CFAIT is treating me and other Canadians is a tragedy. Please consider the following statements of Canadian citizens:

"I don't want to be Canadian anymore," Samson stated publicly after the failure of Canadian Foreign Affairs to assist him properly when he was tortured in Saudi Arabia.

"Canadian politicians are the scum of lowest possible nature," Samson's father, after dealing with Canadian Foreign Affairs.

"It is like I am talking to the air. I feel my words are not being heard by the Canadian government," Stephan Hachemi said, after dealing with Canadian Foreign Affairs concerning torture and murder of his mother in Iran.

"Hiseler is worst human being I have ever met in my life," Michael Kapoustin said, after dealing with Canadian Foreign Affairs in connection to his abuse in a Bulgarian jail.

"It is like listening to a Slovak abuser and talking to the brick wall," I, Jozef Demcak, said, after dealing with Mr. Hiseler in connection to torture I endured in a Slovak jail.

There are many more.

Please read the enclosed correspondence and let me know if you can help me fix this problem.

Thank you for your consideration.

Jozef Demcak, Canadian citizen

The following is my recent letter to Honourable Mr. Lawrence Cannon, minister of foreign affairs, which describes, in short, my hopeless effort.

Jozef Demcak, BA, PO Box 32066 Richmond BC, V6X 3R9, Canada

Tel.: 604 214 0738 E-mail: jozefmagic@yahoo.ca

Fax: 604 214 9333 www.justiceisdead.info

January 31, 2010

Honourable Lawrence Canon, Minister of Foreign Affairs

Sussex Drive, Ottawa, ON, K1A 0G2 Fax: 613 996 9709

Dear Mr. Cannon,

My lawyer from Arvay, Finlay Barristers is sending you correspondence on my request. Please accept for consideration my letter as well, which is more informative. I apologise if I'm using some strong words, as I'm still emotionally affected by the abuse in Slovakia and the way I was treated by Foreign Affairs and International Trade (FAIT) after my release. I trust you will understand why.

With regret, I have to inform you that, in my opinion,

FAIT, namely Mr. Hiseler, acted maliciously or at least unusually with disregard for my rights and interests.

Please consider my case:

In 1998, I was arrested, blackmailed, and tortured in Slovakia. The illegal arrest and abuse was reported to Canadian Foreign Affairs in multiple ways, but very little was done.

By multiple letters from me and my family to the Canadian consulate and to then Prime Minister of Canada Honourable Jean Chretien, it was indicated clearly that I was in a terrible situation, being abused by corrupt Slovak police. I also informed the Canadian consul during his only visit to the prison.

The prime minister's office passed those letters to FAIT, and no steps were taken of any kind to stop or to lessen my suffering.

I'm familiar with some correspondence written by the Canadian consul to the Slovak government, for which I'm thankful, but the most important facts, which are torture and abuse, were not raised in those letters. The consular correspondence focused mainly on illegal or shabby proceedings.

Torture is against the law in Slovakia and is not supported by Slovak government. It is practised by many local, corrupt police and prison guards; therefore, I believe that the Slovak government would have taken some steps to stop it if concerns were raised by Canadian authorities.

The Canadian consul was treated poorly by Slovak authorities, not according to Slovak laws, neither by international agreements Slovakia has signed. My abuser was sitting in the room, denying us the right to have a private conversation. The lawyer who was to defend me did very little and even refused to talk to the consul.

All those practises are clear indications of the fact that

abuse was taking place. Refusing a consular visit was in order to buy time so that visible damage to my body, inflicted by abuse, could become less visible. The presence of the abuser in the room was in order to restrain the prisoner from informing the visitor about the abuse. Complete solitary confinement and not allowing any phone calls were in order to cover up torture and to avoid having any witnesses to it.

Regular telephone calls to me from the consular office would have eliminated abuse completely, because the Slovaks would realize that I could alert Canadian authorities about the abuse when they called me. They only abuse prisoners if they believe that they can cover it up. I received not one single call from anybody. Attempts from my family to reach me were simply refused, but Canadian authorities could have demanded it under diplomatic and consular laws and agreements, but they did not make that attempt.

Most formerly communist countries of the former Soviet block, including Russia and countries of the so-called Soviet satellites, practise similar tactics. I'm familiar with other cases in that region.

Those are the countries to which thousands of Canadians travel frequently and are in danger of being put through similar horrible abuse.

After my release, I spent years trying to persuade Foreign Affairs to do something about it, because other prisoners also suffer in the same prison and because I believe that torture and abuse must stop. It does not matter in which country it takes place.

I was stonewalled by Mr. Hiseler, who has been handling my file right from the beginning. He put me through years of humiliation and stress by mistrusting me, doubting my allegations, and diminishing the seriousness of my testimony, instead mitigating and justifying the Slovaks' illegal activities, including torture.

Not only did he refuse to see evidence of my innocence, but he kept on accusing me of having done something else that I may have done. He just did not know what it could be.

He refused to see RCMP investigative file, because as he claims, it does not matter, for the reason that it is the opinion of one man.

He did not acknowledge the statement of the Canadian consul, who stated to RCMP that I had been arrested to be blackmailed, as is common practise in Slovakia and that region.

He does not recognize the conclusions of the United Nations Convention against Torture, which lists my suffering clearly as physical torture. Mr. Hiseler claims that it was not.

I was also put through mental torture in Slovakia. I offered proof of it and also a detailed description of how it is implicated. From conversation with Mr. Hiseler, I concluded that he had no idea about how mental torture is done or he refuses to acknowledge it. I believe that it would be useful for FAIT officials to know how it is done to be able to identify it when visiting our prisoners, who are being put through it in foreign countries. Nobody wants to hear about it.

The fact is that, when Mr. Chretien's office passed information about my suffering on to FAIT, it stopped right there. Nothing was done.

When Honourable Mr. Stockwell Day ordered RCMP to investigate my case and it was determined that my testimony is legitimate and that FAIT should deal with them, the investigation was stopped and nothing has been done.

Only more humiliation for me.

From my telephone conversation with Mr. Hiseler, I found

out that Mr. Hiseler did not even request to see the RCMP investigative file. Even without seeing it, he claimed that it was worthless. More than 1,700 investigating hours are to be wasted. RCMP was ready to give full cooperation just for asking, but Mr. Hiseler did not ask. He told me that I can send him the file if I get it. They put me through the lengthy process of getting my file through the Access to Information Act.

By correspondence with Honourable Mr. Stockwell Day, Honourable Mr. Peter McKay, and Mr. Sean Robertson, the director of the case management division at Canadian Foreign Affairs, I concluded that Mr. Hiseler is not providing them with all the facts concerning my case, he has even reported wrong information to them. It is the only way I could receive some, to me, morally and humanly unacceptable answers—for example that "my case is a private matter" or that "I should hire a lawyer in Slovakia."

I recognize that traveling abroad is everyone's responsibility, but I also believe that, when injustice and torture is involved, it is everybody's responsibility to help and to try to stop it.

I don't believe that Mr. Robertson knew that the whole Slovak investigative file was bogus and that many documents in it were forged when he wrote to my lawyer that the charge against me was that of a serious nature. He was addressing one accusation. I don't think that

Mr. Robertson was informed that, as part of mental torture, I was accused of almost every possible crime that exists in law books, including murder. Had he known that, he would probably understand better what was going on in that prison.

Mr. Robertson also stated that I had conceded to Mr. Hiseler that I was not tortured. I never would have said such a lie. I know of, and still suffer from, what happened to me. It was Mr. Hiseler who insisted that my suffering was only mistreatment, not me.

Mr. Hiseler told me, "You can basically get whatever opinion you want from people you want, if you only show them documents you want them to see." He was accusing me, but I believe that this is exactly what he has done, and that is the reason why some answers from different officials are, to me, ethically and humanly unacceptable.

The RCMP investigator, after investigating and reviewing my evidence, confirmed, "I have no doubt that you suffered. It could be physical; it could be mental. I have no doubt that there was suffering involved."

He added, "Is it a case against humanity, or did the international community not do enough? We know there was injustice done to you. That is obvious. You have a lot of evidence that shows that, yes, there was great injustice done to you. So Foreign Affairs should get involved. If there is a problem, they can identify the problem with your help. [...] how they failed you, if they failed you, and how they can improve procedures for the next time to prevent it from happening again. So I'm confident that you are telling the truth."

The investigation was abruptly stopped, and Mr. Hiseler refused to ask to see the general conclusion of it. He knew about the torture and injustice virtually from the beginning. I believe that Mr. Hiseler failed to act in a proper manner then, and he is still acting accordingly.

The Slovak prison warden did not deny the torture. He claimed that I can't prove it. But Mr. Hiseler denied that it happened at all, claiming that it was not torture.

After almost ten years of trying, all I have received from FAIT was humiliation, accusations without corroboration, and disappointment. All I have received from FAIT was an offer that, if I write a letter to Slovakia, Mr. Hiseler will mail it for me, but with the condition that I would not mention torture in it and also that I would not mention other prisoners being abused. To me, those are unacceptable conditions, which I cannot agree to. I will never concede that the pain I was intentionally put through was not torture.

The truth is that it—torture or abuse, they can call it whatever they want—was reported to FAIT. After it was reported, they never even phoned me to see if I was still alive or if the abuse continued. A half hour visit in nine months of abuse cannot possibly be enough. How can they still claim that everything was done right?

I'm enclosing my website—www.justiceisdead.info—with many more details, pieces of evidence, and facts, which Mr. Hiseler and anybody from Foreign Affairs refused to see or acknowledge.

I believe that, after reviewing the RCMP and the Canadian consul's conclusions, there is enough evidence that my allegations are legitimate and truthful, which should be enough reason to treat them seriously and act accordingly.

What am I asking my government for?

1. to treat me and all Canadians with honesty and dignity.
2. for consideration of whether compensation and a apology is proper for not attempting to stop or at least lessen my suffering while in prison and for treating me maliciously after I was released.
3. that an official diplomatic protest note (not just my letter as is) be sent to Slovakia for the illegal imprisonment and torture of a Canadian citizen, with a request to investigate Jan Demjan, the policeman who forged official documents to get me into prison and who is still harassing my wife and her family.
4. most importantly, that Canadian authorities do whatever is diplomatically possible to make Slovaks close the specially designed torture chambers in which they abused me and other prisoners. Those chambers are still there and

designed only for one purpose, which is to illegally torture people. It is a moral and human obligation of everybody who knows about it to try to stop the abuse.

5. last, that Canadian Foreign Affairs show initiative and support for amendments to the State Immunity Act, which is a barrier for Canadians who are trying for justice. It is totally unjust that Canadian citizens are on trial, being convicted in absentia in foreign countries. The Canadian government recognizes that, but when we Canadians try for justice in the reverse situation, the Canadian government is spending our hard-earned money to defend morally unacceptable laws that help foreign torturers and murderers avoid punishment and damages us Canadians.

This correspondence is my last hope to get FAIT to deal with my case honestly and to treat me, and all Canadians, with dignity. It is also an attempt to avoid court proceeding to have a jury decide the conclusion I have been fighting for for all these years.

Please respond within two months of this date.

Also to: Prime Minister of Canada

Thank you.

Sincerely,

Jozef Demcak

Please visit www.justiceisdead.info for more details and proof.

(Letters sent January 2010. As of September 2010 there was no reply.)

CONCLUSION

Why Did I Write This Story? The Abuse Must Stop! It makes no difference where it happens or who does it.

What do you get when rabies infect syphilis? — Neocommunist.

I have written my story because of desperation. So many innocent people have suffered and keep on suffering even today. One hundred fifty requests and complaints of mine had no result. I was hoping that there would be somebody, some institution, that could bring those corrupt bastards to justice. No luck.

This way, at least people will know what to expect when traveling to Europe. You are in the hands of the officials of whatever country you are visiting. Most former communist countries have totally corrupt justice systems, and the Council of Europe is hopeless to do anything for you. They will not even consider your suffering until after all the local authorities finish with you. That can take years and years.

What is even more important for me is to bring to an end the suffering of those innocent people who are still being punished just for refusing to falsely testify or for refusing to pay bribes.

There is Jana Visokaiova. She was just an eleven-year-old child when the police abused her. She suffered permanent damage to her mental health and was deprived of a family life, just because she did not know how to lie when she was eleven. Her mom and dad attempted to bring the police to justice; therefore, all of their lives were destroyed.

There are many others who suffer in Slovak prisons. Some are innocent, like I was. They put their hope in me. I do not want them to be forgotten either.

There was my mom. She only wanted freedom for her son—me. She lost her home at the sunset of her life and died as a broken woman, without a feeling of dignity.

Then there is Bibiana, my wife. She also wanted freedom for me and justice for the corrupt officials. Her mom had heart surgery, and she could not visit her. She has been deprived of all basic freedoms, because corrupt people want to punish her for being honest.

And there is me. I have had nine months of abuse in jail; gross damage to my health; And years of writing complaints, looking for justice and punishment for the police who abused the child and caused suffering for so many. My mom was sick and dying in a hospital, and I could not visit. They would have grabbed me if I had.

All innocent people suffer, and criminals who commit these atrocities in the name of the country are free.

If all of this is not crime against humanity, then what is?

It would be nice to see those who caused all that suffering be brought to justice, because they keep on doing it. It is not as important, because God will punish them anyway. There is Demjan, the investigator who fabricates evidence and sends innocent people to jail, where they are abused. Then Danko, former MP of Slovakia, total devil, and informer who rats even his neighbours out. He illegally pulled strings in my case. There is Judge Milko, who made a false file and sent me to prison on its basis, and Judge Jurko, who took my mom's life savings, which she had kept for her own funeral. All she had asked for was that he deal with my case honestly. Soon afterward, he tried to frame me with rape. All of them are still doing their dirty jobs.

What about Meciar? It was all over media that as prime minister of Slovakia, he ordered kidnappings and murder. He kept his MP seat afraid that Lexa will cry out and yell his name as the main evil. Lexa was the one who, as head of SIS, arranged all those horrible crimes. All witnesses to those crimes were murdered. Finally in summer of 2010 citizens of Slovakia had enough of him. Meciar did not make it to parliament of Slovakia. Maybe now he will face justice after all.

I hope you have enjoyed reading my true story. It is not just about terrible crime. It is also about love, which lasts through today, and about believing that truth will prevail.

The proceeds from the sales this book will help those who suffered as innocent victims and are still suffering, because they were hoping for justice. I will look for them and try to help them. It will be a little token, because nobody can ever give them back the years of suffering, their lost health because of hopelessness, or the lives of those who died or were murdered.

Thank you for your consideration.

In the end I would like to remind you of the reactions to all this of those whom many people trust

- European Court of Human Rights: Three judges noticed no broken laws or bridged agreements in this case.
- European ombudsman: The Ombudsman could not do anything, and he knew nobody who could. This should be remembered when you are thinking about traveling to Europe.
- Canadian liberal government of Jean Chretien: They appreciated being informed
- about it.
- Canadian liberal government of Paul Martin: No reply.
- Canadian conservative government of Stephen Harper: They were investigating.
- Slovak President Rudolf Schuster: He noticed nothing unusual in my case.

Some of you will wonder what kind of world we are living in. Why did the Canadian government let it all go by?

Some will ask if it is safe to travel to Europe. Why does the Council of Europe let this anarchy go on?

Please remember that this story is absolutely true, and for every single sentence, I have documented proof.

Most people will ask if this is possible at all. How do corrupt abusers come into this world at all?

I think it is time to explain where the title of my book came from and why I think that I have the right to write on the subject at all. We live in Canada, and here we have restrictions, conditions, or penalties on free speech, the same as European countries have. But there is more. I have firsthand experience, because I grew up in the same country where those monsters were. I also have an education on the subject and years of study.

Here are my conclusions. When the Soviets forced the communist system on all of what became their satellite countries, no thinking or creating was allowed. Only party members were allowed to make decisions. Even artists were told what to paint; songs and books had to be approved by party members.

In the justice system, the cases were concluded even before they were opened. All justice officials were just puppets. For many decades, no judges judged, except party members. Investigators did not investigate, but only framed. Judges could write anything in their judgments, as long as the required results had been met. Their brains were not required to work anymore.

The brain is just like any other organ in our bodies. If it is not being used, it will degenerate. And that's what happened in the decades of not being able to exercise their brainpower. The first generations of people in the communist system were not happy with this situation; therefore, many turned to alcohol. That had a negative effect on their offspring. The communist system had the same effect on the human brain as syphilis has. It degenerated it.

That is the answer to how it is possible that a judge, who is sitting in a robe, cannot even understand a meaning of plain, simple sentence he is writing. Or, when he is at the end of the sentence, he cannot remember the beginning of it. In my case, the judge used a pile of documents from another case and thought that I would not notice it. He concluded that I was just as primitive as he was. Those degenerated brains created the people who wrote all those fabrications and got lost in the whole mess to the point that it was clear that it had all been made up—or hundreds mistakes were made on a 2.5-page document By investigator Demjan.

But it was a new system that topped it all off. The money! It had negative catalytic effect on their brains, which were already damaged, just as if by syphilis. It was the possibility of making a lot of money and the knowledge that there was no watchful eye of some party member over their work that made their brains go berserk. That new freedom to make money had the same effect on them as when you are bit by a dog infected with rabies.

The conclusion of my research: When syphilis gets infected by rabies, the result is a neocommunist.

I will leave on readers to decide if my next observation has anything to do with what I have written above.

The man who was at the beginning of communism died himself of

Syphilis. He was only 53 years old when died but his dogma unravelled the murders of many millions innocent citizens. His name: Vladimir Ilyich Lenin.

(It is important to remember that many honest citizens became communists only because it was necessary just to proceeds with their career to make a living. After disintegration of communist system, they simply went ahead with their lives. None of my opinions are addressing to them. My apology is if my opinion offended them in any way. I'm pointing on "people" types of Danko and Demjan and others whose purpose in life was to take advantage of anything and everything, which was topped with corruption created by Meciar.)

I would like to finish with a quotation from Slovak President at the time Rudolf Schuster. After receiving a request for amnesty from Bibiana and me, in which we described most of the broken laws by Slovak justice officials, he replied:

Bratislava 16 November 1999

c. k. 771/99-72-571

Mr. Demcak,

The Office of the President of the Slovak Republic [Rudolf Schuster] is informing you that the president of the Slovak republic, according to his decision (27/99-PR) from 12.11.1999, did not approve your request or the request of Bibiana Gombosova for pardon, because there were no unusual circumstances discovered that would require an unusual proceeding like be granted pardon by the president of the country.

(Signed) JUDr. Viera Dvorska

I do agree that, in some of those countries, the imprisonment of innocent people by corrupt policemen, investigators, prosecutors, and judges is very usual. Blackmail and extortion by them is a daily occurrence. Using and abusing children and mentally retarded prostitutes in order to frame people must be just as usual for them as destroying innocent people's lives. But I disagree that it is acceptable.

Note: Please understand that my study was limited strictly to those neocommunists whom I got to know in connection with my case and other cases that took place at the time of my suffering.

This is absolutely not a general opinion about Slovak citizens as the whole. I had many friends and classmates who were intellectual, good people. I have also met many smart and able people, whom I've never known before. My opinion is limited mainly to the police and other justice officials who are, in fact, endangering all of those honest citizens.

APPENDICES

I Need a Good Lawyer

My fight for justice is far from over. It has been more than ten years. All of these years, Slovaks have been harassing my wife, Bibiana. On April 1, 2010, they mailed her a charge, which as they claim was fabricated more than 10 years ago. They claim that she ofended whole police station in Trebisov, Slovakia. All that just over one true sentence said more then ten years ago. There are many paragraphs in Slovak law that are proofs that saying that one sentence is not illegal act. In plain words Slovaks illegally persecute Canadian citizen for more than ten years and it is no problem as far as Canadian government is concerned.

Demjan was the one who fabricated the whole illegal charge, forged official files, forged signatures, and of course, blackmailed me. Apparently, he is also offended.

The road to justice is long, but I hope it has an end.

Summaries and Names

Judges: 6
Prosecutors: 10
Policemen: at least 25
Children exploited and damaged: at least 5
Adults grossly damaged: at least 9
Gypsies used: 8
School principals: 2
Psychiatrists and psychologist: 3
Lives destroyed or negatively affected: at least 12
Other officials and people who were involved: many

These are the real names of officials and other people who were swindled, duped, employed, tricked, used, or otherwise involved in and affected by this case because of policemen on their way to frame me. All that damage was done based on false, illegal, forged accusations made by three corrupt individuals, who were then supported or protected by judges, prosecutors, and other corrupt officials of the Slovak Republic

1. Jan Demjan, investigator. He did most of the illegal activities. He fabricated the charge, which was proven to be false right in a Slovak court. Afterward, he fabricated the whole investigative file, forged signatures, and committed many more illegal activities. Some people involved were not even aware that the whole process had been fabricated and was therefore illegal. Some were not even involved at all, but their names were illegally used, and their signatures were forged.

Others were acting based on the request of

2. Jan Danko. He was a member of the Slovak parliament when Prime Minister Meciar created the most corrupt federal government in Slovak history after the fall of the communist system.

   Danko appointed judges, prosecutors, lawyers, investigators, policemen, prison guards, city mayors, directors of hospitals, school principals, and all federal, district, and town jobs. Everyone either owed him a favour or was afraid of being fired. All power was virtually in the hands of this one corrupt man. He was the one who was directing all those dirty happenings in Trebisov. As usual, he was fabricating, directing, publicizing, and creating all that dirt from behind somebody; therefore, his name does not appear on any official document. His illegal activity could be proven only if there was a real investigation and somebody would talk.

3. Jozef Stefanak, a plain policeman. He was present when the child Jana Visokaiova was abused, and he was doing most of the legwork in looking for false witnesses against me.

Imagine: just three corrupt individuals from Trebisov and how much damage they were able to cause to so many innocent people and children.

Following are the real names of 99 people who were involved, were affected, had their names used, or had their signatures forged. I have listed only those names, of which I have official proof in the form of documents. I have not listed those people whose names were used on documents that were confiscated from me in prison. Many more people were approached to participate or to falsely testify.

These include people from the Slovak president, prime minister, general prosecutor, minister of justice, and minister of the interior to provincial and district judges and other investigators, all the way down to plain policemen, doctors, teachers, regular citizens, and gypsies.

All of that was done to find at least one little piece of evidence against me. The result was: absolutely none.

4. mjr. Dziak, policeman, Trebisov. Was Stefanak's partner.
5. JUDr. Jan Milko, judge, Trebisov. Sent me to jail based on illegal and nonexistent documents.
6. JUDr. Jurko Milan, judge, Trebisov. Tried very hard to frame me openly in court and refused to acknowledge all those documents as forged. He found me not guilty but failed to give me the releasing document.

The highest officials of Slovakia were informed about the atrocities and failed to stop it.

7. Mr. Schuster, president of Slovakia. Didn't see anything unusual in corruption.
8. Mr. Dzurinda, prime minister of Slovakia. Unable to correct lawlessness.
9. Mr. Carnogursky, minister of justice. Visited the provincial court in Kosice as well as the prison but avoided seeing my situation.
10. Mr. Pitner, minister of the interior. Visited prison but avoided witnessing the abuse that was taking place there. Later, he lied that he had never heard about my case.

11. JUDr. Maria Pacutova, prosecutor from Trebisov. Her name was just used against me.
12 Mgr. Sabo Maros, prosecutor from Trebisov. Used like a puppet.
13. JUDr. Serecin, prosecutor from Trebisov. Used like a puppet.
14. JUDr. Bicko Frantisek, prosecutor from Trebisov. Illegally protested my release.
15. Unknown young, blond policeman who was with Kovac at the first arrest.
16. pplk. JUDr. Anton Viscur, policeman, Trebisov.
17. kpt. Varga, policeman, Trebisov.
18. pprap. Gazdura, policeman, Trebisov.
19. npor. Sereg Vl., policeman, Trebisov.
20. npr. Kovac, policeman, Trebisov.
21. por. Robert Mesaros, policeman, Trebisov.
22. mjr. Cigle, policeman, Trebisov.

Those who searched my house:
23. mjr. JUDr. Minarik, investigator, Trebisov.
24. mjr. Baco M. policeman, Trebisov.
25. npor. Urban Fr., policeman, Trebisov.
26. npor. Fazekas L., policeman, Trebisov.
27. kpt. Jan Kentos, policeman, Trebisov.
28. Marcel Kucak, policeman, Trebisov.

From the city of Kosice:
29. JUDr. Jan Pernat, provincial prosecutor, Kosice.
30. JUDr. Viera Hockickova, provincial prosecutor's office, Kosice.
31. JUDr. Ondrej Brdarsky, judge, Kosice.
32. JUDr. Jan Popovec, judge, Kosice.

33. JUDr. Jan Liska, judge, Kosice.
34. kpt. Ing. Jaroslav Janosik, Forensic Criminal Institute, Kosice.
35. pplk. Ing. Jan Franko, Forensic Criminal Institute, Kosice.
36. JUDr. Zuzana Hlinkova, provincial prosecutor, Kosice.

From the city of Bratislava and that region:
37. JUDr. Igor Dorica, prosecutor from the general prosecutor's office, Bratislava.
38. Ing. Jarmila Trnovska, Prime Minister Office from Bratislava.
39. JUDr. Lubos Masaryk, prosecutor from General Prosecutor office, Bratislava.
40. Plk. JUDr. Peter Holansky, Ministry of Interior, Bratislava.
41. kpt. Ing Jozef Kuba, Ministry of Interior, Bratislava.
42. Ing. Viera Carnanska, Ministry of the Interior.
43. JUDr. Zdenka Strbkova, Ministry of Justice, Bratislava.
44. JUDr. Viera Dvorska, president of Slovakia's office, Bratislava.
45. JUDr. Jana Pirselova, general prosecutor's office, Bratislava.
46. JUDr. Lubos Masarik, general prosecutor's office, Bratislava.
47. JUDr. Ivan Berier, general prosecutor's office, Bratislava.
48. JUDr. Stefan Minarik, Ministry of Justice, Bratislava.
49. JUDr. Ladislav Jonas, Slovak Helsinski Committee, Bratislava.
50. JUDr. Viera Dvorska, president of Slovakia's office, Bratislava.
51. npor. Miroslav Horsky, foreign police, Rusovce.
52. pprap. Boris Kral, foreign police, Rusovce.
53. pplk. Alzbeta Dzurcaninova, Ministry of Interior, Kosice.
54. mjr. Kapicak, policeman, Bratislava.
55. strzm. Marczy, policeman, Bratislava.
56. pprp. Garay, policeman, Bratislava.
57. Syrt, his dog, Bratislava.
58. kpt. Kubinec, policeman, Bratislava.
59. Bono, his dog Bratislava.
60. pprp. Horvatova, policewoman, Bratislava.
61. JUDr. Viera Fercakova, lawyer, Kosice.
62. JUDr. Stefan Hajdu, lawyer, Trebisov.

Children exploited and damaged by Investigator Demjan:
63. Jana Visokaiova, just turned eleven, Trebisov. Damaged mentally by abuse at the police station and repeated interrogations at school. She was

dropped from my case, but her name was used illegally anyway. She moved out of Slovakia.

64. Anna Demeterova, fourteen years old, Trebisov. Abused by the police at school. She became a prostitute. She was used as a false witness.

65. Lucia Barancikova, ten years old, Trebisov. Illegally interrogated.

66. Marek Mazurkovic, ten years old, Trebisov. Illegally interrogated.

67. Anna Lukacova, twelve years old, Trebisov. Illegally interrogated.

Teachers, other officials, and people duped in my case by Demjan—all from Trebisov:

68. RNDr. Marcela Ferkova, school principal. Used as a witness while Jana Visokaiova was abused at the police station. The police used her school to do their dirty job.

69. mgr. Marta Koscikova, teacher. Stated that Jana was happy after she was abused by the police.

70. mgr. Anna Pekarcikova, teacher. Signed as present when Lucia Barancikova and Marek Mazurkovic were exploited by Policeman Demjan.

71. M. Pivkova. Was named, but not signed as typist when Anna Pekarcikova was questioned October 20.

72. Marta Polakova. Listed as present when mgr. Marta Koscikova and Ms. Ferkova were questioned on October 22.

73. Janette Pircakova, typist at court October 13.

74. Ing. Dusan Polacky, mayor of Trebisov. Signed positive characteristic on me on October 20.

75. Mrs. Gudova. Wrote characteristic for the mayor.

Special examiners duped by Demjan—all from Kosice:

76. Doc. PhDr. Andrej Stancak. made at least five expert examinations.

77. MUDr. Stefan Safku. made expert examination.

78. MUDr. Maria Kilianova. made expert examination.

Citizens:

79. Alena Gradosova

80. Dana Gradosova

Gypsies from Trebisov:

81. Alena Demeterova. Exploited by the police and used as a false witness.

She was dropped from my case, but her name was used anyway. She became a prostitute.

82. Andrea Karickova. The police tried to use her as a false witness. She refused and was not part of any of the proceedings, but in the end, her name was used anyway, illegally.

83. Eva Pukiova. Exploited by the police and used as a false witness. She became a prostitute.

84. Natasa Pukiova. Exploited by the police and used as a false witness. She became a prostitute.

85. Gejza Tancos. Convict used by Policeman Demjan to estimate ages.

86. Anna Demeterova. Exploited by the police and used as a false witness. She became a prostitute.

87. Milan Tancos (Belavi). Pimp to named prostitutes. He attempted to blackmail me. He was used by the police to pass on extortion messages to my family.

88. Radoslav Puky. Apparently received a photo of Eva Pukiova.

Lives destroyed or seriously damaged and affected:

89. Maria Demcakova, my mother. Was in her eighties when fighting for my life. Policeman Demjan and others lied to her face. She moved out of her town to avoid hardship that the justice officials fabricated. She died an emotionally broken lady.

90. Bibiana Demcakova. Fought for my life. She suffered greatly. Slovaks harass her even today.

91. Sona, my sister. Suffered emotionally.

92. Karol, brother-in-law. Suffered emotionally.

93. Alzbeta, my sister. Suffered emotionally.

94. Ondrej, brother-in-law. Suffered emotionally.

95. Milan, my brother. Suffered emotionally.

96. Andrej Milovcik, my mom's brother and my godfather. Suffered emotionally.

97. Jan Visokai, Jana's father. Refused to be a false witness. His family and his life were destroyed by the injustice. He died brokenhearted.

98. Helena Visokaiova, Jana's mom. Refused to be a false witness. Her family and her life were destroyed by the injustice. She attempted to commit suicide. She moved out of her town to avoid the hardship the justice officials created.

99. Marta G. suffers emotionally till present.

100. The policeman who committed suicide after he warned me about danger from the other policemen.

101. S. Volochova.

102. Vilo Biro.

103. Michal Kundrat.

104. Dr. Bobik.

105. All honest citizens who are disgusted or who disagree with the kind of corrupt actions committed by police and officials of justice in Trebisov Slovakia.

All of that just to frame one person—me.

Prisoners:

Peter Mlynar, Poprad. His lawyer would not see him, because Peter had no money.

Miro Mizak, Michalovce. Small-time crook.

Nemec, Michalovce. Small-time crook.

Jane Gore, Kosice. Cut his chest with multiple cuts. Later, he cut his nose open.

Lubo Mrazik, Bardejov. Nice guy who got involved with bad men.

Zdeno Putnoky, Kosice. Arrested because he wanted his daughter to be good.

Arpy Reznises, Tusice. Small-time crook.

Zdeno Vidlicka, Kosice. Small-time crook.

Miro Horvath, Valaliky. Small-time crook. He spent the longest amount of time in the same cell as I was in.

Michal Budaj, Kosice. Small-time crook.

Igor Gregor, Russia. Crook from Russia.

Fero Holub, Spisske Podhradie. His brother and he organized crime. Both were murdered.

Robo Kovac, Roznava. Accused of murdering his partner, who was on the outside, while he was already in prison.

"Zirafa." Used by crooks for fraud concerning a lot of money.

WARNING: This can happen to anybody. My request to honest citizens of the world is that you please help stop atrocities.

Place:
Slovakia and all communist, former communist, former Soviet Union, and former Soviet satellite countries.

Time: From Lenin times until the present.

Crimes:
kidnappings,
extortions, blackmails,
murders, rapes, assaults.

Criminals:
policemen, investigators, crooks.

Accomplices:
judges,
prosecutors, lawyers,
prison wardens, prison guards, appointed psychologists, members of parliament.

Motive:
money, cover-ups,
paybacks, revenge.

Tools: courts, police cars, prisons.

Methods:
physical torture without hitting; mental abuse without the abuser present.
Bogus Witnesses:
children, retarded
gypsies, prostitutes,
pimps, crooks.

Victims: innocent people, children, women, men, whole families, and tourists. This could be you.

Blind Eyes and Deaf Ears: the Council of Europe, the Slovak government, the Canadian government, Amnesty International of Canada and others

Is this story real? It is 100 percent document truth.

Piles of documents were fabricated, number of signatures forged, children abused, families destroyed, just to cover up illegal acts of corrupted Slovak police and other bastards in Slovak justice system to get finances from Jozef.

Jozef is probably most qualifying person in the world to understand what is going on in all communist and post communist jails, because he was in one of them.

He understands how brains of abusers work, because he studied psychology and Marks-Lenin dogma. He had also grown up with some of the abusers. Most importantly he survived torture on his own skin.
All this knowledge and experience is wasted by Canadian Government as they do not want to hear about it.
If they did, somebody could ask the question:- Why didn't they try to stop abuse when it was taking place and why they are defending abusers now.

Jozef has written this story for only one reason. He believes strongly that everybody should do something because
TORTURE and ABUSE MUST STOP.